HTML5 Games: Novice to Ninja

- **Product Manager:** Simon Mackie
- **English Editor:** Ralph Mason
- **Technical Editors:** Franco Ponticelli & Andrzej Mazur
- **Cover Designer:** Alex Walker

Notice of Rights

Notice of Liability

Trademark Notice

Published by SitePoint Pty. Ltd.

48 Cambridge Street Collingwood

VIC Australia 3066

Web: www.sitepoint.com

Email: books@sitepoint.com

ISBN 978-0-9941826-1-6 (print)

ISBN 978-0-9953826-9-5 (ebook)

Printed and bound in the United States of America

About Earle Castledine

Earle Castledine—JavaScript flâneur and internet flibbertigibbet—is back! By day it's serious business while Earle steers the ship as lead engineer at hot startups. By night his attention turns to the world of weird art and wonderful game design.

Author of *Jump Start CoffeeScript*, and the cult classic *jQuery: Novice to Ninja*—as well as speaker at countless JavaScript conferences and meetups all around the globe—he's no novice to brewing up engaging, interesting, and informative creative works.

Now, having been making games with JavaScript long before it was cool, he's here to guide you on your journey to gamedev superstardom.

About SitePoint

SitePoint specializes in publishing fun, practical, and easy-to-understand content for web professionals. Visit http://www.sitepoint.com/ to access our blogs, books, newsletters, articles, and community forums. You'll find a stack of information on JavaScript, PHP, Ruby, mobile development, design, and more.

For Kim Castledine (1948 - 2016)
Thanks for everything, Dad.

Table of Contents

Preface viii

Who Should Read This Book? viii

Conventions Used ix

Supplementary Materials x

Chapter 1:   **Press Space to Start** 1

Game Design 4

A Brief History 6

Games and JavaScript 7

Enough Talk; Let's Make Games 11

Get Ready! 25

Chapter 2:   **Drawing Things** 26

DOM vs Canvas vs WebGL 27

Plain Ol' DOM 28

Canvas API 34

Game Engines vs Reinventing the Wheel 51

Quick, Draw 54

Chapter 3:   **Game Loops & User Input** 55

The Loop 56

User Input 64

Creating Your Game Library 75

A Space Shoot-'em-up 92

Game Over 104

Chapter 4:   Animation, Levels, Maps, Cameras... 106

An Unexpected Proposition...107

De-boilerplating Our Prototypes...108

Sprites with *Zing*!...111

An Unexpected Assignment..121

Sprite Sheets & Animation..122

The Animation Manager..133

Tile Maps..137

Scrolling Maps with a Camera...149

Screens & Game Life Cycle..155

Leveled Up..163

Chapter 5:   Collision Detection & AI................................ 164

Colliding with Things...166

Procedural Level Generation 177

Colliding with Maps 183

AI: The Bots Strike Back 194

Pathfinding 209

Enemies Alive 213

Chapter 6:   **Mathematics & Physics** **214**

Jump Everybody, Jump 215

Fixing Our Time Step 223

Triangles and Vectors 225

Building a Vector Library 226

The Need for Speed (and Direction) 232

Billiard Ball Physics 244

Polar Coordinates 247

Physics Libraries 250

Chapter 7:   **Audio** **271**

Old-school Techniques 272

Audio on the Web 273

An Asset Manager 283

Sound Production 290

The Web Audio API 305

Post Production: Mixing and Mastering.. 319

Fade to Silence 323

Chapter 8:   **Bringing a Game to Life with "Juice"** **324**

Screen Effects...326

Animations, Tweens, and Easing 334

Particle Effects 345

Camera Tricks...350

Platformer Tricks..354

More Tiles..364

Dialogs and Screen Transitions.....................................373

Designing Levels with a Level Editor 378

Got Game...389

Chapter 9: **Optimizing & Packaging**...............................391

Debugging 392

Profiling...398

Speeding Up Your Code..403

Speeding Up Rendering..415

Getting on Devices...426

Getting on the Stores...440

Releasing to the World 442

Chapter 10: **Bonus Round: The Epilogue**......................446

Preface

This book will teach you how to create awesome video games. Games from scratch. Games that run cross-platform, in web browsers, and on phones. Games filled with dynamic sound and music. Games overflowing with impressive visual effects. Fun games.

More importantly, this book will teach you how to *think* about making games. You'll learn to analyze and dissect games—to understand what makes great games great. By the end of the journey you'll have all the knowledge and tools needed to produce engaging, polished *products* that you can unleash on the internet, sell on app stores, or just use to impress your friends.

Aside from creating something cool, gamedev also tantalizes us with the possibility of becoming world-famous indie game superstars! In the '90s, if you wanted fame and fortune you *had* to start an alternative rock band. In the 2000s it was all about being in an electronic music production outfit. But today, all the cool kids are getting a gamedev studio together. The bad news is that you may have wasted all those years learning the guitar, but the good news is that you already know a bunch of JavaScript—and JavaScript is an excellent instrument in the quest for gamedev superstardom.

Whether you want to create games to express yourself and have an emotional impact on your audience, or whether you're just digging for gold looking for the next *Flappy Bird* money-making hit, we all have to start at the same place: the beginning.

"The beginning" for us means establishing a solid codebase for our projects. We'll use it to create a challenging little side-scrolling shoot-'em-up. Then (having got our feet wet) we'll evolve it into a tile-based action game. From there, we'll add gravity to get a fast-paced, dungeon-crawler platform game. And finally, we'll make an entertaining, mobile, penguin-based, physics-based, procedurally generated golf game. Each game builds gradually from the previous, leaving you with a solid foundation for constructing whatever quixotic ideas are swirling around your brain.

Then you'll be a game developer.

Who Should Read This Book?

This book is for anyone who wants to create their own games using tools such as a browser and a text editor. It's expected that you're proficient in HTML and CSS, and are reasonably experienced with JavaScript, but no prior game development experience is assumed.

Acknowledgments

I'd like to thank Amelia for supporting (and tolerating) me throughout this long long journey. Really, thank you!

Also thanks to Simon Mackie for your professionalism, good ideas, and for being the voice of reason whenever I was stuck.

Thanks to Gaëtan Renaudeau for helping kickstart this project and giving it a great foundation to build on, and Franco Ponticelli and Andrzej Mazur for all your fantastic advice and formidable tech knowledge: it was great working with you both.

A huge high-five to everyone who let me use screen shots of their beautiful games and artworks in the book - it wouldn't be the same without it, and I can't wait to see what you all come up with next.

Shout-outs to the early-morning café crew: Warren and Madoo (for keeping my spirits up), and Anthony (for making good coffee).

Finally, thanks to Disasterpeace for the FEZ OST. I listened to it a million times over the course of this project. The perfect soundtrack for writing a gamedev book.

Conventions Used

You'll notice that we've used certain typographic and layout styles throughout this book to signify different types of information. Look out for the following items.

Code Samples

Code in this book is displayed using a fixed-width font, like so:

```
<h1>A Perfect Summer's Day</h1>
<p>It was a lovely day for a walk in the park.
The birds were singing and the kids were all back at school.</p>
```

Tips, Notes, and Warnings

 Hey, You!

Tips provide helpful little pointers.

 Ahem, Excuse Me ...

Notes are useful asides that are related—but not critical—to the topic at hand. Think of them as extra tidbits of information.

 Make Sure You Always ...

... pay attention to these important points.

 Watch Out!

Warnings highlight any gotchas that are likely to trip you up along the way.

Supplementary Materials

- https://github.com/spbooks/html5games1 is the book's code archive, which contains code examples found in the book, plus game library that we'll build in the book.
- https://www.sitepoint.com/community/ are SitePoint's forums, for help on any tricky problems.
- **books@sitepoint.com** is our email address, should you need to contact us to report a problem, or for any other reason.

Press Space to Start

If you only have a few seconds to learn game development, here's the super-condensed version. Fetch user input. Move everything just a tiny bit. Check if anything overlaps. Draw everything. Repeat this 60 times every second.

If you have a couple of extra minutes, then here's the expanded version. A computer can do a *lot* of things, very quickly. It can update the individual positions of an army of enemy tanks, or flock of virtual bunnies. It can launch missiles or grow carrots or spawn beautiful particle effects. It can detect any collisions that occur. And it can draw everything on screen. All in *one sixtieth of a second*.

Game development is analogous to orchestrating a real-time, interactive, stop-motion animation film. Every screen update (called a **frame**, and generally lasting only around 16 milliseconds) the actors all move just a tiny amount. The tiny amounts add up, so playing them back at high speed creates the *illusion* of motion. Game development is almost entirely about creating illusions. If you want something to "walk", first display an image of a character with open legs for a few frames, then switch to an image of closed legs for a few frames. If you're careful about timing (and art style) you'll have a convincing *walk cycle*.

1-1. A headless walk cycle

Animating and moving is only one thing we must do every frame. At the highest level, a main game loop (that runs once per frame) looks like this:

Loop:

Fetch user input

Move everything a tiny bit

Respond to collisions

Draw everything

1-2. The main game loop

This high-level loop doesn't explain how to coordinate and manage all those operations (we'll cover them soon enough), but it's a simple model for starting to think about how games work at their core.

This is all you need for a game. Don't overthink it, don't over-architect it. Just realize that a computer can do a *lot* of things in one sixtieth of a second, and a bunch of small animations and interactions quickly becomes more than the sum of its parts: the human brain is great at attributing life to inanimate objects. Start with a square moving across the screen, add other squares moving in the opposite direction, and it's not much of a stretch of the imagination to see how it becomes *Super Mario Bros.*!

1-3. The addictive world of game development

 This Might Seem Strange to You

If you have a functional programming or web background, the idea of doing everything sequentially in a loop might seem a bit "procedural", but that's only at a high level. Games are ultimately a big ball of *state*. You can model that state however you want. But seriously: *keep it as simple as possible* for your first few games!

Game Design

How can we apply this high-level idea of a "main loop" to making something that actually resembles a game? Video game design, as a field, is still very young, but it's had enough time to develop and refine a set of, well, not "laws", but more like rules, guidelines, adages, best practices, academic theories, myths, and legends.

Game *design* (as distinct from game *development*) is about exploiting this collective knowledge in the pursuit of improving your games. Fortunately, you don't need to be versed in the entire field of game design to start doing it effectively—just as you don't need to know music theory to start a band and make great songs. But the more you learn, the faster you can figure out *why* some things do or don't work. The more rules you know, the more rules you can break—and be reasonably confident in your choices.

I'm not going to delve too far into the nitty-gritty of game design; there are plenty of amazing resources for that. And, like all academic endeavors, it's a deep rabbit hole once you get started. There are volumes devoted to simply defining what a "game" is! If you want to kick off the adventure, start with *The Art of Game Design: A Book of Lenses*[1] by Jesse Schell. At this early stage, we're primarily concerned with picking up the *language* of game design so we can move through our gamedev journey and all be on the same page.

Arguably the most important aspect of a game is its *mechanics*. A **game mechanic** refers to a specific gameplay element. It's the goal or purpose of a single facet of your game—the thing that enforces the rules or encourages exploration to understand the game. Typically, you'll have a whole bunch of mechanics that collectively comprise the overall gameplay, but the element (or elements) that define the *essence* of what makes your game special is called the **core mechanic**.

For example, in a platform game "jumping" is a mechanic (a pretty crucial one!). Perhaps in your game your *core mechanic* is that the player can jump further when they're also running. This allows you, as the game designer, to invent situations where the player needs to choose if they should do a long jump or a short jump, and react accordingly. You need to be very careful when adding, modifying or removing mechanics, as these drastically change the entire shape of your game.

Closely related to game design is **level design**. Designing levels isn't so much about *making* levels as *thinking* about making levels! Once you've defined your game's mechanics, you can start to sculpt them into the overall experience you're aiming to offer the player. Perhaps the first few levels will require a few long jumps, but they become more and more necessary as the game progresses—until the player is almost only performing long jumps. Then, at a crucial moment,

---

[1] https://www.amazon.com/The-Art-Game-Design-Edition/dp/1466598646/

throw in some alternating long/short/long jumps to shock and surprise them and keep them on their toes.

Level design is used to control the game's *pacing*. **Pacing** is how the game flows over time. Where are moments of high tension? Where are moments of peacefulness? How naturally are they combined? Figure 1 shows the classic movie plot tension cycle. It can't just be all about explosions and car chases, or it'll quickly get dull. You have to vary the difficulty—perhaps starting easily and then ramping it up. But not for too long, else the player will get exhausted. There should be periods of relief, and surprise—highs and lows. Pacing is what stops the player from getting bored after they master the core mechanics.

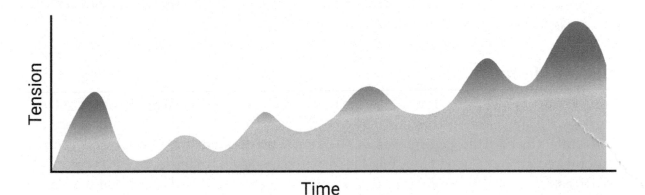

1-4. Classic movie plot tension cycle

With our mechanics and pacing sorted, we need to talk about art. Throughout this book I'll make a distinction between *graphics* and *aesthetics*. They are related, but very different. **Graphics** comprises the images that the artist creates—the pixels that make up the characters, the logos, the backgrounds. **Aesthetics** is concerned with the look and feel of the game at a higher level—the overall themes presented, the mood it generates, the use of colors, symbols, and imagery for artistic purposes.

Aesthetics is almost always more important than graphics. A game with a consistent and coherent aesthetic can be visually enjoyable and impressive even with less-than-stellar graphics. Which is great news for a lot of us who are terrible at Photoshop.

Finally, **juice**. This term probably won't turn up in much academic literature, but it's essential for creating great-feeling games. Juice is the polish, the attention to detail, the necessary unnecessaries, the love. It's the shaking screen when things explode, the small particle trails following the player as they run, the smooth bouncing animations and effects in the user interface. Many of these are extremely easy to add on top of your core mechanic, and we'll be adding heaps of them as we go along.

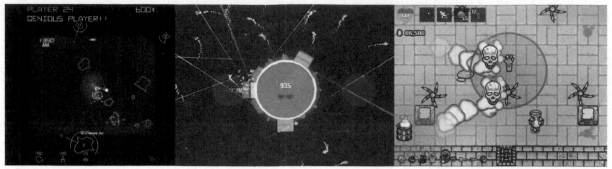

1-5. Juicy games

Now that we have the lingo down, let's define our primary goal for the book (and for your first few games): to create a simple but interesting *core mechanic*, coupled with compelling *level design*, good *pacing*, a pleasing *aesthetic*, and a whole bunch of *juice*!

A Brief History

The viability of producing (and selling) games by yourself has waxed and waned over the years. The original commercial video games and home consoles (such as the Atari 2600, released in 1977) birthed many of the game genres we know today: **platformers** (running and jumping on platforms, collecting coins and treasure, and searching for the end of the level), **RPGs** (role-playing games, exploring rich worlds and developing your character's skills), and side-scrolling **shoot-'em-ups** (blasting bad guys and getting more powerful weapons). All of these had their genesis as simple blocky squares in the '70s.

The machines were new and complex beasts with very limited capabilities, and programming them required intimate hardware knowledge. The home computer revolution in the '80s brought more power, better graphics, and easier development. It sparked the first wave of solo developers and small teams making smash-hit games.

The '90s brought us the 16-bit era, and things got a lot more complicated. Mastering the hardware architecture was far more difficult, and the graphic and sound capabilities of the new machines were an order of magnitude more impressive than their 8-bit brethren. Game development teams got bigger and bigger, and the games themselves became expensive productions. One-person hits (such as Éric Chahi's *Another World*[2], or *Out of This World*) became increasingly rare.

---

[2] https://en.wikipedia.org/wiki/Another_World_(video_game)

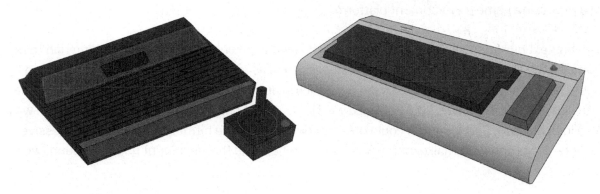

1-6. Atari 2600 and the Commodore 64

Advancements in hardware gave us the likes of the Nintendo 64 and the PlayStation—machines you couldn't develop for even if you if you were a coding and graphics god. They required expensive, hard-to-obtain licensed dev kits and specialized development hardware. Giant game production houses ruled the gaming world. Employees in teams of *thousands* worked as tiny cogs in a mighty game-development machine, creating epic, movie-like productions. The era of the "AAA game" was here, and the days of the lone coder was over—banished to the world of "shareware" and small Flash games.

But then, in the mid-2000s, something strange happened. The world began to tire of AAA game franchises rehashing the same titles over and over again. Games started feeling stale and boring. Suddenly there was an opening for interesting and fresh ideas—even if they didn't have the massive development budgets of *Tired Shooter, XVII*! Around the same time, the release of the original iPhone opened up a whole new market for mobile games—and this time players were actually willing to *pay* for them (unlike shareware). In another part of the internet, the opening of a digital-only game distribution store called *Steam* facilitated the online delivery of new games to millions of customers. The perfect storm had hit, bringing with it a tide of games made by small teams, without publishers or financial backing. The era of the "indie game developer" had begun.

Games and JavaScript

JavaScript and the Web are notably absent from this history. Games used the internet as a data transfer mechanism (and of course web browsers needed to host the Flash plugin) but that was about it. Where JavaScript was used for games, it was for simple point-'n'-click affairs—card and board games, or small experiments. That's not to say it wasn't possible to make "real" games back then. The 2004 release of *DHTML Lemmings*[3] proved it was possible to create arcade-style games, a faithful reproduction of a classic game—including animations, sounds, and even particle explosions. As impressive as it was, it was regarded as a novelty rather than as the birth

---

[3.] http://kap.dyndns.org/lemmings/

of a promising game development platform.

The biggest hurdle to games on the Web was the lack of pixel-level access. Everything had to be done via the *DOM* with standard HTML elements such as `div` containers and images. It wasn't possible to create or manipulate existing graphics in any meaningful way. This changed with the introduction of the Canvas 2D API (which we'll look at next chapter) and then WebGL (which we'll also look at later). Suddenly you could draw shapes, manipulate bitmaps and create impressive effects, all at runtime. Small experiments were hatched, and the JavaScript games groundswell began.

It wasn't so long ago that mentioning "games" and "JavaScript" in the same sentence would have you laughed out of any respectable game development forum. "Real games are written in C++", the reasoning went. "C# may be acceptable, but just *forget* about dynamic languages: they're too slow to do anything good!" ... which, admittedly, was very true once, but much less so now. The introduction of Google Chrome sparked a whole new era of browser wars, each browser maker implementing faster and faster JavaScript and rendering engines, bringing near-native speeds to the Web.

The arguments against JavaScript have been evaporating ... though don't expect many of the low-level, old-school coders on the gamedev forums to have noticed yet! The shift of JavaScript from toy to seriously productive tool happened pretty fast, and most people weren't watching. Now it's a viable language for making big games that can easily be deployed to any platform.

Strengths of JavaScript

The most obvious strength of JavaScript is that it's everywhere. It's unavoidable. It's almost *mandatory*. Thanks to the twists and turns of computer history, JavaScript is one of the most popular languages in the world. If a device can be programmed, it can most likely run JavaScript.

Being ubiquitous is nice, but it's not the reason why JavaScript is good for games.

JavaScript is a dynamic, prototype-based language. As games get larger, people are realizing the problems associated with traditional object-oriented programming. It can lead to complicated, incomplete class hierarchies that are inflexible and limit code reuse. There are many patterns and best practices surfacing to avoid these problems in gamedev, but the good news is that JavaScript comes with flexibility baked in by default. It lets us sculpt our requirements as we go, rather than define them from the beginning. We can change, tweak, and compose components and functions easily—which is excellent for prototyping and experimenting with game ideas.

We're also witnessing a grand period of core language improvement. Since ECMAScript 2015 (aka ES2015, ECMAScript 6 and ES6), the language approval process has been sped up and streamlined, allowing for a whole host of improvements and features that address many of JavaScript's shortcomings, while building on the language's strengths. We now have modules, classes, improved scoping powers, nicer syntax (and new features) for functions and objects, maps and sets, proxies … the list is huge. But the upshot is that we can now write clearer, terser code with less chance of bumping into the historical warts of JavaScript.

The other huge benefit of JavaScript is its implicit partnership with the Web. Writing games in JavaScript means we get all the power of the Web for free. Every new feature and API added to the browser is immediately available for us to use in our games. Whatever we make can be easily distributed to, and accessed by, a huge global audience! We even get a few APIs specifically designed for making games: the Gamepad API implements game controller support; the Pointer Lock API lets us handle mouse movements like a native app (for making mouse-controlled games without losing focus); and, though not intended solely for games, the Web Audio API finally makes sound a first-class citizen on the Web.

Limitations of JavaScript

Every language and coding environment has its trade-offs. (That's why there's more than one language!) So it's important to understand the good and the bad parts of your toolkit. The biggest weakness of JavaScript is also its strength: its dynamic nature.

Dynamic typing is great for playing and sculpting a game into shape. But once the shape is known, it's hard to enforce it. For example, we might know that the player's lives should be a number (`player.lives = 3`), but there's nothing that stops us from saying `player.lives = "hello"` , even though it doesn't make sense. **Static typing** helps us reason about the *correctness* of a program. If the compiler knows the "rules" of what every value can be, it can analyze your source and detect errors before the code is even run. A language with a strong type system avoids runtime messages like the classic `undefined is not a function` .

 Bringing Static Typing to JavaScript

There are currently several attempts to bring static typing to JavaScript—the most popular being TypeScript and Flow. These tools allow you to add type information to your source code, which it uses to enforce the correct types. This code is converted to standard JavaScript before it's deployed to the browser. Personally, I embrace the rock-and-roll dynamic nature of JavaScript—but you should certainly evaluate it for yourself.

Another fun part of web life is getting things working 100% correctly across all browsers. This can be especially hard when relying on bleeding-edge features not yet formalized by the W3C and not fully implemented by the browser makers. So although you can still play *DHTML Lemmings* from well over a decade ago, many demos using brand new HTML5 features are prone to breaking, as it takes time for the specifications to be finalized, and browser makers interpret the requirements differently.

The cross-browser issues also extend to other *platforms* you might want to deploy to. JavaScript can run *everywhere*, but the capabilities and deployment process will be radically different between your browser and, say, your JavaScript-enabled toaster! It's possible (and fun) to run your HTML5 games as native apps on phones, tablets, and consoles, but each platform has its own idiosyncrasies. While there are frameworks and services to make things easier, there's no one-size-fits-all solution.

The Future of HTML5 Games

If you're exploring your options for starting your game development career, HTML5 is an excellent choice. The features and power available to web-based games is constantly increasing and improving. It may not yet be as mind-blowingly fast as native C++ code targeting the latest low-level graphics APIs, but the gap is always closing. If you're just starting out now, the Web is going to be ahead of your needs for a long time to come.

The Web has been a viable deployment target for many game studios for a long time now. Way back in 2012, Green Heart Games released their addictive "gamedev simulator", *Game Dev Tycoon* on Steam, to almost universal praise; it still has 95% positive ratings today. A gamedev simulator game written in JavaScript in 2012 is pretty subversive!

Other early pioneers include Lost Decade Games' action RPG, *A Wizard's Lizard*, which was also released on Steam. These games were written from scratch (just as we'll do in this book)—because there was no alternative! Later impressive efforts like *Airscape: The Fall of Gravity*, *The Next Penelope* and *The Curious Expedition*[4] are all exquisite, very different games with plenty of depth. They proved that limited technology didn't have to be a barrier to creating polished games.

More recently, there's been a rise in so-called **.IO games**, which are casual MMOs (massively multiplayer online games) that generally have a `.io` domain name, hence the name. Examples include Slither.io[5], and the beautiful pixel-art, hack-'n'-slash game Wilds.io[6], by JavaScript gamedev pathfinder Przemysław Sikorski (aka Rezoner).

---

[4]. http://store.steampowered.com/app/358130/The_Curious_Expedition/
[5]. http://slither.io/
[6]. http://wilds.io

1-7. Big HTML5 games

If you look at these games through the various app stores, or read their promotional material, you won't see a single mention of HTML5 or JavaScript—not because they aren't proud of it, but because it's not important! Ultimately, nobody cares what technology you use to create your game, as long as it's good.

HTML5 simply provides a powerful, flexible ecosystem that serves as the foundation for making great games.

Enough Talk; Let's Make Games

If you're still here then you're burning to make some games. It's best to keep things as simple as possible so you can easily start working whenever some idea randomly pops into your brain. Our plan is to start completely from scratch and write everything from the ground up. As we progress, we'll separate out elements we encounter that aren't game-specific (that is, things that can be reused from game to game). These elements will go into a small library that we'll create and build upon for future projects.

 These Are Just Guidelines

PLEASE NOTE! Every single thing we do in this book—how we organize our project, the library we build, how we name our methods and write every line of code, the overall architecture, the number of enemy spaceships we spawn, and how many bullets it takes to explode them—it's *all* just a guideline, a suggestion. Don't be afraid to rip things up, do things your own way, move things around. *Experiment relentlessly*. The best way to get comfortable with new ideas is to rewrite them yourself. Feel free to follow along on our beaten path, but don't be afraid to go off-road.

Let's start our game with an HTML skeleton that all of our examples will derive from. Although we're making games, we're still using web technologies. We still need HTML, CSS, and JavaScript. The only difference is that we'll combine them in a way that *looks* more like a game than a web page. Game development is all about creating illusions!

The general structure of our games will go like this:

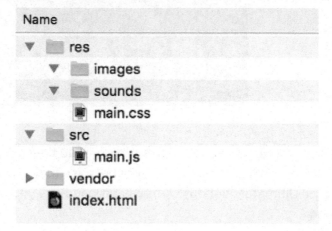

1-8. Base project structure

We have a source directory *src* for our game-specific files, *vendor* for any third-party libraries we might need, and finally *res* for game resources such as images, stylesheets, and audio files. The *index.html* file contains some very simple markup to get us started:

```
<!DOCTYPE html>
<html>
<head>
  <meta charset="utf-8" />
  <title>Game</title>
  <link rel="stylesheet" href="res/main.css" />
</head>
<body>
  <div id="board"></div>
</body>
</html>
```

Here's a first reminder: this is *just a guideline*! You probably already know how you like to structure your HTML documents—so go with that. The only interesting piece is the *board* div that we'll use as the container element for our games. (It's called "board" because that's what I started calling my "game board" area a million years ago, and it stuck.) It has some minimal styling via the stylesheet in *res/main.css* to center it on the page, and to stretch it to a desired dimension:

```
#board {
  width: 640px;
  height: 480px;
  margin: auto;
}
```

There are many tricks we can use to maintain the illusion our game is a cohesive, seamless artifact—but the power of CSS is one of the easiest. The background of the web page can be left a solid color, or it can be styled to match the *aesthetic* of the game. The area surrounding `#board` might be blank, or it might display colorful panels like the ones that decorated old arcade game cabinets. Use whatever works for your game, and whatever helps the player get lost in the experience. We won't spend too much time on CSS—but don't forget it's always available to you.

The last step in our project skeleton is to add some code—a simple JavaScript file that will be the main entry point for our games. In honor of JavaScript's shared C language heritage, we'll save this in our `src` directory as `main.js`:

```
const gameType = "awesome";
alert(`Let's make ${ gameType } games!`);
```

Our first snippet of code may be unfamiliar to some. The `const` keyword (which defines a variable as constant, non-mutable) and the template literal strings (strings enclosed with backticks that allow embedded substitutions) are part of the ECMAScript 2015 standard for JavaScript (see the SitePoint book *JavaScript: Novice to Ninja*[7] if you'd like to read more about newer JavaScript features). Our games will take advantage of modern JavaScript, so it's important to make sure it's executing correctly. To verify that it runs, include the source file as a JavaScript module in `index.html`:

```
<body>
  <div id="board"></div>
  <script type="module" src="src/main.js"></script>
</body>
```

---

[7] https://www.sitepoint.com/premium/books/jsninja2

Modules

At the time of writing, the JavaScript *module* implementation has been finalized as part of the ECMAScript 2015 standard, but browser support is not universal. Code samples for the book have also been compiled to "regular old JavaScript" via the Babel JavaScript compiler—but this is intended as a short-term solution that will not, eventually, be necessary. Consult the "Build Tools and Workflow" section later in this chapter for more information.

If you've got the popup alert working, that's good enough for a project base! Let's quickly hack some logic to make one of the least exciting games in the whole world: the good ol' "What number am I thinking of?" game. Remove the `alert` and replace it with our game code:

```
const myGuess = Math.floor(Math.random() * 20) + 1;
let guesses = 0;
let guess;
```

First we set up variables to hold the total number of guesses and pick a number between 1 and 20. Now we ask for the user's guess and compare it to ours:

```
while (guess !== myGuess) {
  guess = parseInt(prompt("What number am I thinking of?"), 10);
  guesses++;
  if (guess < myGuess) {
    alert("Higher.");
  } else if (guess > myGuess) {
    alert("Lower.");
  }
}

alert(`Well done! You got it in ${ guesses }!`);
```

First parse the user's guess as an integer. If the guess is too high or too low, alert the appropriate message. If it's correct, say "Well done!" The game is boring (though *slightly* more funny if you change `myGuess` from 1-in-20 to 1-in-99999999!) and the user interface based on `alert`s and `prompt` dialogs is extremely annoying. But despite this, it contains the main elements we need for *all* games: an infinite loop, some game logic, and a render system.

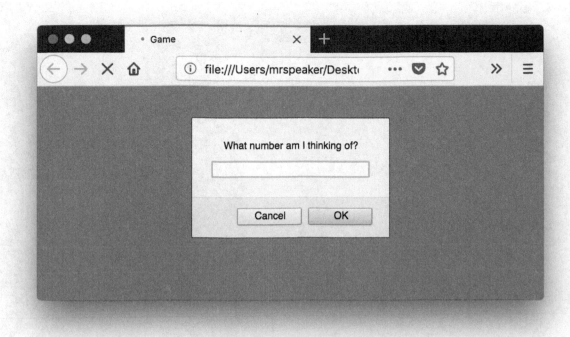

1-9. What number am I thinking of?

The `while` loop runs until we get the answer correct: it's our **main game loop**. The `prompt` is our **user input mechanism**; the game logic will determine if we have a **collision** (a correct guess); and `alert` is our **render system**, giving feedback to the player. To make a real game, we only need to swap out the alerts with image drawing, and input prompts with keyboard controls ... and hey presto—a video game!

Hopefully at this stage you're psyched to get your big ideas on screen. But first we have a few administrative tasks we need to get in order before we go wild. We need to choose some basic tools, and we need to set up a productive project *workflow*. If at any point you're feeling sleepy, skim forward to the aptly-titled section "Staying Motivated".

Making Art

For our first few games, we can get by with basic geometric shapes—such as squares and circles—but we'll quickly want to move on to something more impressive. And don't be too quick to dismiss simple shapes either, as they can be used to good effect. The hit indie game *Thomas Was Alone*[8]

[8.] http://www.mikebithellgames.com/thomaswasalone/ was populated entirely by rectangles and circles—yet the *aesthetic choices*, storytelling, and narration infused so much emotion and personality into those simple shapes.

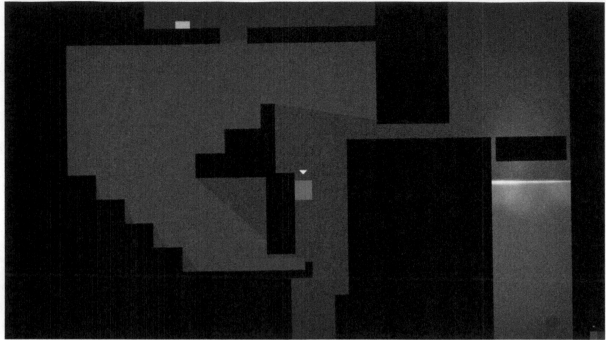

1-10. Thomas Was Alone

But let's assume that rectangles ain't gonna cut it. We want some art. Perhaps you're an artist who can draw well and you're a wizard with graphical editing software … But more likely (like me) you'll be capable of producing *programmer art*. I could *try* to draw, say, a horse—and anyone I asked would probably guess that it's a horse—but it's not going to win any awards for "Best Horse Drawing". If that's also the case for you, it's best to start off with either simple *vector illustrations* or low-res *pixel art*. Neither are "easy", but with a bit of work you can produce some nice results—and with a lot of work you can produce some great results.

Vector illustrations are created by combining and manipulating basic shapes, polygons, and paths. Because the image is described by points (rather than actual pixels), things can be colored, stretched, resized, and edited without losing any information. Objects can easily be copy-pasted and reused without loss of quality.

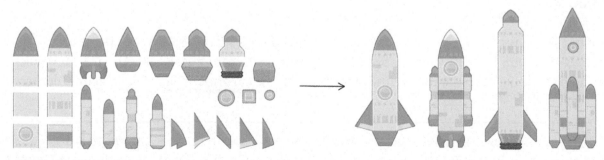

1-11. Kenney.nl Rocket Kit

There are several good vector-based editing software packages around. Inkscape[9] is the go-to free and open-source vector editor I'd recommend. It's under constant development and improvement, and you'll find plenty of resources around to help master it. There are also some great commercial alternatives. Adobe Illustrator (the Photoshop of vector editing) is used by a lot of professional design houses, as are Affinity Designer[10] and Sketch[11].

The concepts between all of these suites are basically the same—and general tutorials for *any* software will often be applicable to all. If you want to learn to start making graphics for your games, head over to the very excellent 2D Game Art for Programmers[12] site for some beginner-friendly vector editing tutorials on making all sorts of game assets.

 Rasterizing

When using vector software, you'll most likely need a **rasterizing** step, because the vectors will ultimately be displayed in your game as bitmap images (*unless* you're using SVGs—which I'll say a bit about in the next chapter). Usually, rasterizing simply requires selecting the **export as PNG** function from your vector software package.

If you're looking for a different aesthetic, but still want to keep things *reasonably* simple, you can try your hand at low-res pixel art. **Pixel art** is artwork created at the *pixel level*—placing individual pixels by hand, as opposed to using large paint brushes that do things like antialiasing and smoothing for you. It's a style that originated back in the early days of video games, when video game characters had to be designed on graph paper!

9. https://inkscape.org/
10. https://affinity.serif.com/en-gb/
11. https://www.sketchapp.com/
12. http://2dgameartforprogrammers.blogspot.com/

128	64	32	16	8	4	2	1		
			■	■				16 + 8	= 24
	■	■	■	■	■	■		64 + 32 + 16 + 8 + 4 + 2	= 126
			■	■				16 + 8	= 24
		■	■	■	■	■	■	32 + 16 + 8 + 4 + 2 + 1	= 63
	■	■	■	■				64 + 32 + 16 + 8	= 120
■		■	■	■	■			128 + 32 + 16 + 8 + 4	= 188
	■	■			■	■		64 + 32 + 4 + 2	= 102
	■	■			■	■	■	64 + 32 + 4 + 2 + 1	= 103
								DATA 24, 126, 24, 63, 120, 188, 102, 103	

1-12. Graph-paper Sprites

The actual technical definition of pixel art is not critical (you can argue about that on the internet), but for us it's useful as an aesthetic option for creating games that feel "8-bit" and retro. It's a style that I'm a big, unapologetic fan of!

Good pixel art is incredibly difficult to do. Reasonable-and-usable programmer pixel art is not so hard … and very good fun to try. The number-one tip when starting out is this: the worse you are at art, the lower you should keep the image resolution. If you have a large canvas for your game's character, you need to hand place a lot of pixels, and you have to be good at drawing. If you make a *tiny* canvas—say 16x16 pixels—you can make more abstract, iconic representations of game characters. With a bit of work, they can even look pretty good! As you improve, you can up the canvas size. 16 pixels *is* really small, though, so you might need to resize the images before using them in the game.

To create pixel art, you have a few options. You can use a dedicated pixel art editor such as the excellent Aseprite[13] editor, which is designed especially for pixel art. All of its tools and features work at the pixel level. You can also use more general image editors, such as GIMP[14] (free and open source), Paint.NET[15] (for Windows), and Pixelmator[16] (for macOS)—which *can* work as pixel

---

[13.] http://www.aseprite.org/
[14.] http://www.gimp.org/
[15.] http://www.getpaint.net/index.html
[16.] http://www.pixelmator.com/

art editors, though you'll need to configure their tools to draw and erase single pixels.

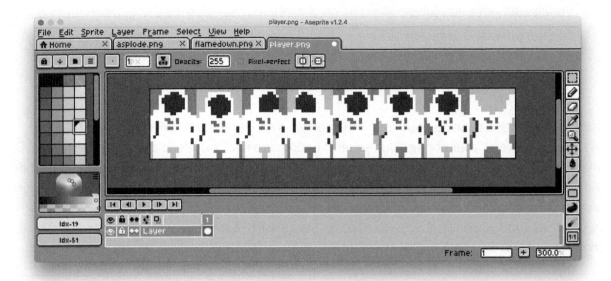

1-13. Aseprite pixel editor

An easier option, of course, is to just use someone else's art—a very tempting option when you can't draw! There are various online resources that supply game art under various licenses. The most well known is <u>Open Game Art</u>, which has a large collection of user-submitted content that can be used in your games. Another is the free, ever-growing art collection of Kenney[17], the asset-producing virtuoso.

1-14. Kenney.nl platform game graphics

---

17. http://kenney.nl/assets

Copyright

Please be careful when using art you haven't created. Artwork (including music and sound effects) is covered by licensing and copyright law. Be sure to check the license attached to these works. You don't want to get in legal trouble for releasing a game with assets you don't have the right to use.

Using preexisting art can be good for motivation when you first start making games. Things *instantly* improve as your boring "blue square" becomes a cool, futuristic cyborg chicken ninja. Or whatever. The problem is, this approach doesn't scale well. The chicken might be great, but when you want to add an underwater level for the chicken to explore, you'll need to go looking for more assets. Even if you find some great underwater assets, they'll have a style of their own. As your game grows (and you pull from more sources), things will become less consistent. You'll have nice graphics, but bad *aesthetics*.

I promise that, in the end, it will be more rewarding to struggle through with your own programmer art (or at least find an artist to collaborate with). Any futuristic cyborg chicken ninjas will be your own.

1-15. Futuristic cyborg chicken ninja

Build Tools and Workflow

The games we'll create will be written in standard JavaScript. To run them, you just load the game page in your web browser—*in theory*. If you're reading this book in "the future" (that is, in the years following 2018, when I wrote this book) it will be true *in practice* too. Each code example has an `index-native.html` file that will run in modern browsers (you may need to still *serve* the page so it's accessed via `http://` rather than `file://` . More details are available in the code repo). At the time of writing, support for some of the new JavaScript language features is not yet universal, so as boring as it sounds, we need to set up some tools for managing our games project.

The solution for working with tomorrow's features today is to *transpile* our code into a form that works on older targets. **Transpiling** is a term that means *to compile code to the same level of abstraction* (rather than to a lower level, such as C to assembly). Transpiling is like converting source code to source code. We convert from source code that will only run in modern browsers to source code that will run in both new and older browsers.

As your projects become more complex, getting them into their final, runnable form becomes harder. Tools that manage your overall project are called **build tools**. They *build* your project from source and resources into the final product—transpiling and minifying your files, copying over art assets, stripping out debugging information, running code-formatting verification tools across your codebase, and so on. Although a lovely aspect of JavaScript and the Web is that it's not *necessary* to use any build tools, in reality you either *need* to run them (for example, to transpile to older targets) or often *want* to run them (to streamline the game-making workflow). In JavaScript land, this pretty much means using npm[18].

npm is a general package manager for JavaScript that's part of the Node.js ecosystem. It's a set of tools for working with JavaScript packages and projects—as well as a giant repository of other people's code you can conveniently slot into your own projects! To install the ecosystem, head over to nodejs.org and follow the instructions on the front page. There are installers (and source code) available for macOS, Windows, and Linux.

Assuming the installation process went swimmingly and was pain free (the communities for Node and npm are very friendly if you get stuck), we can take npm for a test run. npm keeps track of meta information (such as which files belong to a specific project) by means of a special `package.json` file that lives in the root directory. You can manually add this file, or use the command line tool to generate one for you via `npm init` (from *inside your project folder*):

```
npm init
```

npm will respond with a wizard that asks you for some required and optional data about the project. Once done, it creates the `package.json` file with the metadata you entered. Third-party packages and tools can now be brought into your project by installing them with another `npm` command. For example, a handy package is the small web server (which we'll be using in all of the examples in this book) called Budo[19]. Budo is "a dev server for rapid prototyping". It serves up our game page as if it were up in the cloud. It also has some extra cool features, like live reloading: the web page will magically reload whenever you save a change in your code. To install it, use the `npm install` command:

---

18. https://www.npmjs.com/
19. https://github.com/mattdesl/budo

```
npm install --save-dev budo
```

npm install <package name> is how we install third-party packages for inclusion in our project. But notice we also added the flag *--save-dev*. This indicates that Budo *is only needed while developing*—that is, it's not to be included when our game is finished and we want to distribute a final build. To run Budo, we'll take advantage of another benefit of *npm* —the ability to run scripts for managing our project flow. In *package.json*, find the *scripts* object and add the following *start* command:

```
"scripts": {
  "start": "budo src/main.js:build.js --live"
},
```

It instructs Budo to run and to load the *src/main.js* file. If this file includes any other files, it will also load them—and serve everything as a single *build.js* file.

```
npm start
[0000] info   Server running at http://192.168.1.161:9966/ (connect)
[0000] info   LiveReload running
[0000] 35ms   1459B (browserify)
```

Typing *npm start* will execute the command and serve our game up at a URL. If you navigate to the URL, the game will load! But actually, it will still be pointing at the module *src/main.js* —because that's what we told it to do in *index.html*. To make it use our new *build.js* file, change the script tag in *index.html* to *<script src="build.js"></script>* . This will now fetch the bundled *build.js* project file.

That's not very interesting on its own (though the live reloading is pretty cool), but we can now extend Budo to use features like Babel[20] Babel is the primary tool in the JavaScript world for transpiling our code for older targets, allowing us to use all the latest and greatest features from the new versions of the JavaScript language.

```
npm install --save-dev babelify babel-core babel-preset-env
```

Babel is an extremely modular tool that makes it very flexible ... but also unbelievably confusing to new users. If you install those three packages above (*babelify* , *babel-core* , and *babel-preset-env*) you should be good to go. To make Babel compile our code for older targets, modify the *start* command to pass flags we need for babelfication:

---

[20] https://babeljs.io/

```
budo src/main.js:build.js --live -- -t [ babelify --presets [ env ] ]
```

 Bypassing Budo

When it comes time to release your game, you'll need to bypass Budo and use the mechanism *it* uses under the hood for running code in the browser: *Browserify*. This whole build-setup thing is getting boring, though, so I won't go into detail. Have a look at the example repo for how I've done this, and run `npm run build` to save the `build.js` file to disk!

Phew, okay, yes. Setting up tools can be a drag—but once everything's running smoothly, these tools become invaluable. We can grab helpful libraries from other people and easily integrate them into our games, we can extend the `npm scripts` sections to automate and simplify our development workflow, and we can export our *own* code packages that other people around the world can use. Pretty cool.

Version Control Systems

Regardless of your build system (or lack thereof), you'll also eventually need to master a *version control system (VCS)*. A **VCS** tracks changes in your codebase over time. When you make some changes to your code, you *commit* the change with a message about what you did. This might sound a bit annoying, but it allows you to revert to any point in your project's history and run your game from there. This feature is an absolute lifesaver when you make some breaking change at 3:00 a.m. before a hard deadline and can't *for the life you* figure out what you did to break it. It also makes working with teams a lot more manageable, as you can all work on the same codebase and merge your changes as you go.

There are lots of systems available, but one of the most popular is **Git**. It was created by Linus Torvalds (creator of Linux) as a tool for distributed developers to work on the Linux kernel. It's mostly a command line tool, but there are graphical interfaces available for all platforms. These days, Git support is often built directly into your code editor, so you can commit changes without leaving your code.

Git also spawned the fantastic online service GitHub. **GitHub** provides an easy way to store and share your version-controlled code with the world. There are lots of resources available if you're just getting started, such as ReadWrite's *GitHub For Beginners*[21] article.

---

21. http://readwrite.com/2013/09/30/understanding-github-a-journey-for-beginners-part-1

> ### 📌 Valuable Time Spent
>
> Getting up to speed with a VCS and various build tools is one of the best investments you'll make in your developer life. Once you master them, you'll wonder how you survived without them. But to play devil's advocate for a moment, I'll also point out that time spent learning project tools is time spent *not developing your game*. If you've never made a game before, I won't tell anyone if you postpone learning Git for a while in favor of getting something moving on the screen!

Staying Motivated

The final thing you need before we begin is motivation. Motivation is what drives you to get stuff done. Perhaps your motivation is just money—creating a breakout hit on the App Store and never having to work again. Perhaps it's fame—to be recognized in the gamedev field as a developer rockstar. Perhaps it's art—to make something the world has never seen before, or challenge society's beliefs. Perhaps you just want to finish a game.

Because we're all different, and we have a long way to journey together, I'll just assign us a common group motivation for the duration of this book. Here goes …

The evil AAA game studio conglomerate, *Exploitative Games, Inc.*, has decided it's time to crush the indie game market … and all the developers in it. This concerns you directly, because you're a professional indie game developer. You've decided to quit your day job (and in spectacular fashion: you can *never* go back) to start your very own game development studio, *MomPop Games*.

Having procured some co-working space, an old laptop, and some takeout coffee, you arrive on your first day of your new life.

Upon entering the lobby, you bump into an ominous, white-suited figure who you recognize instantly as *Guy Shifty*, CEO and owner of the world-renowned *Exploitative Games, Inc.* (which just happens to be located in all of the 34 floors above your office). He pauses and looks at you suspiciously for some time. An associate leans over and whispers something into his ear. Finally he says, cryptically, "Don't get too settled in. I plan to become king of the indie scene and get rid of the amateurs like you once and for all … *MomPop Games*."

He and his entourage shuffle past, leaving you staring at your coffee.

Looks like we've got a bit of friendly competition on our hands! We'd better get started.

Get Ready!

Now that we're all suitably motivated, here we go. Our mission is clear: we need to learn how to create amazing, captivating, successful video games, and we need to learn fast. We already have our project set up and ready to go. Our workflow is in place. We've got the tools, we've got the talent. Now we just need some good ideas, and a tiny bit of knowledge.

Fortunately, in just a few hundred pages you'll walk out of here with the know-how for creating absolutely *any* hair-brained game you can imagine.

Drawing Things | Level 2

Having settled into your brand new office space, your fellow co-workers are starting to ask you some hairy questions—such as, "Can we see some of your work?" The problem is, so far we have *nothing to show* (don't show them that "what number am I thinking of?" game, please). We don't even have a logo. It's important to have great game ideas—but ideas alone are not enough. We need to get them out of our head and onto the screen as soon as we can. Before we can run, we need to learn to walk. For us, that means displaying some simple graphics. We need to start drawing things.

The first thing to realize is that you can make a game with just about *any* technology that exists. The "how to make a game" list from the previous chapter was *very* short: in a loop, *get user input* ... to *move everything a tiny bit* ... then *respond to collisions* ... before you finally *draw everything*. If you understand the core of a game at this level, it's not surprising that people create games that run in all sorts of weird places: in spreadsheets, on LGR's old Ti-83 calculator[1] on Plonat Atek via an oscilloscope[2] ... If you can add logic and visuals to something, you can use it for games.

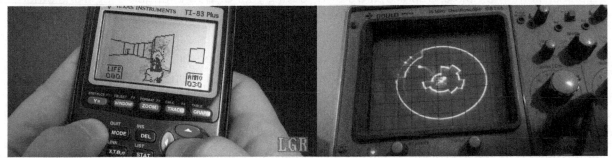

2-1. Strange place for a game!

 Don't Get Pigeonholed

Try not to pigeonhole yourself to a particular technology. Whenever you read a tutorial or see some code, think about how you can apply the *general ideas* to any situation (or any programming language). That way, you'll never find yourself locked into one solution, and you'll gain insights from more sources.

DOM vs Canvas vs WebGL

These days there are several excellent options available for us when it comes time to push some pixels into the eyeballs of our players: plain ol' web page elements (via images, containers styled with CSS, or SVG elements), the Canvas 2D API, and WebGL. Each of these comes with wildly different features, costs, and benefits. Ideally, the way you architect your game will be fairly

---

[1.] https://www.youtube.com/watch?v=nduMTX86ZI0
[2.] https://s-ol.itch.io/plonat-atek

render-agnostic so that it's possible to take your game and render it to different environments without modifying too much of the core code.

If you have a webdev background, the most obvious way to get things on screen is via DOM elements in a web page. Using standard image elements, for example, we can position and move things around the screen. We can take advantage of DOM events, CSS transitions and animations. The downsides to this approach are possible poor performance (if you have a lot of things happening on screen), and no direct access at the pixel level: you can mostly only work with *existing* images. They can't be wildly manipulated at runtime.

On the other end of the spectrum is WebGL. WebGL is an effort to bring the power of GPU processing to the web. Your computer's CPU is great at processing general-purpose instructions for running software, but when you need raw number-crunching speed to manipulate zillions of pixels at 60 frames per second, you need to run on the GPU. WebGL provides a way to render graphical elements via the graphics card's GPU, leaving your CPU free for game logic and other tasks.

WebGL has recently found its way into most modern web browsers and mobile devices, making it a promising and powerful target for our games. It's a target that will become more important as we start pushing our games to the limits. WebGL's downside is that it has a *very* steep learning curve—and an arcane, low-level API.

For the most part, we'll be using a third option to make our games: the Canvas API. It doesn't have the raw processing power of WebGL, but it's simple to use, provides the ability to draw basic shapes and manipulate pixels, and does all the important stuff we need for making games quickly. But again, don't get too bogged down in the details: our goal is to make fantastic games. The technology we choose is just a means to an end!

Plain Ol' DOM

Before we get lost in the innards of the Canvas API, let's have a look at how we could make a game the "old fashioned" way. It's still viable (and sometimes even preferable) to make your games with standard DOM elements. It's especially viable if you're a web developer: you already know how to get things on screen and move them around.

Elements in an HTML document are organized logically in a tree structure. This organization is called the **Document Object Model** (DOM). It's a tree because the document starts with a *root* node, that contains one or more *child elements*. Each of these child elements can themselves be containers that have further child elements. At the bottom of each branch are the *leaf nodes* that contain the content to display on screen. However, the tree doesn't dictate *where* an element appears on screen. It's CSS that allows you to put them pretty much wherever you want. Having a model with a separation between logical organization and on-screen display is good for modeling web pages, but it also works well for making games.

Using DOM elements is a little different from other drawing environments, because it's a "set and forget" approach. In most rendering systems (including Canvas and WebGL) you have to re-draw the screen manually *every frame*. But the DOM takes care of this for us! So if you place your evil boss character in the center of the screen, he'll stay there being evil for ever and ever.

If we want to use the DOM for games, our primary task is to keep our game's *logical model* (in JavaScript) synchronized with its *actual on-screen position*. When we create a new game character in our game code (or remove an old one) we dynamically add or remove a corresponding DOM node via the standard DOM methods `appendChild` and `removeChild`. We keep a reference to the DOM elements in our JavaScript code, and then keep everything in sync as they move about in the game.

To put this to the test, and to prove we can make a game in any ol' tech, let's make a quick DOM-based game—*Rick Clicker 2000*. The goal of *Rick Clicker 2000* is to click and remove all the Rick Astleys from the page as quickly as possible. If you have webdev experience, you probably already see how this will work: it's some images with a click event handler.

2-2. The raw excitement of Rick Clicker 2000

We'll begin with our base project from Chapter 1, but remove all the existing code in `src/main.js`, leaving us a with blank slate:

```
<div id="board">
  <span id="remain"></span>
</div>
```

The only addition to the base code's HTML file is a *span* with ID `remain`. This is where we'll show how many Ricks to click. Now, let's write some code:

```
let clickers = 50;
let startTime = Date.now();

// position element in the DOM
function sync (dom, pos) {
  dom.style.left = `${pos.x}px`;
  dom.style.top = `${pos.y}px`;
}
`${pos.x}px`
```

First, we set up two global variables: one is the number of Ricks to click, and other is the time the game starts (so we can tell the player how long they takes to finish). We also add the all-important `sync` function that is the heart of our DOM renderer. `sync` moves an absolutely positioned DOM element (`dom`) to a given position with `x` and `y` coordinates by setting its `left` and `top` CSS properties respectively. In our tiny game the Ricks don't move, so we'll only need to call the function once per Rick. But if you were making an action game, it would be necessary to call `sync` *every time Rick moved* to keep the DOM elements up to date.

```
function addClicker () {
  const pos = {
    x: Math.random() * 500,
    y: Math.random() * 300
  };
  const img = new Image();
  img.src = "res/images/rick.png";
  img.style.position = "absolute";
  img.addEventListener("click", removeClicker, false);

  document.querySelector("#board").appendChild(img);
  sync(img, pos);
}
```

The `addClicker` function creates a new Rick and assigns him a screen position with random `x` and `y` coordinates stored in a variable called `pos`. An HTML image is created using `new`

Image() . It has an event listener attached that listens for a "click" event, and is styled to be absolutely positioned (so we can move it around by altering its *top* and *left* properties).

Finally, we can add the Rick to the page. We're using the *document.querySelector* method to select the *board* element from the page, and *appendChild* to inject the image. We correctly position Rick via our *sync* helper (if this were an action-based game, we'd have to update the *pos* variable as Rick moved around, and then re-call *sync*). The *pos* variable is the *logical model* and the DOM image node is the rendering system.

 Finding DOM Elements

The *querySelector* method accepts a query selector string and searches the page for *the first* match (its partner *document.querySelectorALL* is similar, but searches for *all* matches). The query string can be any valid CSS selector.

Because this is the DOM, we have to remember our normal website-making rules. The image for the game has to go in the correct folder (*res/images/*), and it's absolutely positioned via CSS. This means the image location will depend on the parent container it's *relative to*. Because *#board* has no styling, the relative container is the main *body* element. But we want the images to appear inside our game board, and for that we make *#board* relatively positioned.

```
#board {
    /* additional styles for Rick */
  position: relative;
  background-color: #8CD;
}
```

We've added a bit of CSS in *res/main.css* to make the images relative to the game *#board* . And we'll add a background color for our game for good measure. A nice sky-blue feels appropriate. With that fixed, any absolutely positioned elements will be aligned relative to *#board* . Perfect.

```
function removeClicker (e) {
  e.target.parentNode.removeChild(e.target);
  clickers--;
  checkGameOver();
}
```

When the user clicks on an image, the *removeClicker* function is called. This function receives the mouse event for the click, which we can use to find the event *target* —which is the correct Rick element to remove via *removeChild* . Finally, we call our *checkGameOver* function to see if all the Ricks are gone.

```
function checkGameOver() {
  document.querySelector("#remain").innerHTML = clickers;
  if (clickers === 0) {
    const taken = Math.round((Date.now() - startTime) / 1000);
    alert(`De-rick-ed in ${taken} seconds!`);
  }
}
```

Now for a bit of game logic. The remaining total of Ricks is displayed. If that's *zero*, the game is finished and we calculate the time it took to clear the screen. The only thing left is to add a whole bunch of Ricks to start things rolling:

```
// Add all the Ricks!
for (let i = 0; i < clickers; i++) {
  addClicker();
}
```

So this is (technically, at least) a game—but notice that we didn't have to add an infinite loop anywhere. Earlier we said this was a *primary requirement* for making games, so what's going on? The trick is that the DOM is doing the loop for us behind the scenes. It has its own **event loop** that sits around waiting for the user to do things (like click an element) and dispatches the events to us. We say that the Web is **event-driven**. Our game *only* reacts to events: it doesn't do anything by itself. This turns our core game loop on its head:

2-3. Modified game loop

Traditional game programming tends to be more sequential than this. We'll make our own explicit loop to show the difference in Chapter 3.

But being able to use the browser's event loop is actually a terrific reason to use the DOM for games: we get the benefits of the event handling for free! The browser captures clicks for us—and these events target *individual page elements* (such as each Rick). When it comes time to do this in a procedural way (with Canvas or WebGL), it will be up to *us* to do this logic manually. If we want to know if the player clicked a Rick, we'll have to get the current mouse position and figure out which elements occupy *that space* using our logical model (the `pos` variable), and *then* figure out which of those is on top.

With a bit of imagination and a liberal sprinkling of graphics and CSS transitions, we could turn *Rick Clicker* into a more entertaining game. *Cold Snap: Vegas Ruleshttp://www.mrspeaker.net/dev/ld31* is a DOM-based game from the *Ludum Dare* game jam competition, featuring a clicking mechanic similar to *Rick Clicker*—but with a bit more polish. It could also be the start a terrifying Clicker game—perhaps something like *Universal Paperclips*[3], but with Ricks.

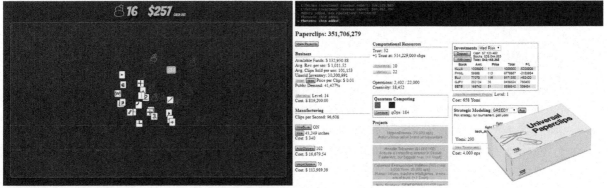

2-4. Clicking can be fun

The games we've made so far are not very good. When starting game development, it's critical to start small. *Really small. Really really small.* It's so tempting jump right in and try to make a something epic (or at least "medium sized"). But small steps are the key to getting games finished ... and getting games finished is *the hardest part of gamedev.*

To maintain your sanity through your initial, potentially boring games, you *must* add your own style and flair to everything you touch. *Rick Clicker* is bad, but at least *a little bit* funny. Play with every image, every variable, and make them your own! If you keep in mind your game's aesthetic, you can add character and interest to even the simplest of ideas.

Why Not DOM?

So the DOM looks like a pretty nifty way to make games. We get a lot of browser power for free. It's easy to add event handlers, and we can use our existing knowledge of CSS animations and

[3.] http://www.decisionproblem.com/paperclips/

effects. The flip side to this power is performance and extensibility. Action-packed games might have hundreds (or thousands) of things moving on the screen at once—goodies, baddies, explosions, particle effects ... Each time something moves in a DOM document it triggers a **reflow** of the entire page. The browser needs to recalculate the correct position for all the elements on the screen and repaint them. This potentially takes a lot of time and limits how many things we can move smoothly.

Additionally, we don't really have any direct access to the pixels on the screen: we can add and remove elements, but we can't easily create our own images from scratch or do processing on existing ones. We can partly get around this restriction by using SVG (Scalable Vector Graphics). SVG provides a rich drawing API for shapes and paths (as well as regular DOM nodes for event handling) ... but we still don't get access at the pixel level, and it's also relatively slow.

If these problems are acceptable (or nonissues) for game ideas you have, then *by all means* use the plain ol' DOM (or SVG). It's a perfectly valid choice for getting things on screen!

Canvas API

In this book we'll largely be using the Canvas API for drawing. Introduced by Apple in 2005 for the dynamic creation and display of graphics and images, it was standardized in HTML5 and is now supported on most modern web browsers. The API sports a variety of features for drawing shapes, text, images, paths, and gradients. It's fairly comprehensive, but we only need to know a subsection of it for getting started making games.

Our project skeleton from Chapter 1 includes an HTML page containing a single div element. Let's add a canvas element inside that:

```
<div id="board">
  <canvas width="640" height="480"></canvas>
</div>
```

Just like any DOM element, we need to get a reference to it if we want to play with it. Let's do that with `document.querySelector` inside `main.js` and then log the variable to the debug console to double-check the reference is correct.

Using the Console

If you're not familiar, a **web console** is an interface for logging messages while your code runs. It's not a standard part of the Web, so you shouldn't leave it in your final code output—but it's a very powerful tool for debugging. Most modern web browsers include support for functions like `console.log` (for general log messages) and `console.error` (for logging scary-looking messages). Find out how to access your browser's web console, and memorize the keyboard shortcut for opening it!

```
const canvas = document.querySelector("#board canvas");
const ctx = canvas.getContext("2d");
console.log(ctx.canvas);
```

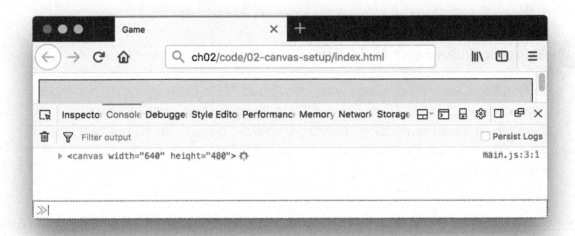

2-5. Canvas in the console

With the canvas element in our hands, we ask for a *context* for drawing via `canvas.getContext("2d")`. The canvas element is designed to allow various APIs to be layered on top of it; it's like a general container for drawing stuff. We've asked for the drawing context called *"2d"*, but we could ask for others (for example, if we had "webgl" we could get access to the WebGL API). There also may be other APIs accessed in this manner in the future. But for now, we just want to draw some 2D shapes.

Using the Context

Notice that we can also get the original canvas element back from the context (`ctx.canvas`). This is handy for getting attributes like the canvas *width* and *height* programatically.

Drawing Some Shapes

You use the Canvas API in a *stateful* way: many settings you make—such as defining the paint color, or the amount of transparency—is done once and then remains in effect until you change it. To make things appear, there's a host of primitive drawing instructions (with names like `fillRect` , `arc` , `path` , `text` , and `drawImage`). Composing a complete image is a process of making changes to the settings and then calling the drawing instructions until you achieve your final result.

Skim the Following if You're Super Impatient

What follows are instructions on using the Canvas API to draw things. It's not about making games, but just drawing things. It's really interesting, and well worth learning—in the spirit of "doing things from scratch". *But* ... if you're impatient and itching to get on with it, feel free skim through. It's some good stuff though, so don't skim too fast!

Many Canvas drawing instructions only define the *path* of the shape, not information on its visual characteristics. To get something on screen you need to specify if you want to *stroke* the path (paint the outline of the shape), or *fill* the path (paint all of the insides of the shape). If you want to do both, you need to do two separate drawing instructions.

Before we define our shapes, we first have to set some global colors for drawing:

```
ctx.strokeStyle = "black";
ctx.fillStyle = "red";
```

The `strokeStyle` property sets the outline color of the shape we'll draw, and `fillStyle` sets the shape's solid fill color. Again, these are stateful properties, so once we've assigned them, all further drawing operations will use `red` and `black` until we reassign them to something else. The valid values for colors are any supported CSS Color DOM String[4] **named values** ("red", "black" etc., as above), or RGB strings (such as `0xFF00FF` , or `rgb(255, 0, 255)`). We'll also be

---

[4.] http://dev.w3.org/csswg/css-color/—usually

using some other formats as we go, to get alpha support and for making some nice color palettes for our games.

With the colors set, we can at last be rewarded with an image on screen:

```
ctx.fillRect(300, 200, 50, 50);
ctx.strokeRect(300, 200, 50, 50);
```

The first instruction, `fillRect`, draws a filled rectangle in the color of the current fill style (red). The next instruction, `strokeRect`, then draws an outline of a rectangle over the top of this, in the current stroke style (black). Both operations expect the same set of four parameters: `x position`, `y position`, `width`, and `height`. All values are in pixels.

The coordinate system starts in the top left of the screen. We've asked for our rectangle to start 300 pixels in from the left, and 200 pixels down from the top. So we'll end up with a 50x50 pixel square, starting at screen location 300x200 and ending at 350x250—kind of in the middle of the screen.

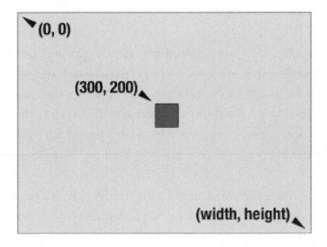

2-6. A canvas square

Our first game character—what a lil' rascal! I hope you're a little excited now that we're drawing! Probably not going to win any art prizes with this little guy, but a journey of a thousand miles starts with a single rectangle. Many a great game prototype has featured the trusty square protagonist. And if it's fun with rectangles, it's going to be extra cool with real art.

Naturally, a square is nothing without its beloved partner in crime, the circle. There's no `circle` method on the Canvas API. Instead, we have to make a circular *path* with `arc`:

```
ctx.beginPath();
ctx.arc(325, 170, 25, 0, Math.PI * 2, false);
ctx.fill();
ctx.stroke();
```

Oh, this looks a bit more complex than the rectangle. We're using a canvas path to create a circular shape. The steps for making a general path are to start by calling `beginPath`. We then define the path shape—in this case using then `arc` drawing instruction. And finally we call `fill` or `stroke` (or both) to render the path in the appropriate color.

The `arc` method is a flexible way to draw circles or sections of a circle. The six parameters it expects are `x`, `y`, `radius`, `start`, `end`, and `antiClockwise`. `x` and `y` are the locations of the *center* of the circle. `radius` is the radius from the center. The `start` value indicates the angle on the imaginary circle the path begins, and `end` where it finishes. From 0 to `Math.PI * 2` represents an entire circle (see the "Degrees vs Radians" section that follows). The last parameter is optional and dictates the direction of the arc: clockwise by default, but you can change it by setting `antiClockwise` to true.

Degrees vs Radians

Let's take a brief aside to discuss degrees vs radians. We may as well get this out of the way now: in game development, anything that involves angles is usually expressed in *radians* rather than *degrees*. If you remember from school, a circle has 360 degrees—or 2π *radians*. Radians is just another unit of measure for angles. If we move clockwise, then 0 radians lies due east, π x 0.5 is south, π is west, π x 1.5 is north, and 2π is back where we started. The value π is accessible in JavaScript via the method `Math.PI`.

It's easy to convert between degrees and radians: if a full circle is 360 degrees, or 2π radians, then a semicircle is 180 degrees or π radians. So to get radians from degrees, `π/180 * degrees`, and to get radians from degrees it's `180/π * radians`:

```
const deg2Rad = deg => (Math.PI / 180) * deg;
const rad2Deg = rad => (180 / Math.PI) * rad;
```

You can do all of your planning in degrees and convert them to radians at the last minute. But radians are so ubiquitous that it's probably better if you just get used to thinking in radians!

The ability to draw simple shapes like circles and rectangles might not seem super exciting to begin with, but they can easily be composed into more impressive forms. Additionally, they're very helpful for debugging (for outlining images and shapes when doing collision detection, for example) and can also be used for some simple and cool effects. Let's make a starfield (starting with our project skeleton):

```
const canvas = document.querySelector("#board canvas");
const ctx = canvas.getContext("2d");
const { width: w, height: h } = canvas;
```

Like our rectangle + circle friends above, we start by getting a reference to the canvas element, then fetch the width and height (by destructuring and renaming the canvas's width and height as `w` and `h`). Next, we set up some colors:

```
ctx.fillStyle = "black";
ctx.fillRect(0, 0, w, h);
ctx.fillStyle = "#555";
```

We fill the entire screen with black, using the instruction `ctx.fillRect(0, 0, w, h)`. This fills a rectangle starting at the top left and ending in the bottom right. Then we change colors to a suitably cosmic gray, ready to draw some stars:

```
let x, y, radius;

for (let i = 0; i < 550; i++) {
  x = Math.random() * w;
  y = Math.random() * h;
  radius = Math.random() * 3;

  // draw the star!
  ...
}
```

We set up some variables and then loop a lot of times (because there's a lot of stars in space). For each star we pick a random `x` and `y` position and radius. All that's left to do is draw some circles:

```
// draw the star!
ctx.beginPath();
ctx.arc(x, y, radius, 0, Math.PI * 2, false);
ctx.fill();
```

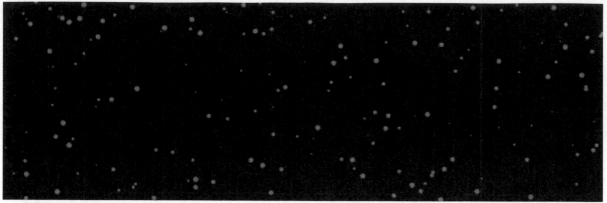

2-7. Point-y starfield

A simple starfield background like this can add depth to your scene, and it also highlights a nifty lesson in game development: a simple thing repeated a lot of times can add up to more than the sum of its parts. Add "static starfield" to your bag of tricks. It'll come in handy, I promise.

The Canvas API also has the ability to draw text. It's a useful feature for both providing information to the player (in the form of head-up displays, scores, or instructions) and information to *us* as debug messages during development. Just as we can set the fill and stroke color, we set font information via the `font` property. This is a string that defines the font you want to use, as well as its size. By default, it's "10px sans-serif", but you can change it to whatever you want:

```
ctx.font = "20pt courier";
```

By default, the font families available are restricted to the fonts on the user's computer. Just like with regular CSS, we have the ability to include custom fonts. This is helpful for adding style and individuality to our games and to ensure the fonts look the same to all players.

After setting it to the best font available to us for now (monospaced fonts are the best of course—so computer-y!), we then fill or stroke (or both) a message with *fillText* and *strokeText*:

```
const center = w / 2;
ctx.textAlign = "center";

for (let i = 0; i < 11; i++) {
  ctx.fillText("if you're in the game", center, i * 40);
}
ctx.strokeText("strokes the word", center, h - 30);
```

2-8. Text rendering

The parameters for the `text` method are a string with the message we want to display, followed by the `x` and `y` coordinates to plot at. The text will start from the location provided, but the alignment can be modified if needed. In our example, we modify it by setting the `textAlign` property to `center`. This way, the text is balanced on either side of the `x` coordinate.

Images

Okay, finally we've made it. Here comes the big one! Circles and squares are fine for debugging and testing, but in general we won't be making our game assets out of simple shapes. The vast majority of assets in our games will be beautiful art we create elsewhere and then import. The Canvas API supports a few useful image-drawing operations, the most basic of which takes an HTML image and plots it at a given location.

Sounds great, but there's one small catch: the image needs to be already loaded *before* we can draw it. As we move though our game development journey, we'll see better ways to tackle asset loading. For now, we'll just wait for the image `load` event using `addEventListener`:

```
const img = new Image();
img.src = "res/images/rick.png";
img.addEventListener("load", draw, false);
```

Starting from our project skeleton again, with our friend `rick.png` copied into the `images` directory, this snippet of code will create a new DOM image and load the given URL. Once loading is complete, it will call the `draw` function, which looks like this:

```
function draw() {
  for (let i = 0; i < 100; i++) {
    const x = Math.random() * w - 50;
    const y = Math.random() * h - 100;
    ctx.drawImage(img, x, y);
  }
}
```

Jackpot! Step one in our plan for gamedev world domination is complete: we can draw a game character on screen! The `drawImage` method takes the image object along with the `x` and `y` coordinates and plots the image to the canvas at that point.

But `drawImage` can do oh-so-much more. It also has some optional parameters for *cropping and stretching* the image that's rendered. For example, if we supply two extra parameters— `width` and `height` —we can change how the image is scaled. By default (if you don't supply the parameters) they are the correct pixel dimensions of the image. But if you want to double the width of the image, you can multiply it by 2. If you want to halve the height, divide it by 2 ... and so on.

Most of the time we'll keep the multiplier value the same for both width and height so things are scaled uniformly. Let's test this out by creating another starfield example ... only this time as a snowfield. A snowfield of snowflakes:

```
const img = new Image();
img.src = "res/images/snowflake.png";
img.addEventListener("load", draw, false);
```

The setup is similar to our last example: load the image, then call the `draw` function:

```
for (let i = 0; i < 100; i++) {
  let x = Math.random() * w;
  let y = Math.random() * h;
  let scale = Math.random();

  ctx.drawImage(img, x, y, width * scale, height * scale);
}
```

2-9. Snowfield

Our starfield just got a lot cooler (geddit?). This time we have a loop with 100 snowflakes. Each snowflake gets a random `x` and `y` position, as well as a random scaling factor. `Math.random()`

will return a number between 0 and 1: we multiply the snowflake's dimensions by this factor to get the final output size.

Besides scaling, there's one more trick up *drawImage* 's sleeve. It can accept a call with *nine* parameters for getting very precise control over what's drawn on screen:

```
ctx.drawImage(image, sx, sy, sw, sh, dx, dy, dw, dh);
```

Phew, that's a lotta parameters. There are really three "sets" here. First is the image, which we already know. The remaining parameters are two sets of *x* , *y* , *width* and *height* parameters: a "source" and a "destination". This *source* lets you specify a *piece* of the original image, and the *destination* specifies where on the final canvas to draw (and to what scale).

```
// Draw the original
ctx.drawImage(img, 170, 140);

// Draw cropped images
for (let i = 0; i < 22; i++) {
  ctx.drawImage(
    img,
    // source
    32, 0, 53, 75,
    // destination location
    i * 20, i * 10,
    // destination scale
    i * 0.2 * 53, i * 0.2 * 75
  );
}
```

2-10. '80s video effects!

This example crops a Rick head from the original image: from 32 pixels in from the left and 0 pixels down from the top—then 53 pixels across and 75 pixels down (this defines the *source* area). It takes this crop and moves and scales it to create the crazy '80s video effect. We'll be using this technique a lot when making animations from grids of images: a single image will contain all the animation frames, but we'll crop out individual cells to display like a flip book.

The last cool thing about `drawImage` is that the `image` parameter isn't restricted to DOM images; you can also use another canvas element as the image source. This is really useful when doing procedurally generated assets, or adding static effects to existing images.

Transformations

There are still a few power features we need before getting down to making games. The Canvas API provides us with a set of features for performing transformations on the drawing surface. We can *translate* (move), *rotate* and *scale* (as well as perform more advanced general matrix transformations) our drawing operations. These affect the canvas surface itself—like keeping the "pen" still and moving the "paper" underneath.

The effects of transformations are cumulative (the order that you perform them is important) and permanent (so every subsequent drawing operation is affected). Because of this, we also get a way to undo stateful changes: `save` and `restore` . These methods create a *stack* of canvas states: we can push and pop from the stack to ensure we don't get cumulative weirdness—like making a 1-degree rotation that accumulates every frame, sending our game spinning uncontrollably. (Of course, this might be *exactly* what you want!)

To see the stack in action, start with 100 squares drawn in the current `fillStyle` :

```
function draw() {
  for (let i = 0; i < 100; i++) {
    const x = Math.random() * w;
    const y = Math.random() * h;
    ctx.fillRect(x, y, 50, 50);
  }
}
```

Now we'll draw black rectangle, followed by some red ones, and then `restore` the context:

```
ctx.fillStyle = "black";
draw();

ctx.save();
```

```
ctx.fillStyle = "red";
draw();
ctx.restore();

// Back in black!
draw();
```

Here we wrapped the red rectangles in a save and restore. When we *restore*, we go back to the original state. In this case, the `fillStyle` is returned to black. The result is three layers of rectangles: the background and foreground in black, the middle ground in red. We could easily do this manually without `save/restore`, but it becomes tedious when we want to perform a whole bunch of temporary changes.

Sometimes the cumulative nature of canvas transformations is useful, and we don't want to `save` and `restore` our changes. Here's an example where repeatedly applied transformations give us a nice kaleidoscope effect:

```
const { width: w, height: h } = canvas;
ctx.translate(w / 2, h / 2);
```

The first step is to move the origin of the canvas with `translate`. By translating to half of the width and half of the height, we've effectively offset all our subsequent drawing operations relative to the middle of the screen. Drawing a rectangle at point 0x0 will plot in the center, not in the top left.

```
for (let ring = 1; ring < 28; ring++) {
  ctx.fillStyle = `hsl(${ring * 25}, 90%, 50%)`;
  for (let dots = 0; dots < ring * 6; dots++) {
    ctx.rotate((Math.PI * 2) / (ring * 6));
    ctx.beginPath();
    ctx.arc(0, ring * 15, 7, 0, Math.PI * 2, true);
    ctx.fill();
  }
}
```

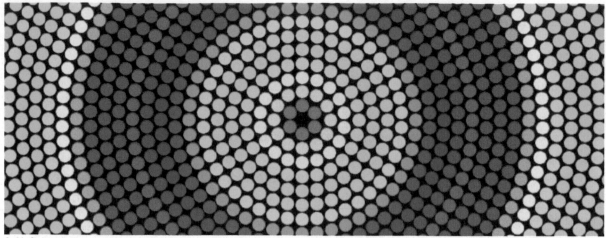

2-11. Color rings

Next we do a nested loop of "rings" and "dots". Each time we draw a dot, we rotate the canvas a small amount. It's important to note the rotation is in degrees, not radians (see earlier). Each ring has 6 dots, times the ring number (so the inner-most has 6, the next has 12 etc.)—so our rotation amount is a full circle (`Math.PI * 2`) divided by 6. We draw each dot at `x` position 0, and `y` position dependent on the current ring number. Because the canvas itself is rotating, we get a circle pattern.

 HSL

The color of each ring is set using HSL values. **HSL** (an alternate to RGB for defining a color) stands for "hue, saturation, lightness", and is a great gamedev trick for picking random colors that aren't terrible! The *saturation* and *lightness* values range from 0 to 100%, and the *hue* ranges from 0 to 360 (as in degrees in a circular color-wheel)—with 0 being red, and 360 also being red, with all the colors of the rainbow in between. We'll talk more about colors as we progress, but notice in our example we modify the hue while keeping the saturation and lightness constant.

Blending and Alpha

Now that we've nailed the basics, we can look at some quick-'n'-easy effects to add to our repertoire. The Canvas 2D API features some more "artistic" functions that are required to compose nice-looking scenes.

By default, everything we plop onto our canvas is drawn fully opaque. Images drawn with `drawImage` will have the correct transparency (if transparency exists in the original source image), but we don't have control over this at runtime. To control transparency ourselves, we need the `globalAlpha` property. The `globalAlpha` number value ranges from 0 (completely invisible) to 1 (fully opaque). As its name suggests, it applies *globally* to any drawing operations we do.

```
ctx.save();
ctx.save();
ctx.globalAlpha = 0.3;
ctx.fillStyle = "blue";
draw();
ctx.fillStyle = "orange";
draw();
ctx.fillStyle = "green";
draw();
ctx.restore();
ctx.fillStyle = "lemonchiffon";
draw();
```

Because the `globalAlpha` is less than 1, initial shapes are see-through. When we `restore` them, `globalAlpha` returns to 1, so the final draw call is solid.

2-12. Alpha circles

Let's look at one final cool trick of the Canvas API. In the example above, each layer of shapes is drawn over the top of another. In the intersecting areas, orange has precedence over the blue, and green has precedence over orange. But this behavior can be altered via the `globalCompositeOperation` operation.

The *composite operation* will be familiar if you've ever used Photoshop or similar image editing software that can change how layers are blended when things are drawn over the top of each other. In the Canvas API, the default value is `source-over`, meaning that the new image (the source) is rendered over the existing (destination) image. There are lots of other values available. Here's an example of some of the possible composite operations:

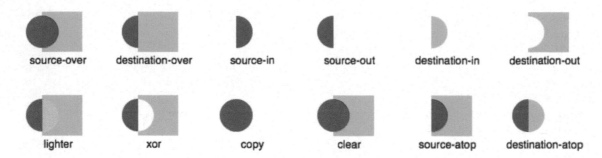

2-13. Composite operations

It's best to play around with these—some have more obvious effects than others. For example, setting `ctx.globalCompositeOperation = 'destination-over';` means that when you draw a shape, the *background* will end up in front of the new shape! You might not need to change these too often, but they can be useful for creating some interesting effects and game ideas. For example, here's a screen shot from the game *Zmore*. In the game the entire scene is invisible. But the player can use a laser gun (powered by the `destination-out` composite operation) to shoot bubbles that render parts of the wall visible:

2-14. Composite operations in effect in Zmore

Recently, browsers have begun to implement additional composite functionality called **blending modes**. They work the same, but are more concerned with how *colors* are mixed. Because they're relatively new, not all modes are fully supported on all browsers, so you should check out the results on browsers you want to target before shipping your game.

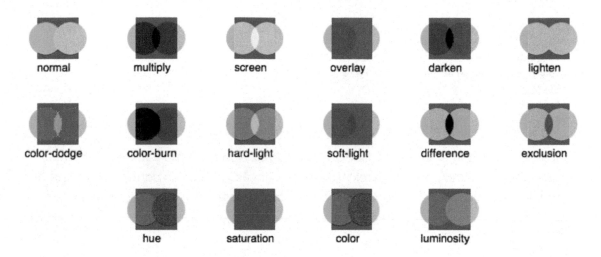

2-15. Blending modes

To test out the composite operations, we'll get down to business and create ourselves a new company logo. This is going to show up at the start of all our games, and be printed out and sticky-taped to our office door—so it had better be good! First, we'll define the main shape of our logo as two stacked words—MOM and POP—in big letters:

```
// Draw the words as a mask
ctx.font = "bold 70pt monospace";
ctx.fillStyle = "black";
ctx.fillText("MOM", 10, 60);
ctx.fillText("POP", 10, 118);
```

Next, we'll change the composite operation to `source-atop`, which takes the source and only draws it where you're trying to draw. So our initial words will act as a mask:

```
// Draw lines over the mask
ctx.globalCompositeOperation = "source-atop";

// Rainbow!
for (let i = 0; i < 6; i++) {
  ctx.fillStyle = `hsl(${i * (250 / 6)}, 90%, 55%)`;
  ctx.fillRect(0, i * 20, 200, 20);
}
```

```
`hsl(${i * (250 / 6)}, 90%, 55%)`
```

This gives us some nice rainbow text. But now we need a drop shadow. By switching to *destination-over* , we re-draw our words in black, offset by a few pixels, and only the shadow will be visible:

```
// Draw the shadow behind the logo
ctx.fillStyle = "#999";
ctx.globalCompositeOperation = "destination-over";
ctx.fillText("MOM", 13, 62);
ctx.fillText("POP", 13, 120);
ctx.font = "30pt monospace";
```

The last step is to add the "games" byline under the logo. Now we jump back to the default composite operation and print some text. However, Canvas gives us no control over the font's letter-spacing attribute, and the default is too tight for our logo. So we'll do our own letter spacing, by plotting individual characters in the right place!

```
// Back to default
ctx.globalCompositeOperation = "source-over";

// Add characters (so they're evenly spaced)
"games".split("").forEach((ch, i) => {
  ctx.fillText(ch, i * 37 + 12, 145);
});
```

2-16. A home-made logo for MomPop Games

Ah, the perfect logo. Our neighbor Guy Shifty at *EGI Games* is going to be mighty jealous of this masterpiece. Let's print it out and stick it on the door. You can perform some great visual trickery with the various features of the Canvas API, so it's a good idea to spend some time figuring out how to use them. You never know when your game might call for some zany effects!

Performance Considerations

If you spend any time around gamers, it won't be long before they start talking about **FPS** (frames per second) in games. This is the number of times the screen will be redrawn every second. There needs to be a minimum amount to fool the human eye into seeing movement. The "gold standard" at the moment is 60 frames per second—though many argue that 30 frames per second is enough to be smooth ... as long as the game is good!

Canvas is powerful and pretty fast. You can easily make complex games, with lots of images and effects, all running at 60 frames per second. But there are limits. If you do too many `drawImage` calls (or other CPU-intensive operations) you'll start to notice things slowing down. For now, we're not worried about performance *at all*. Getting some experience under our belt is priority number one. But at some point in the future, on larger projects, you'll notice your game start to get sluggish. When that happens, jump to Chapter 9 for some killer performance tips.

Game Engines vs Reinventing the Wheel

At this point you might be wondering why we're reinventing the wheel by making our own game library from scratch. Hasn't someone else already done it? It's a valid question, and one you should consider carefully. Indeed, there are many excellent existing game libraries and engines for creating games. The hard work of writing a rendering engine and game framework has already been done for us; we could just plop in our graphics and write some game logic.

There's a saying in the gamedev world: "Make games, not engines." As computer programmers, we love to hack and tinker with things. We like to understand how *everything* works. It's a noble trait, but it can sometimes obscure our larger, long-term goals—like actually finishing a game. We can save vast amounts of time (and get more impressive results, at least initially) by surrendering some control and using the tools already available to us.

So, why are we doing it from scratch?! First, it's because we love to tinker and understand how everything works! The goal of this book is not to create a new JavaScript game library. It's to understand the fundamentals of *how* a game library works. To do this, you have to be able to dive in, and play, and experiment with *every aspect* of the code. A third-party library may include its source, but the project is already built. It's already huge. Everything is already in its place and it's hard to know *why* it was structured that way and how you could modify it.

By building it ourselves, we'll know *everything* about our library. We can tinker and change it however we want, and make it do whatever we want.

More crucially, a framework is a set of constraints. Game development is a highly creative undertaking, and frameworks and engines are like starting a painting with a base layer of paint-by-numbers: the end results can still be beautiful and interesting, but there will still be some essence of those initial boundaries. Frameworks can shape how you think about *the possibilities* of your games.

It's a trade-off. Ultimately, anything you can do to get games *completed* is good. Just don't forget the drawbacks. Many of the biggest indie hits (such as *Braid* and *Fez*) worked because of a quirky core mechanic that would have been hard (or even impossible) to implement in popular frameworks at the time. If you constrain yourself to thinking in a framework, you make it harder to think about experimenting with crazy ideas.

Okay, that's enough for the warning. With the explosion in popularity of HTML5 games, we've seen several excellent libraries and frameworks bubble to the top. It's been a rapid boil, though, so be sure to keep your eyes peeled for other newcomers to the field. And even if you don't use them, they're useful for ripping off good ideas for your own library!

Game Libraries and Engines

The quantity and quality of HTML5 game libraries is growing rapidly. At the time of writing, Phaser.io[5] has (by far) the most traction in the JavaScript game-making community. Phaser will render to Canvas or WebGL and has built-in physics and particle engines, handles user input and triggering sounds, and has helpers for managing your game entities, and lots more.

Impact[6] is another mature project, with a consistent and full-featured API. It has support for animations, images and sprites, sounds, physics ... everything you'd need for making games. It's not free (it's still US$99 at the time of writing) but the cost includes the game engine, a cool level editor, and the source code for both. It was created by Dominic Szablewski (responsible for several great gamdev-related projects—notably *Ejecta*, which we'll cover when it comes time take our games to mobile devices), and has a large and loyal community behind it.

[5.] http://phaser.io/
[6.] http://impactjs.com/

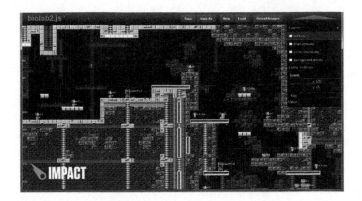

2-17. Phaser.io and Impact.JS

Now—have you considered non-JavaScript options? I won't judge, because getting projects *finished* is the primary objective. If some game-making software works for you, use it! One of the most prolific and easy-to-get-started packages is Game Maker[7]. It has been responsible for some massive Indie hits including *Undertale*, *Nuclear Throne*, *Gunpoint*, *Hotline Miami*, and *Spelunky*. A similar, web-based package is Construct3[8] which has a growing userbase.

If you want to "get serious", then the king of the indie world at the moment is Unity[9]. Unity is primarily a 3D (though recently its support for 2D is getting better) game-making engine and IDE that's extremely popular amongst indie game developers. Games can be exported cross-platform, to iPhone and Android, and there's even an exporter to HTML5 (though it's pretty flaky—at least at the time of writing).

 Godot

Another up-and-comer in this space is the Godot[10] game engine. It's a free and open-source environment that's looking to take on Unity. It's growing in popularity, and is worth keeping an eye on.

Finally, if you want to stay with trusty JavaScript but don't want to do *everything* yourself, you might consider Pixi.js[11]. Pixi.js is a 2D WebGL renderer (it falls back to Canvas if the browser doesn't support it) that's designed solely with the intent of rendering your game super fast. If you find yourself hitting the limits of canvas performance, Pixi.js is where you should turn next!

[7.] https://www.yoyogames.com/gamemaker
[8.] https://www.scirra.com/
[9.] https://unity3d.com/
[10.] https://godotengine.org/
[11.] http://www.pixijs.com/

Quick, Draw

That'll do us for drawing. Canvas provides us a fast and flexible rendering environment that's pretty fun to work with. It might not be the Ferrari (or Tesla Roadster) of the rendering world, but it's perfectly capable of handling our game requirements—at least for our first dozen or so games.

Anyway, enough drawing. Let's go make some games.

Game Loops & User Input

Level

3

There's a knock on the frosted-glass office window. It's Guy Shifty and his shiny white teeth. "Hey, friend!" he croons, "we've got a little Friday two-hour game jam going on this afternoon. Fancy showing us what you're made of? I don't expect you can do anything under that kind of time pressure, but I'll buy a copy of the winner's game for a dollar. You in?"

Good news! We've just been commissioned to produce our first ever game. If we earn that dollar, we'll (technically) be professional game developers! Also, it's our first *game jam*. **Game jams** are organized events where people get together to make games, either solo or in teams, online or in person. They sometimes have themes or other restrictions, and they always have a time limit. A fixed deadline is a great incentive to start *and finish* making a game.

We're getting ahead of ourselves. We still have a several missing pieces to figure out before we can claim our dollar prize money.

3-1. High-level loop

We can draw a static scene, but that's far from a game. To create the illusion of movement and interaction, we must enter the mind of the *cartoonist*—composing a collection of static scenes, where the actors move ever so slightly each frame. If we carefully consider timing and expression, we can *move everything a tiny bit* in a way that looks and feels alive.

The Loop

Here it is—*the* number one most important step in our list of game-making requirements: the *infinite loop*. Inside the loop is where we animate things, fetch periodic input from the outside world, and perform the necessary calculations to make our scene respond appropriately. In the following sections, we'll build up a generic loop system that can power our games.

There are many ways to loop—from the quick and dirty, to the ridiculously over-architected. Just as with our rendering engine, how far you go will depend on your specific requirements. Just remember not to get lost in the details at the expense of making games. A quick and dirty solution that powers a fun game is more valuable that an elegant system with no game attached.

 The Loop Exists

As mentioned in Chapter 1, even if you aren't writing the loop yourself, it exists. In the case of our *Rick Clicker* game, the browser's built-in event loop was running in the background, updating the view and responding to user input.

The Old-school Way

The quickest and dirtiest way to loop in the browser is with the `setInterval` and `setTimeout` methods. Not so long ago, these were the *only* way to do animation in JavaScript without blocking the main UI thread. (An infinite `while` loop, for example, could control a game, but because JavaScript is single-threaded it would lock up the entire page!) The `setInterval` and `setTimeout` don't block, and both work in a similar way:

```
setInterval(() => {
  // Run your game loop!
}, 1000 / 60);
```

The first parameter is the function that will run after a certain time has elapsed. The second parameter is the delay time in milliseconds. If we specify 5000, for example, the function will be called once every five seconds. By specifying `1000/60`, we're asking for a loop that runs every 16 or so milliseconds. A thousand milliseconds in a second, divided by 60, gives us *60 frames per second*. `setInterval` will run unceasingly and forever.

To interrupt the loop, you need a reference to the *timer ID* returned from calling `setInterval`. This is an integer that we can then pass to `clearInterval` to break the infinite loop. This gives us some control. Let's use that control to play a game called "*How many milliseconds does your luck last for?*" Starting at 0, time will accumulate until you're unlucky and the game's over:

```
const start = Date.now();
const timer = setInterval(() => {
  // Clear the screen
  ctx.fillRect(0, 0, w, h);
  // Write the time
  ctx.strokeText(Date.now() - start, 20, 80);
```

```
    if (Math.random() < 0.01) {
      ctx.strokeText("Game Over!", 160, 180);
      clearInterval(timer);
    }
  }, 1000 / 60);
  "Game Over!"
```

3-2. Game over!

The game begins by taking the current time (in milliseconds) with `Date.now()`. The `setInterval` loop runs until you're unlucky (that's when our friend `Math.random` gives us a very small number). Theoretically, if you're extremely lucky, the game will *never* finish—but practically, it takes a couple of seconds. My high score is 6424. Yet another boring game, but you should be a little excited, because we're seeing our *first bit of animation*. Something is changing on screen at 60 frames per second!

An alternative to `setInterval` is `setTimeout`, which works in a similar way but loops *only once*. If you want to loop again, you have to re-call `setTimeout`. To facilitate that, we convert the anonymous function into a named function, `loopy`, and have `setTimeout` call `loopy`:

```
const start = Date.now();
function loopy () {
  ctx.fillRect(0, 0, w, h);
  ctx.strokeText(Date.now() - start, 20, 80);

  if (Math.random() < 0.01) {
    ctx.strokeText("Game Over!", 160, 180);
  } else {
    // Loop
    setTimeout(loopy, 1000 / 60);
  }
}
loopy(); // Start things running!
```

This construct is a bit more verbose than `setInterval`, but it affords us more control over when and how things loop. If you want to pause and resume the action, for example, it's just a matter of not calling `Loopy` until it's time to start again.

These days there are better options than `setInterval` and `setTimeout`. But if you find yourself just wanting to get something looping without thinking about it (say, if you've just been thrust into a last-minute game jam), then these will work happily in all browsers, old and new.

Looping with HTML5

The problem with `setTimeout` and `setInterval` is that they're a bit unreliable. They weren't really designed for doing very high-precision animations. Also, they'll just keep on running if the user switches browser tabs—unnecessarily draining their battery and using up CPU cycles. Thankfully, HTML5 has given us an improved timer specifically for running animations— `requestAnimationFrame`. Our general game loop structure (that we'll use throughout the book) will look like this:

```
// Game setup code
...

function loopy (t) {
  requestAnimationFrame(loopy);

  // Game logic code
  ...
}
requestAnimationFrame(loopy); // Start things running!
```

A call to `requestAnimationFrame` says "I'd like my callback function to run on the next frame, please." It runs at 60 frames per second in the browser (perfect for games) and it calls a function passing a single parameter of type `DOMHighResTimeStamp`. The timestamp is the amount of time that has elapsed since the page loaded. Note that to start things running we didn't call `Loopy` directly, but rather we invoked it via `requestAnimationFrame`. This is so we always have a correct value in our `t` (time) parameter.

Let's give it a whirl by creating our first bit of real animation—a small visual effect entitled "*fading raindrops in the cold, cold night.*" It's some white circles randomly plotted on a black background. But the black background is also painted with a very low opacity wash (by setting Canvas's `globalALpha`), creating a pleasant transition of slowly fading splotches.

3-3. Rain splotches

```
// Game setup code
ctx.fillStyle = "#000";
ctx.globalAlpha = 0.02;
```

In our game setup code, we set the Canvas state for drawing: a black background (`#000`), and a very low global alpha level. Inside the `Loopy` function we can do the "game logic". Here's where we *move everything a tiny bit*:

```
// Game logic code
ctx.save();
ctx.fillRect(0, 0, w, h);
ctx.fillStyle = "#fff";
ctx.globalAlpha = 1;
```

The background is painted all black, the color set to solid white (by making `globalAlpha = 1`). Now we can splatter our circle to a random location, at a random size:

```
// Random circle
const x = Math.random() * w;
const y = Math.random() * h;
const radius = Math.random() * 20;

ctx.beginPath();
ctx.arc(x, y, radius, 0, Math.PI * 2);
ctx.fill();

ctx.restore();
```

The effect works because we paint the background with a very low alpha, but paint the circles with a very high alpha. This results in the "raindrops" becoming washed out over time. Experiment with all of the values to see the impact.

Commit This Loop to Memory

You should commit the simple `requestAnimationFrame` loop to memory. It's a couple of lines that you'll use over and over again, and having it in your brain will help when you find yourself taking part in something like the Zero Hour Game Jam[1], a contest that takes place as daylight savings time moves back an hour. Start making your game at 2 a.m., and when you finish an hour later, it's 2 a.m. again!

An Even More Accurate Loop

The `requestAnimationFrame` timer is good enough to get started, but it still has some limitations that affect how your game works on different computers. This is especially true when we come to doing physics, where small timing issues can compound, until the game catastrophically fails—usually in a hilarious and explosive fashion.

We can alleviate most problems by keeping track of how much time elapsed between the previous frame and the current frame. If we account for this elapsed time in our animation code, things will animate correctly—even with different frame lengths. By multiplying our game object's speed by the *delta time between frames*, a short frame (one that executes quickly) will only move the object a short distance. Conversely, if the frame takes a long time to complete, the delta time will be greater and the object will move further. The net effect is consistent movement regardless of frame length.

```
// Game setup
...
let dt = 0;
let last = 0;
function loopy (ms) {
  requestAnimationFrame(loopy);

  const t = ms / 1000; // Let's work in seconds
  dt = t - last;
  last = t;

  // Game logic code
  ...
}
requestAnimationFrame(loopy);
```

`requestAnimationFrame` gives us a timestamp containing the current time in milliseconds. We divide the timestamp by 1000 to get the current time in seconds. *This was an API decision.* (It's

---

[1]. http://0hgame.eu/

another decision I've made that you're free to disagree with. Many game engines leave everything in milliseconds, and you may want to as well.) I've chosen seconds because it can be more natural when thinking about how fast things should move.

We then calculate the **delta time** (`dt`)—the time elapsed since the last frame—by subtracting it from the `last` frame time. The delta time will be a factor used to correctly position our game objects. The total time, `t` , is also useful for many time-based calculations and effects that we'll need in our games.

To visually see the difference when using a delta time, we'll conduct a race between two squares—one using a fixed amount of movement every frame, and one using our new dynamic delta time:

```
// Game setup code
const speed = 64;
let p1 = 0;
let p2 = 0;
```

The `p1` and `p2` variables represent the position of each square. Every frame, the square will move by a constant amount (`speed`) multiplied by the delta time amount. The delta tells us the time that's passed in seconds, so a `speed` of 64 effectively means "64 pixels per second". Because the canvas is 640 pixels wide, it should take exactly 10 seconds to complete one lap.

To further illustrate what's happening, and to make it a bit more exciting, let's add some stats to the top of the screen that display the *frame length* and *total time*:

```
// Game logic code
ctx.fillStyle = "#000";
ctx.fillRect(0, 0, w, h);
ctx.strokeText(`Frame length: ${(dt * 1000).toFixed(2)} ms`, 70, 50);
ctx.strokeText(`Total time: ${t.toFixed(2)}`, 70, 90);
```

This canvas code will render the delta time `dt` (in milliseconds) and `t` (in seconds) on the screen. The JavaScript method `toFixed` will chop off a number at the given number of decimal places; we don't need too much precision for this example! And now for the big race:

```
p1 += speed * dt;
p2 += speed * (1 / 60);
if (p1 > w) p1 -= w + 50;
if (p2 > w) p2 -= w + 50;
```

```
ctx.fillStyle = "#f00";
ctx.fillRect(p1, 120, 50, 50);
ctx.fillRect(p2, 190, 50, 50);
```

 Tiny Movement

Before we analyze the results, let's reflect on the implications of `p1 += speed` . The square's initial position is 0. After one frame its position is *slightly more than zero*. You know what that means? It means we've just covered the second item in our list of core requirements for making games: "Move everything a tiny bit"!

The most crucial part of this snippet is the first two lines: both squares have their position increased a tiny bit adding `speed` multiplied by a factor. Square one has a dynamic factor based on the length of the previous frame. Square two has a fixed factor. Following this we do a little more game logic. We check if either square has gone past the edge of the screen. If they have, we send them back to the start of the screen by subtracting the width of the screen from their current position.

In an ideal world, these two squares would behave *exactly the same*, because `requestAnimationFrame` is supposed to loop at 60 frames per second. But if you run the program for a while (and depending on your browser and computer) you'll notice this isn't the case.

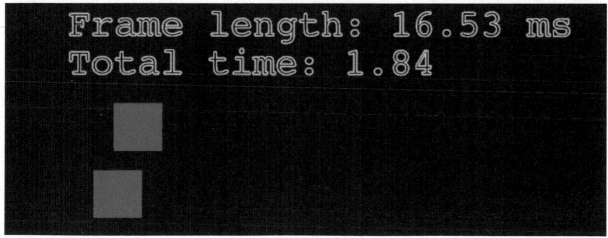

3-4. Racing squares

Switch Tabs

To really see the effect of this, switch tabs in your browser (causing `requestAnimationFrame` to pause). When you return, you'll notice that square one—thanks to the large `dt` —moves to the correct position and still finishes a lap on every 10th second. Square two—thanks to being paused—starts lagging behind.

Using a delta time like this helps to ensure a game plays fairly regardless of the user's computer speed. Our version is basic and useful enough, but there are some hidden issues with it that we'll address later (we'll need to be especially careful when we implement physics in Chapter 6). If you're feeling loopy, you should also dive into the oft-cited resource on game loops, Glen Fiedler's *Fix Your Timestep* article[2].

User Input

Our racing squares demo is alarmingly close to being a game. The next step is user input. The inherent fun of games centers around how the player's reactions affect things on screen. It's a feedback loop: their reactions influence the state of the game, resulting in a new state that requires further reactions. The challenge for the game designer (you) is to craft a compelling set of states, and provide a satisfying input system for the users to react *with*.

Writing a simple input system is really easy. Writing a *good* input system is really tough. When judging/rating/criticizing your games, the *second* thing people will comment on is the controls. (The first, unfortunately for me and my poor art skills, is graphics.) Making controls that *feel* perfect is as much art as science, and it varies wildly from game to game.

A notable example of great-feeling controls is in the indie game *Super Meat Boy*[3] by Team Meat. (I recommend you go play it if you haven't already.) *Super Meat Boy* is an infuriatingly difficult platform game where you die a lot. Despite the difficulty, the game is never overly frustrating, because the controls are so *tight*: every tiny movement of the game controller translates seamlessly to the on-screen character. When you die, you don't feel like it was the game's fault; you feel like it was your own personal failing, and you just *have* to try again.

---

2. http://gafferongames.com/game-physics/fix-your-timestep/
3. http://www.supermeatboy.com/

3-5. Super Meat Boy going through the grinder

A counter example, where *extremely difficult* controls make a game feel great is *Getting Over It with Bennett Foddy*[4]. Here the controls *do not* feel good…they make you want to throw your mouse out the window! But they're fair, so it keeps you coming back for more. The controls *make* the game.

3-6. Having some trouble getting over it

Keyboard Input

Capturing raw user input is easy in HTML5, because the event-handling systems are provided by the browser. But as we covered earlier, the web is **event-driven**—meaning that nothing happens until the user presses something or does something. That doesn't fit with the sequential flow processing of our core game loop: get input, move things, check collisions, draw everything. If a user presses a key during the "check collisions" phase, we can't jump back to the "move things" phase.

---

[4] http://www.foddy.net/2017/09/getting-over-it/

Instead of responding directly to keyboard events, we update our *model of the input state*. Then, when the loop comes around for the next frame, we can poll the current state, and everything gets processed in order. To handle keyboard inputs, we listen to the standard `keydown` and `keyup` events, and maintain an object of which keys are currently being pressed. In our code we can ask "Is key X being pressed?" Asking (rather than being told) has the added bonus that we don't have to deal with browsers' *key repeat* events that fire if we hold a key down too long.

We'll model our keyboard state in a class called `KeyControls`. It can live in a new file called `KeyControls.js` in our `lib` folder. It's in the library folder because it will be a general keyboard handler. It won't have logic that's specific to one particular game, and we can reuse it for anything that needs keyboard control.

 Structuring the Code, or Not?

This is the first time we're creating a separate file for code. Although it's in the interests of modularizing and structuring our codebase, it's still introducing complexity that isn't *strictly* necessary for our first game. We could just handle the keyboard state inline in the `main.js` without an external class. That becomes messy and hard to follow as the game grows, but it works. In fact, an exercise after you've finished this chapter is to un-make and distill our game into the simplest form possible you can. Write a small game in one file. It'll cement your understanding and reinforce that there are many approaches to structuring a game. There's no "one true way".

```
class KeyControls {
  constructor () {
    this.keys = {};
    // Bind event handlers
    ...
  }
  // Handle key actions
  ...
}
export default KeyControls;
```

Creating a new `KeyControls` instance will allocate an object literal (`keys`) that's a map from the key's **key code** (effectively an ID for the key, constant for all keyboards) to a boolean value— `true` if the key is currently down, `false` if it's not. So if the player presses the X key (which happens to be key code 88) then `keys[88]` will be `true`. We can then use this state in our games to control the characters.

```
// Bind event handlers
document.addEventListener("keydown", e => {
  if ([37,38,39,40].indexOf(e.which) >= 0) {
    e.preventDefault();
  }
  this.keys[e.which] = true;
}, false);

document.addEventListener("keyup", e => {
  this.keys[e.which] = false;
}, false);
```

The event handlers will fire for each key the player presses (*keydown*) or releases (*keyup*). The callback functions get given a keyboard event that contains a property *which* , the key's *key code*.

That strange *[37, 38, 39, 40].indexOf(e.which)* check is a trick to stop the browser scrolling if the game is embedded in a web page that has scrollbars. The numbers represent the key codes of the *keyboard arrow keys*. The array method *indexOf* will return the index in the array of a match, or -1 if it's not found. If one of the arrow keys *is* pressed, we call the event's *preventDefault* method, preventing the browser's default behavior from happening. The web browser's default behavior for arrow keys is to scroll the entire current web page—making it very hard for the player to concentrate on the game!

Now we have a simple generic key press handler that we can use in our game. To figure out what a given key's key code is, you can put a *console.log(e.which)* inside the *keydown* handler. For example, if the space bar is down (key code 32), fire! If the left arrow key is down (key code 37), move left. And so on.

```
if (keys.keys[32]) {
  // Space bar is being pressed!
}
```

However, this highlights the fact that key codes aren't very intuitive. 32? What's that?! When we're writing a game, it would be nicer if we were able to use something more meaningful. To this end, we'll add some helpful *get* properties inside the *KeyControls* so we don't have to remember all those codes:

```
// Handle key actions
get action () {
  return this.keys[32];
}
```

The `action` property will tell us if the space bar is currently being pressed. Inside a game, we can now ask for its status:

```
if (keys.action) {
  // Jump, or shoot, or …
}
```

Often there should be *multiple* key codes mapped to the same game action. If the player wants to move left, they should be able to hit the A key (key code 65—for the ever-popular WASD arrangement) *or* the left arrow key (key code 37). These can be grouped together as getters as well. Rather than return boolean values, we'll have them return some useful information about the nature of the player's intent—namely, which *direction* they want to move:

```
get x () {
  // left arrow or A key
  if (this.keys[37] || this.keys[65]) {
    return -1;
  }
  // right arrow or D key
  if (this.keys[39] || this.keys[68]) {
    return 1;
  }
  return 0;
}

get y () {
  // up arrow or W key
  if (this.keys[38] || this.keys[87]) {
    return -1;
  }
  // down arrow or S key
  if (this.keys[40] || this.keys[83]) {
    return 1;
  }
  return 0;
}
```

`keys.x` and `keys.y` are used to check when the player wants move horizontally or vertically. If the player moves *left*, `keys.x` will return `-1` . If the player moves *right*, it will return `1` , otherwise it returns `0` . Likewise, if the player moves *up*, `keys.y` will return `-1` , while *down* will return `1` and neither up nor down will return `0` . These values can be used conveniently in calculations for the *speed* of a character, which we'll do soon!

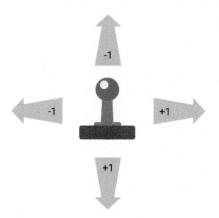

3-7. Direction offsets

We can add as many of these helper methods as makes sense for our game, and each game will likely have different control requirements. But you can easily reuse the logic from game to game. I've made the decision to hardcode the WASD/arrow controls into `KeyControls` for a few reasons:

1   They're very applicable to many action games—and all of the games in the book will use them.

2   Creating a general solution (with redefinable keys, for example) complicates the code too much at this stage.

3   Making this class more general is a good challenge. Do it yourself!

 Game Genre Doesn't Really Matter

Yes, most of the games in this book will be action- or arcade-style games. Perhaps that's not your preferred genre, but it really doesn't matter. The *ideas* behind making games are all that matter. The core loops, the techniques for handling input, and rendering on screen—they'll work for *Sim* games, *Rouge*-like text adventures, mobile zombie walking simulators ... *anything*. Don't get overly focused on one genre or technology when you're starting out. There are lots of great tutorials around for all sorts of game mechanics, engines, and programming languages. Watch as many as you can, and try to steal (and apply) their good ideas for your own games!

To use the Controls object, import the file at the top of `main.js` (with `import KeyControls from "../lib/KeyControl.js"`). Then create a new instance with `new KeyControls()`. In this example, we'll map the keyboard keys to a rectangle's `x` and `y` location, and just for fun we'll have its color be controlled by the space bar:

```
// Game setup code
let x = w / 2;
let y = h / 2;
let color = 0;
const controls = new KeyControls();
```

We have a new `KeyControl` instance ready to roll. Inside the main loop we can check for key presses, and draw our colorful square:

```
// Game logic code
x += controls.x;
y += controls.y;
if (!controls.action) {
  color += 10;
  if (color > 360) {
    color -= 360;
  }
}

// Draw the rectangle
ctx.fillStyle = `hsl(${color}, 50%, 50%)`;
ctx.fillRect(x, y, 50, 50);
```

We add the value of `controls.x` and `controls.y` to the square's position every frame. Remember that the helper properties return -1, 0, or 1. If no movement keys are pressed, the values will be 0 and the rectangle will remain stationary. Otherwise, it will move in the direction that the keys are being held down—and we have some user-controlled movement! Next, we add a conditional check for the space bar. If `controls.action` isn't active (the space bar is not being held down) we increment the variable `color`. The hue in the `hsl` color format ranges from 0 to 360; we wrap around if we exceed that.

When the square is stationary it pulses with color. If you move the arrow keys it leaves a beautiful rainbow trail in its wake. Holding down the action key will stop the color cycling and allow you to paint in a solid color.

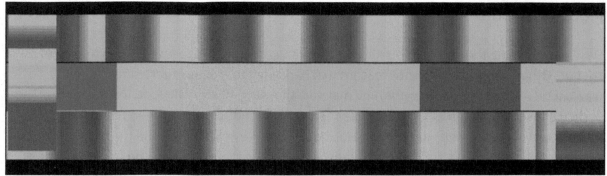

3-8. Crazy trails!

Mwahahaha! The next step towards our gamedev world domination plans is complete—actually controlling an on-screen object! Our keyboard handler is really just a map of `KeyCode -> boolean` that wraps `keydown` and `keyup` . The benefit of putting it in a module is we can extend it as our requirements change. For example, perhaps we also want to handle *other keys* without making special properties for them (like we did for `action` , `x` , and `y`). We'll make and "advanced mode" for getting or setting a key's state directly:

```
key(key, value) {
  if (value !== undefined) {
    this.keys[key] = value;
  }
  return this.keys[key];
}
```

The `key` function will return the state for the key code you ask for. If you wanted to know if the 1 key is down (key code 49) you can ask `if (keys.key(49) { ... }` . `key` also has some bonus functionality, in that you can *set* the state—which you might need to do if you want to reset a key so it doesn't fire again until the user lifts their finger and presses it again: `key.keys(32, false)` . Sometimes we might also want to do this for *all* keys that are currently being held down:

```
reset () {
  for (let key in this.keys) {
    this.keys[key] = false;
  }
}
```

This will set *everything* to `false` , so effectively no keys are being held down. The player will have to re-press a key if they want it to fire again. This ensures they don't, say, accidentally start a new game because they hit the start button the instant the title screen appears. (We don't have a title screen yet—but we will soon enough.)

Mouse Controls

We won't be using the mouse in our first few games, so feel free to jump ahead to the next section. Otherwise, you'll be happy to learn that handling the mouse is very similar to our `KeyControls` : wrap the DOM events and maintain the relevant state needed for our games. The particular events of interest are `mousedown` , `mousemove` , and `mouseup` . When the player moves their mouse over the page, we track the position. When they click or release the mouse button, we update the state. This state can be queried in the game loop in exactly the same manner as our key codes:

```
class MouseControls {
  constructor(container) {
    this.el = container || document.body;
    // State
    ...
    // Handlers
  }
}
export default MouseControls;
```

`MouseControls` takes a DOM element as a parameter. If one isn't passed, it uses `document.body` . This means that the mouse position would be reported relative to the top left of the entire web page (not the game canvas)—so it's better to pass a reference to the canvas element. Don't forget to export the class out so it can be included in `main.js` .

```
// State
this.pos = { x: 0, y: 0 };
this.isDown = false;
this.pressed = false;
this.released = false;
```

There are a few things needed to track the state of the mouse system. The first is `pos` (position) for the `x` and `y` location of the mouse pointer. The others are boolean variables: `isDown` is `true` anytime the mouse held down; `pressed` is only `true` for the *first frame* the mouse is pressed (it's only `true` once per click); and `released` is only `true` on the frame the mouse is released. `pressed` and `released` need to be calculated based on the state of `isDown` at the end of every game loop.

```
// Handlers
document.addEventListener("mousemove", this.move.bind(this), false);
document.addEventListener("mousedown", this.down.bind(this), false);
document.addEventListener("mouseup", this.up.bind(this), false);
```

For the mouse event handlers, the *mousemove* event listener will call the class's *move* method. (This method is bound to the class using the *bind* function, so the context inside the *move* function will be *this* —the class instance. If we didn't bind it, *this* would be the global window object and it would throw an error.) In turn, *move* calls a helper method (*mousePosFromEvent*) that sets the current mouse *pos* in relation to the game canvas:

```
mousePosFromEvent({ clientX, clientY }) {
  const { el, pos } = this;
  const rect = el.getBoundingClientRect();
  const xr = el.width / el.clientWidth;
  const yr = el.height / el.clientHeight;
  pos.x = (clientX - rect.left) * xr;
  pos.y = (clientY - rect.top) * yr;
}

move(e) {
  this.mousePosFromEvent(e);
}
```

The *clientX* and *clientY* coordinates come from the native mouse event. From these we subtract the DOM element's position (obtained by calling *getBoundingClientRect*). We also have to consider any canvas stretching that might be done by CSS. By finding the ratio of the *clientWidth* and *clientHeight* to the element's dimensions we can account for this and determine the correct current position of the mouse in the game screen.

 Why are we doing this every frame?

It might seem strange to call *getBoundingClientRect* every frame. The reason is that the *top* and *left* properties will change when the screen is resized. An optimization would be to also handle screen resize events and update the cached coordinates then. This is left as an exercise for the reader!

Next up we have to handle the other two mouse events: *mousedown* and *mouseup* . This is where we update the state of the mouse clicks (and call *mousePosFromEvent* again to ensure we're hitting the correct pixel):

```
down(e) {
  this.isDown = true;
  this.pressed = true;
  this.mousePosFromEvent(e);
}
```

```
up() {
  this.isDown = false;
  this.released = true;
}
```

When the user clicks, `isDown` and `pressed` are true. When the user *releases*, `isDown` is false and `released` is true. The last thing to do is to add an `update` method that needs to be called at the end of your game loop—to set the correct values for `pressed` and `released`, as these need to be cleared so they're not *true* for multiple frames in a row:

```
update() {
  this.released = false;
  this.pressed = false;
}
```

Let's replace the `KeyControls` for `MouseControls` in our last painting demo to get some nice mouse-control paint brushes happening. (Perhaps you could extend it to *also* use `KeyControls` for changing paint colors and brush sizes?) Don't forget to pass the `canvas` into the `MouseControl` constructor:

```
const mouse = new MouseControls(canvas);
```

The controls can be used in a similar way to the `KeyControls`, with the exact position coming from the `pos` variable:

```
// Game logic code
const x = mouse.pos.x;
const y = mouse.pos.y;
if (mouse.pressed) {
  color += 10;
  if (color > 360) {
    color -= 360;
  }
}

// Draw the rectangle at `x` and `y`:
...
// Don't forget to update at the end!
mouse.update();
```

If you change `mouse.pressed` to `mouse.isDown`, the color cycling will happen for as long as you hold down the button, rather than just once per click. The last—and very important—thing we do is call `mouse.update()` at the end of the loop. Without that, `pressed` would not be reset to `false` and therefore would act exactly the same as `isDown` .

Both our `KeyControls` and `MouseControls` are minimal implementations, and we'll hit their limits as we use them in real games. When this happens, we have two choices: augment the code with these requirements (so the new functionality will also be available for future games), or write completely custom controls that *only* work for our current project. Both approaches are valid. We'll extend our controls handlers where it makes sense—but good game controls are so vital to the playability of a game that sometimes you just have to bite the bullet and start from scratch!

Creating Your Game Library

Hold on tight, because we're about to change gears. We're approaching a fork in the road, or some other driving metaphor. At this point we've covered *4 out of 5* of the core steps in making a game:

Loop:

Fetch user input

Move everything a tiny bit

Respond to collisions

Draw everything

3-9. High-level loop: nearly there

You might be hoping we just get straight to "respond to collisions" and call it a day, but instead it's time to take a step back. It's time to get serious. Hopefully you can see how games are formed using our core steps. Doing each step in order, in one page, is fine for a couple of squares, but it'll become a giant mess for each new feature you have to jam in.

Making a giant mess is fine (I encourage you to do it!) because you'll learn a lot before reaching the conclusion that there must be a better way. But in the interests of making bigger games faster, we're going to start implementing one possible *better way*. As you progress, you'll find yourself creating some pieces of code over and over, and in the spirit of "Don't Repeat Yourself" it's best to group them together into a library or toolkit.

When to Add Things to Your Library

A good rule of thumb that will keep you focused on writing games, and not needlessly wasting time bloating your game library, is to only add things *the second time you need them*.

The next section is going to be quite tough. We'll cover a lot of the most important concepts in constructing a game engine. It's a huge jump from drawing a few rectangles, but the payoff will be worth it. It's also not essential you grasp everything all at once. As we start making games with our framework, it'll be more obvious how the pieces fit together.

Our Game Architecture Idea

Having a library reduces code duplication, but it's also where we can add some underlying structure and design principles. An overarching architectural idea will make it easier to decide where things live in a project, and how best to wrangle all the elements of a game. One common, high-level approach is to model all the pieces of your game as a *tree*.

A **tree** is a hierarchical structure made up of a root *node* which contains zero or more child nodes. The core idea behind our library will be a tree that maintains all of the elements in our game. **Nodes** in our system will be *container* elements that can hold either game elements (like players or bullets) *or other containers*. The game elements are leaf nodes in our tree. Similar game elements (for example, all of a player's bullets) can be grouped into a container. This system is sometimes called a **scene graph**. We can easily recurse over the tree to update the game elements ("move everything a tiny bit") or render them ("draw everything").

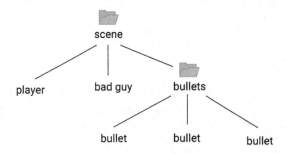

3-10. Scene graph

In this scene graph there's a root-level "container" called `scene` that holds a few game entities: a player, a bad guy (this game only has one bad guy, apparently), and another container called `bullets`. Every time someone shoots, a new bullet object goes into the `bullets` container. Every frame cycles through each child—and updates it. `Player` will handle user input, `bad guy` might calculate some AI, the `bullets` container will then get a chance to update each of its children—and so on down the tree.

One Approach of Many

This approach is just one of a huge number of ways to tackle the problem of building a game framework. Your game library will work better for you if you develop it gradually (even if you start with a spaghetti code mess!), incorporating ideas and techniques that make the most sense to you. Our approach here is fairly common, but as you'll see, it's also fairly complex. Try your own ideas, and test other libraries and frameworks to get a feel for alternate ways of doing the same things.

Core ideas and project structure are all well and good—but the *most critical* aspect to any game library is the name, of course. `MomPop Games` needs to maintain its brand identity. So unless anyone has a better idea, our library is called *Pop*. That pops! Let's rejig (and rename) our `lib` folder to look more like this:

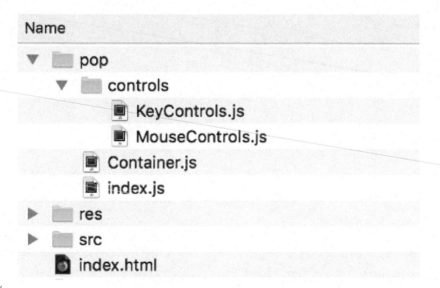

3-11. Base library

`pop` will hold all the source files of our game library. The `index.js` file will simply re-export all of the library files so everything is grouped under a single module:

```
import KeyControls from "./controls/KeyControls.js";
import MouseControls from "./controls/MouseControls.js";

export default {
  KeyControls,
```

```
    MouseControls
};
```

Then, for example, to make some keyboard controls you'd access it via `pop.KeyControls` . Eventually every file in our library will be exported out from here. Any new module we create needs to be added and re-exported.

With the name locked down, we're ready to implement the guts of Pop. The primary item—the thing we'll use most—is the `Container` class (`pop/Container.js`). You'll see a lot of containers in the coming chapters. A `Container` will be a general "bag" to group related things in. It has couple of properties: a `pos` structure that holds its `x` and `y` screen position, and an array `children` that holds the child objects. These can include "things" like players, bad guys, explosions, and bullets. It can also include *other containers*. By nesting containers we have our game tree structure:

```
class Container {
  constructor() {
    this.pos = { x: 0, y: 0 };
    this.children = [];
  }

  // Container methods
  ...
}

export default Container;
```

 Variable Names

In general, it's considered bad form to shorten variable names. *pos* is just a short form of *position* , so it would be clearer to write it out if full. But I'm going to make a few exceptions to the rule: *pos* instead of *position* , and *w* and *h* instead of *width* and *height* . The reason is partly because they're used so frequently that it becomes a pain to type out the full word, and partly because I'm just lazy. You can obviously name things however you like!

All items in our library must also be exported from the main *Pop/index.js* file to become part of *Pop* . Add *Container* to the list:

```
import Container from "./Container.js";
```

```
import KeyControls from "./controls/KeyControls.js";
import MouseControls from "./controls/MouseControls.js";

export default {
  Container,
  KeyControls,
  MouseControls
};
```

The API for our `Container` is pretty small: `add`, `remove`, and `update`. Through these we'll manage *all* of the items in a game: adding and removing heroes and enemies, and updating each so they can perform their per-frame logic. The implementation of the `add` and `remove` methods simply gets game elements in and out of the `children` array:

```
// Container methods
add (child) {
  this.children.push(child);
  return child;
}

remove (child) {
  this.children = this.children.filter(c => c !== child);
  return child;
}
```

Calling `add` will push an element into the list, and calling `remove` will use the JavaScript array `filter` method to remove a matching element. It works by calling a function once for every child element. If the function evaluates to `true`, the element will remain in the returned list. Otherwise, it's excluded and it will no longer be a child of the container.

 Returning the Same Item

> Note that `add` and `remove` *return the same item* we passed to it as a parameter. This might seem a bit redundant, but it allows us to use the value when applying it with functional methods such as Array's `map`. For example, we might use an array to initialize a series of Spaceships. Because we return the Spaceship from `add`, each object becomes part of the returned set: `const ships = [1, 2, 3].map(() => scene.add(new Spaceship())`. We just transformed 1, 2, 3 into three spaceships!

Next we can update the children. The main loop will call `update` every frame. This is how stuff actually happens; this is how we "move everything a tiny bit". Our `update` method traverses our tree structure, updating all of the containers, and sub-containers, and sub-sub-containers ... until everything has been notified and given a chance to do its thing. We also pass along the delta time (`dt`) and total time (`t`) from our game loop so they can be accessed when doing movement calculations:

```
update (dt, t) {
  this.children.forEach(child => {
    if (child.update) {
      child.update(dt, t);
    }
  });
}
```

The key piece of code here is the call to `child.update` . All of the elements in our game can (optionally) have an `update` method. If they do, the container will call it and the element can do whatever it needs to do—such as move itself a tiny bit. Additionally, our container objects *also* have an `update` method (that one we just wrote) so elements can be either "entities" that will update themselves appropriately *or* another container that will have its own children. The `update` method will be recursively called until there's no one left to update.

To use our structure in a game, we need to create a new instance of it. Then we can add, remove, and update game "things":

```
import pop from "../pop/index.js";
const { Container } = pop;

// Game setup code
...
```

The first step is to always import our fancy library. By importing `../pop/index.js` , all items are available via the `pop` accessor. We can then do `new pop.Container()` to make a container object. However, it's a bit cleaner if we then extract out the pieces we want to use as standalone variables (`const { Container } = pop;`) so our code isn't littered with lots of `pop` s.

Using the container looks like this:

```
// Game setup code
const scene = new Container();

// Example game element to manipulate
const player = {
  update: function () {
    console.log("updated!");
```

```
    }
};

scene.add(player);
scene.update();
scene.remove(player);


console.log(scene.children); // Empty list
```

`Container` is really just a way to manage an array, but it makes our life easier in a few ways. The root container gives us a nice *entry point* into all of the things in our game. Containers also let us group related things so we can apply logic to only certain containers. For example, we can easily check for collisions on only specific types of objects by putting, say, all the player's bullets in one container and all the bad guy's in another.

Additionally, the scene graph approach is very flexible: it doesn't dictate exactly what goes into the containers. We can treat background assets (such as scrolling background images) the same way we treat player and bullet objects.

The Renderer

The next big piece for our library is the *renderer*. One approach to rendering is to simply let our game objects render themselves inside their `update` function: as long as they somehow knew about the Canvas `context`, we could ask them to draw themselves every frame. They're self-contained, and have all the information they need to just call the relevant Canvas drawing functions.

Another approach (spoiler, it's the one we're going to choose) is to completely separate our *update phase* from our *rendering phase*. A specialized system—called a **renderer**—will separately traverse the game tree and decide how to draw each object. The advantage of this approach is that all of the drawing complexity is contained in one subsystem without spilling into the game logic. The "racing squares" from earlier, for example, know they have a width and a height—but they don't have to know what `ctx.fillRect()` is.

The beauty of this approach is that it's possible to have *multiple* renderers that have different render targets. One renderer (our main one) knows how to draw a square using Canvas's `ctx.fillRect()`. Another renderer may know how to draw it as a texture using super-fast WebGL (which we'll cover in <ins>Chapter 9</ins>). Another might even know how to render a racing square as ASCII text in a text console! In each case, the game logic stays exactly the same.

Create another new folder inside `pop` called `renderer`. Inside this folder create

`CanvasRenderer.js` . (Don't forget to re-export this in `Pop/index.js` .) We can also now remove the static canvas tag in the `index.html` file of our project skeleton. Because we want the ability to have multiple types of renderers, it makes sense to create the type of element required *in code* rather than directly in the HTML. The `index.html` body should look more like this:

```
<div id="board"></div>
```

The `CanvasRenderer` will be responsible for rendering all the visuals for our game onto an HTML5 canvas element. But how do we define a "visual" element? The plan is to create models for each "type" of thing we want to display in our game—images, sprites (coming soon), text, and so on. These will be the **leaf nodes** of our game tree. Any renderer must know how to draw every leaf type to correctly render the game.

Our leaf nodes will live in the library root directory. Each leaf node will hold all the information needed for any renderer to draw them on screen. The first leaf type we'll create is for text. A `pop.Text` element will be used to display text for messages, high scores, speech dialogs ... whatever. Add a new file `Text.js` (and re-export it from `Pop/index.js` !):

```
class Text {
  constructor(text = "", style = {}) {
    this.pos = { x: 0, y: 0 };
    this.text = text;
    this.style = style;
  }
}

export default Text;
```

All of our types will have a position (`pos`) object so they can be correctly positioned on screen. The `Text` type also has an associated `text` string and some `style` information about how it should look. We'll need to choose which properties we expect in the `style` object. For a start, we'll support a `fill` property (for the color of the text), a `font` property (for the font information), and maybe optionally an `align` property for horizontally aligning the text. We can add support for more text features later if we need them.

Following Canvas's Conventions

The style properties we defined are similar—but not the same—as those supported by Canvas. `fill` will be the same as Canvas's `fillStyle` , and `align` will be the same as `textAlign` . For the most part, it's just convenient for us to follow Canvas's conventions. But remember that the leaf nodes *should not need to know* about our rendering technology. Each should simply describe itself. It's up to the renderers to convert that description into something it can display.

Our old approach was to directly call `ctx.fillText` to render text with Canvas. Moving forward, we only want to *describe* the text and someone else renders it. We can make a new Text object by instantiating it in the `main.js` file, and passing in a message string with some style information:

```javascript
import pop from "../pop/index.js";
const { Container, Text } = pop;

const scene = new Container();
const message = new Text("The Renderer!", {
  font: "40pt monospace",
  fill: "blue",
  align: "center"
});
message.pos.x = w / 2;
message.pos.y = h / 2;

scene.add(message);
```

We've added something in our `scene` container—a `Text` object with some styled text and a position. At this stage, all we have is a *model* of a text message. Nothing is on screen. It's just an object inside the container's `children` array.

Now we can get down to the serious business of actually *rendering* our root container. The end goal of the renderer is to recursively traverse our tree and render any leaf nodes (currently just a `Text` message). To begin with, we have to create the canvas element and set up our environment in `CanvasRenderer.js` :

```javascript
class CanvasRenderer {
  constructor (w, h) {
    const canvas = document.createElement("canvas");
    this.w = canvas.width = w;
    this.h = canvas.height = h;
```

```
    this.view = canvas;
    this.ctx = canvas.getContext("2d");
  }
}
export default CanvasRenderer;
```

Here's the start of our `CanvasRenderer` . The logic should look familiar from Chapter 2, but instead of finding an *existing* canvas element in the web page, we create it with `document.createElement` . The renderer itself is now responsible for setting up everything it needs to render. We keep a reference to the canvas element (as `this.view`) as well as the context (`this.ctx`).

 Thinking Beyond Canvas

> Why assign the canvas element to `this.view` and not `this.canvas` ? When we make another renderer that doesn't use HTML5 canvas, it would be nice to keep our external API consistent ("view" sounds a bit more general than "canvas"). It doesn't matter if we're using Canvas or plain ASCII: we'd still get the main rendering element via `renderer.view` .

The width and height are set on the canvas element itself and (at the same time) on the object's `this.w` and `this.h` properties. This concludes the setup: we have a canvas context that we can use to draw some `Text` (or any other leaf node). To start this process, we call the renderer's `render` method, passing in our game tree container:

```
render(container) {
  const { ctx } = this;
  function renderRec (container) {
    // Render the container children
    ...
  }
  ctx.clearRect(0, 0, this.w, this.h);
  renderRec(container);
}
```

When `render` is called, we set up an alias to the renderer's context (because we access this a lot), then clear the screen with `ctx.clearRect` . `clearRect` is a Canvas action that works in a similar way to `fillRect` , but instead of using a fill color, it makes the area *transparent*. It clears the screen. And finally we start the ball rolling by calling the internal `renderRec` ("render recursive") function.

Why is there an internal function? Because our main data structure is a tree, and a very elegant way to traverse a tree (to render all the leaf nodes) is recursively. We pass the container to the internal `renderRec`, and somewhere inside *that* function, it will call `renderRec` with any child containers, and so on, until we only have leaf nodes.

```
// Render the container children
container.children.forEach(child => {
  ctx.save();
  // Draw the leaf node
  ...

  // Handle the child types
  if (child.children) {
    renderRec(child);
  }
  ctx.restore();
});
```

Inside the recursive function, we loop over and process each child item. The canvas context is saved and restored so any modifications to the state will not affect subsequent children. If the `child` of a container happens to have a `children` property, it's also a container—so we re-call `renderRec` to draw all of *its* children too. Until our tree is fully rendered.

Before we draw the contents of the leaf node, we'll *translate* the canvas to the correct position:

```
// Draw the leaf node
if (child.pos) {
  ctx.translate(Math.round(child.pos.x), Math.round(child.pos.y));
}
...
```

If the child element has a `pos` variable, we move the canvas's drawing location to the correct `x` and `y` position. The positions are rounded with `Math.round` so we don't draw things on "half pixels". We'll talk more about how translating works in the next chapter.

```
if (child.text) {
  const { font, fill, align } = child.style;
  if (font) ctx.font = font;
  if (fill) ctx.fillStyle = fill;
  if (align) ctx.textAlign = align;
  ctx.fillText(child.text, 0, 0);
}
```

Finally, some actual drawing! We'll end up with a bunch of checks here to determine what we need to render. Our first (and currently only) case is to look for the `child.text` property. If a child element has this property, it means it's a `Text` leaf node.

At this point, we have access to the renderer's canvas context (`ctx`), a screen position to draw (it's `0, 0`, because we've already translated the canvas to the correct position offset), and the font style information (`child.style` —containing, optionally, `font` , `fill` , and `align` properties). That's everything we need to draw some text in Canvas.

 Font Baseline

After testing this out, I made an executive decision to add the line `this.ctx.textBaseline = "top";` to the constructor of `CanvasRenderer` . This modifies the *vertical baseline* when calling `fillText` . By default, it's set to `bottom` , which renders from the bottom-left corner. In this case, setting a `Text` entity's position to `message.pos.y = 0` aligns the *bottom* of the text to `y` position 0 (so you don't see the message). By changing the baseline to `top` , it draws from the top-left corner—which is consistent with how other entities in our engine will be rendered.

We can put our `CanvasRenderer` to work in the `main` game file with our game scene.

```
import pop from "../pop/index.js";
const { Container, CanvasRenderer, Text } = pop;
```

As always, we extract the components we need from our library. For now, I'm being explicit about importing files and destructuring the library components: but it gets repetitive and takes up a lot of space in the book. Shortly I'll start omitting these, but they'll be in the supporting code examples if you can't figure out where something is coming from.

```
// Game setup code
const w = 640;
const h = 480;
const renderer = new CanvasRenderer(w, h);
document.querySelector("#board").appendChild(renderer.view);
```

We decide on a width and height for our game screen, and pass them as parameters for creating our very first `CanvasRenderer` . As we know, this in turn creates a new HTML `canvas` element referenced by `renderer.view` . We inject that into our HTML page using the DOM method `appendChild` . Our `canvas` view is back!

Take a deep breath, because here comes our *scene graph*. We create our root `scene` container and add one child leaf node—a `Text` message—with its `pos` position set to the center of the screen:

```
// Game objects
const scene = new Container();
const message = new Text("The Renderer!", {
  font: "40pt sans-serif",
  fill: "DarkRed",
  align: "center"
});
message.pos.x = w / 2;
message.pos.y = h / 2;
scene.add(message);
```

Reread the above code carefully and make sure you follow everything that's happening; it's using all the *most important parts* of our game engine. The scene graph's root node is the `Container` called `scene`. Next is a leaf node, `message` —a `Text` entity, with its `pos` position set to the center of the screen. The call `scene.add(message)` adds the leaf node to the container's children.

```
// Render the main container
renderer.render(scene);
```

Aaaand finally we can call `renderer.render(scene)`, which renders all the entire scene graph (just a single `Text` object so far) to the canvas context.

The Renderer!

3-12. The renderer in action

Phew. If you've made it to this point, then I have some good news: everything is easier from here on. It might seem like a *ridiculous* amount work to get something to appear on the screen (especially seeing as we were already doing a bunch of more interesting stuff last chapter!). But it's important to grasp the importance of what we've built here. We've abstracted our *game model* and our *rendering phase* so they're completely decoupled. Additionally, we have a base architecture that we can build upon—something that gives us structure and lets us more easily decide where pieces of our game code should go.

Bonus Renderer Features

Our renderer is going to grow and evolve as we create new entity types and encounter new requirements. We don't want to complicate the renderer unnecessarily at this stage, but there's a couple of features that I know will come in handy as we progress.

The first is a boolean flag called `visible` that can be applied to indicate the entity should *not be rendered*. By setting `message.visible = false` you hide the text. This could be used to hide the `Game Over` text until you died, or perhaps you miss the `<blink>Blink Tag</blink>` from HTML and could periodically toggle the message on or off.

```
container.children.forEach(child => {
  if (child.visible == false) {
    return;
  }
  ctx.save();
  ...
});
```

If a child entity is marked as not-visible, we don't need to process it at all. We don't even need to save/restore the canvas, and we can simply move on to the next child. This also means that, if the child is a `Container`, the container won't be processed; all of *its* child elements will also be hidden as well.

The other feature we'll add (which is mostly for debugging and experimenting) is to make the `ctx.clearRect` call optional. `clearRect` clears the canvas so you have a blank slate at the start of each frame. *Usually* this is exactly what you want, but occasionally (as in our *fading raindrops* example) it's desirable to overwrite the current canvas. We'll pass a flag in that can be set to `false` if you ever want to accumulate rendering across frames:

```
render(container, clear = true) {
  ...

  if (clear) {
    ctx.clearRect(0, 0, this.w, this.h);
  }
}
```

Adding the Loop

We're not quite done yet. At the moment, we're only rendering a static scene for a single frame. Where's our infinite loop? To integrate that, we have to wrap the last line (`renderer.render(scene)`) in our `requestAnimationFrame` game loop from earlier. The game loop no longer contains any game processing or drawing of its own. It delegates those tasks to our new scene graph system. The game loop only executes `scene.update(dt, t)` to move everything a tiny bit, and then `renderer.render(scene)` to draw everything:

```
let dt = 0;
let last = 0;

function loopy (ms) {
  requestAnimationFrame(loopy);

  const t = ms / 1000;
  dt = t - last;
  last = t;

  scene.update(dt, t);
  renderer.render(scene);

}
requestAnimationFrame(loopy);
```

The text is now rendered 60 times per second. It's hard to tell, because our `Text` leaf node doesn't have an `update` method. It's not being "moved a tiny bit", it just sits there being boring. To make it more alive, you have to add an `update` function to the `message` element:

```
message.update = function (dt) {
  this.pos.x -= 100 * dt;
  if (this.pos.x < -420) {
    this.pos.x = w;
  }
};
scene.add(message);
```

 The update Method

If any game object has an `update` method it will be called in by its parent container. *How* it gets an `update` method is up to you. Above we added it directly to the instance, but you can also create an object with a prototype (or use a custom `class`) that has an update method and it will call that. That's what we'll mostly be doing as we move forward.

The scrolling text message proves our engine is up and running! It works because our leaf node now has an `update` function that's executed when its parent container (`scene`) loops through all its children. We use the delta time (`dt`) to move the message at 100 pixels per second, then wrap around once the text goes off screen (the amount `420` was determined by scientific trial and error).

Game Entities

The guts of our game library are in place, and the hard work is done. Now we can begin to build on it with more fun, game-related stuff. It's time to implement the concept of a game *entity*. An **entity** is a *thing* in a game (we've been calling them "things" or "objects" or "items", but that doesn't sound game-designer-y enough). Players, bullets, bad guys, bonus pickups, weapons, glittery particles, rain drops, magic potions ... a game entity is something that has a *position* and some *dimensions*. It doesn't have to have a visual element, though. For example, a "trigger" entity is invisible, but performs some action when a player touches it.

A game entity that *does* have a visual element is called a **sprite**. The image associated with a sprite is commonly called a **texture**. We want to use lots of sprites in our games. Sprites are the bread and butter of nearly all 2D games, so let's model these game entities and add them to our library as `Texture.js` and `Sprite.js` respectively:

```
class Texture {
  constructor (url) {
    this.img = new Image();
    this.img.src = url;
  }
}

export default Texture;
```

`Sprite` is also quite simple, and accepts a `Texture` as an input rather than a URL:

```
class Sprite {
  constructor (texture) {
    this.texture = texture;
    this.pos = { x: 0, y: 0 };
  }
}

export default Sprite;
```

Just like our `Text` model, we're creating simple interfaces here—a representation of elements in our game. If we wanted to write a WebGL renderer, we'd still keep on using our `Sprite` and `Texture` objects in our game. They'd just be handled differently by each renderer.

The `Texture` is modeled as a simple DOM image. (You can just call it `Image` if you like. The term "texture" is a bit more generic, and is used often in other contexts like WebGL.) The texture accepts a URL path to the resource to load. For the following examples, we'll draw a spaceship (called *spaceship.png*) and place it in the */res/images/* folder.

Textures are useful on their own to display static images in our game, but we'll also use one in our *Sprite* object. A *Sprite* is an image with a bunch of game-specific properties. At the moment, the properties consist only of a screen position, but we'll be adding more functionality soon. It's required that you pass a texture object to the sprite when you create it:

```
// Game objects
const scene = new Container();

const texture = new Texture("res/images/spaceship.png");

for (let i = 0; i < 50; i++) {
  const ship = new Sprite(texture);
  ship.pos.x = Math.random() * w;
  ship.pos.y = Math.random() * h;
  scene.add(ship);
}
```

This is *gamedev*: why have only *one* when you can have 50? The more the merrier! The fifty *Sprite* objects all using the same *Texture* entity. The texture needs be drawn on screen in the correct position. But this is just our *model*. The renderer doesn't yet know how to draw a texture (it only knows how to draw text). To remedy this, inside the renderer's *recRender* function we need to handle this new case:

```
// Handle the child types
if (child.text) {
  ...
}
else if (child.texture) {
  ctx.drawImage(child.texture.img, x, y);
}
```

Any new leaf node we create for our library *must* be added here if we want it to be displayed. When an entity passes through the renderer, and it has a *texture* property (as all our sprites will), it will be drawn as the image inside the *Texture* model—at the correct *x* and *y* position—using Canvas's *drawImage* method.

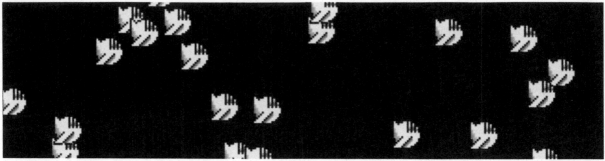

3-13. Spaceships ahoy!

Adding Some Action

The base sprite object currently doesn't have any logic associated with it; it doesn't have an `update` method. We already saw this when we added the `update` function to our `Text` object to create a scrolling message. Adding an `update` method is how our update system communicates with the entities:

```
const speed = Math.random() * 150 + 50;
const ship = new Sprite(texture);
...
ship.update = function (dt) {
  this.pos.x += speed * dt;
  if (this.pos.x > w) {
    this.pos.x = -32;
  }
};
```

The ships are assigned a random speed. The speed is a random number between 50 (the static component) and 200 (the random component between 0 and 150 *plus* the static component) pixels per second. Thanks to the `update` function, the ships fly to the right. When they exit the screen (`pos.x > w`) they wrap back around to the left.

To wrap around fully, they need a value that's 0 minus the width of the ship itself (32 pixels). If we just set `pos.x` to 0, the ship would suddenly appear in full, rather than scroll in from stage left. As a test, see if you can make them fly to the *left* and wrap back around to the right. How about up and down?

A Space Shoot-'em-up

Suddenly, a loud knock startles you as you're tinkering. Uh oh, Guy Shifty's at the door. "Hooooow's it going, my main indie gamedev?" he laughs, making air quotes. You're not sure which part of the sentence he was air quoting. Maybe all of it. "So, just a heads-up: the comp is starting in ..." he looks at his watch, "oh, 30 minutes ago. There's an hour and half left. The theme is 'Space' or, um, maybe 'Shoot-'em-up' ... I forget now. Anyway, good luck!" And he's gone.

A space-themed shoot-'em-up. The perfect vehicle to test-drive our shiny new library. The requirements for our simple shooter are fairly minimal:

1. A controllable player.

2. Bullets. A lot.

3. Baddies. A lot. All scrolling towards the player.

4. A way to vary the pace of the waves of bad guys.

5. Collisions between baddies and bullets.

6. If a bad guy gets past the player, game over.

Our game will be a **side-scroller** (waves of bad guys start off screen, then relentlessly steamroll toward the player until the player can't keep them from getting past) **shoot-'em-up** (lots of bullets.) Our game will scroll right to left, but you could just as easy to scroll in any direction.

We can easily handle most of the items on the list already: only number five—"Collisions between baddies and bullets"—and number four— "A way to vary the pace of the waves of bad guys"—are new. We only have an hour and a half left in the game jam, so no time to dawdle.

Setting Up the Game

Our project skeleton should be looking fairly familiar now. (So this is the *last time* we'll show the standard *import* statements at the top of the example. If you see references to *Pop* objects, you'll have to remember to import them!) We set up the environment, create a main root *scene* container and then loop. To create a cool "narrow attack corridor of space", this game will be only 300 pixels high.

```
import pop from "../pop/index.js";
const { CanvasRenderer, Container } = pop;

// Game setup code
const w = 640;
const h = 300;
const renderer = new CanvasRenderer(w, h);
document.querySelector("#board").appendChild(renderer.view);
```

```
// Game objects
const scene = new Container();
```

We also have the standard game loop that updates and renders our scene graph. We can copy-paste the entire game loop from the "Adding the Loop" section above. Hmmm, we've used that game loop twice now. *And* we know it's boilerplate code that we'll need for nearly *every* prototype we make. That's a good candidate for integration into our library ... buuut, we're in the middle of an extremely time-sensitive challenge. Let's type it out this one last time and refactor it next chapter, once we've won our $1.

A Controllable Player

First on our list of to-dos is "A controllable player". That's no problem: it's just a *Sprite* entity (which needs a *Texture* to display) whose position is controlled by *KeyControls* . We'll start by loading in some textures that we'll need in the game:

```
// Load game textures
const textures = {
  background: new Texture("res/images/bg.png"),
  spaceship: new Texture("res/images/spaceship.png")
};
```

We've seen the spaceship before, but the background is new. It's a static image that's the same size as our game screen. It sets the scene and tells the story: we're the last bastion of hope for a city facing imminent destruction from marauding kamikaze aliens from outer space. Good enough.

The textures are grouped together in a simple map called, unsurprisingly, *textures* . When we need them in our game we can refer to them with *textures.spaceship* . Later, we'll see how we can be a bit more organized in loading assets, but this works for now.

```
const controls = new KeyControls();

// Make a spaceship
const ship = new Sprite(textures.spaceship);
ship.pos.x = 120;
ship.pos.y = h / 2 - 16;
ship.update = function (dt, t) {
  // Update the player position
  ...
};
```

```
// Add everything to the scene container
scene.add(new Sprite(textures.background));
scene.add(ship);
```

We create the player's spaceship at 120 pixels from the left and half-way up the screen (height divided by 2, minus half the ship's own height) and add both the spaceship and the background image to the scene. (If you forget to add an entity to the scene graph, it won't be processed or displayed!)

The background image, `textures.background`, is going to be stationary. We don't need to keep a reference to it. (That's why we create the sprite directly in the call to `scene.add`.) By default, the Sprite's position will be `0, 0` —the top-left corner of the screen, which is the correct place to draw a background.

As we did earlier, to apply the keyboard movements to the player we modify its `x` and `y` positions inside the `update` function:

```
// Update the player position
const { pos } = this;
pos.x += controls.x * dt * 200;
pos.y += controls.y * dt * 200;

if (pos.x < 0) pos.x = 0;
if (pos.x > w) pos.x = w;
if (pos.y < 0) pos.y = 0;
if (pos.y > h) pos.y = h;
```

There's a few interesting things happening here. The goal is to end up with new `pos` values where the renderer will draw the player's texture. Way back at the start of the chapter we moved a colorful square around with the keyboard—and we're doing the same here. The `pos.x` value is updated depending on the direction of the left (-1) or right (+1) keys held down (`controls.x`), then multiplied by the delta time and the player's speed—200 pixels per second.

 Moving Things

> Changing the `pos` values is the only way we can move things around the screen. As we proceed, we'll make bullets and baddies that will be controlled in a similar way (though they'll be controlled by numbers, not by `KeyControls`).

We then perform a series of checks to *clamp* the player's position inside the screen. If they try to move to a negative `x` position, for example, the position is snapped back to 0. They can't escape through the left side of the screen. The same is done for the other edges.

3-14. Under control

A Player That Shoots

We have "a controllable player", so on to the next item on our list—bullets. Bullets tend to be popular in shoot-'em-ups! Adding bullets is the same as adding the player, except that we'll have lots of them. It makes sense to group them together in a new container.

```
// Load game textures
const textures = {
  ...
  bullet: new Texture("res/images/bullet.png")
};

// Bullets
const bullets = new Container();

// Add everything to the scene container
scene.add(bullets);
```

Bullets (and bad guys) need to be controlled separately. And there needs to be a whole bunch of them. To facilitate this, we'll have a factory function that's responsible for pumping out bullet sprites, and adding their movement abilities (by way of an *update* function).

 Playing Fast and Loose, for Now

It's kind of cheeky to do it this way: we're creating a new *update* function for *every* entity. The function could be named and reused, or it could be part of the object's prototype, or … whatever you want! We're playing fast and loose for this game jam, but we'll fix it next chapter when we start modularizing things in separate code files.

```
function fireBullet(x, y) {
  const bullet = new Sprite(textures.bullet);
  bullet.pos.x = x;
  bullet.pos.y = y;
  bullet.update = function(dt) {
    this.pos.x += 400 * dt;
  };
  bullets.add(bullet);
}
```

To create a bullet, call `fireBullet`, passing the `x` and `y` coordinates of the bullet's origin. The update function will "move the bullet a tiny bit" in the same way as the player moves, only the *speed* is hardcoded to 400 pixels per second. The `pos.y` value isn't changed, so the bullet travels perfectly horizontal. The `fireBullet` factory function also adds the bullet into the `bullets` container for us. Thanks `fireBullet`.

When the player is holding down the `action` button (space bar) it will fire a bullet from the ship's position. *But* … before doing this, we have to consider the *fire rate*. Holding down the space bar would generate one bullet *every frame it's being held down*. 60 bullets per second. That's too many for this particular game. Keeping track of the time of the *last shot* will allow us to regulate when the next shot can occur.

```
// Game state variables
let lastShot = 0;
```

Inside the main game loop we check if the player wants to fire a bullet or not (if `control.action` is true). Additionally, we make sure there's been *at least* 150 milliseconds (0.15 seconds) since the last time they fired. (Feel free to experiment with other firing times!) Then we update `lastShot` and fire a bullet:

```
// Game logic code
if (controls.action && t - lastShot > 0.15) {
  lastShot = t;
  fireBullet(ship.pos.x + 24, ship.pos.y + 10);
}
```

This kind of timer—where we have a variable to track the *last time* an event happened—will show up often in your game dev travels. The initial position of the bullet is *slightly* in front of the player: 24 pixels to the right, 10 pixels from the top of the texture.

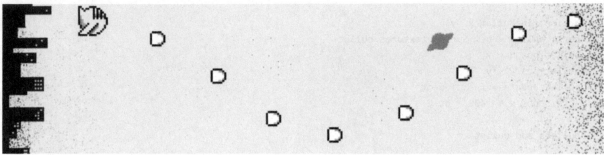

3-15. Fire away!

Removing "Dead" Entities

The gift of shooting is bestowed on the player. It looks great (and it's pretty exciting that we can shoot), but there's a hidden issue. If you hold down the fire button for long enough, your browser will eventually start to slow down and the game will become jittery … and probably crash. The bullets are *never being destroyed*. We end up with thousands and thousands of bullets all drifting off into the infinity of space (and wasting a lot CPU time being updated and rendered for nothing!)

```
// Destroy bullets when they go out of the screen
bullets.children = bullets.children.filter(bullet => {
  return bullet.pos.x < w + 20;
});
```

Our first attempt at a solution (shown above) is to *filter the bullets* out of the `children` array as they pass out of the screen (when their `x` position is greater than the screen width). Now you can shoot an infinite number of bullets and never slow down the browser.

 Optimization

> Deciding *when* to optimize things is a black art. We can sink an exorbitant amount of time into eking out small performance gains. In general, it's best not to worry too much about optimization *until you have a performance issue*. You won't be able to ignore performance considerations forever, but you can ignore them *at least* until we cover them in Chapter 9!

Removing "dead" entities is something common to every game. Instead of handling it manually, we can offload the responsibility to our library. We'll make it that declaring an entity "dead" (i.e. `bullet.dead = true`) will remove the entity after it's finished updating. This will be done as part of our core `Container` update logic. Instead of straight looping over the `children`, we filter them *once* as part of the regular update. Any children that set their `dead` property to `true` will be filtered out of the scene graph:

```
update (dt, t) {
  this.children = this.children.filter(child => {
    if (child.update) {
      child.update(dt, t, this);
    }
    return child.dead ? false : true;
  });
}
```

The *dead* property is nice, because we often deal with groups of entities by looping over them. Any time we encounter an entity we can mark it as *dead* and know that it'll be removed from the *children* array at the end of processing:

```
// while looping over each bullet …
if (bullet.pos.x >= w + 20) {
  bullet.dead = true;
}
```

The Bad Guys Strike Back

Having tackled bullets, adding waves of scrolling kamikaze aliens shouldn't be too tough. (But wait! Take a moment to think about how *you'd* do it.) I say the logic is *identical* to the bullet: we add a new container, create a factory function to generate bad guys, and attach the correct movement pattern (move toward the player rather than away from them):

```
// Bad guys
const baddies = new Container();
function spawnBaddie(x, y, speed) {
  const baddie = new Sprite(textures.baddie);
  baddie.pos.x = x;
  baddie.pos.y = y;
  baddie.update = function(dt) {
    this.pos.x += speed * dt;
  };
  baddies.add(baddie);
}

// Add everything to the scene container
scene.add(baddies);
```

The only difference is that a baddie's speed is not hardcoded, but passed in at creation time. That way, our bad guys move at different velocities, providing some variation for the player.

To control the *pacing* and excitement in the game, we'll schedule the bad guys with some *spawner logic*. It's similar to how we regulated the player's firing rate—but the rate will vary over time. This has the effect of creating peaks and troughs, and *waves* of spawned enemies.

```
// Game state variables
let lastSpawn = 0;
let spawnSpeed = 1.0;
```

We use these inside the game logic in the main loop. The magic numbers are adjusted each time an enemy is spawned. The time between each spawn becomes less and less and the aliens appear more frequently—giving the player a lot of targets to try to hit:

```
// Spawn bad guys
if (t - lastSpawn > spawnSpeed) {
  lastSpawn = t;
  const speed = -50 - (Math.random() * Math.random() * 100);
  const position = Math.random() * (h - 24);
  spawnBaddie(w, position, speed);

  // Accelerating for the next spawn
  spawnSpeed = spawnSpeed < 0.05 ? 0.6 : spawnSpeed * 0.97 + 0.001;
}
```

3-16. Bad guys strike back

When enough time has elapsed, a new bad guy is spawned just off the right side of the screen. Its vertical position is picked at random. So is its speed, to a degree. The bad guy's speed is *negative* (so it moves from right to left) and is modified by a random number to vary the intensity of the attack waves.

A Neat Randomization Trick

`Math.random() * Math.random()` is a very neat trick. `Math.random()` returns a number between 0 and 1; multiplying two together creates a distribution that favors lower numbers. The result is more bad guys moving slowly, with the odd baddie moving superfast.

Every time a bad guy is spawned, the `spawnSpeed` is adjusted—reducing by a factor of `0.97` —until it hits `0.05` seconds (very frequent spawning), then resets to `0.6` seconds (slowish spawning) to give the player a breather. This satisfies our "a way to vary the pace of the waves of bad guys" game requirement.

Collisions—at Last!

It's *looking* fantastic … but there's a big problem. We're nearly out of time for the game jam, but there are no collisions (and no scores). There's no point to it! It *looks* like a game, but it's not a game yet.

```
// Add the score game object
const score = new Text("score:", {
  font: "20px sans-serif",
  fill: "#8B8994",
  align: "center"
});
score.pos.x = w / 2;
score.pos.y = h - 30;
scene.add(score);

// Game state variables
let scoreAmount = 0;
let gameOver = false;
```

Tracking score is important. How else will a player know they're awesome? A `Text` component is positioned in the center of the screen, just above the bottom. That was easy.

What about collisions? Well, that's tougher. It's a complex subject that we'll delve into in Chapter 5, but that's not an answer that Guy Shifty is going accept. The dying minutes of a game jam is the perfect time to break out something quick and dirty: *Pythagoras's theorem!*

If we treat the positions of two sprites as *points* that define a *line* in space, the length of the line (the distance between the sprites) can be calculated by treating the line as a *hypotenuse* formed by making a right-angled triangle with the points:

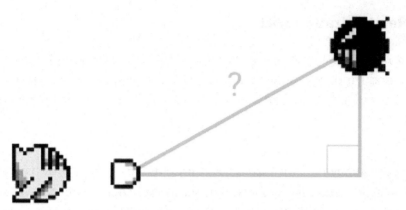

3-17. Collision triangle

For every bullet and for every baddie, we find the hypotenuse formed between them: if the length of the hypotenuse is small, the two entities are very close—so the baddie is dead! To integrate this into our main loop, we'll augment the code that checks if the bullets have gone off screen. Then nest a loop that goes over every baddie and check *each bullet against each baddie*. If they're too close (*or the bullet goes off screen*), they'll be marked as `dead` and be out of the game.

```
// Check for collisions, or out of screen
baddies.children.forEach(baddie => {
  bullets.children.forEach(bullet => {
    ...
    if (/* check for collision */) {
      // A hit!
      baddie.dead = true;
      bullet.dead = true;
    }
  });
});
```

By nesting the loops, we can check the full list of baddies and bullets, and apply Pythagoras's theorem to their positions. If there's a hit, the player gets a reward in the form of points. To make it more fun, the amount of points will depend on how long they've survived (by using `t`). Early kills are not as valuable as later ones!

```
// Check distance between baddie and bullet
const dx = baddie.pos.x + 16 - (bullet.pos.x + 8);
const dy = baddie.pos.y + 16 - (bullet.pos.y + 8);
if (Math.sqrt(dx * dx + dy * dy) < 24) {
  // A hit!
  bullet.dead = true;
```

```
    baddie.dead = true;
    scoreAmount += Math.floor(t);
  }
```

To calculate the length of the *sides* of our right triangle, you subtract the `x` and `y` points of the entities (to get `dx` and `dy`). We take the *center* of each entity and then see if they overlap. (A baddie is about 32 pixels wide—which we'll treat as a diameter—so 16 is the center. A bullet is smaller—about 16 pixels wide, so 8 is the center.) If the hypotenuse (calculated by taking the square root of the sum of the sides) is less than the two radiuses combined (16 + 8), then they overlap, and there's a collision!

 Imperfect Collisions

> It's not a perfect collision. Our sprites happen to be circular-ish. (That's not a coincidence; I made them circular-ish on purpose!) So this radius check is pretty good. We'll go much further into other collision detection techniques in <u>Chapter 5</u>.

Oh my, we have a game! Shooting baddies forever is fun, but will quickly get boring if there's no grander purpose. The goal of our shoot-'em-up is to accumulate points and prevent bad guys from reaching our city. When the city is breached, the player is dead and is shown a good ol' "Game Over" message.

```
function doGameOver() {
  const gameOverMessage = new Text("Game Over", {
    font: "30pt sans-serif",
    fill: "#8B8994",
    align: "center"
  });
  gameOverMessage.pos.x = w / 2;
  gameOverMessage.pos.y = 120;

  scene.add(gameOverMessage);
  scene.remove(ship);
  gameOver = true;
}
```

We create a `doGameOver` function which will be triggered if any of the baddies make it to the left side of the screen where our city folk reside. The perfect place to examine the bad guy's progress is after the bullet-collision check (outside the inner loop.) If they're the first one to make it to the city, the game over code function will be run. In either case, we also set `dead` to true, as they don't need to be rendered on screen anymore.

```
// Check if out of screen
if (baddie.pos.x < -32) {
  if (!gameOver) {
    doGameOver();
  }
  baddie.dead = true;
}
```

There's one slight issue remaining. The player can still spawn new bullets *after they're dead*! To fix this, check the *gameOver* flag before shooting:

```
if (!gameOver && controls.action && t - lastShot > 0.15) {
  ...
}
```

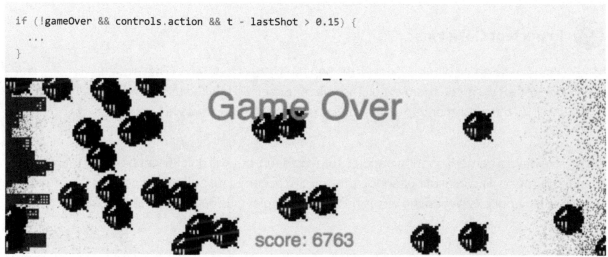

3-18. Shoot-'em-up over

Not bad! Well, there's no way to restart without refreshing the browser, so let's now have a look at adding this new feature ...

Game Over

"Sorry, time's up!" beams Guy Shifty. "Did you get anything working? One of our guys managed to get a cube on the screen, but they assure me they've got the base for a solid AAA game engine there ... Hey, what's that?" He sits downs and plays through a few rounds of your game. His beaming smile reduces to a grimace. "Yeah, that's pretty good," he grumbles. He reluctantly takes out his wallet and gives you the dollar, and sulks out of the room.

Congratulations! You managed to build the base for a powerful game library, become a professional game developer, *and* ruin Guy's weekend. Not bad for one day's work.

This chapter has really covered a lot of ground, and some of the concepts are tricky. Take some time to experiment with the library. See if you can think of how to implement these ideas in other ways. See if you can add a feature to the game (play around with the spawn rates, the direction things move, adding a "pickup" item). See if you can create a game from scratch, with totally new graphics. Try to remember our core checklist and create something only using Canvas *without* any library.

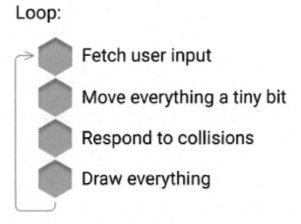

3-19. High-level loop done

We've still got a lot of things to add and a lot of things to learn, but if you understand the concepts covered so far, everything from here on is child's play.

Level

Animation, Levels, Maps, Cameras...

4

In the last chapter, we developed the initial version of our game library and used it to create a nifty shoot-'em-up. Hopefully you're excited about that. It means we have all the essential ingredients needed to make some basic games. And games *do not* have to be complex to be addictive and compelling. *Tetris* and *Flappy Bird* are two examples of games that are fundamentally simple yet have managed to gobble up large chunks of humanity's free time.

4-1. Tetris and Flappy

In this chapter we massively expand our game library. We've covered the core game loop; now it's time to enlarge our bag of tricks to facilitate faster experimentation. We'll add functionality to the renderer for stretching and spinning entities, and implement classic flip-book animation techniques.

After that, we need to start thinking in terms of *finished products*. Actually *finishing* a game is a deceptively hard challenge. It's important to quickly develop a playable, demo-able game that other people can test. Feedback from real-world players is the only way we can know if we're on the right track. To that end, we'll add more exciting backgrounds and levels (via "tile maps") and wrap the whole thing up as a presentable package—with title and game-over screens. Then we'll have a game.

An Unexpected Proposition

"Listen, I don't like you, you don't have to like me."

It's our friend, Guy Shifty, busting through the door. "But I'm in a pickle and I've got no one else to turn to. I sent all my staff on a corporate 'health' retreat to teach them how to work for longer periods of time without sleeping."

He grabs your take-out coffee and has a swig.

"Arrrgh, needs sugar. Anyhoo … a client of mine needs some work done by end of week. I really don't think you're up to it because your last effort was … well, a bit boring. But I'll tell you what: if you can show me *by lunchtime* that you can conjure up some '*zing*'—some movement, stretching, animating … that kind of thing—the gig's yours."

De-boilerplating Our Prototypes

Sounds like we need to get **prototyping**—creating a minimal version of a game idea, in order to test if it's any fun or not. Being able to quickly get a new prototype running is paramount. To facilitate this, let's abstract all of the repetitive boilerplate code from our project skeleton (that we currently have to copy-paste every time we want to start a new game) and make it part of the Pop game library.

Starting a New Game

Our main loop and DOM handling is a pain to set up for each prototype. We'll create a new class— `Game` —that we can reuse across projects. The goal of `Game` is to let us write `main.js` game code like this:

```
const game = new Game(640, 320);
const { scene, w, h } = game;

const ship = new Sprite(new Texture("res/images/spaceship.png"));
scene.add(ship);

// Our old loop!
game.run((dt, t) => {
  ship.pos.x += dt * 0.2;
  if (ship.pos.x > w) {
    ship.pos.x = -32;
  }
});
```

The `Game` class will take care of all the setup details that we were previously doing manually: injecting the canvas element into the DOM, making a scene `Container`, and spinning up the main `requestAnimationFrame` loop. It's just a few lines of code to produce a moving, screen-wrapping spaceship. We're just hiding a bit of the boilerplate, but it's a *serious* time saver as you experiment and play with new ideas.

Skip Ahead if You're Impatient

Generalizing this code makes it easier to make new games, but if you're impatient to get to *actually making new games*, you can skip the implementation details of this for now. Either keep copy-pasting the ol' skeleton, or better yet, if you understand the small code snippet above, just use the new `Game.js` and revisit this section later!

`Game.js` will hold the helper class (remember to re-export it from Pop's `index.js`). To make a new game, you'll need to provide a width and height for the display as well as (optionally) the identifier for the parent DOM container the game should live in.

```
import Container from "./Container.js";
import CanvasRenderer from "./renderer/CanvasRenderer.js";

class Game {
  constructor (w, h, parent = "#board") {
    ...
  }
}

export default Game;
```

Inside the constructor, we take care of some of the basic scene setup:

```
this.w = w;
this.h = h;
this.renderer = new CanvasRenderer(w, h);
document.querySelector(parent).appendChild(this.renderer.view);

this.scene = new Container();
```

Each new `Game` will create a new instance of a `CanvasRenderer` and inject the canvas element into the page as a child of the `#board` DOM element. (All the examples in this book will use `"#board"` from our HTML skeleton. If this were a library for general use, I'd probably default it to `"body"` —but it's up to you!) It also creates a default `Container` object called `scene` . Next we need to handle the main game loop:

```
run(gameUpdate = () => {}) {
  ...
}
```

This is done via a method called `run` . Run takes a *function* as a parameter. The function will be called every frame. It receives the familiar delta time `dt` and game time `t`. There's a default value provided (an empty function `() => {}`) so you can also call `game.run()` without any per-frame logic:

```
let dt = 0;
let last = 0;
const loopy = ms => {
  requestAnimationFrame(loopy);

  const t = ms / 1000; // Let's work in seconds
  dt = Math.min(t - last, MAX_FRAME);
  last = t;

  this.scene.update(dt, t);
  gameUpdate(dt, t);
  this.renderer.render(this.scene);
};
requestAnimationFrame(loopy);
```

Inside `run` is the bulk of our boilerplate code from last chapter. It's the main game loop—with a few tweaks. The whole purpose of the loop is to "move everything a little bit" (by updating the `scene` container) and "to render everything" (by drawing the children of `scene` container). As a bonus feature, after the scene update we *also* call the `gameUpdate` function provided. This will execute any extra logic we specify from `main.js` (such as moving the `ship` earlier). *Mostly* we won't have code in `main.js` (it'll be delegated to other children containers), but it can be useful for quick experiments and especially for debugging.

The other sneaky tweak is a little fix that we've so far been ignoring— `dt = Math.min(t - last, MAX_FRAME)`. What's this `Math.min` doing here? It's actually forcing a *maximum frame time* of `MAX_FRAME` milliseconds, which we'll set to five times our expected frame time of 60 frames per second. This is defined as a constant at the top of the file. (We'll be playing with this more when we get to Chapter 6, *Mathematics & Physics*.)

```
const STEP = 1 / 60;
const MAX_FRAME = STEP * 5;
```

Having a `MAX_FRAME` prevents extremely large delta times from breaking your game. For example, if you change tabs in the middle of playing a game and come back an hour later, `dt` will be 60,000 instead of 0.0166: anything you multiplied by that `dt` would go berserk! `Math.min` is acting as a fail-safe for us.

A Little Help with the Children

While we're tinkering with our core library, let's add one more timesaver to the `Container` class. Another requirement we'll see again and again is to apply logic to *every child* of a container. Currently we do that explicitly by accessing the `container.children` array. Let's encapsulate that via a helper method called `map`:

```
map (f) {
  return this.children.map(f);
}
```

This simply runs JavaScript's array `map` over the children for us. For any container, we can iterate over each child object using this new helper. For example, the code in our shoot-'em-up from last chapter becomes more concise:

```
bullets.map(bullet => {
  baddies.map(baddie => {
    if (/* is a collision? */) {
      bullet.dead = true;
      baddie.dead = true;
    }
  });
});
```

It might not seem like a huge change, but it removes more boilerplate code and makes the intended logic clearer. Additionally, users of the library don't *have* to know how the `Container` class does things under the hood.

Sprites with *Zing*!

As it stands, our minimal `Sprite` class is only able to render an image *exactly* as it appears on disk. But as we saw in Chapter 2, the Canvas API is capable of more: translating, scaling, and rotating. These are all built into Canvas, and thus can easily be baked into our library too. Messing around with our sprites could then look something like this:

```
const ship = new Sprite(texture);
ship.scale = { x: 3, y: 0.5 };
ship.rotation = Math.PI / 4;
```

We can stretch and spin our art assets in funky, creative, and useful ways—without having to crack open Photoshop.

Affine Transitions

Often you'll see the following set of operations labeled "affine transforms". **Affine transforms** are a *general* way of representing various planar transforms. Under the hood, these transforms are performed via a transformation matrix. You can set this matrix manually with `ctx.setTransform();`, but support for reading it (via `ctx.currentTransform`) is still limited.

Sprite Translation

Translation is altering the position of a sprite. That doesn't sound very exciting, because we already have this functionality in our engine—it's how we offset our entities before we draw them with `ctx.translate()`. *Translating* works by shifting the (0, 0) point from the top left of the canvas to the point we want to draw. It affects any and all drawing operations that follow—as if we've moved the "paper" below our "pen".

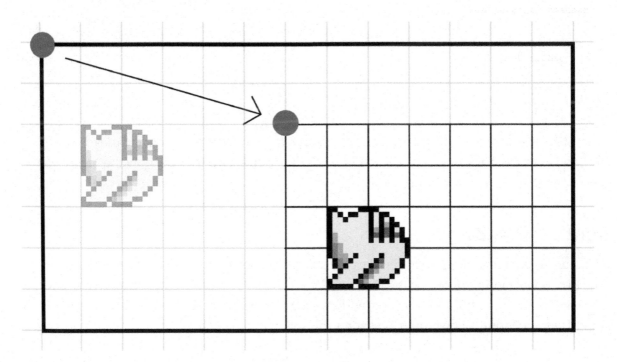

4-2. Translating an entity

Because we're recursively rendering any children of an element from *inside* the `ctx.save()` and `ctx.restore()` calls, any children will be translated relative to their parent's position.

Scaling Sprites

Scaling means making things bigger or smaller by some factor. A factor of `2.0` makes an image twice as big, `0.5` makes it half as big. There are also a few interesting cases: if the scaling factor is 1.0, it will return to the original size. If 0, the image will be invisible. If it's *less* than 0, the image will flip! That's quite a lot of power for one operation. We can perform some very useful effects with it—such as flipping an image in the direction the player is facing, or making a quirky animated "wobble".

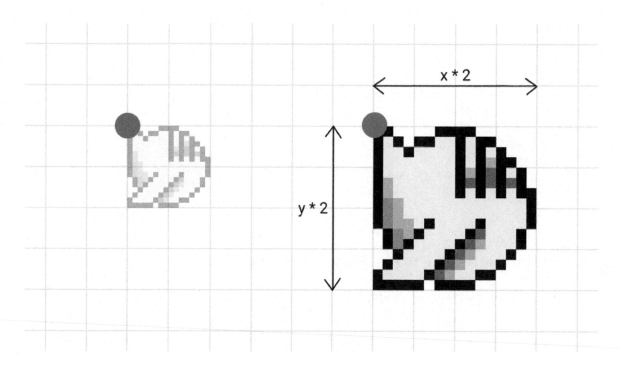

4-3. Scaling an entity

To implement scaling, we have to add it to our entity model, then add corresponding support for rendering. First, make `scale` a property of our `Sprite` class. We can scale things in either the `x` or `y` (or both) directions. The default, non-scaled value is 1.

```
class Sprite (texture) {
  this.texture = texture;
  this.pos = { x: 0, y: 0 };
  this.scale = { x: 1, y: 1 };
}
```

Now we need to handle this in our renderer. Directly after the call to `ctx.translate` we can add the code to scale things. Scaling works exactly the same as translation—except that we use the Canvas `scale` operation. Just like `translate`, `scale` accepts `x` and `y` parameters.

```
if (child.pos) {
  ...
}
if (child.scale) {
  ctx.scale(child.scale.x, child.scale.y);
}
```

We apply the same logic to scaling as translating: if a child element has a `scale` property, we perform the operation on the canvas context. Because there are both `x` and `y` parameters, we scale dimensions independently. To illustrate this, let's make our sprite go all wobbly by adding a scale amount based on sine waves:

```
// Make a spaceship
const ship = scene.add(new Sprite(textures.spaceship));
ship.pos = { x: 80, y: 120 };
ship.update = function(dt, t) {
  // Wobbly ship
  const { scale } = this;
  scale.x = Math.abs(Math.sin(t)) + 1;
  scale.y = Math.abs(Math.sin(t * 1.33)) + 1;
};
```

 Creating and Adding to the Scene in One line

> Notice how we're assigning `ship` the return value of `scene.add`? We're taking advantage of the fact that our Container API returns the same object you passed (in this case, the new `Sprite` object). This lets us create and add to the scene in one line.

The only new piece of code here is updating the `scale` amount. Often we'll want to change the scale factor to a static amount (for example, by setting both `scale.x` and `scale.y` to 2 to double the size of the sprite), but doing it dynamically in the Sprite's `update` method is more fun. We change the `x` amount slightly differently than the `y` and the `Math.abs` keeps the scaling positive (try without it!). This makes the sprite stretch differently horizontally and vertically, creating a rubber-band effect suitable for a time warp bonus (or for when your main character is a rubber band!).

Scaling can be used for various art tricks. Scaling things smaller the further away they are is how we can model perspective to make things look 3D. Another useful effect is to generate scenery by repeating an item many times with random scale amounts. Let's add a scrolling cityscape behind our wobble-ship. Create a container and fill it with 20 or so sprites of buildings. The scale amount for each building will be random, but they'll all scroll at the same speed so it looks like our ship is flying by.

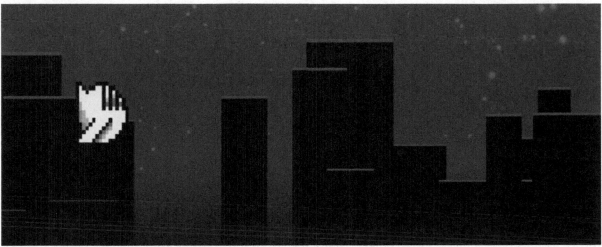

4-4. Scrolling cityscape

```
const buildings = scene.add(new Container());
const makeRandom = (b, x) => {
  // Place the building at x position, with random scale
  ...
};

game.run(dt => {
  buildings.map(b => {
    b.pos.x -= 100 * dt;
    if (b.pos.x < -80) {
      makeRandom(b, w);
    }
  });
});
```

Start with a new *Container* just for our city. We'll have a helper function (*makeRandom*) to place and scale each building—once when it's created, and then once again every time it loops out of the screen. There's a lot of random things to calculate, and frankly, *Math.random* is getting a bit repetitive. It's time to move it into the library!

Math Helper Functions

There will be a lot of math-related helper functions in the chapters ahead, so let's put them in a new file in */utils/math.js* (you'll have to create the *utils* folder too). Every function we create will be exported for use in our games:

```
function rand(min, max) {
  // return random integer
}
function randf(min, max) {
  // return random float
}
export default {
  rand,
  randf
};
```

The two functions we'll create to help with random numbers is *randf* and *rand*. *randf* will return a floating point number between our *min* and *max* values. If we don't give it any parameters, it will work exactly the same as `Math.random`, generating a number between 0 and 1. If we supply a *min* and *max*, the number will be constrained in this range; and if we only call it with a single value, it will return a number between 0 and the number provided:

```
...
const { math } = pop;

math.randf(); // Same as Math.random()
math.randf(1, 10); // between 1.0 and 9.99999...
math.randf(100); // between 0 and 99.999...
```

The only non-trivial case is when we have a *min* and a *max* value. To calculate this, we need to get the difference between the two and choose a random number from the result. We then *add* the minimum to offset everything: the smallest number we can get is *min* (if the random number is 0, the result is the offset) and the highest number we can get is *max* (the difference + the offset).

```
function randf(min, max) {
  if (max == null) {
    max = min || 1;
    min = 0;
  }
  return Math.random() * (max - min) + min;
}
```

The initial *if* conditional swizzles the input for the different cases when we provide 0, 1, or 2 parameters—making *min* 0 if it's not supplied, and *max* 1 if it's not supplied. The *rand* function simply calls *randf*, and then floors the result, giving us a whole number.

```
math.rand(1, 10); // between 1 and 9
```

```
math.rand(100); // between 0 and 99
```

 Zero-based Random Numbers

We've made another executive decision for the *rand* function to return numbers from *min* to *max - 1*. We're so used to dealing with zero-based random numbers that it just seemed more natural for *math.rand(10)* to go from 0 to 9 than it seemed weird for *math.rand(1, 10)* to not include a 10! If it annoys you, feel free to change it!

While we're here being random, we'll use *rand* to make two more random-y functions that I happen to know will be convenient in the future. The first is a boolean function that returns *true* with given odds. Say 1 in 10 times it will return *true*; otherwise it will return *false*. Let's call it *math.randOneIn*. If we wanted a 1-in-100 chance to alert a message, we'd write *if (math.randOneIn(100)) alert("winner!")*.

```
function randOneIn(max = 2) {
  return rand(0, max) === 0;
}
```

The second, soon-to-be-handy function picks a random *element* from a given array. It's called *math.randOneFrom*. For example, at the time of writing this book, *math.randOneFrom(["pick", "me", "please!"])* returned the element "please!". (Your results might vary.)

```
function randOneFrom(items) {
  return items[rand(items.length)];
}
```

Any time we come up with some handy little math functions throughout the book, we'll add them here. We'll probably have some other *utils* files too—for example, for dealing with entities. That's why we've put it in a folder. Anyhoo, back to work. We can use our new helpers to scale and place our initial armada of buildings:

```
const makeRandom = (b, x) => {
  b.scale.x = math.randf(1, 3);
  b.scale.y = math.randf(1, 3);
  b.pos.x = x;
  b.pos.y = h - b.scale.y * 64;
};
```

The building scale is a random float value between 1 and 3. It will never be smaller than original, but can be stretched up to 3 times its size. The y positions now need to consider the sprite's y scale so that it can be drawn flush against the ground. The building image is 64 pixels high, so multiplying by the scale gives its real height:

```
for (let x = 0; x < 50; x++) {
  const b = buildings.add(new Sprite(textures.building));
  makeRandom(b, math.rand(w));
}
```

50 random buildings later, we've got ourselves a city. We give each of them a random integer x value from 0 to the screen width with the handy new `math.rand` function.

Anchor Points

Another practical use for scaling is to *flip* the sprite so it faces whichever direction the player is facing. When the scale amount of an axis is `-1` we have a mirrored image from the original. But scaling happens from the *top-left corner*, so flipping an image on its x axis means it will be rendered right-to-left. If you quickly flip between a scale amount of 1 (normal) and -1 (flipped), you'll see it jumps around instead of taking up the same screen space.

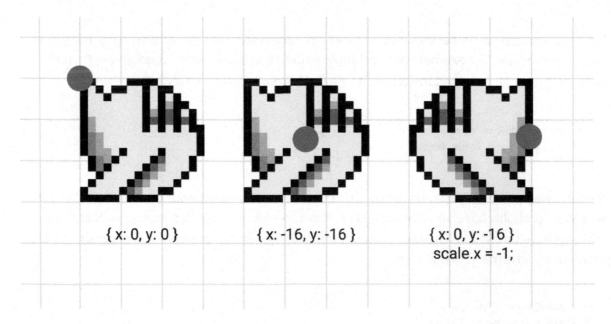

{ x: 0, y: 0 }   { x: -16, y: -16 }   { x: 0, y: -16 }
                                                    scale.x = -1;

4-5. Entity anchor points

To work around this (and to give us some flexibility in where we finally render a texture) we'll introduce the concept of an **anchor point**. This will be an *offset* for the drawing location of the sprite's image. When we invert an image, we can also modify the texture offset so the flipped version is rendered in the same place as the original.

```
function Sprite (texture) {
  this.texture = texture;
  this.pos = { x: 0, y: 0 };
  this.anchor = { x: 0, y: 0 };
  this.scale = { x: 1, y: 1 };
}
```

The anchor point is just a way to "fine tune" the drawing position without affecting the sprite's *pos* world position. This is done with another *translate* by the offset amount provided in *anchor*:

```
if (child.pos) { ... }
if (child.anchor) ctx.translate(child.anchor.x, child.anchor.y);
```

Having an anchor point is great for entities like a *cross hair pointer*, where you want the *center* of the cross hair image to be located at *pos*. By negatively offsetting the origin of the drawing location, the canvas "paper" is moved under the "pen". A call to *drawImage* will render such that the *anchor point* (the middle of the cross hairs) will be located at (0, 0). The same idea applies to fixing our flipped sprites: positively offset the texture whenever the sprite is flipped to match its non-inverted position:

```
const cross = scene.add(new Sprite(textures.crosshair));
cross.anchor = { x: -16, y: -16 };

const flipped = Math.random() < 0.5;
spaceship.scale.x = flipped ? -1 : 1;
spaceship.anchor.x = flipped ? 32 : 0;
```

The extra fine-grained control over where a texture is drawn also comes in handy when we want to implement visual effects without impacting collision-detection calculations.

Sprite Rotation

In many graphics systems, "rotation" means busting some math with sine and cosine. But thanks to Canvas, it's just a call to the *ctx.rotate* method. This accepts an angle (in radians, naturally) to rotate by. If any of our entities have a *rotation* property, we'll pass it directly to *rotate*:

```
...
if (child.rotation) {
  ctx.rotate(child.rotation);
```

```
   }
```

Any non-zero *rotation* value will be used to rotate the entity. Rotation occurs from the origin in a clockwise direction. Don't forget that we need to give the angle in radians, not degrees! If you skipped that section, it's in Chapter 2 when we drew some circles.

The *origin* of the rotation is the top-left corner by default. To adjust this, we need to add a **pivot point**. This is similar to the anchor point, in that it changes the origin of the drawing operation. If you have a basketball sprite, for example, you'll want it to rotate around the *center* of the ball image. And if your sprite is a giant robot's forearm, you want it to rotate around its giant robot elbow.

The sprite model gets a new property, *this.pivot = { x: 0, y: 0 };* . Inside the rotation code we can account for the change in pivot offset:

```
if (child.rotation) {
  const px = child.pivot ? child.pivot.x : 0;
  const py = child.pivot ? child.pivot.y : 0;
  ctx.translate(px, py);
  ctx.rotate(child.rotation);
  ctx.translate(-px, -py);
}
```

The canvas is translated to the *pivot* position, and the point (0, 0) is now where the rotation will occur. Once the canvas is rotated, we *undo* the translation so that subsequent operations aren't affected. As a test, draw 10 circle-ish spaceships and set their pivot points to the center of the image: *{ x: 16, y: 16 }* :

```
for (let i = 0; i < 10; i++) {
  const ship = ships.add(new Sprite(textures.spaceship));
  ship.pivot = { x: 16, y: 16 };
  ship.pos.x = i * 48;
}
```

Changing the ship's *rotation* property will now rotate the ship around its center. Try different pivot values to see the (wobbly) results!

```
const rps = Math.PI * 2 * dt; // One revolution per second
ships.map((s, i) => {
  s.rotation += i * rps;
});
```

4-6. Rotated entities

When transforming objects, order is important. The result of scaling *then* rotating is different from rotating *then* scaling. (Don't take my word for it. Try it out!) Scaling or rotating will change the "paper" under our "pen"—so that future operations will also be scaled and rotated. For example, scaling by 2 then translating 10 pixels will actually translate *20* pixels. The most useful order for our engine will be to *translate* to the correct position, *scale* to the correct size, then *rotate*. If we rotated first before scaling, our pivot point would be incorrect.

An Unexpected Assignment

"Holy moly!" exclaims Guy Shifty, peeking over your shoulder. He spills some coffee—the same coffee he swiped from you earlier. "You made all that just now? Okay, you've got the gig."

"My friend needs a game," he continues. "An *arcade game*—for Serious Biz Con, that's happening *this weekend*. She wants a 1980s-style game to put in an arcade cabinet for people to play. You know what I'm talking about? Three lives, 'game over—insert coin', high scores, blah blah blah ... that kind of thing. Something catchy, with a catchy name and a marketable main character. And she needs the code by *close of business, Friday*. Don't let me down!"

Our very first game that will be seen by the outside world! We want it to be ambitious, but we don't have a lot of time. We should acknowledge our current limitations:

- collisions can only be distance-based (like our bullet collision detection)
- entities have to be circles (because of the previous point)
- enemies have to be pretty stupid (we don't have any AI tricks in our toolbox yet).

That's fine: with a bit of imagination we can embrace these constraints and do something interesting, for sure. Hmm, there's a couple of other blocking issues, though:

- the game can't restart, and there's no game over screen
- the game world can only be as big as the viewport (no scrolling)
- there's no animation.

It'd be a stretch to say these weaknesses are actually strengths. We have to bite the bullet and figure them out. Time to crack open a caffeinated drink product and get to it.

Sprite Sheets & Animation

If we're going to wow the crowds at Serious Biz Con, we need a game with a memorable main character. Something identifiable. Something lovable. Something round. Actually, come to think of it, the '80s were a time of confusion and ridiculousness, so really any old nonsense should be fine. Let's go with … *SquizzBall*. That has a nice ring to it. SquizzBall is a ball. A ball trapped in a post-apocalyptic wasteland where the earth is so desolate that it literally disintegrates as you traverse it. Waves of wild flying wildebeest sweep the air, destroying anything they touch. How long can SquizzBall survive this test of endurance?!

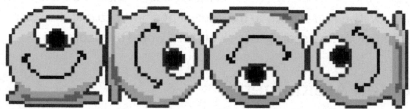

4-7. The original SquizzBall

Awww, perfect. At least we have a character! And when it's a huge success we can release *SquizzBall Jr.* and *Ms. SquizzBall.* (Ka-ching!)

Naturally, we'll need to make SquizzBall move—not merely float around the screen, but *become animated*. This requires some art skills. Each element needs to be painstakingly designed by an artist (us!). Then, once we have the animations looking great, every individual frame has to be rasterized and exported from our art tool. There may eventually be hundreds or thousands of frames, so we have to think a bit about how to organize our assets. One of the oldest (but still very useful) ways is via a "sprite sheet".

Sprite Sheets

In a **sprite sheet**, all of the individual frames or cells of the sprite are packed into a single image and aligned to a grid. With a bit of math magic (and with the help of Canvas's `drawImage` cropping ability), we can maintain a *pointer* to which frame we want displayed at any given time, like a flip book.

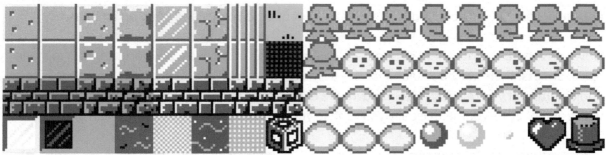

4-8. An example sprite sheet (CC0, from OpenGameArt.org)

The benefit of using a sprite sheet is that it's easier to edit when you're prototyping a game (all of your frames are in a single image), and the math required to cut up the frames is very straightforward. We could have every frame on the file system and load them by a name (for example, `run-left-01.png`, `run-left-02.png`, and so on), but we save a lot of HTTP requests this way!

The downside of a grid-based sprite sheet is that every frame needs to be *as big as your biggest image* (or at least *some multiple* of that size, as you can stitch a few cells together to make a larger image). This is a problem if you have a character that does some huge moves, like a frantic, lunging punch. Now all your images will have a bunch of needless whitespace around them. A similar approach that avoids this issue is a *sprite atlas*. In an atlas, the images are tightly packed into a single image, but the packing is done via a tool into which you feed all of the individual image files.

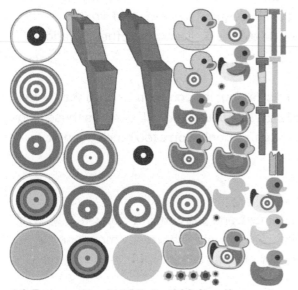

4-9. Texture atlas with XML file (CC0, from Kenney.nl)

Along with the output image is a file containing a set of metadata coordinates to assist with dissecting the image into frames. We're going to stick with sprite sheets for simplicity, but you'll hopefully see that it's not too difficult to take a set of coordinates and chop up an atlas.

How you create a sprite sheet depends on your software. If you use a pixel art program to make sprite sheets, there will be defaults for the frame sizes, as well as options for the number of rows and columns. If you're using a standard image editor, you'll need to calculate the frame pixel width and heights yourself. Usually you'll make your own grid template that you can draw in.

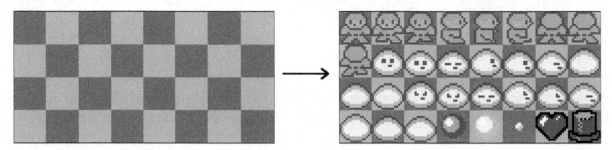

4-10. Sprite sheet template

In the example above, we have a blank sprite sheet with five rows and five columns, each 32x24 pixels in size. The grid lines are *included* in the total area, so once you've drawn a sprite in a box you need to remove any remaining grid line pixels. Otherwise, they'll show up in the game!

There are no "correct sizes" for the cells, but there are some common dimensions that have emerged over time—mostly due to long-outdated technical reasons, but some that still make sense today. For example, the original Nintendo Entertainment System allowed sprites to be either 8x8 or 8x16 pixels in size (so, very small). A lot of subsequent systems had similar restraints: powers of two are common (16x16, 32x32, 64x64) as well as some other variations such as 32x24 or 32x48.

These days there's certainly no hard limitations on cell sizes, but it's common to keep the overall output image size as a power of two (for example, 512x512) because WebGL expects these kinds of textures. This is more of a WebGL optimization, though, so don't worry too much about it.

 Where to Get Sprite Sheets

Sprite sheets are very common in game development, and you can find many examples and resources on the Web. A popular free resource I've already mentioned is Open Game Art[1], which maintains a large directory of game assets you can use in your games, including stacks of sprite sheets.

---

[1]. http://opengameart.org/art-search?keys=tileset

Depending on the scope and requirements of your game, you may have only need a single sprite sheet for all your assets, but it's more likely you'll have a handful—perhaps one for "baddies", one for "game objects" or one for small sprites, one for big sprites ... how you arrange them is up to you and your workflow.

Creating the TileSprite

If we loaded our sprite sheet image as a texture and gave it to *Sprite* , the *entire grid* would appear on screen. We need a new kind of sprite that only renders a *cropped portion* of the texture. For this, we'll create *TileSprite.js* —another core type in our library. *TileSprite* really is an awful lot like like a regular *Sprite* , just with some extra information relating to the grid: the width and height of a single cell frame, as well as the *x* and *y* cell *indexes* to render.

 Why is it called a "tile" sprite?

Why is it called a "tile" sprite? Sprite sheets are also sometimes called "tile sheets", or "tilesets", because they can be used to make large designs made up of repeated cells, like decorative tiles on a floor. In fact, we're going to be creating level maps using this technique shortly. (See the "Tile Maps" section below.)

```
import Sprite from "./Sprite.js";

class TileSprite extends Sprite {
  constructor (texture, w, h) {
    super(texture);
    this.tileW = w;
    this.tileH = h;
    this.frame = { x: 0, y: 0 };
  }
}

export default TileSprite;
```

Because *TileSprite* extends *Sprite* , it will also have a *texture* property and will therefore be rendered identically to a sprite (that is, the entire sheet will be drawn). But we only want to render a *part* of the image—based on the current *frame* . We have to modify *CanvasRenderer* . If during our child node tests a child has a *tileW* property, we assume it's a *TileSprite* and draw the *cropped frame*. Otherwise, it's a regular sprite and we can draw the whole thing as before.

```
const img = child.texture.img;
if (child.tileW) {
```

```
ctx.drawImage(
  img,
  child.frame.x * child.tileW,  // source x
  child.frame.y * child.tileH,  // source y
  child.tileW, child.tileH,     // width & height
  0, 0,                         // destination x & y
  child.tileW, child.tileH      // destination width & height
);
} else {
  ctx.drawImage(img, 0, 0);
}
```

Oooh, that looks complex. It's not bad if you break it down into the `drawImage` parameters. If the child element is a `TileSprite`, we use the advanced version of `drawImage` (which we covered in Chapter 2) to draw a *cropped* section to the screen. The parameters for `drawImage` are the image, the source area's `x` position, `y` position, width, and height, followed by the destination area's `x` position, `y` position, width, and height. The cropped size is determined by multiplying the frame indexes by the cell dimensions. From this coordinate, it draws an image exactly the size of one frame (`tileW` x `tileH`).

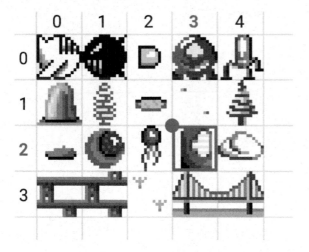

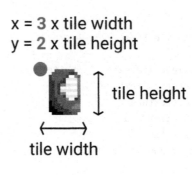

4-11. TileSprite crop

For example, the *default* `frame` property points to `x` index 0, and `y` index 0, which represents the *first cell* in the sprite sheet. The frame indexes get multiplied by the tile width and height (respectively) to give the *source point* of the image crop. The *destination* dimensions are those of a single cell (`tileW` x `tileH`). We can choose any tile index to draw. If we have `frame.x = 1`, the image *source position* will be `1 * tileW` and `1 * tileH` and the image will start on the second cell of the sprite sheet.

```
const { Game, Texture, TileSprite, math } = pop;
...
const texture = new Texture("res/images/player-walk.png");
const squizz = new TileSprite(texture, 32, 32);

scene.add(squizz);
game.run(() => {
  squizz.frame.x = math.rand(3);
});
```

Although the actual texture is large, we only show 32x32 pixels of it at a time—the size of a single frame. Setting the coordinates in `squizz.frame` allows us to draw any frame in the sprite sheet. It's hard to tell with our current demo, though: there's just a blur on the screen because the `TileSprite` is updated 60 times every second! To slow it down (and make sure we're *actually* drawing sprite frames) we'll modify it so that it updates at random times:

```
if (math.randOneIn(20)) {
  squizz.frame.x = math.rand(3);
}
```

 Different Sprite Sheet Formatting

Not all sprite sheets you'll find on the internet will be formatted as beautifully as ours. Some will have extra padding between each cell, or perhaps margins around the entire image. We're not going to support this in our library, but if you're feeling keen then go ahead and add these features to the `TileSprite`. To do so, you'll need to add some properties for padding and margins and then factor these extra sizes in the `drawImage` call.

Cell-based Animation: the Easy Way

The tweaked-out, random-frame `TileSprite` is technically "animated", but it's pretty silly. How about instead of *random* frames, we loop in a *linear order* to achieve an animation? The sprite sheet technique makes it easy to do "flip book" style animation, sequentially displaying carefully drawn images to give the illusion of fluid movement:

```
game.run((dt, t) => {
  squizz.frame.x = Math.floor(t / 0.1) % 4;
});
```

Wow! We're animating! What sorcery is this? If it's unfamiliar to you, then pay attention: it's an old-school staple for performing timing tricks. The remainder operator (`%`) is a fantastic tool any time you need a repeating cycle or counter. This is especially useful for simple animation effects when we tie it to the current time (`t / 0.1`). *No matter how big time gets*, the remainder operator will always wrap it after a certain value (in this case, before it gets to `4`). It takes the remainder of time—altered by a factor to get the correct speed (the lower the number, the faster the animation)—and rounded to the nearest integer (`Math.floor`). `frame.x` will cycle forever between 0, 1, 2, 3, and back to 0 again, flipping every 0.1 seconds.

Using Remainder

By using the "remainder of time" for animating, we don't need extra state variables just to manage timing. To make something blink, we can write `sprite.visible = Math.floor(t * 0.08) % 2` (the `visible` property will toggle between 0 and 1 every 80 milliseconds). To make something wrap around the screen, we can write `sprite.pos.x = (sprite.pos.x + 10) % w` . Whenever you need something to cycle, or repeat, or blink, or toggle, think about the remainder operator.

Rather than have our main game loop be responsible for animating our SquizzBall, we'll let SquizzBall look after itself. Our game is going to end up fairly large, so it's a good time to think about some organization. Create a new folder called `entities` in the project and in it, our first real entity, `Squizz.js` . `Squizz` is a `TileSprite` at heart, so it will inherit from `TileSprite` in the same way that `TileSprite` inherited from `Sprite` :

```
import pop from "../../pop/index.js";
const { TileSprite, Texture } = pop;
const texture = new Texture("res/images/player-walk.png");

class Squizz extends TileSprite {
  constructor() {
    super(texture, 32, 32);
  }
  update (dt, t) {
    this.frame.x = Math.floor(t / 100) % 4;
  }
}
export default Squizz;
```

A `Squizz` has all the functionality of a `TileSprite` , and therefore it works out of the box in our render system. More importantly, Squizz-specific logic can now be contained in here. We don't need to manually add an `update` method via a factory function (as we've been doing so far). It's just another way to group logic together. To create and add new Squizzes to the main scene, make a container and `.add()` them:

```
import Squizz from "./entities/Squizz.js";

const balls = scene.add(new Container());
for (let i = 0; i < 100; i++) {
  const squizz = balls.add(new Squizz());
  squizz.pos.x = math.rand(w);
  squizz.pos.y = math.rand(h);
}
```

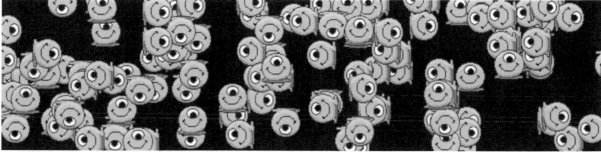

4-12. A SquizzBall party

100 animated SquizzBalls! They look fantastic. We may be on a tight deadline (we're *always* on a tight deadline) but how about we procrastinate a little and expand this into a mini shooting gallery game—kind of a *Rick Clicker II: Flying SquizzBalls*. The goal is to shoot the balls as they whiz past.

Cell-based Animation: A More Powerful Way

First step, let's beef up our animation system a little. Flipping through `frame` frames via a simple remainder means all of our animations are required to be *sequential* cells in the sprite sheet. You can't use a random cell (that's located in another part of the sprite sheet) as part of your animations.

A more flexible approach is to sequence the frames ourselves, and keep check of how much time has elapsed by hand. *We* decide when we should flip to the next frame in the animation. It's more complicated (with more variables) but far more flexible and extensible.

Add a new variable (`rate`) to the `Squizz` class. This indicates how many seconds each frame should be displayed for. (The lower the rate, the faster the animation will run.) A separate variable (`curTime`) will *accumulate the delta time* each frame of our game. When the accumulated amount of time is greater than the rate, update the frame pointer (`curFrame`) to the next frame and start all over again.

```
// Animation variables
this.rate = 0.1;
```

```
this.curTime = 0;
this.curFrame = 0;
this.frames = [
  { x: 0, y: 0 },
  { x: 1, y: 0 },
  { x: 2, y: 0 },
  { x: 3, y: 0 },
];
this.frame = this.frames[this.curFrame];
```

frames is an array of frame pointers indicating which cells of the sprite sheet should be displayed, in which order. You can have as many frames as necessary, and they can point to any cell in the sheet. The animation variables are manipulated in the sprite's *update* method. Here's where time is accumulated and frames flipped. (It's all very manual at the moment, but we'll automate it after we understand it.)

```
const { rate, frames } = this;
// Animation handling
this.curTime += dt;
if (this.curTime > rate) {
  this.frame = frames[this.curFrame++ % frames.length];
  this.curTime -= rate;
}
```

Whenever we want the sprite to be animating, we take the delta time (*dt*) from *update* and accumulate it in *curTime* . Eventually, this amount will be greater that the frame rate *threshold*. Then *frame* is changed to the next frame in the sequence. We use our new *remainder* friend (*%*) to wrap the sequence index back to 0 whenever it's greater than *frames.length* .

The last step is to reset the *curTime* accumulator whenever the frame is updated. You might be tempted to set this counter back to 0. That would work, but it would introduce a subtle timing bug: we also need to consider the *amount* that it goes over the threshold by. Otherwise, each frame duration will be ever so slightly different. To account for this, just subtract the *rate* from the *curTime* , rather than setting it to 0: *this.curTime -= rate;* .

You Can Use This Mechanism Everywhere

This timer mechanism we just implemented can be used e-v-e-r-y-w-h-e-r-e! A variable counts up (or down) until it hits a threshold, then is reset. It can be used for flipping animation frames, periodically spawning enemies, controlling AI decisions (such as "wait 3 seconds, then attack") ... anywhere you need to delay execution for a given amount of time. Much later in the book, we'll abstract this mechanism and give it a nice API (where we don't require additional state variables).

Time	Index	Frame	Image
0.0	0	{ x: 0, y: 0 }	
0.1	1	{ x: 1, y: 0 }	
0.2	2	{ x: 2, y: 0 }	
0.3	3	{ x: 3, y: 0 }	
0.4	0	{ x: 0, y: 0 }	
0.5	1	{ x: 1, y: 0 }	

4-13. Calculating frames

For the shooting gallery game, we want SquizzBalls to fly past at random speeds. Clicking on them once will stun them; twice, they're dead. Flying around at random speeds is easy: choose a random number, move them by that amount in *update* . We probably *should* pass the SquizzBall's speed in as a parameter—so it's more general—but because this is a temporary mini-game, let's just cheat and set it inline:

```
this.speed = math.rand(20, 100);
```

Our random helpers are really paying off now! We set the SquizzBall speed to between 20 and 100 pixels per second. Then in *update* we add the speed (times *dt* as always) and update the animation variables:

```
const { pos, speed, rate, frames } = this;
pos.x += speed * dt;
```

That's it for the SquizzBalls. The rest of the game logic will be implemented in *main.js* . This will

be our first mouse-based game, so we import _MouseControls_ instead of the usual _KeyControls_ .
MouseControls requires the _renderer.view_ object for calculating the click offsets. (See Chapter
3 if this is all news to you!)

```
const mouse = new MouseControls(game.renderer.view);
```

For the main game loop, the logic for the game goes like this: every frame, we move the
SquizzBalls a tiny bit (hmm, sounds familiar). If they go out of the screen, we _wrap them back
around_ and increase their speed by (say) 10%. "Shooting" a SquizzBall means we clicked on it. We
have to check for the _mouse.pressed_ property. (Don't forget that we have to call _mouse.update_
at the end of the _game.run_ loop. Otherwise, _pressed_ will never be reset to _false_ .)

```
// game logic
const { pressed, pos } = mouse;

balls.map(b => {
  if (b.pos.x > w) {
    b.pos.x = -32;
    b.speed *= 1.1;
  }
  // Check for collision
  ...
});

mouse.update();
```

So far, so good. Things are flying and accelerating. The last thing is shooting—which means
"respond to collisions", with our friend _Math.sqrt_ . Hey, we already did this once before. You
know what that means? Time to generalize it and put it in the library! Take the distance
calculation from our shoot-'em-up and add it to the _math.js_ file as a new function called
distance :

```
function distance (a, b) {
  const dx = a.x - b.x;
  const dy = a.y - b.y;
  return Math.sqrt(dx * dx + dy * dy);
}
```

distance will take two points (objects with _x_ and _y_ properties) as parameters, and will return
the distance (in pixels) between them using the method we discussed last chapter. Now our
collision detection code is much cleaner. We can check the distance between the mouse click
position and the SquizzBall:

```
if (pressed && math.distance(pos, b.pos) < 16) {
  if (b.speed > 0) {
    b.speed = 0;
  } else {
    b.dead = true;
  }
}
```

 Adjusting the Anchor Point

This will find the distance between the mouse-click location and the *top-left* corner of the sprite. Remember from earlier that we can adjust the anchor point of the sprite to offset the texture for situations like this. In `Squizz.js`, add `this.anchor = { x: -16, y: -16 };` so it looks like we click on the *center* of the `Sprite`.

If it's the first time we click on a SquizzBall (its speed is greater than 0), we stop it dead in its tracks (`b.speed = 0`). In this case, we don't accumulate the delta time in the animation logic, so the SquizzBall's animation stops too. If the speed is *already* zero when you shoot it, then it's double-killed. Remove it by setting `dead` to true. So long, SquizzBall!

The Animation Manager

So what happens when you want to have *two different* animations for your entity? What if you want a *rolling animation* while the SquizzBall rolls around but a *stunned animation* when it's stunned (rather than just having it stop animating entirely)? Instead of a single array containing the animation frames sequence (`this.frames`), we could create an object containing *multiple arrays* and switch them based on the current animation.

Adding this kind of logic for *every entity* that we ever want to animate sounds really un-fun. It's yet another job for the Pop library! We need to create an API for an "animation manager". An **animation manager** exposes a more friendly API that allows the user of the library to create, play, and stop multiple animations. Like this:

```
if (entity.speed > 10) {
  entity.anims.play("run");
} else if (entity.speed > 0) {
  entity.anims.play("walk");
} else {
  entity.anims.stop();
}
```

As end-users of the library, we only have to define the frames that make up an animation, and not bother with managing all the timing and frame variables by hand. `AnimManager.js` is responsible for the API methods, as well as wrangling the individual animations via its internal state. `Anim` will be a class *only* used directly by `AnimManager` . (In fact, we might even just define `Anim` inside `AnimManager.js` .) There'll be one `Anim` class instance *for every animation* in a given `TileSprite` . (That is, we'll have an `Anim` instance for "run" and another instance for "walk".)

```
class Anim {
  constructor(frames, rate) {
    this.frames = frames;
    this.rate = rate;
    this.reset();
  }

  update(dt) {
    const { rate, frames } = this;
    if ((this.curTime += dt) > rate) {
      this.curFrame++;
      this.frame = frames[this.curFrame % frames.length];
      this.curTime -= rate;
    }
  }
}
```

We pass in the frame sequence that makes up the animation and set the playback rate. The update logic is exactly the same as our manually controlled version. When we create a new `Anim` it calls `this.reset()` , which will reset the animation variables, including moving the frame pointer back to the beginning of the current animation. `reset` is its own method, so `AnimManager` can also call it when the animation needs to be reset.

```
reset() {
  this.frame = this.frames[0];
  this.curFrame = 0;
  this.curTime = 0;
}
```

The `Anim` class won't be used directly by us; a bunch of them can be bundled together and controlled by the `AnimManager` . We just tell `AnimManager` what we want to do.

```
class AnimManager {
  constructor(e) {}
  add(name, frames, speed) {}
  update(dt) {}
```

```
  play(anim) {}
  stop() {}
}
```

AnimManager organizes the *Anims* and determines which *frame* should be displayed at any given time. To achieve this, we need to pass a sprite (*e* , for "entity" in the constructor) as a parameter. *AnimManager* keeps a reference to the sprite's *frame* object so it can update the values, and finally our *CanvasRenderer* will use the frame reference to draw the image. Whatever *AnimManger* says to display, will be displayed.

```
constructor(e) {
  this.anims = {};
  this.running = false;
  this.frameSource = e.frame || e;
  this.current = null;
}
```

As well as keeping the reference to the frame source, it creates an object (*anims*) to hold all the different individual animations, and sets a flag (*running*) to indicate if the animation should be playing or not. This way, we can *stop* when necessary.

```
add(name, frames, speed) {
  this.anims[name] = new Anim(frames, speed);
  return this.anims[name];
}
```

Before we can play an animation, we need to *add* it. An animation has a name (such as "jump", "idle"), an array of frames, and the speed it should play at. We can add as many different animations to a sprite as we want.

```
play(anim) {
  const { current, anims } = this;
  if (anim === current) {
    return;
  }
  this.current = anim;
  anims[anim].reset();
}

stop() {
  this.current = null;
}
```

Besides *add* , we can also play and stop animations. Starting an animation will reset the counter variables and keep a note of the current animation. Note that if we play the same animation again (*anim === current*) it ignores it. So it doesn't matter if we call *play* in a game loop with the same animation name. Stopping the animation is done by clearing the *current* animation. Inside *update* , if there's no animation, we bail.

```
update(dt) {
  const { current, anims, frameSource } = this;
  if (!current) {
    return; // bail!
  }
  const anim = anims[current];
  anim.update(dt);

  // Sync the TileSprite frame
  frameSource.x = anim.frame.x;
  frameSource.y = anim.frame.y;
}
```

On to the most important part of the whole animation system. We ask the current animation to update itself (to do its animation timing calculations) and then set the *frameSource* to the *calculated animation frame*. Remember that *frameSource* will point to the *TileSprite.frame* property—it's a reference—so now we've changed the object *pointed to* by this reference to the correct sprite sheet indexes for the animation frame.

In practice, the *AnimationManager* isn't even used directly by us. Only *TileSprite* s care about frame animation, mostly. Inside the constructor of *TileSprite* we create a new animation manager:

```
this.anims = new AnimManager(this);
```

All of a sudden, *TileSprite* s are aware of animations! Inside its *update* method, we must also update the animation manager (*this.anims.update(dt)*). Because this is happening in a parent class, we can no longer forget to call *super.update(dt)* from the *TileSprite* if we want our animations to work.

That's the grunt work done with. *All* of our *TileSprite* s now have the ability to be animated easily. We can assign our various animations via the *this.anims.add* API method, passing the *animation name*, the *frame sequence*, and the *speed*.

```
const { anims } = this;
anims.add("walk", [0, 1, 2, 3].map(x => ({ x, y: 0 })), 0.07);
```

```
anims.add(
  "idle",
  [{ x: 0, y: 0 }, { x: 4, y: 0 }, { x: 4, y: 1 }, { x: 4, y: 0 }],
  0.15
);
anims.play("walk");
```

The above example is quite interesting, so take a moment to make sure you understand it. We define two animations for the sprite, `walk` and `idle`. The `walk` animation consists of four animation frames, going from `{x: 0, y: 0}` to `{x: 3, y: 0}`, and plays at a rate of 0.07 seconds per frame. (Notice how we .*map* the frames, just because they are sequential—we don't have to manually create each object.) The `idle` animation is also four frames, playing at 0.15 frames per second. Here the frames are *not* sequential so the `x` and `y` indexes are specified explicitly. We kick off the animation by calling `anims.play("walk")`. At any time in our game we can switch animations by calling `play` with the animation name:

```
if (x || y) {
  anims.play("walk");
} else {
  anims.play("idle");
}
```

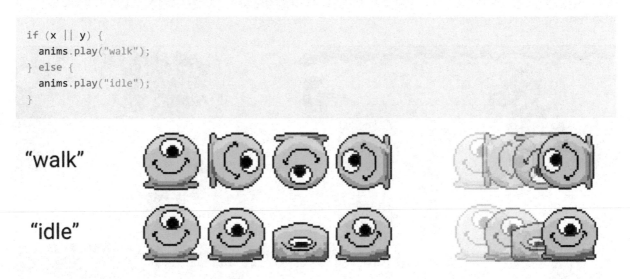

4-14. Multiple animations

This sure beats manually tracking delta times and current frames. We can quickly and easily get animations into all our new prototypes. It can also be expanded to do things like playing non-looping animations, firing callbacks when an animation loops, or doing ping-pong animations.

Tile Maps

Enough goofing around shooting and animating things: back to *SquizzBall*. *SquizzBall* is going to be **tile based**—which means the background level (and general game logic) will be modeled as a *2D grid*. Each frame of a sprite sheet acts as a "brush" that can be painted into any cell. Each frame of the sprite sheet can appear many times to create a background mosaic.

This technique was originally used to overcome the memory limitations of early game systems. But it remains an effective way to generate varied graphics from a small set of art resources, and is still used widely today. In some games (like the outlandish *Crashlands*, by Butterscotch Shenanigans) the grid is fairly obvious and you use it to craft your base. In others (such as *Stardew Valley*, by ConcernedApe) the clever use of graphics makes the grid harder to spot.

4-15. Base-building in Crashlands

4-16. Stardew Valley, with grid

If you look closely, you can see where tiles are reused. From a gamedev perspective, it means we can create just a handful of tile assets and reuse them to maximum effect. Additionally, doing math in a rigid grid is nice and simple—helping with things like pathfinding, and modeling interesting systems based on neighboring cells (for example, the classic cellular automaton *Conway's Game of Life*).

Implementing a basic version of a tile map is quite straightforward if we repurpose our existing library elements. We can think of a tile map as *a collection of sprites* that are neatly organized as a 2D matrix. If we position everything carefully, it creates the *illusion* of a seamless background.

Thinking in terms of data structures, we want a simple solution that lets us easily imagine in code what our background will look like on screen. The most straightforward (and old-school) approach is to create an array with elements that point to the tile frames we want to draw.

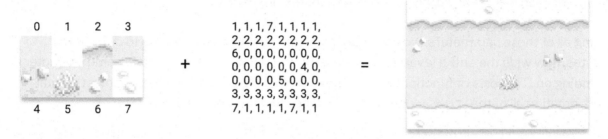

4-17. Tilesheet to tilemap

In our engine, a tile map will be a `Container` whose children are `TileSprite`s all stacked next to (and on top of) each other to make the final picture. To "draw" a level using the above example, each number in the array will need to somehow be mapped to the corresponding *frame* for the `TileSprite`. In the level data, `1` might map to a "solid rock" tile, which is at offset `{x: 0, y: 0}`, and `2` is a "ladder" tile that maps to, say, frame `{x: 1, y:1}`. Anywhere in the level data you put a `2`, the game will draw a ladder. The final definition of a "level" layout will be an *array of frame data*.

The tile map itself will be managed by a new library item, `TileMap.js`. It's a `Container` that positions `TileSprite`s into a grid. To properly define a tile map, we need to supply several pieces of information:

```
class TileMap extends Container {
  constructor(tiles, mapW, mapH, tileW, tileH, texture) {
    super();
    this.mapW = mapW;
    this.mapH = mapH;
    this.tileW = tileW;
    this.tileH = tileH;
    this.w = mapW * tileW;
    this.h = mapH * tileH;

    // Add all TileSprites
    ...
  }
}
```

The first parameter `tiles` is a big array of *frame data* to draw: `[{x:1, y:0}, {x:1, y: 0}, …]`. The number of elements in this array will be the width of the map multiplied by the height of the map. These parameters are also passed as `mapW` and `mapH`. If the map is ten tiles across and ten tiles high, the `tiles` array will contain 100 elements.

The remaining parameters define the `TileSprite`s that will comprise the level: the width and height of each *individual* tile, and the sprite sheet texture to draw.

Using all of these parameters, we can figure out a lot of useful things: where to draw all the sprites, how wide the entire level is in pixels (`mapW * tileW`), what tile a certain game character is standing on ... all sorts of functionality we'll need for making games. First up, the most critical part: creating all of the `TileSprite` children and positioning them as a grid:

```
// Add all TileSprites
this.children = tiles.map((frame, i) => {
  const s = new TileSprite(texture, tileW, tileH);
  s.frame = frame;
  s.pos.x = i % mapW * tileW;
  s.pos.y = Math.floor(i / mapW) * tileH;
  return s;
});
```

`TileMap` is a `Container`, so it has an array of child elements that the `CanvasRenderer` will render. To populate the array, we iterate over the `tiles` frame data. For each element, make a new `TileSprite` and initialize it with `tileW`, `tileH` and the `frame` object.

Finding the tile's grid position requires a bit of math. The `x` position is calculated by taking the remainder of the map width (`mapW`) for the current tile index (`i`). This returns a value *between 0 and the map width*. Multiplying this index by the a single tile's width (`tileW`) gives us the correct grid `x` position on screen.

The `y` position is calculated by dividing the index by the map width. The number of times `i` goes into `mapW` gives us the *row* it should be on. We floor the result (to snap to the grid) and multiply by `tileH` to get the final `y` pixel position. As an example, let's calculate the position for the 13th element (the only `1`) in this simple map that has a width of 5:

```
0,0,0,0,0,
0,0,0,0,0,
0,0,0,1,0,
0,0,0,0,0
```

`13 % 5 = 3 (4th column) * 32 (pixels) = 96`. The `x` position for the fourth column is 96. Similarly, `13 / 5 = 2 (3rd row) * 32 (pixels) = 64` gives the `y` position of the third row as 64. Repeat for every element in the map and you have your level! To show it off in action, we'll create a map made up of random tiles covering the full height and width of the viewport:

```
const texture = new Texture("res/images/tiles.png");
const tileSize = 32;
const mapW = Math.floor(w / tileSize);
const mapH = Math.floor(h / tileSize);
```

The tiles in our sprite sheet are 32x32, so to get the map width we divide the viewport width by 32. Same for the height. Now we can create frame data for each cell in the map. For now, the x and y values will point to random tiles in the image.

```
// Make a random level of tile indexes
const level = [];
for (let y = 0; y < mapH; y++) {
  for (let x = 0; x < mapW; x++) {
    level.push({
      x: math.rand(5),
      y: math.rand(2)
    });
  }
}
```

The array `level` now contains `mapW * mapH` elements with random x and y frame data. We now have enough data to create a tile map: the array of frame data, the map width and height, the tile width and height, and the sprite sheet image.

```
const map = new TileMap(level, mapW, mapH, tileSize, tileSize, texture);
scene.add(map);
game.run();
```

4-18. Random tilemap

Every time you refresh the page, you get a random level of tiles that take up the entire screen! I personally love this. As soon as tiles fit together, they seem to be more impressive than the sum of their parts. As homework, find other tilesets on game asset sites and test them out here too. It can be very motivating to wrangle professional-quality assets to make weird worlds!

Our map is cool, but creating the level (and calculating map width and heights) is making the `main.js` messy. *SquizzBall* will be a fairly large game, so we need to keep things tidy as we go along. Move the `TileMap` code into a new file called `Level.js`. A `Level` will be a `TileMap` with all the related code needed to make the *SquizzBall* levels.

```
const texture = new Texture("res/images/tiles.png");

class Level extends TileMap {
  constructor(w, h) {
    // tile map setup
    ...
    super(level, mapW, mapH, tileSize, tileSize, texture);
  }
}
```

Back in `main.js`, we can delete all the map-related code and replace it with our brand new `Level`:

```
const level = new Level(w, h);
scene.add(level);
game.run();
```

With a nice backdrop, let's now introduce our main character back into the world. We can import it and add it to the scene *after* we add the level. (If we added it *before*, the level would be on top of the player, and you wouldn't see it!)

```
const controls = new KeyControls();
const squizz = new Squizz(controls);
const level = new Level(w, h);

scene.add(level);
scene.add(squizz);
```

If you test this out, you'll see that it looks really cool, but that the player can just wander off screen and be lost forever. To enforce our world boundaries, we'll get `Level` to store where we think the edges of the level should be. Based on the size of a tile and the width and height of the map, we assign an object property *bounds* in `Level.js` *after* the call to *super*:

```
this.bounds = {
```

```
    left: tileSize,
    right: w - tileSize * 2,
    top: tileSize,
    bottom: h - tileSize * 2
};
```

This dictates that (for example) the furthest *left* that SquizzBall will be allowed to go is *tileSize* pixels (which is 32 pixels for our tile sheet). The idea is that we'll check `bounds` when moving and disallow moving into the *first column* of the screen; we'll draw a wall tile there. The net result is it *looks* like the wall tile is blocking the player.

 Tile Map Eye Candy

The tile maps we're creating in this chapter are just for show: they sit in the background and look pretty. That's why it's necessary to manually define the level "bounds". In the next chapter, I'll introduce real collisions and interactions with tiles. This is when the configuration of the background goes from eye candy to *level design*. We'll delve more into level design as we go, and find some tools so we don't have to make elaborate tile maps by hand!

```
game.run(() => {
  const { pos } = squizz;
  const { bounds: { top, bottom, left, right } } = level;
  // Confine player pos to the bounds area
  ...
});
```

Inside the game loop, extract the level bounds (using nested destructuring to get `level.bounds`, and then from that getting `bounds.top`, `bounds.bottom`, `bounds.left`, and `bounds.right`). These can then be used to stop the player from running off screen.

Clamping Down

To restrict the player to the level bounds in the horizontal direction, we make sure the player's `x` position is not less than the level's left edge, and not greater than the level's right edge. Doing both of these checks at once is called **clamping**. It's a function that should definitely be in the core math library:

```
function clamp(x, min, max) {
  return Math.max(min, Math.min(x, max));
}
```

clamp takes three parameters: the "current" value of the thing we're clamping, the minimum value it's allowed to be, and the *maximum* value it's allowed to be. We then do a funky trick to combine the calculations. First, we find the smaller value (with *Math.min*) out of the "current" value, and the *maximum* value (so if we're greater than *max* , it returns *max*). We then look for the larger value (with *Math.max*) of our *min* value and the result from the first calculation. If the result is *less* than *min* , we'll take *min* .

```
// Confine the player pos to bounds area
pos.x = math.clamp(pos.x, left, right);
pos.y = math.clamp(pos.y, top, bottom);
```

To clamp the position to the level bounds, we set the left and right level values as *min* and *max* and clamp the player's position between them. And we do the same for the top and bottom values. The player is trapped inside our arena!

Snapping to a Grid

Being trapped inside the arena is not enough. The game relies on things being in rows and columns; it's not a free-range SquizzBall. In order to feel more '80s, we want to stick to the grid. SquizzBalls should *snap* to the correct location, so they're always moving along either a row or a column. We'll give Squizz a speed (measured in "number of seconds it takes to travel one tile") and a direction object:

```
this.speed = 0.15;
this.dir = {
  x: 1,
  y: 0
};
```

The direction (*dir*) will have an *x* and *y* component that can be -1 (for left or up), 0 for no movement, and 1 (for right or down). We'll make sure that only one of the components can ever be non-zero at a time, by resetting the opposite direction whenever the keys are pressed:

```
const { x, y } = controls;
if (x && x !== dir.x) {
  // Change to horizontal movement
} else if (y && y !== dir.y) {
  // Change to vertical movement
}
```

Here's where we'll be tricky: if the player presses a key in a new horizontal direction, we'll set the *dir.x* property to the direction, and set the *dir.y* property to 0. No more moving vertically.

Additionally, we'll *snap* the player's y position to the closest "tile". Snapping is a requirement that you'll encounter frequently—especially when making tile-based games.

```
dir.x = x;
dir.y = 0;
pos.y = Math.round(pos.y / 32) * 32;
```

Snapping is done by dividing the position by the tile size (32 pixels in our case) and then rounding it. When we re-multiply by the tile size, the remainder part from the division will be gone—so the player will be exactly aligned to the nearest "y" tile. We do the same for the vertical check too. The player position is then updated depending on the direction they're traveling:

```
pos.x += dir.x * dt * (32 / speed);
pos.y += dir.y * dt * (32 / speed);
```

As a single tile is 32 pixels wide, we multiply the direction by *32 / speed* . If speed were 1, it would take 1 second to travel the 32 pixels. We can decrease this as the game plays so it gets faster and harder for the player.

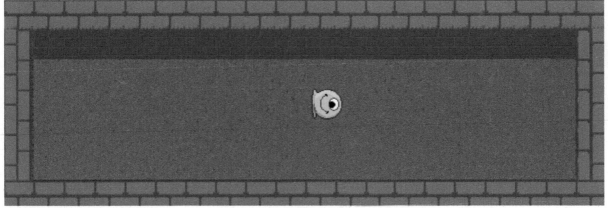

4-19. Tilemap level

Tile Map Helpers

The player is racing around the world. The next task is to *alter the ground behind them* so they can never go back—like the snake game on old mobile phones: no eating your tail.

For this, we need some extra functionality on the *TileMap* for finding which tiles are at which screen positions. Being able to modify a tile map dynamically enables the creation of all sorts of fun game mechanics, so it goes straight into the library. We'll define three sets of helpers, each having two functions—one for working with pixel references (for example, "player is at pixel screen position *{x: 400, y: 300}* ") and another for working with map references (for example, "player is at map grid cell *{x: 2, y: 3}* ").

```
pixelToMapPos(pos) {
  const { tileW, tileH } = this;
  return {
    x: Math.floor(pos.x / tileW),
    y: Math.floor(pos.y / tileH)
  };
}

mapToPixelPos(mapPos) {
  const { tileW, tileH } = this;
  return {
    x: mapPos.x * tileW,
    y: mapPos.y * tileH
  };
}
```

The first of the helpers converts between pixel coordinates and grid cell indexes. *pixelToMapPos* takes a position *x* and *y* , and divides each by their *tileW* and *tileH* . These are then floored to give the map reference. If the player is at screen pixel *{x: 48, y: 48}* and the tiles are 32x32, they are converted to *48 / 32 = 1.5* . Flooring gives *1* . So the player is standing in the second column of the second row (*{x: 1, y: 1}*). Converting back (*mapToPixelPos*) is easier: just multiply by the tile dimensions.

Next up, we often want to get the actual *TileSprite* that's at a given position (perhaps you need to check if the player is standing on solid ground, for example). Returning the correct element from the container's *children* array involves finding the map *x* and *y* position and converting it to an array index.

```
tileAtMapPos(mapPos) {
  return this.children[mapPos.y * this.mapW + mapPos.x];
}

tileAtPixelPos(pos) {
  return this.tileAtMapPos(this.pixelToMapPos(pos));
}
```

If we have a map position, it's the map *y* position multiplied by the *mapW* (each row down we need to move *mapW* elements through the array) and then add the *x* offset to get to the correct element. The formula *y * w + x* emerges often when working with 2D grids! To convert from a pixel position, we call the same function, but first convert the coordinates using *pixelToMapPos* .

Finally, we'll add some functions to set a new frame at a given position. In *SquizzBall*, we want to leave a trail behind the player as they move. We can change any tile the player is standing on from a "dirt" image to an "empty" image. This is a matter of updating the frame *{x, y}* reference:

```
setFrameAtMapPos(mapPos, frame) {
  const tile = this.tileAtMapPos(mapPos);
  tile.frame = frame;
  return tile;
}

setFrameAtPixelPos(pos, frame) {
  return this.setFrameAtMapPos(this.pixelToMapPos(pos), frame);
}
```

setFrameAtMapPos uses *tileAtMapPos* to first get the tile, then replaces the *frame* property. If we only have a screen pixel position, we call *setFrameAtPixelPos* —which calls the same function after converting the position with *pixelToMapPos* . That's a good set of *TileMap* helpers to get us started. As always, we'll expand on them as needed!

To put this into practice, we'll add a function to the *Level* called *checkGround* . We'll make the level responsible for remembering where the player is and if they've moved to a new square. If the current tile returned from *tileAtPixelPos* is the same as *this.lastTile* , it's the same square, so we don't have to do anything. If not, it's a new square. The square gets converted to a "blank" tile (*this.blank = { x: 0, y: 0};*) via our helper function *setFrameAtPixelPos* . The player won't be allowed to go back there again.

```
checkGround(pos) {
  const { blank, lastTile } = this;
  const tile = this.tileAtPixelPos(pos);
  if (lastTile === tile) {
    return "checked";
  }
  this.lastTile = tile;
  if (tile.frame !== blank) {
    this.setFrameAtPixelPos(pos, blank);
    return "solid";
  }
  return "cleared";
}
```

For every frame in the main game, we ask the level to report the status of the ground the player is standing on, using *const ground = level.checkGround(squizz.pos)* , and clear the ground underfoot. Take some time to revise the helper methods and how we're modifying the level map. Getting good at chopping and changing level maps opens the door to all sorts of fun game mechanics and visual tricks.

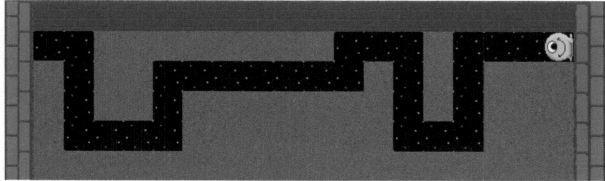

4-20. Tilemap level destroying

Entities Utilities

In its current state, you'll see there's an issue. (Isn't there always?) The SquizzBall is positioned at the top-left corner of the `TileSprite` . For our purposes, it would make sense if we checked for the ground from the *center* of the player. Getting the center of an entity in our engine is something we'll need *a lot*. So, let's stick it in the library.

But where? It's a math-related function, so it could happily live in `utils/math.js` . But it's the first math function that needs to know about the structure of Pop entities; it's not just pure math. We'll make another API design decision to include a *different file* for entity-related utilities, called `utils/entity.js` . Here we add a function, `center` , that returns the *center* of an entity. With it, we can get the ground under the center of the player with `level.checkGround(entity.center(squizz))` .

```
function center (entity) {
  const { pos, w, h } = entity;
  return {
    x: pos.x + w / 2,
    y: pos.y + h / 2
  };
}

export default {
  center,
};
```

Nothing magic about this: it takes an entity as a parameter and returns the entity's position with half its width and half its height added to it—or, in other words, its center! Sounds pretty handy. While we're here, let's give *center* a friend: `entity.distance` . It's the same function as `math.distance` , but rather than being between points, we'll make it between entities:

```
function distance (a, b) {
  return math.distance(center(a), center(b));
}
```

Helper functions like this can greatly reduce the amount of cruft in your game code. On the other hand, if you add everything you could ever possibly need, you end up with a bloated "kitchen-sink" API. Deciding what to include in a "utilities" module is more art than science!

Scrolling Maps with a Camera

The game worlds in our minds are vast, expansive fields, treacherous mazes, exotic plains, and post-apocalyptic dungeons. They're not going to fit on a single screen. We need a way to move around the level and see more of what exists outside the realms of the canvas window. One way to do that is to move *everything* in the world by the same amount every frame, while keeping the player fixed in place. But a nicer answer is to leave everything where it is and implement a **camera**.

Just like a movie camera, we should be able to pan around our level and focus on important parts of our game. Generally this will involve simply tracking the player, but cameras can also be used to frame the on-screen action in different ways—for example, highlighting imminent danger or areas of interest. Cameras can be as nuanced as game controls. They can make or break a game. Our initial camera attempts will be very simple (but useful). Just like controls, though, don't be afraid to experiment and re-implement from scratch if your game calls for it!

Start with a new file in the library directory called `Camera.js` . A camera is a `Container` that contains all of the elements in the game that should be "filmable". (That is, they'll be affected by the position of the camera.) This will include all of our game items, but not UI components (such as scores or instructions) which will stay in a fixed position.

```
class Camera extends Container {
  constructor(subject, viewport, worldSize = viewport) {
    super();
    this.w = viewport.w;
    this.h = viewport.h;
    this.worldSize = worldSize;
    this.setSubject(subject);
  }
  setSubject(e) {}
  focus() {}
  update(dt, t) {}
```

```
}
export default Camera;
```

The camera requires a few things to work properly. The `viewport` will be an object with width (`w`) and height (`h`) representing the size of the camera screen. For us, it'll be the size of the game canvas. The `worldSize` is also an object of `w` and `h`, but it's the *entire* world—the limits of how far the camera can pan.

The *subject* is what the camera should follow. It will usually be an entity in our game (and most likely the player), but may be some other position object if you want to have greater control over what the game is highlighting. There's a method, `setSubject`, in case we want to change the target entity during game play. It accepts an entity or a position. If it's an entity, we assume it has dimensions—and so we want to focus on the center of it using an offset:

```
this.subject = e ? e.pos || e : this.pos;
this.offset = { x: 0, y: 0 };

// Center on the entity
if (e && e.w) {
  this.offset.x += e.w / 2;
  this.offset.y += e.h / 2;
}
if (e && e.anchor) {
  this.offset.x -= e.anchor.x;
  this.offset.y -= e.anchor.y;
}
```

📌 **Camera Subject**

`setSubject` will first try to get the position from an entity if we passed it (`e.pos`). Otherwise it will assume `e` *is already* a position (for example, if we passed in our own custom x/y object). If `e` is neither, we just use the camera's own position: it doesn't try to follow any external entity, and you can just control it manually.

If the subject has a width, the offset becomes the middle of the entity (`e.w / 2` and `e.h / 2`). If it also has an anchor point set, we need to take this into consideration too—as the center won't be correct otherwise. The camera will be updated every frame (because it's a `Container`). In the update method, we'll call a new method— `focus` —that will do the grunt work of following the subject:

```
super.update(dt, t);
if (this.subject) {
  this.focus();
}
```

There are some calculations to do to keep the *center* of view focused on the subject. The core idea is to position the camera so the `subject` (plus the `offset`) will be in the center of the viewport (`w / 2`). The exception to this is when the subject is *near the edges* of `worldSize`. The camera should stop panning if it would otherwise show "blank" areas outside the world. To achieve this, clamp the position at `worldSize.w - w` so that once the camera is "one viewport width" away from the right edge it will go no further. Then do the same in the vertical direction.

```
const { pos, w, h, worldSize, subject, offset } = this;

const centeredX = subject.x + offset.x - w / 2;
const maxX = worldSize.w - w;
const x = -math.clamp(centeredX, 0, maxX);

const centeredY = subject.y + offset.y - h / 2;
const maxY = worldSize.h - h;
const y = -math.clamp(centeredY, 0, maxY);

pos.x = x;
pos.y = y;
```

4-21. Unclamped (left) vs clamped (right) camera

The camera container is now centered on the center of the player. Because it's recalculated every frame, it follows the player wherever they go. In our game, the camera should follow our main character, `Squizz`. The size of the viewport will be the full canvas size, and the size of the world is the *pixel size* of the level. The camera needs to be added to the main *scene*, but now `squizz` and `level` should be added to the camera, not directly to the scene.

```
const squizz = new Squizz(controls);
const level = new Level(w * 2, h * 2);
const camera = new Camera(
  squizz,
  { w, h },
  { w: level.w, h: level.h }
```

```
);

scene.add(camera);
camera.add(level);
camera.add(squizz);
```

SquizzBall is designed to be played in an arcade cabinet with a joystick, so we'll ditch the `MouseControls` and shooting and bring back our `KeyControls`. Because the level is twice as big as the screen view, when `Squizz` moves around, the camera will track them.

 A Hidden Issue

Although the level looks fantastic, there's a hidden issue that would bite us if we were making a bigger game. Currently, our renderer renders *all* of the children of a container every frame. This means our *entire* level gets rendered, even if parts of it are off screen. Because our levels are currently small, we'll ignore it—but very large worlds will definitely result in a reduced frame rate. In Chapter 9 (which focuses on performance) we'll address it.

Grid-based Baddies

The game is shaping up. Now we need some challenges. The two things in *SquizzBall* that will kill the player are "backtracking" over your own trail, and getting hit by the patrolling bad guys in the sky. The bad guys will move in *rows and columns* so the player can safely pass next to them. Our `entities/Baddie.js` will be very similar to the bad guys from Chapter 3—a sprite that simply flies in a straight line (depending on the `xSpeed` and `ySpeed` we provide):

```
class Baddie extends TileSprite {
  constructor (xSpeed, ySpeed) {
    super(texture, 32, 32);
    this.xSpeed = xSpeed;
    this.ySpeed = ySpeed;
  }
  update (dt) {
    const { pos, xSpeed, ySpeed } = this;
    pos.x += xSpeed * dt;
    pos.y += ySpeed * dt;
  }
}
export default Baddie;
```

Nothing new here. In fact, hopefully it's starting to become familiar how we think about creating the elements of a game. We need a flying bad guy, so we look into our box of tricks and see what works best. In this case, it's a `TileSprite`, because we have art assets in a sprite sheet so it's easy to integrate. Inside `update`, we describe the behavior we want the bad guys to have ("move everything a tiny bit"). The baddies will fly horizontally and vertically. To do this, we'll make either their `ySpeed` or `xSpeed` equal to 0.

Having designed an enemy type, we now have to think about how we *spawn them*. This happens back in `main.js`:

```
// Add roaming baddies
const baddies = addBaddies(level);
camera.add(baddies);
```

The baddies get their own `Container` to keep them organized. Where and when we spawn them is up to you! Changing how many enemies there are, where they spawn from, how fast they go ... this *is* game design. Tiny tweaks can radically change how the game plays. In the interests of making SquizzBall enemies ominous, we'll try an attack "grid" of evenly spaced bad guys that fly over the arena:

```
function addBaddies(level) {
  const baddies = new Container();
  // Horizontal bad guys
  for (let i = 0; i < 5; i++) {
    const b = baddies.add(new Baddie(32 * 5, 0));
    b.pos.y = Math.floor(level.h / 5) * i + level.tileH * 2;
  }
  // Vertical bad guys
  for (let i = 0; i < 10; i++) {
    const b = baddies.add(new Baddie(0, 32 * 5));
    b.pos.x = Math.floor(level.w / 10) * i + level.tileW;
  }
  return baddies;
}
```

This is just one idea (the first one I had—you should really try out some of your own ideas). The horizontal bad guys have a speed of "5 tiles per second" (`32 * 5`) and a vertical speed of 0. They'll start on the left side of the screen and fly relentlessly to the right. The vertical baddies have 0 horizontal speed, and a positive vertical speed—to make them fly from the top of the screen straight down.

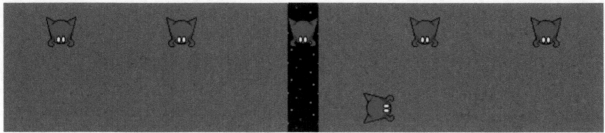

4-22. Wave of baddies

Ooooh, scary! Only problem is, the baddies fly straight off the screen and never come back. Also, there's no collision detection with the player. Not very scary. We can use our `entity.distance` helper to see if there's a collision. We kill the player (by setting their `dead` property to `true`) and send the baddie backwards off the screen. If the bad guy has traveled too far off screen, we wrap them back around again—just like we did in our mouse-controlled clicker game earlier:

```
this.baddies.map(b => {
  const { pos } = b;
  if (entity.distance(squizz, b) < 32) {
    // A hit!
    squizz.dead = true;

    // Send off screen for a bit
    if (b.xSpeed) pos.x = -level.w;
    else pos.y = -level.h;
  }

  // Screen wrap
  if (pos.x > level.w) pos.x = -32;
  if (pos.y > level.h) pos.y = -32;
});
```

The other way the player can die is if they step on their own trail. Each frame, we ask the `Level` what tile the player is currently standing on (via `Level.checkGround`). If it returns the string `cleared`, it means the player has been here before, and therefore they're doomed!

```
// See if we're on new ground
const ground = level.checkGround(entity.center(squizz));
if (ground === "cleared") {
  squizz.dead = true;
}
```

At this point, it's worth remembering that the rules we've implemented—the rules for the player, for the bad guys, for the controls ... *everything*—are totally arbitrary. They have nothing to do with making a game library; they're only about game design. They are ideas we made up. It's *here* you need to put your game designer hat on—to think about mechanics and aesthetics. Start asking questions—like *why* things are flying at our SquizzBall, or why we're confined to a grid. What can you add that supports the game's theme? What needs to be removed or modified? This is the exciting part! Don't be afraid to tweak and change anything and everything and discover what works and what doesn't. There are no wrong answers!

Screens & Game Life Cycle

"Oooh, hey, look at this! Let me have a go!" says Guy Shifty, swooping in to play-test your game. But it doesn't take long for his facial expression to sour. "What am I supposed to be doing? ... Hmm, what just happened? I was controlling that ball, then I moved around, and now I'm dead? What's going on?"

He's not impressed. He's confused about the rules, and doesn't know what he's supposed to do. As much as we dislike him, he's right. We have a working *prototype* for a game, with a simple mechanic, and some good controls, but we don't have a *game*. It's time to take a step back and look at the big picture. We're getting *dangerously close* to possessing all the tools we need to complete a polished, impressive-looking game. What we're missing now is the game's life cycle—a title screen with instructions, resetting levels when the player dies, a "game over" screen, and a way to start the whole process over.

Game Screens

Up until now, when our games have started we've thrown the player into the deep end. The action starts as soon as the browser finishes loading. If you're not the one developing the game, that's stressful and confusing. To remedy this, we'll introduce the notion of a **screen**. Each section of game logic can go into a re-startable screen that we can call when needed. All of the game logic we currently have can be moved out of the `main.js` root file and placed in its own file `GameScreen.js` in a new folder called `/screens`.

 Put Yourself in the Player's Shoes

As soon as you have your core mechanic functioning, you need to start putting yourself in the shoes of a *new player*—someone who knows nothing at all about your game. Think about how *they* will experience things, and how you can make things more intuitive and enjoyable.

```
class GameScreen extends Container {
  constructor(game, controls) {
```

```
    super();
    // Initialization code
  }

  update(dt, t) {
    super.update(dt, t);
    // Game screen update logic
  }
}
```

We don't need a new core type for screens; we'll just reuse our good ol' `Container` . All of our
game elements (including UI and camera) will go inside. This will replace the main `scene`
container we've been using so far. All of the elements that were added in `main.js` can now be
moved to `GameScreen.js` . The `level` , `camera` and `SquizzBall` will now need to be defined as
class properties, rather than free variables. So they'll need to be set in the `GameScreen`
constructor:

```
// Keep references to things we need in "update"
this.level = level;
this.camera = camera;
this.squizz = squizz;
```

With the entire game moved into a screen, `main.js` now looks very bare: it creates the `Game` ,
some root game objects (a new `KeyControls` to control our `SquizzBall` , and the new game
screen), then starts the main loop:

```
import GameScreen from "./screens/GameScreen.js";

const game = new Game(640, 480);
const controls = new KeyControls();

game.scene = new GameScreen(game, controls);
game.run();
```

The Circle of Life

When we refactored the `GameScreen` , we changed our main `scene` from our static reference
(that we originally created in `Game.js`) to a new instance of the `GameScreen` . By switching this
reference, we can manage the *flow* of screens in our game. Our `Game` object calls `scene.update`
and `scene.render` every frame, so we just have to change what `game.scene` is pointing at to set
the *active screen*.

We can make some helper functions that will reassign *scene* to the correct game screen:

```javascript
import LogoScreen from "./screens/LogoScreen.js";
import TitleScreen from "./screens/TitleScreen.js";
import GameScreen from "./screens/GameScreen.js";
import GameOverScreen from "./screens/GameOverScreen.js";

const game = new Game(640, 480);
const controls = new KeyControls();

function titleScreen () {
  game.scene = new TitleScreen(game, controls, newGame);
}

function gameOverScreen (result) {
  game.scene = new GameOverScreen(game, controls, result, titleScreen);
}

function newGame () {
  game.scene = new GameScreen(game, controls, gameOverScreen);
}

game.scene = new LogoScreen(game, titleScreen);
```

This defines a bunch of new screens—most of which don't exist yet, but we're getting to that! When we call any of the functions, the new screens will become active (because they're now *game.scene* , which is what our system passes to *CanvasRenderer*).

Notice that we pass in some other useful things to each screen: a reference to the *game* object (so the screen can get width and height information if it needs it); the *controls* objects; and *a reference to another screen-changing function*. For example, *LogoScreen* has a reference to the *titleScreen* function. Inside *LogoScreen* , we'll call this when it's time to *leave the logo screen*. This function creates a new *TitleScreen* and passes a reference to the *newGame* function. *GameScreen* gets a reference to the *gameOverScreen* function, and *GameOverScreen* gets a reference back to the *titleScreen* function.

This is the flow of our game. *LogoScreen -> TitleScreen -> GameScreen -> GameOverScreen ->* back to *TitleScreen* .

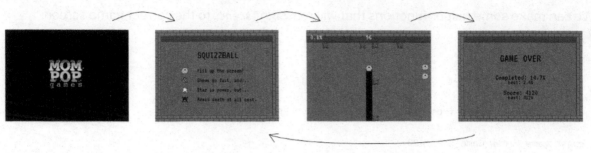

4-23. Game screen flow

As an example, `screens/LogoScreen.js` will hold the screen that just displays our company logo for a couple of seconds the first time the game loads (because we really need to do some self-promotion!). You can get creative here and add whatever you want—throwing in some movement, or a starfield, or some other effects to accompany the company logo.

```
const texture = new Texture("/res/images/logo-mompop.png");

class LogoScreen extends Container {
  constructor(game, onDone) {
    super();
    this.onDone = onDone;
    this.life = 2;
    const logo = this.add(new Sprite(texture));
    logo.pos = { x: 220, y: 130 };
  }
}
```

Once again we're implementing our timing mechanism from earlier. For each frame in `update`, we subtract the delta time from the `life` counter. After two seconds, `life` will be less than 0 and we call the `onDone` function that we set in the constructor:

```
update(dt, t) {
  super.update(dt, t);

  this.life -= dt;
  if (this.life < 0) {
    this.onDone();
  }
}
```

Remember that `onDone` is a reference to the `titleScreen` function from `main.js`. Calling this sets the `game.screen` to a new `TitleScreen` instance, which in turn is called in our main `Game` loop ... and the game begins! We can do the same again for the title screen. The `titleScreen` function also passes in a reference to the `KeyControls` so that we can wait for the user to hit a key to begin:

```
class TitleScreen extends Container {
  constructor(game, controls, onStart) {
    this.onStart = onStart;
    this.controls = controls;
    controls.reset();
  }
}
```

 Stopping Accidental Skipping of the Title Screen

We call `controls.reset()` in the screen initialization phase. This "unpresses" any keys the user might be holding down as the game is loaded. Without this reset, there's a danger the action key would *already be down* and the title screen would be skipped without the user ever seeing it.

The title screen (`screens/TitleScreen.js`) is your first point of contact with the player, so feel free to get creative. Our title screen has a few elements to it: the "SquizzBall" title, an animated SquizzBall, and a few lines of instructions.

 Don't Overuse Text

Don't offer too much text if you can avoid it. Players tend never to read text—*ever!* You need to catch their attention, and convey any absolutely necessary information as effectively as possible. Seriously, players *won't read your text*.

We take care of animations inside *update* (in this case bobbing the *title* image with *Math.sin*) and check the user input to see if the player is ready to begin!

```
const { title, controls } = this;
title.pos.y += Math.sin(t / 300) * 0.3;
if (controls.action) {
  this.onStart();
}
```

The last screen in our flow is `screens/GameOverScreen.js`. In `main.js` you'll notice that the helper function accepts a parameter— `results` —which gets passed into the screen creation. This is how we can *transfer data across screens*. In the game we maintain a list of statistics (about scores and times):

```
this.stats = {
  pellets: 0,
  maxPellets: level.totalFreeSpots,
  lives: 3,
  score: 0
};
```

When the player gets some points, we increment `stats.score`. When they clear a tile, we increment `stats.pellets`. (I chose "pellets" because the changing tiles are kind of like *Pac-Man's* pellet system: you have to collect them all!) When the player dies, this object is passed over to `GameOverScreen`:

```
this.gameOver(stats);
```

Finishing Touches

Well, we've met all the requirements of our brief and we *could* call it a day—but unfortunately it's not that simple. With the core mechanics in place, it's inevitable that you'll get excited and want to add more. New features, improvements, entire new concepts … that's great! Embrace it! Try things out, move things around, cut things out, go nuts! With our limited time remaining, we've decided to add a few embellishments to the core game: a high-score system, bonuses, power-ups, explosions, and a SquizzBall who starts off slow and speeds up over time.

 Do It Yourself

We'll only cover these features in overview, but they're all variations of the mechanics and techniques we've already covered. There's nothing you couldn't figure out for yourself—and please try to do so!—but it's also all included in the example code for your reference.

There are two types of high score: a points achievement and a percentage-of-the-arena-filled achievement. These get displayed at the top of the in-game screen as well as on the game-over screen. To track the high scores over multiple plays, we could either pass the data around the screens or create a new file (`hiscore.js`) with a shared `hiscore` object and import it in `GameOverScreen`:

```
const highscore = {
  bestScore: 0,
  bestComplete: 0
```

```
};
export default highscore;
```

When a player's `stats.score` is greater than `highscore.bestScore`, they've earned a new high score. We didn't create a system to enter your initials like in the olden days, but that would be a cool feature to add!

We've also added some pickups, power-ups, and obstacles that affect SquizzBall—"shoes" to make you run faster, a "powerball" that lets you smash the flying bad guys and retrace your steps with impunity, and a deadly skull that must be avoided at all costs. These are implemented in a single `entities/pickup.js` file, and they randomly get generated and added to a `pickups` container, with the logic for each pickup handled in the `GameScreen` when there's a collision.

The powerball mode gets a cool "blinking cool-down" effect using a trick we learned in the "Cell-based Animation: the Easy Way" section earlier in this chapter. When the player gets the power pickup, we set a timer (another timer!) and change animation to the power animation:

```
this.powerupTime = seconds;
this.anims.play("power");
```

Then in `update`, when the `powerupTime` is nearing its end, we blink SquizzBall using the remainder (another remainder!) combined with the remaining power-up time:

```
// Powerball blink mode!
this.visible = true;
if (this.powerupTime > 0) {
  const time = this.powerupTime -= dt;
  // Blink when nearly done
  if (time < 1.5) {
    this.visible = Math.floor(t / 100 % 2);
  }
  if (time < 0) {
    anims.play("walk");
  }
}
```

The player will flash on and off (because we toggle the `visible` property of the sprite). When the time runs out, the blinking stops and we play the normal "walk" animation again.

Another touch is a separate pickup— `entities/Jackpot.js` —that sprinkles the letters J A C K P O T S around the arena. When you collide with a new letter, it's added to the left of the screen and gives you a free life when you collect all 8. Finally, we've added a cloud explosion effect when you die or smash a baddie. This entity— *entities/Cloud.js* —is a simple *Sprite* with the image of a dust cloud. Each cloud gets a *life* amount (using *yet another timer*) and a position to draw itself:

```
class Cloud extends Sprite {
  constructor (pos, life = 1) {
    super(texture);
    this.life = life;
    this.pos.x = pos.x - 16;
    this.pos.y = pos.y - 16;
  }
  update (dt) {
    // Jiggle!
    ...
  }
}
export default Cloud;
```

For each frame, the cloud is "jiggled" a little bit to give the impression of chaotic movement. Its *life* is decreased until it has no life—it's dead and gone. The effect is that of a cartoonish explosion at the location of a collision.

```
// Jiggle
this.pos.x += math.randf(-1, 1);
this.pos.y += math.randf(-1, 1);

if ((this.life -= dt) < 0) {
  this.dead = true;
}
```

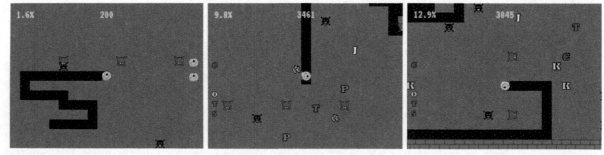

4-24. Game screens

Small touches like this make a *monumental* difference to how the game looks and feels. I've been a bit hand-wavy with how they're implemented—but it's meant to whet your appetite! We're going to be covering many, many more of these vital finishing-touch techniques as we go along, especially in Chapter 8, where we discuss "juice".

Leveled Up

"My my, this game is perfect!" beams Guy. "We'll just rip out that MomPop logo, slap in a few EGI banners, and get this over to Serious Biz Con! Oh, by the way, you realize that the waiver you signed means you surrender any and all rights to *SquizzBall, SquizzBall Jr., Ms SquizzBall,* or any future games featuring 'Squizz' or 'Ball' or associated or definitive depictions or merchandising, in perpetuity ... right?"

Guess we should have read the fine print!

Phew wee! What a chapter. We've really fleshed out our Pop game library and can transform our simple prototypes into fully playable games—with backgrounds, animations, screens, and a complete game life cycle. It's enough to start sharing our games with other people—to play-test, elicit feedback, and iterate on our ideas.

That's when the real work begins! In the coming chapters, we'll add more depth, more features, and more finishing touches to our library. But even with the simple tools at our disposal we must now starting thinking like *game designers*—and use our tools to delight, surprise, and entertain our players.

Collision Detection & AI

Level

5

After a marathon work week, you pat yourself on the back and pack up your stuff, ready to enjoy the lazy weekend ahead. As you get up to leave, you're startled to discover Guy Shifty perched like the Cheshire Cat on the edge of your desk.

"Hey hey! Where are you off to? It's the Lucky Dare Game Jam Competition this weekend. Don't tell me you're not doing it? You *of all people* need to build out your portfolio. Besides, this is the most fun game jam of the season. All my employees love doing it every year—which is why I made it mandatory."

He might not be selling it well, but game jams definitely are good fun. Building small but *complete* games in a limited time forces you into the habit of getting games finished—the most elusive gamedev skill of all.

"48 hours to make a game," Guy continues. "Voting just finished a few moments ago. The chosen theme is 'Scared to Death'. You should really get cracking if you want to make something decent."

There will be other weekends to relax, I suppose. Let's do it!

 Game Jams

If you're hankering to go in a real game jam, there are plenty around! My favorites are the *absolutely huge* Ludum Dare[1] competition (with a 48-hour time limit), and Js13kGames[2]: an annual JavaScript-focused challenge where your entire game must fit in a 13Kb zip file! It's run by Andrzej Mazur who also puts out the excellent Gamedev.js Weekly[3] newsletter.

We still have couple of problems to tackle if we want more interesting games. Firstly, we need to expand our rudimentary collision detection methods to work with non-circular entities. That includes being able to collide with walls and other solid objects in our fancy new tile maps. And secondly, the baddies in our games thus far have been ... uninspiring. They're no match for us. They just float around, oblivious to the fact we're even trying to shoot them. (Hmm, are *we* the bad guys?!) Anyway, this chapter addresses the two largest chunks missing from our game development repertoire: collision detection and AI.

---

[1] https://ldjam.com/
[2] http://js13kgames.com/
[3] http://gamedevjsweekly.com/

Colliding with Things

It's possible to make games that don't require collision detection: puzzle games, card games, old-school text-adventure games ... But come on, colliding with things (and *avoiding* colliding with things) is really fun! Yet it turns out that writing *good* collision detection code is actually quite difficult. After "control feel" and graphics, collision detection is one of the most oft-critiqued aspects of an action game. Players will be very unhappy if they feel they were unfairly killed (or unfairly denied a kill) because of a poor collision detection algorithm.

Paradoxically, you don't want your collision detection code to be *too* good, either.

An enemy bullet overlapping the hero by just a single pixel *should* be enough to make them explode. But you may consider conveniently ignoring "close shaves" against the player, in order to improve the user's overall *experience*. Players will blame you if they're unfairly killed, but they'll attribute near misses to their skillful mastery of the game.

This doesn't just apply to bullet hit areas. For example, in a platform game you might want to make the player's ground-collision area a bit wider than the graphic that represents it: when the player goes for a huge running jump, there will secretly be a few *extra pixels* on the edge of the platform. They'll launch into a spectacularly satisfying leap, rather than plunging to their death.

Of course, this a balancing act. If you go overboard, the player knows you're holding their hand. If you do it subtly—and these scary moments fall in favor of the player—they'll feel awesome and want to keep playing and improving.

Bounding-box Collisions

We've sort of cheated with collisions so far. To avoid introducing a lot of new code, we've stuck to the a basic *circle collision* algorithm. We covered this in Chapter 3, and then added it to our library as `math.distance`. It works well (it's mathematically perfect, actually) for detecting collisions between two circles. But it turns out that circles are not the go-to shape for 2D game development. Rectangles are. And the most common collision algorithm used in 2D games is called the *axis-aligned bounding box* (AABB).

Axis-aligned means that it doesn't work for independently rotated shapes (both entities must have the same rotation, their axes aligned), and they must be rectangles (their shape defined by a **bounding box**). Why is this preferable to circle collisions? When an entity has the same height and width, circles will generally be adequate for defining a hit area. But if the entity is very tall or wide, a circle hit area will have a lot of empty space. Collisions with the empty space will report a false positive.

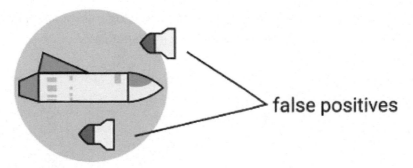

5-1. Bounding circle showing false positives

 Why Use AABB?

There's a historical reason AABB was primarily used in 2D games—even for roundish game objects. Circle collision detection requires a square-root operation—something that was very expensive in terms of CPU instructions. (If you could get away with it, you could use an *approximation* of the distance to avoid the square root.) Even today, collision detection can consume a significant portion of your frame processing time. AABB is very fast to calculate. Saving cycles is still important!

To detect if two rectangles are overlapping, we have to compare each of their corners. The results of the comparisons can be used to determine where the entities sit in relation to each other.

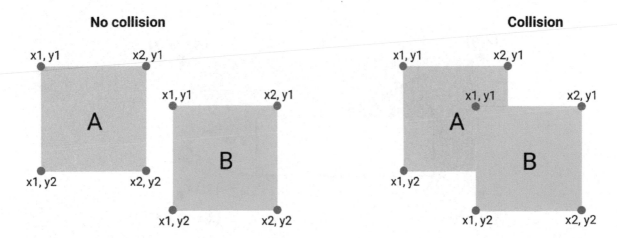

5-2. Bounding box vertices

There are four expressions (two horizontal and two vertical) that *all must be true* if the rectangles intersect. First we check if a's right edge is past b's left edge, then if a's left edge is before b's right edge. If these two clauses pass, the rectangles overlap somewhere on the x axis. They may be above or below each other, so we have to do the same logic vertically. If both horizontal and vertical checks show an overlap, the rectangles are intersecting:

```
if (
  a.x2 >= b.x1 &&
  a.x1 <= b.x2 &&
  a.y2 >= b.y1 &&
  a.y1 <= b.y2) {
    // A hit!
}
```

The && Operator

Notice that, in JavaScript, the `&&` operator is a short-circuit operator. This means that if *any* of the expressions are false, the remaining expressions don't get evaluated. This is important for collision detection routines, as they'll usually be called *a lot* of times every frame and can become a performance bottleneck. We'll talk more about this in Chapter 9.

In our game engine, a `Sprite` object has a `pos` property with the `x` and `y` coordinates that represent the *top-left corner* of the graphic. We don't *have* `x2` or `y2` properties. To figure out the other three corners, we need to provide some more information—namely, the entity's width (`w`) and height (`h`). Given this, we can then calculate all four points of the rectangle:

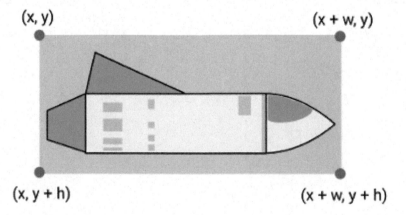

5-3. Bounding box with dimensions

In our system, to find "a.x2" we actually need to use `a.pos.x + a.w` (the `x` position plus the width).

Quick demo time. To test the collision detection logic, spin up a new project with a new *Game* instance in `main.js`. We'll do our tests here. Our game will be called *Who stole my cheese, seriously?* You're a mouse, there's some cheese. Every time you reach your goal (a collision is detected), the cheese is teleported away and reappears somewhere in the distance, for ever and ever. It's a metaphor or something.

 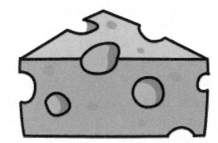

5-4. Mouse and cheese. It's complicated

Add a couple of new files for our collidable entities— *Mouse.js* and *Cheese.js* . These will both be *Sprites* , and will only have a single frame each as a graphic. *Mouse* and *Cheese* will be *very simple* objects. If you wanted to, you could also just model them inline rather than as standalone files, as we did in Chapter 3.

The cheese has no logic in it. It's just cheese. However, we'll add in the new *w* and *h* properties that represent the pixel size of the *cheese.png* file:

```
const texture = new Texture("res/images/cheese.png");

class Cheese extends Sprite {
  constructor () {
    super(texture);
    this.w = 74;
    this.h = 50;
  }
}

export default Cheese;
```

That's some good cheese. The cheese now has width (*w*) and height (*h*) properties so it can be used in our collision computations.

Hopefully creating new entities makes sense now. Any time you want to get something to display on the screen, create a *Texture* for it and give it to a *Sprite* (or *TileSprite*). The *Game* system takes care of updating it (if needed) and the *CanvasRenderer* takes care of drawing it for us.

Avoiding Manual Effort

It's worth noting that adding size parameters manually could be avoided by taking the dimensions *directly from the texture image*. In the core library we could return the texture image's width and height as the `w` and `h` properties. We won't do this now, as having some manual control is useful, but it's something we'll add after we implement an asset-loading system.

It might seem like a hassle to make a file and extend a class, but now it's easy to add functionality to the cheese when you later decide the cheese should fly, or shoot, or transform into a Camembert monster or something. The mouse is a bit more complicated (though you may notice that the logic closely resembles our *spaceship* from Chapter 3):

```
const texture = new Texture("res/images/mouse.png");

class Mouse extends Sprite {
  constructor(controls) {
    super(texture);
    this.w = 100;
    this.h = 51;
    this.controls = controls;
  }
  update(dt) {
    const { pos, controls } = this;
    const { x, y } = controls;
    const speed = 100;
    pos.x += x * dt * speed;
    pos.y += y * dt * speed;
  }
}
```

Again, we've added the width and height of the image, but other than that, it's really our spaceship in disguise as a mouse. Each frame in `update`, we get the user's input and move ourselves a tiny bit. Then, as always, the entities must be added to the scene graph. We'll put them in the main `scene` container. Remember that the `add` function returns the entity itself, so we can add it to the container and assign it to a variable in the same expression:

```
const game = new Game(640, 320);
const { scene, w, h } = game;
const a = scene.add(new Mouse(new KeyControls()));
const b = scene.add(new Cheese());

game.run(() => {
```

```
    // Bounding-box detection
});
```

A sprite will default to position `{x: 0, y: 0}` (the top-left corner of the screen). Before we run the game, move the `Mouse` and `Cheese` somewhere random on the screen. To do this, set both the `x` and `y` properties to a random value between 0 and the screen width/height (with `math.rand`). Rather than doing it manually to both entities, we'll make a little function that does it for us for *any* entity:

```
const relocate = e => {
  const { pos } = e;
  pos.x = math.rand(w);
  pos.y = math.rand(h);
};
relocate(a);
relocate(b);
```

We can control our mouse friend around the screen, and of course that makes us hungry. We want to eat some cheese, using *AABB* to react to collisions. Because this is just a test, we'll plop it inside the `game.run` main loop. (There's no need to make a whole `GameScreen` unless you feel like building this out into bigger game!)

```
// Bounding-box detection
if (
  a.pos.x + a.w >= b.pos.x &&
  a.pos.x < b.pos.x + b.w &&
  a.pos.y + a.h >= b.pos.y &&
  a.pos.y < b.pos.y + b.h
) {
  // Hit!
  relocate(b);
}
```

When a hit is detected, the magic cheese instantly teleports to a new location. The important piece is the bounding-box test: each corner of the sprite is calculated using the entity's `w` and `h` settings, along with their `pos`, to determine if any edges overlap. If they do, "Hit!" Take a minute to follow along with this logic and match the corners (x1, y1, x2, y2) to make sure it makes sense.

Drawing Rectangles

All this talk of boxes highlights that there's currently no way in our library to *draw* a simple rectangle. Rectangles are very versatile. They can be used as backgrounds to text messages so things are easy read, they can be placeholder protagonists when you're testing out a new game idea, and they can be debugging aids to figure out *where* the AABB collisions will actually occur. We should have rectangles in Pop.

Adding a new core type is a mundane task for us now! The two steps are: create the *model* for the type, and handle it in the *renderer*. We'll call our type `Rect`, and it can live in `Rect.js`:

```
class Rect {
  constructor(w, h, style = { fill: "#333" }) {
    this.pos = { x: 0, y: 0 };
    this.w = w;
    this.h = h;
    this.style = style;
  }
}
```

The `Rect` model has a width, a height, and some style information. We'll simply support a fill color for now. The color will be set in the `CanvasRenderer` and the rectangle drawn with `ctx.fillRect`. If the renderer finds a leaf node in our scene that has *width*, *height* and *style* information, it draws the rectangle:

```
...
else if (child.style && child.w && child.h) {
  ctx.fillStyle = child.style.fill;
  ctx.fillRect(0, 0, child.w, child.h);
}
```

Adjusting the Bounding Box

For collision detection, a rectangle shape is a better fit for our entity than a circle, but it's still not great. If you look closely (and move slowly) you'll find occasions where a "hit" is detected even where pixels *don't actually overlap*. This will be especially noticeable if your shape is not very boxy, or has some sort of protrusion (such as a mouse's tail) leaving a lot of empty pixels in the rectangle. The easiest and sneakiest way to fix this is to reduce the size of the bounding box so that it's smaller than the image that represents the entity.

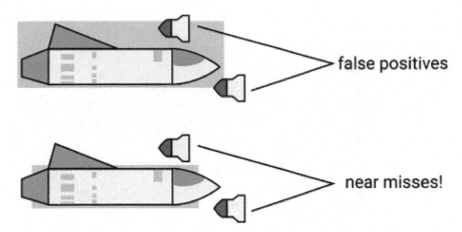

5-5. Reduced bounding box

Depending on your image, there might still be empty pixels, but by playing with the size and position of the box you can *dramatically* alter the feel of the game. To control the collision area, we maintain a second rectangle that we'll call the **hit box**. We'll make a distinction between the *bounding box* (that is, the rectangle that the entity's texture can fit into) and the *hit box*—the tweaked rectangle used to improve the feeling of the game collision detection:

```
class Mouse extends Sprite {
  constructor(controls) {
    ...
    this.w = 100;
    this.h = 51;
    this.hitBox = {
      x: 18,
      y: 8,
      w: 70,
      h: 35
    };
  }
}
```

The hit box is a new object property that maintains the bounds of the collision area *relative to the position* of the `Sprite` itself. Usually the width and height properties will be smaller or equal to the bounding box dimensions, but there are some cases where it might be larger—for example, where you have a `trigger` sprite that fires when you're near it. Here's our sprite with the hit box highlighted to show where a collision will occur:

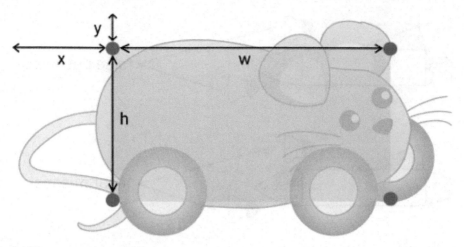

5-6. The mouse's hit box

 Bounding Box Highlighting

Highlighting the bounding box like this makes it easier to tweak and test collision settings. To facilitate this, I've added a helper in `utils/entity` to display the bounding box and hit box of a sprite. Calling `entity.addDebug(mouse)` will highlight the boxes on our mouse. It relies on the sneaky fact that our renderer will render anything in a `children` array, even if it's not actually a `Container`. So create the array and add a debug `Rect`.

Any AABB calculation must account for the hit box area. The relative offsets of `hitBox` should be added to the `Sprite`'s position and dimensions. Rather than adding all of this directly into the collision detection test, we'll create a temporary object that holds the calculated values:

```
const { hitBox: aHit, pos: aPos } = mouse;
const a = {
  x: aHit.x + aPos.x,
  y: aHit.y + aPos.y,
  w: aHit.w,
  h: aHit.h
};
```

We've effectively created a *new* bounding box that can be incorporated into the collision test. Once we do the same with the `Cheese`, both of these new bounding boxes can be fed into the previous AABB check.

Compared with our initial AABB implementation, this feels far better. The bounding boxes can overlap slightly, but a collision isn't triggered until the *hit boxes* intersect. You can still find cases where a hit is detected where no pixels are intersecting; but a dirty gamedev secret is that nearly *all* games have this limitation. Computing simplified collision areas is fantastically more efficient than checking actual pixels, and (paradoxically) a tweaked hit box will often feel more "correct" to the player than precise pixel collision detection.

It's extremely important to play around with the size of the hit boxes on all your entities. It has a big impact on *tightness* and the general feel of the game's controls. As a rule, your players will be happy if the enemy hit boxes are bigger than their own!

Collision Testers

Once you've internalized how AABB works, it's not much fun writing collision tests by hand. It should be handled in a helper function somewhere deeper in our library. Because collisions are between entities (with a `w` , `h` , and `pos`) it makes sense to put them into `utils/entity.js` . As we've seen, the first step to computing a hit box collision is to extract the new bounds of the entity based on its `hitBox` property:

```
function bounds(entity) {
  const { w, h, pos, hitBox } = entity;
  const hit = hitBox || { x: 0, y: 0, w, h };
  return {
    x: hit.x + pos.x,
    y: hit.y + pos.y,
    w: hit.w - 1,
    h: hit.h - 1
  };
}
```

The `bounds` function is a way to extract the collidable position and dimensions of an entity. If an entity doesn't have a `hitBox` , get its full width and height. The *or* operator (`||`) is a short-circuit operator, so if `hitBox` *is* defined, it's immediately returned. Otherwise, the new object is assigned.

 Off-by-one

Our original hit tests suffer from an off-by-one error: `w` and `h` are not zero-based, so they are one pixel too large! I omitted this important information just to keep the core ideas (and code) clear, but I've snuck in the fix by subtracting one from `hit.w` and `hit.h` for the final `w` and `h` bounding values.

The `bounds` are calculated and used inside an AABB collision checker, `hit` , a function that takes two entities and returns a boolean indicating if the entities are hitting each other:

```
function hit(e1, e2) {
  const a = bounds(e1);
  const b = bounds(e2);
  return a.x + a.w >= b.x &&
    a.x <= b.x + b.w &&
    a.y + a.h >= b.y &&
    a.y <= b.y + b.h;
}
```

To test for collisions, first grab the bounds of both entities (with `bounds`), then run them through our now-familiar AABB test. All of the inline tests can now be taken out of the `game.run` game code and replaced with the `hit` tester:

```
if (entity.hit(mouse, cheese)) {
  relocate(cheese);
}
```

Ah, that's much nicer! If we wanted to have many cheeses (who wouldn't?), we can add them all to a *cheeses* container and then test each child:

```
cheeses.map(cheese => {
  if (entity.hit(mouse, cheese)) {
    relocate(cheese);
  }
});
```

However, knowing how `hit` is implemented, you might notice something inefficient. We're recalculating the *bounds* of the player sprite for *every* child in the container, even though it never changes. It's not a good idea to worry too much about performance at this stage (we'll do plenty of worrying about it in Chapter 9), but I can't let this one go.

```
function hits(entity, container, hitCallback) {
  const a = bounds(entity);
  container.map(e2 => {
    const b = bounds(e2);
    if (
      a.x + a.w >= b.x &&
      a.x <= b.x + b.w &&
      a.y + a.h >= b.y &&
      a.y <= b.y + b.h
    ) {
      hitCallback(e2);
```

```
      }
   });
 }
```

The logic of *hits* is similar to *hit* , but applied to each child of a *Container* . Because there's more than one possible entity to collide with, we can't just return a single boolean. Instead, we call a callback function for *every* child element that collides. The reference to the *bounds* of the initial entity is stored (so we don't unnecessarily recompute it) and then we map over the children, doing an AABB check for each. When something collides, the callback is called. This function also receives the *entity we collided with*. Often this is useful information in you game logic—such as when we have many cheeses and want only to teleport the cheese that was hit by the mouse:

```
entity.hits(mouse, cheeses, cheese => {
  relocate(cheese);
});
```

Moving the collision detection code into the core library means it's convenient to use in future games—though it's still important to understand how the algorithm is working under the hood. That knowledge lets you confidently customize things to fit your game's specific use case, if necessary—and people will praise (or hopefully not even notice) your game's excellent collision detection.

Procedural Level Generation

Time is ticking on the game jam clock, and all we have so far is "Spooky Cheese". Let's bin that idea and come up with a new concept—a hair-raising, procedurally generated, labyrinth-based action-adventure game … with bats and ghosts and goblins, and creepy things that shoot fireballs. Naturally we'll need an intrepid explorer as the main character. Someone brave and determined, yet humble. Perhaps a little fragile. And probably egg-shaped—because that's all I can draw … introducing *Q.B. Bravedigger: explorer extraordinare*! Or Bravedigger for short.

Bravedigger will avoid the scary dungeon dwellers while raiding their cavernous vaults of gold. The dungeon will be modeled on our *Level* tile map from the last chapter (the arena in *SquizzBall*). First, we need to create a suitable tileset. We at least needs some dungeon walls, but we can also noodle around and brainstorm some ideas for characters.

5-7. Initial Bravedigger tileset

Yep, these look sufficiently scary (in a weird cute way). The `Level` will be a `TileMap` like SquizzBall, but the `TileSprites` will be arranged to look like a labyrinthine dungeon. The easy way to do this is to create our layouts by hand. We choose where each tile goes and carefully arrange them in clever maze patterns. But we want our levels to be different *every game*. How do we do that without creating a million levels by hand?

The answer is *procedural generation*. An algorithm (rather than a human) will design elements of the game. Procedural generation algorithms range from extremely simple to mind-bendingly complex. The simplest way we could generate a level is via `Math.random()` : each cell in our "maze" is picked at random. Not very playable, but a good place to start.

 Procedural Generation

Procedurally generated levels are not easy to do *well*. It's tempting to think we can delegate game design to a function and save all that time. In reality, you can lose *a lot* of time tweaking your algorithms, and even then, well-designed, hand-made levels are almost *always* more satisfying for the player. There are exceptions. Some games do procedural generation really well. *Spelunky*[4], from 2013, is a "rogue-lite" platform game that feels very "human" in its brutal level creation. Other bigger efforts like the epic space exploration game *No Man's Sky*[5] take procedural world generation to impressive lengths.

To start our dungeon, we first fill out the `TileMap` boilerplate (map width and height, tile width and height, and a texture). To create the level data, we'll add some extra information to our frames. Not only do we specify the sprite sheet indexes (have a look at the tileset above to see which frames point to which graphic tile), but we also add identifiers for tiles. Later we can use them to get certain tiles by their ID.

```
const tileIndexes = [
  { id: "empty", x: 0, y: 2 },
  { id: "wall", x: 2, y: 2 },
  { id: "wall_end", x: 3, y: 2 }
];

const level = Array(mapW * mapH).fill(0);
// Make a random dungeon
...

super(
  level.map(i => tileIndexes[i]),
  mapW,
  mapH,
  tileSize,
  tileSize,
  texture
);
```

For the remainder of the book, we'll use an object like `tileIndexes` to hold the *metadata* about our tiles. `TileMap` expects us to give it an array of tile `frame` offsets to draw the correct tile from the tileset image. But a tile is more than just a pretty face: it can have other properties too. For example, we may add a `walkable` flag to the `empty` tile (which we'll do later in this chapter) so that entities can pass over it. (Otherwise, they're blocked from walking on it.)

As we add features to our tile-based games, there will be more per-property metadata associated with each tile. They'll all go in `tileIndexes`. We can refer to the tiles in our level simply by the *offset* in the `tileIndexes` tiles array. For example, we initialized our `level` variable to an array of size `mapW * mapH` and mapped each element to `0` (using Array's nifty `fill` method). This means the entire map will be drawn as the first `tileIndexes` element (which is the "empty" tile). The entire level is empty. If we make some of the elements `1`, these will point to the *second* tile—a "wall" tile.

---

4. http://www.spelunkyworld.com/
5. https://www.nomanssky.com/

A little help

I've kept it simple by using the array index. However if you look in the code examples you'll find a helper function called `getIdx` that will return the index for a given ID, so you can write `getIdx("wall")` instead of just `1`. This reads a lot nicer and will keep working if you change the order of the `tileIndexes` array.

The actual transformation between the offset and the tile object is done when we call `super` : `level.map(i => tileIndexes[i])` . All of the indexes (`i`) get mapped to the corresponding tiles. Creating a random level can then be done by assigning either a 0 (blank) or 1 (wall) tile to every space on the map:

```
// Make a random dungeon
for (let y = 0; y < mapH; y++) {
  for (let x = 0; x < mapW; x++) {
    // Define the dungeon walls
    level[y * mapW + x] = math.randOneFrom([0, 0, 1]);
  }
}
```

The level data is expected to be a one-dimensional array, but it's better to think of it as a two-dimensional matrix representing the rows and cells of the map. To convert from `x` and `y` grid *coordinates* to the correct *array element*, multiply the `y` component by the map width (because each row has "width" elements in it), then add the `x` offset: `y * mapW + x` . To this element we assign either a 0 (empty) or a 1 (wall).

Weighting

Notice that we chose tiles randomly from the array `[0, 0, 1]` : two 0s and one 1. This is to *weight* the choice in favor of a 0 (resulting in more empty space in the level). This would be the same as if we had used `math.randOneIn(3)` , or even `Math.random() < 0.3333` . It doesn't matter how you weight things, as long as it gets you the results you're after. Sometimes `randOneFrom` is helpful when you'd like to choose from non-sequential items—for example, `math.randOneFrom([0, 1, 2, 2, 4])` . In this case, 0, 1, and 4 all have a 1-in-5 chance of being chosen, and 2 has a 2-in-5 chance.

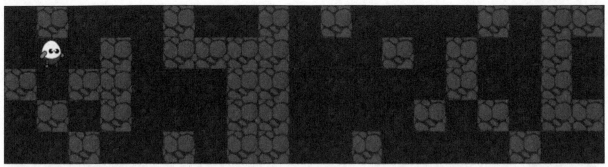

5-8. Random tilemap

Okay, that doesn't look much like a maze, and doesn't look like much fun to traverse as a player. This is the double-edged sword of procedural generation: your levels will only be as good as your algorithm! Game design is an art form, and you're outsourcing some of your art generation and game design skills to the algorithm.

That said, we can do a lot better than `Math.random()` ! We're going to use a very simple maze-ish generator for our levels. I say "maze-ish", because maze enthusiasts (yes, there are many) wouldn't consider it strictly a maze. There's no start, no finish, and it's not *perfect*. A perfect maze has no loops where you can double back on yourself. But our algorithm is simple, consisting of three steps:

1. Draw the map borders (add a wall around the perimeter).

2. Add grid "posts" (add a wall in *every other cell*, making a grid).

3. Add some side walls. For each grid post, randomly pick a direction and add a wall.

This logic generates a satisfying level for such a small amount of code. Step 1 is to draw the walls of the level. In our nested `for` loops, we check the `x` and `y` loop variables and see if they lie on the perimeter.

```
// Define the dungeon walls

// 1. Map borders
if (y === 0 || x === 0 || y === mapH - 1 || x === mapW - 1) {
  level[y * mapW + x] = 1;
  continue;
}
```

The big `if` statement here checks four cases—one for each "direction". If `y === 0` , we're on the very first row of the level. If `x === 0` , we're on the very first *column* of the level. Similarly, we check if we're in the last row or column. If so, draw a wall and `continue` on to the next loop item.

The level will look like this:

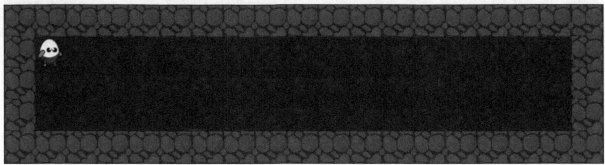

5-9. Maze perimeter wall

If it's *not* a wall item, the `if` statement will be false and we can move on to step 2—adding grid posts. The idea of this step is to make a consistent grid of walls spaced evenly so there's a one-space gap between each of them. To do that, we check `y % 2 || x % 2` . This will be true in every *odd* cell. In these cases, we `continue` and leave them blank.

```
// 2. Grid points - randomly skip some to make "rooms"
if (y % 2 || x % 2 || math.randOneIn(4)) {
  continue; // don't draw a wall, please.
}
level[y * mapW + x] = 1;
```

We also do something extra: we randomly *don't* draw some of the grid points. Wherever this occurs (when we have `math.randOneIn(4)` in our example, but you can play with this value) there will be a gap in the grid posts. In the final level, this will look like "room". It doesn't look much like a room at the moment though. After adding grid posts, the level will look like this:

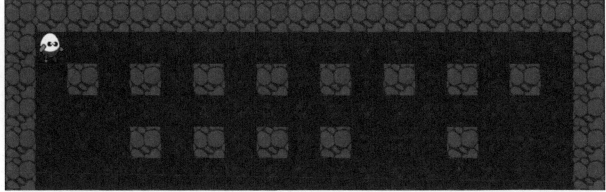

5-10. Maze grid posts

Better than our first random level, but a little too open. Step 3 involves adding in some side walls. We've just drawn the grid post; now we take a random direction—north, south, east, or west—and make *that* a wall too.

```
// 3. Side walls - pick a random direction
const [xo, yo] = math.randOneFrom([[0, -1], [0, 1], [1, 0], [-1, 0]]);
level[(y + yo) * mapW + (x + xo)] = 1;
```

The direction *north* is represented by the array `[0, -1]`, which is the x/y offset from the current position. The cell to the north is at location `x + 0` (no change in the `x` position) and `y + (-1)` ("up" one in the `y` position). South is `[0, -1]` ("down" one in the `y` position). East is `[1, 0]` ("right" one in the `x` direction), and west is `[-1, 0]`. The directions are all stored inside another array, and `math.randOneFrom` picks one for us.

5-11. 'Mazed

Getting the Faux-3D Look

After the map was designed, I did *another* pass over the level data and checked if there was a wall tile *below* each tile. If the space was free, then I converted the wall tile into a `wall_end` tile which gives the faux-3D look.

The transformation is complete! Refresh the page over and over; each time, a new design. It's quite impressive to get such satisfying results from so few rules (and so little code!). It's not foolproof, but will serve well for a base for our game jam entry. Hopefully it gives you a taste for what procedural generation is about. If you'd like to see more of what can be done with algorithms, check out Reddit's lively Procedural Generation subreddit[6].

Colliding with Maps

To make the walls of the maze solid, we need to add collision detection between Bravedigger and

---

[6.] https://www.reddit.com/r/proceduralgeneration/

the map's `TileSprite`s. But collision *detection* isn't enough; we also need to perform *collision resolution*. **Collision resolution** is how we *resolve* an entity's position after a collision is detected. Our spooky cheese magically teleporting is kind of a resolution (hey, it certainly isn't colliding anymore), but it's not very useful. In a maze, we don't want to teleport to a random location every time we touch a wall!

The secret to doing collision resolution is to test the *intended* movement of the player, *before* they make it. Depending on the result of the test, you can either *allow* the move (if the tile area is clear), or *reject* (or modify) it if they hit a solid tile.

Getting the collision detection and resolution perfect for tile maps is complex, but the task can be broken into three pieces: *basic collisions* (determining when we would be "stuck in a wall"), *snapping back* to perfectly rest against the edge of a tile, and *"wall sliding"* (allowing horizontal movement when you're only blocked vertically, and vice versa).

For the first part—basic collisions—you might think we could just do our AABB test against every tile in a map. Yep, that *would* work for sure. But tile maps can be very large, and checking every tile against every entity quickly becomes a huge computational task. Thanks to the grid-like nature of a tile map, it's more efficient for us to work against the *model* of the entire map, rather than consider each entity individually.

For example, if we know a player wants to move to map position `{x: 1, y: 1}`, there's no need to do a full AABB test between the player's `Sprite` and the `TileSprite` at location `{x: 1, y: 1}`: we could just store metadata in the `TileSprite`'s `frame`, then look up if it's "walkable" or not. No calculations necessary! If a tile is "walkable", the player is allowed to move. Otherwise, they're stopped in their tracks.

```
const tileIndexes = [
  { id: "empty", x: 0, y: 2, walkable: true },
  { id: "wall", x: 2, y: 2 },
  { id: "wall_end", x: 3, y: 2 }
];
```

The first step is to annotate the `tileIndexes` metadata with suitable attributes. Designating a tile as `walkable` indicates that the player is allowed to move freely over this type of tile. To make walls obstruct a player, we don't give them the `walkable` attribute.

```
const tile = this.tileAtPixelPos({ x: pos.x, y: pos.y });
const canWalk = tile.frame.walkable;
```

This will tell us if the player's top-left corner is touching a `walkable` block, or if it's a solid wall.

But because a player has *two dimensions*, they're likely touching more than one tile in any given frame. Assuming they're smaller than a single tile, they can be intersecting with up to four tiles at any given moment:

5-12. Edge tile collisions

In this image, the entity's top-left corner is touching tile 1, the top-right corner is touching tile 2, the bottom-left corner is touching tile 3, and the bottom-right corner is touching tile 4. This means we have to check *each corner* of a `Sprite` to get the full set of possible collisions.

 Keeping Things Simple

For simplicity, our engine is going to maintain the assumption that the entities will be the same size or smaller than a tile. If the entity is larger, it's possible that a collision with the middle of the entity is not detected. To fix this, you have to check more than just the corners: you must check the full range that covers the number of tiles the entity could possibly cover.

Finding the tiles that an entity is touching can be the responsibility of the `TileMap`. To check each corner, we need the bounds of the entity (the result of calling `entity.bounds`) and, optionally, an `x` and `y` offset from the bounds. The reason for the offset will be explained shortly.

```
tilesAtCorners(bounds, xo = 0, yo = 0) {
  return [
    [bounds.x, bounds.y], // Top-left
    [bounds.x + bounds.w, bounds.y], // Top-right
    [bounds.x, bounds.y + bounds.h], // Bottom-left
    [bounds.x + bounds.w, bounds.y + bounds.h] // Bottom-right
  ].map(([x, y]) => this.tileAtPixelPos({
    x: x + xo,
    y: y + yo
  }));
}
```

The four corners are placed in an array, then mapped to a function that retrieves the tile at that location with `tileAtPixelPos`. The end result is an array of the top-left, top-right, bottom-left, and bottom-right tiles that the entity is standing on. Depending on where the player is, they might all be the *same* tile (if the player is carefully placed in the center of a tile) or they could be four different tiles (if the player is on an intersection of the tiles).

```
const bounds = entity.bounds(player);
const tiles = map.tilesAtCorners(bounds);
const walks = tiles.map(t => t && t.frame.walkable);
const blocked = walks.some(w => !w);
```

The `tiles` array contains a bunch of information about the tiles, but for now we're interested in "walkability". We map over the tiles and extract only if the `frame` is walkable or not. We then check each of these values to see if *any* of the tiles are blocking us (that is, any of the `walks` values are `false`). Now we know if any tiles below the entity are solid!

Additionally, because the `tiles` represent the corners of the entity, we can use the `walks` array to glean more useful information about *how* the entity collides. For example:

```
const hitYourHead = walks[0] || walks[1]; // TL or TR
const feetInTheGround = walks[2] || walks[3]; // BL or BR
const collidedLeft = walks[0] || walks[2]; // TL or BL
const collidedRight = walks[1] || walks[3]; // TR or BR
```

So, back to `tilesAtCorners`. What are those `xo` and `yo` offsets for? They're there to facilitate collision resolution. It's too late for us if the player is *already* standing inside a wall: we should have checked *before* we let them get themselves stuck. The `xo` and `yo` offsets represent the amount the player *would like* to move. For example, the player might ask us "am I allowed to move to the left 5px and down 2px this frame?" and we check with `xo = -5` and `yo = 2`. If any of the tiles are not walkable, we say "Sorry, no."

Asking questions about the tiles you *would* be touching—and responding accordingly before it happens—is collision resolution.

We'll generalize the idea of "intended movement" as a function that can be reused by multiple entities (and in multiple games). Inside the entity's *update* function, we call the function with the amount the entity *would like* to move. This value may come from the player's *controls* , or from gravity in a physics system. It might be the amount generated from an AI movement function, or it may be derived from specific logic in our game: "if the player is swinging a sword, is the tile in the direction the player facing a magic tile?"

The movement function will compute the result of trying to move by the intended amount, and then return the *allowed amount* the entity can move. For now, if the space is clear, the results will be the same as the inputs. ("Sure, you can move left 5px and down 2px.") If the entity is blocked, the function will return zeros. ("Sorry, you can move left 0px and down 0px.") In a later section, we'll return more fine-grained results.

Collision detection code varies greatly between your games, and you'll eventually need to write your own that matches your game's requirements. But there are some common cases that we should include in the Pop library too. They can go in a new folder called *pop/movement/* . Our first attempt will be called *deadInTracks.js* . It stops the player dead in their tracks when they touch a wall:

```
function deadInTracks(ent, map, x = 0, y = 0) {
  const bounds = entity.bounds(ent);
  const tiles = map.tilesAtCorners(bounds, x, y);
  const walks = tiles.map(t => t && t.frame.walkable);
  const blocked = walks.some(w =>!w);
  if (blocked) {
    x = 0;
    y = 0;
  }
  return { x, y };
}
```

The function accepts the entity, the map they're testing against, and the amount they *want* to move. It returns the amount the player is *allowed* to move. If any of the tiles aren't walkable, the allowed movement will be *{x: 0, y: 0}* . If it's all clear, the allowed movement will be the full amount the player requested to move— *{x: x, y: y}* . The result can then be added to the entity's position so they either move or get blocked:

```
class Player extends TileSprite {
  constructor(controls, map) {
    super(texture, 48, 48);
    this.controls = controls;
    this.map = map;
    // ...
  }
  update(dt, t) {
    let { x, y } = controls;
    const xo = x * dt * speed;
    const yo = y * dt * speed;
    // Can we move to this position?!
  }
}
```

Normally, we'd simply add the `xo` and `yo` to `pos` and be done: the player can move wherever they want. But when implementing collision resolution, we'll ask our function if we're *permitted* to make a move before our position is updated:

```
// Can we move to this position?!
const r = deadInTracks(this, map, xo, yo);
pos.x += r.x;
pos.y += r.y;
```

Notice that the value returned from *deadInTracks* is added to *pos* . *deadInTracks* is the boss of how far we're allowed to move. It needs the entity that's trying to move (*this* , the player), the map that's trying to stop it, and the amount of *intended movement*. When any of the tiles aren't walkable, *blocked* is *true* and *x* and *y* are set to 0. Otherwise, they stay unchanged from the value passed in. Either the player can move according to its speed, or it's stopped dead in its tracks. Now they can't walk through walls.

Finding Empty Tiles

The clock is still ticking, and we have no goal in our game yet. Rule number 1 of game jams is "Make sure you get enough sleep, otherwise going to work on Monday will be a nightmare." But rule number 2 is "Add a win/lose state as quickly as possible!" The goal will be "help Bravedigger find as much treasure in the dungeon as you can." Several treasures should be sprinkled around the maze and—upon collecting it all—it respawns. Everyone likes infinite treasure.

Picking things up is an effortless task for us now. (Skip forward if this is old news!) *Pickup* is a class that extends *TileSprite* and which points to the correct *frame* graphic. It doesn't have any extra logic. Pickups will be added in the main *GameScreen* to a special container, called *pickups* :

```
this.pickups = this.add(new Container());
this.populate();
```

To spawn the pickups, we have the *populate* helper method to position the treasure. There will be five treasure pickups per spawn. These are randomly positioned to free spots (walkable tiles) on the map:

```
populate() {
  const { pickups, map } = this;
  for (let i = 0; i < 5; i++) {
    const p = pickups.add(new Pickup());
    p.pos = map.findFreeSpot();
  }
}
```

The *map.findFreeSpot* function is new. It returns a random *walkable* (non-wall) tile. It wouldn't be very fair if we spawned treasure inside a wall! Because *findFreeSpot* will rely on the tile metadata, it's game-specific. So it lives in the *Level* class (not in the parent *TileMap*). *findFreeSpot* doesn't take any parameters, and it returns the *{x, y}* position of an empty space on the map:

```
findFreeSpot() {
  const { mapW, mapH } = this;
  let found = false;
  let x, y;
  while (!found) {
    // Choose random tile
  }
  return this.mapToPixelPos({ x, y });
}
```

It uses a *while* loop to search the map until it finds a free spot. When it does, it converts the map position into a pixel position:

```
x = math.rand(mapW);
y = math.rand(mapH);
const { frame } = this.tileAtMapPos({ x, y });
if (frame.walkable) {
  found = true;
}
```

To find an empty space, choose a *random tile* and see if its frame has the *walkable* property. If not, try again. If there happens to be no free spaces in the entire map, this function will run forever. (Your homework is to cap the amount of searching it will do!)

Inspecting Metadata

Although we're looking for walkable tiles here, this approach will work for any other game logic too. For example, if you wanted to find a specific *type* of tile, say a "wall", you could ask `if (frame.id === "wall")`. The key is inspecting the metadata for the properties you need.

With pickups placed on the map, we can finally check for collisions. (Thank you again, `hits` collision helper method.) If the player has retrieved all of the treasure (and `children.length` is 1—that is, it will be 0 once this pickup is removed) then we call `populate` again to add some more:

```
// Collect pickup!
entity.hits(player, pickups, p => {
  p.dead = true;
  if (pickups.children.length === 1) {
    this.populate();
  }
});
```

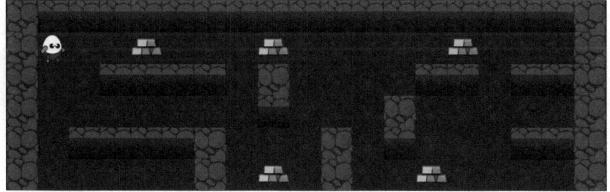

5-13. Maze, now with treasure!

Wall Sliding

Great! We have a goal for the game, and Bravedigger can explore and interact with the maze. But it doesn't "feel" quite right. When you hit a wall, you stop, dead in your tracks—even if you're moving diagonally. This means you need to lift your fingers off the arrow keys and press them again every time you hit a wall. You'd expect that you should still move in the non-blocked direction. This is known as **wall sliding**.

To implement wall sliding, we *break the collision detection into two pieces*: a vertical check, and a horizontal check. The vertical check ignores the amount of "intended x movement" (temporarily assuming it's 0) and only looks for collisions moving up or down. If there *is* a collision, set the y amount to 0 to prevent moving into the wall. Next, check the horizontal movement using both the intended x amount *and* the y amount allowed from the vertical direction check. Here's the skeleton for our `movement/wallslide.js` implementation:

```
function wallslide(ent, map, x = 0, y = 0) {
  let tiles;
  const bounds = entity.bounds(ent);

  // Final amounts of movement to allow
  let xo = x;
  let yo = y;

  // Check vertical movement
  if (y !== 0) { }

  // Check horizontal movement
  if (x !== 0) { }

  // xo & yo contain the amount we're allowed to move by
  return { x: xo, y: yo };
}
```

It's the same structure as `deadInTracks`, but this time we'll do two checks—one if the entity wants to move vertically (`y !== 0`) and one if the entity wants to move horizontally (`x !== 0`):

```
// Check vertical movement
tiles = map.tilesAtCorners(bounds, 0, yo);
const [tl, tr, bl, br] = tiles.map(t => t && t.frame.walkable);

// Hit your head
if (y < 0 && !(tl && tr)) {
  yo = 0;
}
// Hit your feet
if (y > 0 && !(bl && br)) {
  yo = 0;
}
```

First, the vertical test: the player wants to move up or down. We check `tilesAtCorners` with the y amount, but we temporarily assume there's *no horizontal movement* (that is, we hardcode 0 as the x parameter)—even if there is. This is to *only* test for vertical collisions. If the vertical direction is blocked, it gets set back to zero, and no vertical movement will be allowed.

Destructuring Results

Rather than dealing with the result of the `tilesAtCorners` —"an array of four values that represents the top-left, top-right, bottom-left, and bottom-right"—we destructure the results into variables `tl`, `tr`, `bl`, `br`. This makes it easier to perform logic like "will the entity's head be hitting a non-walkable tile?"

Having conducted our vertical tests, we can then do the same for the horizontal direction:

```
// Check horizontal movement
tiles = map.tilesAtCorners(bounds, xo, yo);
const [tl, tr, bl, br] = tiles.map(t => t && t.frame.walkable);

// Hit left edge
if (x < 0 && !(tl && bl)) {
  xo = 0;
}
// Hit right edge
if (x > 0 && !(tr && br)) {
  xo = 0;
}
```

The only (and crucial) difference is we use the intended horizontal amount for `x` but the *new* vertical amount for `y` (that is, the amount returned from the vertical test, not hardcoded to `0`). Effectively, we've tested the entity's movement in two steps—allowing it to move in either direction even if one is blocked.

Try this out and compare it to our `deadInTracks` effort. The difference is night and day. Hold down multiple directions at the same time and you can wall slide around much more smoothly, traversing the maze without getting trapped on every surface.

Snap to Edges

One subtle issue remains with tile map collisions that needs addressing—and you may not even notice it if your player's movement speed is low.

Say the player is moving horizontally at a rate of 5 pixels per frame. They run into a wall on the right (so `xo` is 5). The `wallslide` code checks if they're clear to move, and it says "No! You hit the wall! Sorry, but your `x` movement is 0!" Depending on where the player was located in the *previous* frame, they could currently be stopped up to 5 pixels away from wall, leaving a gap:

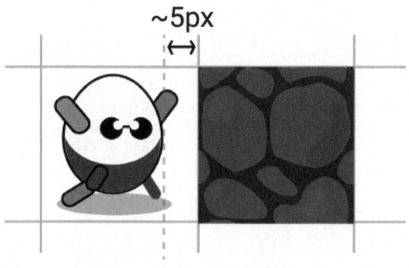

5-14. Wallslide Gap

The faster the speed, the bigger the gap can be. To correct this, rather than setting *xo* or *yo* to *zero* when there's a collision, determine the correct number of pixels between the entity and the tile and subtract that from the intended distance to move. The result is the *exact amount of space* the player can move without being stuck, and without leaving a gap:

```
// Hit your head
if (y < 0 && !(tl && tr)) {
  tileEdge = tiles[0].pos.y + tiles[0].h;
  yo = tileEdge - bounds.y;
}
// Hit your feet
if (y > 0 && !(bl && br)) {
  tileEdge = tiles[2].pos.y - 1;
  yo = tileEdge - (bounds.y + bounds.h);
}
```

To calculate the distance to move, take the position of one of tiles we would hit and subtract our current position. For example, if we hit our head we move 1 pixel below the tile above us (The extra pixel is because the tile height is not zero-based). For example, if we hit our head we move 1 pixel below the tile above us. If we hit our feet we move 1 pixel above the tile below us. The same idea is applied to the horizontal checks for the left and right edges:

```
// Hit left edge
if (x < 0 && !(tl && bl)) {
  tileEdge = tiles[0].pos.x + tiles[0].w;
  xo = tileEdge - bounds.x;
}
// Hit right edge
```

```
if (x > 0 && !(tr && br)) {
  tileEdge = tiles[1].pos.x - 1;
  xo = tileEdge - (bounds.x + bounds.w);
}
```

Any collision with a tile will now situate the entity snugly against the correct edge. As you can see, there's quite a lot of complexity in getting collision resolution working perfectly. Thankfully, it's something that will apply to all of our future tile-based games, and something that's now handled by the Pop game library.

 `wallslide.js` **Isn't a Catch-all**

Your future games will have some specific needs that won't be addressed by `wallslide.js`. Good collisions are *vital* to a great-feeling game, so don't be afraid to copy-paste this and use it as a base. If you create new features that are general to many games, add them back into the library!

If you've understood wall sliding, you're in an excellent position to implement all kinds of `TileMap` features. One of my favorite resources on this subject is an *extremely old* set of articles titled *Tonypa's tile-based tutorials*[7]. They were written for Flash (and the code is in ActionScript) but the core ideas are easy to port over to our system!

AI: The Bots Strike Back

We have all the tools at our disposal now to make fantastically detailed worlds to explore and inhabit. Unfortunately, our co-inhabitants haven't proved themselves to be very worthy opponents. They're dumb: they show no emotion, no thought, no *anima*. We can instill these characteristics via graphics, animation, and above all, artificial intelligence (AI).

Artificial intelligence is a huge and extremely complex field. Luckily, we can get impressive results even with a lot more *artificial* than *intelligence*. A couple of simple rules (combined with our old friend `Math.random`) can give a passable illusion of intention and thought. It doesn't have to be overly realistic as long as it supports our game mechanics and is fun.

Like collision detection, AI is often best when it's not *too* good. Computer opponents are superhuman. They have the gift of omniscience and can comprehend the entire state of the world at every point in time. The poor old *human* player is only able to see what's visible on the screen. They're generally no match against a computer.

---

7. http://www.gotoandplay.it/_articles/2004/02/tonypa.php

But we don't let them know that! They'd feel bad, question the future of humanity, and not want to play our games. As game designers, it's our job to balance and dictate the flow of our games so that they're always fair, challenging, and surprising to the player.

Intentional Movement

Choosing how sprites move around in the game is great fun. The `update` function is your blank canvas, and you get godlike control over your entities. What's not to like about that!

The way an entity moves is determined by how much we alter its `x` and `y` position every frame ("move everything a tiny bit!"). So far, we've moved things mostly in straight lines with `pos.x += speed * dt`. Adding the speed (times the delta) causes the sprite to move to the right. Subtracting moves it to the left. Altering the `y` coordinate moves it up and down.

To make straight lines more fun, inject a bit of trigonometry. Using `pos.y += Math.sin(t * 10) * 200 * dt`, the sprite bobs up and down through a sine wave. `t * 10` is the frequency of the wave. `t` is the time in seconds from our update system, so it's always increasing linearly. Giving that to `Math.sin` produces a smooth sine wave. Changing the multiplier will alter the frequency: a lower number will oscillate faster. `200` is the *amplitude* of the waves.

You can combine waves to get even more interesting results. Say you added *another* sine wave to the y position: `pos.y += Math.sin(t * 11) * 200 * dt`. It's *almost* exactly the same as the first, but the frequency is altered very slightly. Now, as the two waves reinforce and cancel each other out as they drift in and out of phase, the entity bobs up and down faster and slower. Shifting the frequency and amplitude a lot can give some interesting bouncing patterns. Alter the `x` position with `Math.cos` and you have circles.

The important aspect of this is that movements can be *combined* to make more complex-looking behaviors. They can move spasmodically, they can drift lazily. As we go through this chapter, they'll be able to charge directly towards a player, or to run directly away. They'll be able to traverse a maze. When you combine these skills (a bobbing motion used in conjunction with a charge-at-player), or sequence them (run away for two seconds, then bob up and down for one second) they can be sculpted into very lifelike beings.

Waypoints

We need to spice up these apathetic ghosts and bats, giving them something to live for. We'll start with the concept of a "waypoint". **Waypoints** are milestones or intermediate target locations that the entity will move towards. Once they arrive at the waypoint, they move on to the next, until they reach their destination. A carefully placed set of waypoints can provide the game character with a sense of purpose, and can be used to great effect in your level design.

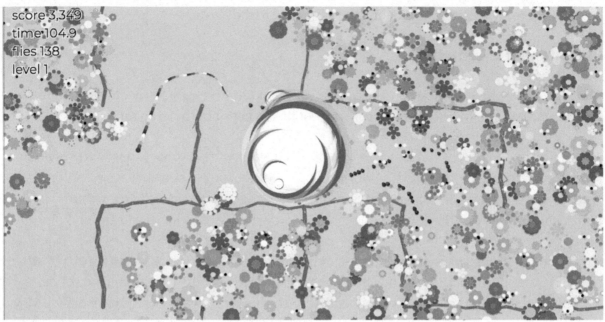

5-15. The waypoint-following bombs of Franco Ponticelli's FlyMaze

So that we can concentrate on the concepts behind waypoints, we'll introduce a flying bad guy who's *not* constrained by the maze walls. The scariest flying enemy is the mosquito (it's the deadliest animal in the world, after humans). But not very *spooky*. We'll go with "bat".

Bats won't be complex beasts; they'll be unpredictable. They'll simply have a single waypoint they fly towards. When they get there, they'll pick a new waypoint. Later (when we traverse a maze) we'll cover having multiple, structured waypoints. For now, bats waft from point to point, generally being a nuisance to the player.

To create them, make a new entity based on a `TileSprite`, called `Bat`, in `entities/Bat.js`. The bats need some smarts to choose their desired waypoint. That might be a function that picks a random location anywhere on screen, but to make them a bit more formidable we'll give them the `findFreeSpot` functions, so the waypoint will always be a *walkable* tile where the player might be traveling:

```
const bats = this.add(new Container());
for (let i = 0; i < 5; i++) {
  bats.add(new Bat(() => map.findFreeSpot()))
}
```

We have a new `Container` for the bats, and we create five new ones. Each gets a reference to our waypoint-picking function. When called, it runs `map.findFreeSpot` and finds an empty cell in the maze. This becomes the bat's new waypoint:

```
class Bat extends TileSprite {
  constructor(findWaypoint) {
    super(texture, 48, 48);
    this.findWaypoint = findWaypoint;
    this.waypoint = findWaypoint();

    ...

  }
}
```

Inside `Bat.js` we assign an initial goal location, then in the bat's `update` method we move towards it. Once we're close enough, we choose another location to act as the next waypoint:

```
// Move in the direction of the path
const xo = waypoint.x - pos.x;
const yo = waypoint.y - pos.y;
const step = speed * dt;
const xIsClose = Math.abs(xo) <= step;
const yIsClose = Math.abs(yo) <= step;
```

How do we "move towards" something, and how do we know if we're "close enough"? To answer both of these questions, we'll first find the difference between the waypoint location and the bat. Subtracting the x and y values of the waypoint from the bat's position gives us the distance on each axis. For each axis we define "close enough" to mean `Math.abs(distance) <= step`. Using `step` (which is based on `speed`) means that the faster we're traveling, the further we need to be to be "close enough" (so we don't overshoot forever).

 Using Absolute Value for Distance

> We take the *absolute value* of the distance, as it could be negative if we're on the other side of the waypoint. We don't care about direction, only distance.

```
if (!xIsClose) {
  pos.x += speed * (xo > 0 ? 1 : -1) * dt;
}
if (!yIsClose) {
  pos.y += speed * (yo > 0 ? 1 : -1) * dt;
}
```

To move in the direction of the waypoint, we'll break movement into two sections. If we're not too close in either the x or y directions, we move the entity towards the waypoint. If the ghost is above the waypoint ($y > 0$) we move it down, otherwise we move it up—and the same for the x axis. This doesn't give us a straight line (that's coming up when we start shooting at the player), but it does get us closer to the waypoint each frame.

```
if (xIsClose && yIsClose) {
  // New way point
  this.waypoint = this.findWaypoint();
}
```

Finally, if both horizontal and vertical distances are close enough, the bat has arrived at its destination and we reassign `this.waypoint` to a new location. Now the bats mindlessly roam the halls, as we might expect bats to do.

This is a very simple waypoint system. Generally, you'll want a list of points that constitute a *complete path*. When the entity reaches the first waypoint, it's pulled from the list and the next waypoint takes its place. We'll do something very similar to this when we encounter path finding shortly.

Moving, and Shooting, Towards a Target

Think back to our first shoot-'em-up from Chapter 3. The bad guys simply flew from right to left, minding their own business—while we, the players, mowed down the mindless zombie pilots. To level the playing field and make things more interesting from a gameplay perspective, our foes should at least be able to *fire projectiles at us*. This gives the player an incentive to move around the screen, and a motive for destroying otherwise quite peaceful entities. Suddenly we're the hero again.

Providing awareness of the player's location to bad guys is pretty easy: it's just `player.pos`! But how do we use this information to send things hurtling in a particular direction? The answer is, of course, trigonometry!

```
function angle (a, b) {
  const dx = a.x - b.x;
  const dy = a.y - b.y;
  const angle = Math.atan2(dy, dx);

  return angle;
}
```

Trigonometry

In this chapter, we'll see a couple of trigonometric functions for achieving our immediate goals of "better bad guys"—but we won't really explore *how* they work. This is the topic of next chapter … so if you're a bit rusty on math, you can breathe easy for the moment.

In the same way we implemented `math.distance`, we first need to get the *difference* between the two points (`dx` and `dy`), and then we use the built-in arctangent math operator `Math.atan2` to get the angle created between the two vectors. Notice that `atan2` takes the `y` difference as the first parameter and `x` as the second. Add the `angle` function to `utils/math.js`.

Most of the time in our games, we'll be looking for the angle between two *entities* (rather than points). So we're usually interested in the angle between the *center* of the entities, not their top-left corners as defined by `pos`. We can also add an angle function to `utils/entity.js`, which first finds the two entities' centers and *then* calls `math.angle`:

```
function angle(a, b) {
  return math.angle(center(a), center(b));
}
```

The `angle` function returns the angle between the two positions, in radians. Using *this* information we can now calculate the amounts we have to modify an entity's `x` and `y` position to move in the correct direction:

```
const angleToPlayer = entity.angle(player.pos, baddie.pos);
pos.x += Math.cos(angle) * speed * dt;
pos.y += Math.sin(angle) * speed * dt;
```

To use an angle in your game, remember that the cosine of an angle is how far along the `x` axis you need to move when moving one pixel in the angle direction. And the sine of an angle is how far along the `y` axis you need to move. Multiplying by a scalar (`speed`) number of pixels, the sprite moves in the correct direction.

Knowing the angle between two things turns out to be mighty important in gamedev. Commit this equation to memory, as you'll use it a lot. For example, we can now shoot directly *at* things—so let's do that! Create a `Bullet.js` sprite to act as a projectile:

```
class Bullet extends Sprite {
```

```
constructor(dir, speed = 100) {
  super(texture);
  this.speed = speed;
  this.dir = dir;
  this.life = 3;
  }
}
```

A `Bullet` will be a small sprite that's created with a position, a velocity (speed and direction), and a "life" (that's defaulted to three seconds). When life gets to 0, the bullet will be set to `dead` ... and we won't end up with millions of bullets traveling towards infinity (exactly like our bullets from Chapter 3).

```
update(dt) {
  const { pos, speed, dir } = this;

  // Move in the direction of the path
  pos.x += speed * dt * dir.x;
  pos.y += speed * dt * dir.y;

  if ((this.life -= dt) < 0) {
    this.dead = true;
  }
}
```

The difference from our Chapter 3 bullets is that they now move in the direction given when it was instantiated. Because `x` and `y` will represent the angle between two entities, the bullets will fire in a straight line *towards the target*—which will be us.

The bullets won't just mysteriously appear out of thin air. Something needs to fire them. We need another new bad guy! We'll deploy a couple of sentinels, in the form of *top-hat totems*. Totems are the guards of the dungeons who watch over the world from the center of the maze, destroying any treasure-stealing protagonists.

5-16. Top-hat totems: Toptems

The `Totem.js` entity generates `Bullets` and fires them towards the `Player`. So they need a reference to the player (they don't know it's a player, they just think of it as the `target`) and a function to call when it's time to generate a bullet. We'll call that `onFire` and pass it in from the `GameScreen` so the `Totem` doesn't need to worry itself about `Bullets`:

```
class Totem extends TileSprite {
  constructor(target, onFire) {
    super(texture, 48, 48);
    this.target = target;
    this.onFire = onFire;
    this.fireIn = 0;
  }
}
```

When a new `Totem` is created, it's assigned a target, and given a function to call when it shoots a `Bullet`. The function will add the bullet into the main game container so it can be checked for collisions. Now Bravedigger must avoid `Bats` and `Bullets`. We'll rename the container to `baddies` because the collision logic is the same for both:

```
new Totem(player, bullet => baddies.add(bullet)))
```

To get an entity on screen, it needs to go *inside a* `Container` to be included in our scene graph. There are many ways we could do this. We could make our main `GameScreen` object a global variable and call `gameScreen.add` from anywhere. This would work, but it's not good for information encapsulation. By passing in a function, we can specify *only* the abilities we want a `Totem` to perform. As always, it's ultimately up to you.

 Don't lose your entities

There's a hidden gotcha in our `Container` logic. If we add an entity to a container *during that container's own update call*, the entity will not be added! For example, if `Totem` was inside `baddies` and it tried to add a new bullet *also to `baddies`*, the bullet would not appear. Look at the code for `Container` and see if you can see why. We'll address this issue in Chapter 9, in the section "Looping Over Arrays".

When should the totem fire at the player? Randomly, of course! When it's time to shoot, the `fireIn` variable will be set to a countdown. While the countdown is happening, the totem has a small animation (switching between two frames). In game design, this is called **telegraphing**—a subtle *visual indication* to the player that they had better be on their toes. Without telegraphing, our totems would suddenly and randomly shoot at the player, even when they're really close. They'd have no chance to dodge the bullets and would feel cheated and annoyed.

```
if (math.randOneIn(250)) {
  this.fireIn = 1;
}
if (this.fireIn > 0) {
  this.fireIn -= dt;
  // Telegraph to the player
  this.frame.x = [2, 4][Math.floor(t / 0.1) % 2];
  if (this.fireIn < 0) {
    this.fireAtTarget();
  }
}
```

There's a one-in-250 chance every frame that the totem will fire. When this is true, a countdown begins for one second. Following the countdown, the `fireAtTarget` method will do the hard work of calculating the trajectory required for a projectile to strike a target:

```
fireAtTarget() {
  const { target, onFire } = this;
  const totemPos = entity.center(this);
  const targetPos = entity.center(target);
  const angle = math.angle(targetPos, totemPos);

  ...
}
```

The first steps are to get the angle between the target and the totem using `math.angle`. We *could* use the helper `entity.angle` (which does the `entity.center` calls for us), but we also need the center position of the totem to properly set the starting position of the bullet:

```
const x = Math.cos(angle);
const y = Math.sin(angle);
const bullet = new Bullet({ x, y }, 300);
bullet.pos.x = totemPos.x - bullet.w / 2;
bullet.pos.y = totemPos.y - bullet.h / 2;

onFire(bullet);
```

Once we have the angle, we use cosine and sine to calculate the components of the direction. (Hmm, again: perhaps you'd like to make that into another math function that does it for you?) Then we create a new `Bullet` that will move in the correct direction.

That suddenly makes maze traversal quite challenging! You should spend some time playing around with the "shoot-at" code: change the random interval chance, or make it a timer that fires consistently every couple of seconds ... or a bullet-hell spawner that fires a volley of bullets for a short period of time.

Flexible Mechanics

Throughout this book, we've seen many small mechanics that illustrate various concepts. Don't forget that game mechanics are flexible. They can be reused and recombined with other mechanics, controls, or graphics to make even more game ideas—and game genres! For example, if you combine "mouse clicking" with "waypoints" and "fire towards", we have a basic tower defense game! Create a waypoint path for enemies to follow: clicking the mouse adds a turret (that uses `math.distance` to find the closest enemy) and then fires toward it.

Smart Bad Guys: Attacking and Evading

Our bad guys have one-track minds. They're given a simple task (fly left while shooting randomly; shoot towards player ...) and they do the same thing in perpetuity, like some mindless automata. But real bad guys aren't like that: they scheme, they wander, they idle, they have various stages of alertness, they attack, they retreat, they stop for ice cream ...

5-17. Skeletons at work—and rest—in Mozilla's BrowserQuest

One way to model these desires is through a *state machine*. A **state machine** orchestrates behavior changes between a set number of states. Different events can cause a *transition* from the current state to a new state. *States* will be game-specific behaviors like "idle", "walk", "attack", "stop for icecream". You can't be attacking *and* stopping for ice cream. Implementing state machines can be as simple as storing a state variable that we restrict to one item out of a list. Here's our initial list for possible bat states (defined in the `Bat.js` file):

```
const states = {
  ATTACK: 0,
  EVADE: 1,
  WANDER: 2
};
```

We Don't Actually Need to Define States

It's not necessary to define the states in an object like this. We could just use the strings "ATTACK", "EVADE", and "WANDER". Using an object like this just lets us organize our thoughts—listing all the possible states in one place—and our tools can warn us if we've made an error (like assigning a state that doesn't exist). Strings are fine though!

At any time, a bat can be in only one of the `ATTACK`, `EVADE`, or `WANDER` states. Attacking will be flying at the player, evading is flying *directly away* from the player, and wandering is flitting around randomly. In the function constructor, we'll assign the initial state of `ATTACK`ing: `this.state = state.ATTACK`. Inside `update` we switch behavior based on the current state:

```
const angle = entity.angle(target, this);
const distance = entity.distance(target, this);

if (state === states.ATTACK) {
  ...
} else if (state === states.EVADE) {
  ...
} else if (state === states.WANDER) {
  ...
}
```

Depending on the current state (and combined with the distance and angle to the player) a `Bat` can make decisions on how it should act. For example, if it's attacking, it can move *directly towards* the player:

```
xo = Math.cos(angle) * speed * dt;
yo = Math.sin(angle) * speed * dt;
if (distance < 60) {
  this.state = states.EVADE;
}
```

But it turns out our bats are part chicken: when they get too close to their target (within 60 pixels), the state switches to `state.EVADE`. Evading works the same as attacking, but we negate the speed so they fly *directly away* from the player:

```
xo = -Math.cos(angle) * speed * dt;
yo = -Math.sin(angle) * speed * dt;
if (distance > 120) {
  if (math.randOneIn(2)) {
```

```
    this.state = states.WANDER;
    this.waypoint = findFreeSpot();
  } else {
    this.state = states.ATTACK;
  }
}
```

While evading, the bat continually considers its next move. If it gets far enough away from the player to feel safe (120 pixels), it reassesses its situation. Perhaps it wants to attack again, or perhaps it wants to wander off towards a random waypoint.

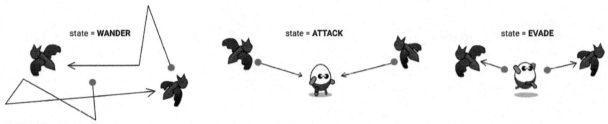

state = WANDER   state = ATTACK   state = EVADE

5-18. When bats attack

Combining and sequencing behaviors in this way is the key to making believable and deep characters in your game. It can be even more interesting when the state machines of various entities are influenced by the state of other entities—leading to **emergent behavior**. This is when apparent characteristics of entities magically appear—even though you, as the programmer, didn't specifically design them.

 Emergent Behavior

An example of this is in *Minecraft*. Animals are designed to EVADE after taking damage. If you attack a cow, it will run for its life (so hunting is more challenging for the player). Wolves in the game also have an ATTACK state (because they're wolves). The unintended result of these state machines is that you can sometimes see wolves involved in a fast-paced sheep hunt! This behavior wasn't explicitly added, but it *emerged* as a result of combining systems.

A More Stately State Machine

State machines are used a lot when orchestrating a game—not only in entity AI. They can control the timing of screens (such as "GET READY!" dialogs), set the pacing and rules for the game (such as managing cool-down times and counters) and are very helpful for breaking up any complex behavior into small, reusable pieces. (Functionality in different states can be shared by different types of entities.)

Dealing with all of these states with independent variables and `if … else` clauses can become unwieldy. A more powerful approach is to abstract the state machine into its own class that can be reused and extended with additional functionality (like remembering what state we were in previously). This is going to be used across most games we make, so let's create a new file for it called `State.js` and add it to the Pop library:

```
class State {
  constructor(state) {
    this.set(state);
  }

  set(state) {
    this.last = this.state;
    this.state = state;
    this.time = 0;
    this.justSetState = true;
  }

  update(dt) {
    this.first = this.justSetState;
    this.justSetState = false;

    ...
  }
}
```

The `State` class will hold the current and previous states, as well as remember how long we've been in the *current state*. It can also tell us if it's the *first* frame we've been in the current state. It does this via a flag (`justSetState`). Every frame, we have to update the `state` object (the same way we do with our `MouseControls`) so we can do timing calculations. Here we also set the `first` flag if it's the first update. This is useful for performing state initialization tasks, such as reseting counters.

```
if (state.first) {
  // just entered this state!
  this.spawnEnemy();
}
```

When a state is set (via `state.set("ATTACK")`), the property `first` will be set to `true`. Subsequent updates will reset the flag to `false`. The delta time is also passed into `update` so we can track the amount of time the current state has been active. If it's the first frame, we reset the time to 0; otherwise, we add `dt`:

```
this.time += this.first ? 0 : dt;
```

We now can retrofit our chase-evade-wander example to use the state machine, and remove our nest of *if* s:

```
switch (state.get()) {
  case states.ATTACK:
    break;
  case states.EVADE:
    break;
  case states.WANDER:
    break;
}
state.update(dt);
```

This is some nice documentation for the *brain* of our `Bat` —deciding what to do next given the current inputs. Because there's a flag for the *first* frame of the state, there's also now a nice place to add any initialization tasks. For example, when the `Bat` starts `WANDER` ing, it needs to choose a new waypoint location:

```
case states.WANDER:
  if (state.first) {
    this.waypoint = findFreeSpot();
  }
  ...
  break;
}
```

It's usually a good idea to do initialization tasks in the `state.first` frame, rather than when you transition *out* of the previous frame. For example, we could have set the waypoint as we did `state.set("WANDER")` . If state logic is self-contained, it's easier to test. We could *default* a `Bat` to `this.state = state.WANDER` and know the waypoint will be set in the first frame of the update.

There are a couple of other handy functions we'll add to `State.js` for querying the current state:

```
is(state) {
  return this.state === state;
}

isIn(...states) {
  return states.some(s => this.is(s));
}
```

Using these helper functions, we can conveniently find out if we're in one or more states:

```
if (state.isIn("EVADE", "WANDER")) {
  // Evading or wandering - but not attacking.
}
```

The states we choose for an entity can be as granular as needed. We might have states for "BORN" (when the entity is first created), "DYING" (when it's hit, and stunned), and "DEAD" (when it's all over), giving us discrete locations in our class to handle logic and animation code.

Controlling Game Flow

State machines are useful *anywhere* you need control over a flow of actions. One excellent application is to manage our high-level game state. When the dungeon game commences, the user shouldn't be thrown into a hectic onslaught of monsters and bullets flying around out of nowhere. Instead, a friendly "GET READY" message appears, giving the player a couple of seconds to survey the situation and mentally prepare for the mayhem ahead.

A state machine can break the main logic in the `GameScreen` update into pieces such as "READY", "PLAYING", "GAMEOVER". It makes it clearer how we should structure our code, and how the overall game will flow. It's not necessary to handle everything in the `update` function; the switch statement can dispatch out to other methods. For example, all of the code for the "PLAYING" state could be grouped in an `updatePlaying` function:

```
switch(state.get()) {
  case "READY":
    if (state.first) {
      this.scoreText.text = "GET READY";
    }
    if (state.time > 2) {
      state.set("PLAYING");
    }
    break;

  case "PLAYING":
    if (entity.hit(player, bat)) {
      state.set("GAMEOVER");
    }
    break;

  case "GAMEOVER":
    if (controls.action) {
      state.set("READY");
    }
    break;
}
```

```
state.update(dt);
```

The *GameScreen* will start in the *READY* state, and display the message "GET READY". After two seconds (*state.time > 2*) it transitions to "PLAYING" and the game is on. When the player is hit, the state moves to "GAMEOVER", where we can wait until the space bar is pressed before starting over again.

Pathfinding

Our entities have become sentient and can make decisions for themselves. But they don't have a lot of vision. They lack a long-term plan. One of the most useful (and fun) ways to make AI-controlled entities smarter is to give them the brains to navigate intelligently from one point in a maze to another.

In grid-based games, this is most effectively done via a **pathfinding algorithm**. As the name implies, this class of algorithms calculates how to navigate a path from one point in our game to another. Pathfinding algorithms operate on a *graph of nodes* that represent space in your game level. Our graph is a simple 2D grid. You can find paths through a 2D grid efficiently with the **A* (pronounced "A star") algorithm**.

The concepts of A* are not too difficult to understand and implement. The idea is to treat the game tile map as a mathematical graph. The algorithm uses a system of weights to traverse the graph and find the most direct path between any two nodes (map tile positions). We won't implement one here; we've got games to make. But if you're interested in diving into the hows and whys, there's a lot of information on A* available online[8].

There are many A* libraries for JavaScript, and they all work in more or less the same way:

1. create an instance of the pathfinding library

2. convert your game level to the correct format for the algorithm

3. set the start and end nodes on the graph

4. call the function to calculate the path and get a result.

What's returned is a *list of cells* that represent the shortest path from the start point to the end point. How cool is that!

We're going to use a recent and well-maintained A* library called EasyStar.js[9]. EasyStar is "an

---

[8]. http://www.policyalmanac.org/games/aStarTutorial.htm

asynchronous A* pathfinding API written in JavaScript for use in your HTML5 games and interactive projects". It's efficient and has a feature-rich API. To use it, install it from *npm* by running the following command in your project from the command line:

```
npm install --save easystarjs
```

This adds the *EasyStar* library to your *package.json* file, ready to be imported into your game. Now we can move on to step 1 of 4: "create an instance of the pathfinding library". Go ahead and create a fresh pathfinder object inside our *Level* constructor function:

```
import EasyStar from "easystarjs";

// Create a pathfinding thing
const path = new EasyStar.js();
```

EasyStar expects levels to be modeled as a two-dimensional array of integers that should be passed to a method *setGrid* . Unfortunately, our *map* is stored in a *one-dimensional array*. So step 2 of 4 for pathfinding is "convert your game level to the correct format for the algorithm". This is achieved by "chunking" the original array into map-width sized chunks, appending them to the resulting two-dimensional array:

```
// Translate the one-dimensional level into pathfinder 2d array
const grid = [];
for (let i = 0; i < level.length; i += mapW) {
  grid.push(level.slice(i, i + mapW));
}

path.setGrid(grid);
```

By default, all of the tiles are considered "solid" (non-walkable). We tell EasyStar which tile types are walkable via the *setAcceptableTiles* method. Walkable tiles in our game are defined in the *tileIndexes* metadata. We can map over this array and extract the tile indexes that have the *walkable* property set to *true* :

```
const walkables = tileIndexes
  .map(({walkable}, i) => walkable ? i : -1)
  .filter(i => i !== -1);
path.setAcceptableTiles(walkables);

this.path = path;
```

9. http://easystarjs.com/

Extracting the walkable tile indexes is done in two phases (because we need the *index* of the array element, not just the element itself). First, map `tileIndexes` to an integer value of either the tile's index (if it's walkable) or a `-1` (if it's not). Then filter out all of the `-1`s, leaving just the tile indexes that are walkable.

That's the setup done. If the level changes dynamically during your game (for example, if the player has the ability to build or destroy blocks), you'll have to recalculate the grid with `setGrid` again to update the graph. Our levels are static, so we only need to do it once.

Target the Player

The next step is to "set the start and end nodes on the graph". First we need a new bad guy to give the pathfinding brain to. Pretty sure what we need now is ghosts. Ghosts that (for one reason or another) have the supernatural ability to know where Bravedigger is standing, yet don't have the supernatural power of passing through walls. They're the spookiest because they have to obey alive-human rules.

Ghosts have a `pos` (which will also be the path *start* position) and a `target` (the path *end* position). At any given time, they can ask EasyStar to give them an *updated list of the waypoints* they must pass through to get to the player. EasyStar is an asynchronous library, so the final path is returned to the ghost via a callback function:

```
findPath() {
  // Calculate the pathfinding path
  const { map, target } = this;
  const s = map.pixelToMapPos(entity.center(this));
  const d = map.pixelToMapPos(entity.center(target));
  map.path.findPath(s.x, s.y, d.x, d.y, path => {
    this.path = path || [];
  });
  map.path.calculate();
}
```

The EasyStar API requires a start and end position as tile indexes (`s` is source, `d` is destination). `path.findPath` is the EasyStar asynchronous call that returns either `null` if no path is found, or a list of waypoints that represent the path. This is stored on the ghost's `path` property. To actually make EasyStar do some work, we have to call `path.calculate`.

Pathfinding & Performance

Pathfinding is impressive, but it can be computationally expensive. If you updated a path every frame, on a big level, for large quantities of entities, you'd see your frames per second go down the drain. There are tricks to help (such as only periodically updating paths), but always remember the golden rule when making your first few games: don't waste time optimizing something until it's really a problem!

Moving Along a Path

The final step is to actually follow the path. This works almost identically to our original *Bat* 's waypoint system—except that, instead of a single random waypoint, we use the *head of the list* of the path elements. Once the ghost is "close enough" to the waypoint, we slice this list (which removes the head), and then start moving towards the next waypoint. The result is that the ghost relentlessly hunts down the player. Perfect!

```
followPath(dt) {
  const { map, speed, path, pos } = this;
  if (!path.length) {
    return; // We've finished following the path
  }

  // Move in the direction of the path
  const cell = this.path[0];
  // ... just like we moved towards waypoints

  // If you made it, move to the next path element
  if (closeX && closeY) {
    this.path = path.slice(1);
    if (this.path.length === 0) {
      this.findPath();
    }
  }
}
```

For our game, our ghost is a bit lazy. It only looks for a new path *after* it gets to where the player *was* standing. Obviously the player is not as lazy: they've moved on a long time ago to avoid being struck by totem projectiles! You could make the ghost far more vicious by updating its path more regularly. Updating often enough would result in an unforgiving ghost that the player could never escape. Pathfinding in action is fantastically satisfying.

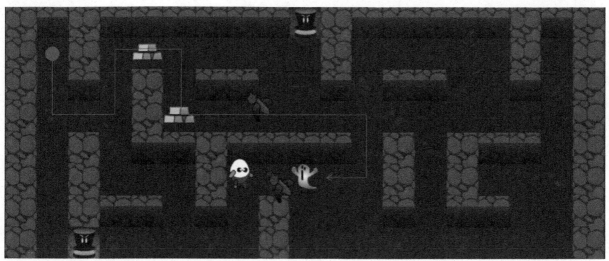

5-19. Pathfinding ghosts

Enemies Alive

It's halfway through the game jam. You should have been asleep many hours ago, but you're having a lot of fun, so you're still at the office. As you rise to leave for some much-needed rest, right on cue our old friend Guy Shifty appears, looking annoyingly wide awake and sprightly.

"Hey, whoa! You heading off already?" He tilts his head back and laughs. "You must be feeling confident. I'd never let my employees off this early. How's it traveling, anyway?"

You let him play through the maze dungeon arena. After several minutes, he looks up at you and asks, "What's with all the dungeons and bats and ghosts and things?"

You remind him of the game jam's theme, "Scared to Death", and his eyes go wide. "Oh—did I say that? Oh, ha ha, nooo … that was *last year's* theme. This year it's, um … 'Let's get PHYSICal'. You know—like physics games with gravity and stuff? Ah, that's funny. Too bad, because I like your dungeon thingy."

You're beginning not to like this guy.

24 hours down the drain. 24 hours to start all over again. On the positive side, you now know a lot more than when you started: how to do bespoke collision detection between rectangles, how to wall slide around a tile map, how to stalk humans by injecting cunning and cleverness into the brains of artificial foes. You can feel the power rising. Use that power for good, not evil!

Mathematics & Physics

Level

6

Well, I won't sugar coat it: we're in trouble. The Lucky Dare Game Jam Competition is 50% over, and it turns out we wasted the entire first day working on entirely the wrong project. We need to pivot and somehow transform our spooky maze crawler into something *physics-based*.

This means emulating the forces that act in the world around us. Good physics can increase player immersion and make a game world feel fluid, natural, and dynamic. Game physics can range from simple (often exaggerated) approximations to elaborate simulations. In this chapter, we'll cover essential math concepts for game development and use them to implement some widely applicable game physics.

As always, game development is 90% smoke and mirrors. If you're creating the next *Kerbal Space Program*, you'll want to dust of your physics textbooks. If you're making something more, uh, out-of-this-world—such as Sos Sosowski's *Mosh Pit Simulator* then reality is not the goal. Accuracy and realism is often undesirable for crafting the user experience we want to provide. All we need is something that *feels* like physics, is fun to control, and meets our artistic needs.

6-1. The lightly-exaggerated physics of Mosh Pit Simulator

Jump Everybody, Jump

Being on a deadline, it seems unwise to completely throw away our *Bravedigger* maze crawler from the end of the last chapter. We're agile (and lazy) and can adapt it to work with the new theme. Instead of a top-down maze explorer, it becomes a side-on platform game à la *Super Mario Bros*. All we need is a bit of gravity and we can call it *Bravedigger II*!

Rather than have Bravedigger's vertical position determined by the *keyboard* (that is, via `controls.y`) it'll be powered by a *jump force* (applied when the player hits the space bar) combined with an opposing *downward force*. Imagine an apple. It falls from a nearby tree and lands on your head. In retaliation to the inanimate object, you pick it up and hurl it into the sky. What does its trajectory look like?

6-2. Apple in flight

The apple starts around ground level. After one instant of time (say, 16.66 milliseconds) it has traveled upwards a large distance. If we drew it on screen it would move, say, `-10` pixels in the vertical direction. But its vertical speed isn't constant. Because gravity is pushing down on the apple, the movement in the next instant will be reduced—say `-9.5` pixels. Then after that even less—perhaps `-8.7` pixels—and so on.

The apple is still moving upwards, but it's slowing down each frame. Eventually, it will be moving vertically by ~0 pixels, only its horizontal position appearing to change. From this point on, the apple starts falling back to the ground, at first slowly—say `+0.1` pixels—but with the force accumulating. It falls faster and faster and faster as it approaches the ground. This sounds vaguely like gravity!

Faking Gravity

It's time to fake some fundamental universal forces. I say "faking" because we won't worry about air resistance, or which planet we're on, or even how heavy we are. We just need something that looks gravity-like. Starting with a minimal new project, we now have to think "side on" rather than "top down". This means removing the ability to move up and down with the keyboard (unless your game also happens to feature a jetpack):

```
const { x } = controls; // Removed `y`!
const xo = x * dt * speed;
let yo = 0;

// Apply some gravity
...


pos.x += xo; // horizontal influenced by the keyboard
pos.y += yo; // vertical influenced by "gravity"
```

The left–right keys still determine the horizontal movement, but now `yo` can only be influenced by gravity. The player is suspended permanently on a vertical plane wherever they spawn. To get them airborne, add some properties for leaping and falling:

```
this.jumping = false;
this.vel = 0;
```

jumping is a flag to track if the player is currently airborne. They can only start a jump if they're not *already* jumping. Otherwise, they could spam the "jump" button and fly right out of the top of the screen.

The other property is the player's velocity— *vel* for short. For now, this is a scalar value, a one-dimensional force (we'll go 2D later in the chapter) that tracks the player's *y* offset, as influenced by gravity. When a jump commences, velocity is set to a large negative number (-10 pixels, for example). This is our *launch force*—the only thing that can get us off the ground. Gravity will reduce the force until we hang in the air and then start falling—just like an apple.

```
if (!this.jumping && controls.action) {
  // Jump!
  this.vel = -10; // Launch force
  this.jumping = true;
}
```

Pressing the space bar triggers a jump and sets the launch velocity. Whenever the sprite is in the process of jumping, any force accumulated in *vel* is added to our temporary variable *yo* . Remember that this amount is finally summed with the player's position, therefore affecting vertical motion on screen.

Now the player is moving upwards, but they are dutifully respecting Newton's First Law of Motion: *a body in motion will remain in motion unless it is acted upon by an external force*. If there were no *change* to *vel* , the player would rapidly depart the top of the screen at a speed of -10 pixels per frame. It's time for gravity to flex its muscles and assert some force over *vel* :

```
if (this.jumping) {
  this.vel += 32 * dt;
  yo += this.vel;
}
```

Here gravity is also a scalar: *32 pixels per second*. Every frame, it gets *added* to velocity. The player's initial launch velocity is -10. After one frame that velocity is increased by *32 * dt* to about -9.46 (depending on *dt*). Like our apple, the player is still moving upwards—but a tiny, tiny bit slower. This accumulates every frame, until velocity is positive and the player starts "falling".

The result is a nice arcing trajectory.

Gravitational Constant

"32" is our game's gravitational constant. But 32 is not the *actual* gravitational constant of earth. (It's about 9.81 meters per second on Earth, at 45 degrees latitude). So what is 32? It's a number I chose because it felt pretty good. 50 felt too heavy, 10 felt too floaty. Test things out, but don't overthink it!

Having applied our force, the final step is to actually *stop* it when the player is on the ground. In the real world, gravity is relentless and unceasing. In the game world it's whatever we want it to be. Real-world forces can be hard to control in the game world, so we'll simplify things. When we decide the player is on "the ground", the jump is finished and gravity no longer exists:

```
// Check if hit ground
if (player.pos.y > h / 2) {
  player.pos.y = h / 2;
  player.jumping = false;
}
```

6-3. Bravedigger in flight

As well as ending the jump, we also set the `y` position to be exactly level with the ground plane (`h / 2`). This is necessary, as the player may be moving very quickly when they land, and could end up with their feet stuck below the floor.

For homework, you should test out various launch velocities and the gravity constants. You'll see they tremendously alter the feel of the player—from moon-like, floaty leaps to heavy, lead-balloon trajectories. What works for you will depend completely on your requirements, and might even change throughout your game.

Jumping Platformer

At this point we have something that passes for gravity, but we need to try it out in a real game environment to see if it plays well. In our game we need the *tile map* to be the judge of when the player is on the ground (rather than some arbitrary ground plane). But last chapter's top-down, procedurally generated maze is no longer appropriate for a side-view platformer. We have to undo the cool maze generation code and create an artisanal, hand-crafted ASCII map that's purpose-built to accommodate a jumping character:

```
const ascii = `
# # # # # # # # # # # # # # # # # # # # # # # #
# # # # #                             # # # #
# # #                       B         # # #
# #                             # #     # #
#               # # # # # # #           # #
#       # #             # # #             #
# B                   # # # #             #
# # #                     # #             T
# # # #         # # T # #     # # # #      #
# # # # #                             # #
# # #                             # # # #
# #         # #                           #
#       # # # # #             # # # # # # #
#     # # # # # # #       T # # # # # # # # #
# X                   # . # # # # # # # # # #
# # # # # # # # # # # # # # # # # # # # # # # #`;
```

Hand-rolling level maps inside code files is pretty good fun. If you squint you can see what the level will look like. The ASCII characters in the string get sliced up into rows and columns. Each cell is converted into the relevant `TileSprite` index that defines the cavernous level. Where there's a `#` will be a solid wall tile. A space will be a walkable tile. The mapping from character to `TileSprite` is completely up to you. The scattered letters will generate spawn points: `X` is where the player spawns, `B` is where the bats will spawn, and `T` where the `Totems` spawn.

```
switch (cell) {
  case "#":
    return 1; // Wall tile
  case "B":
    spawns.bats.push({ x, y }); "B"// Create a bat!
    return 0; // Empty tile...
  case " ":
    return 0; // " "// Empty tile
}
```

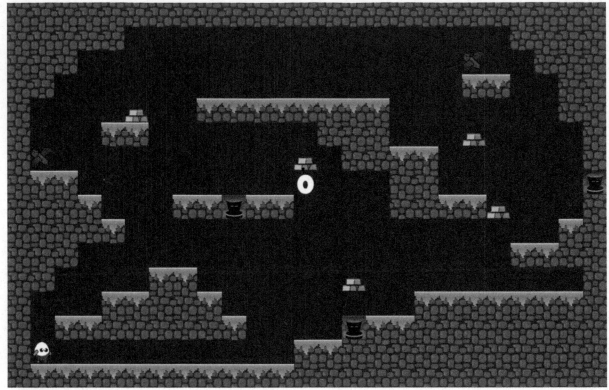

6-4. Artisinal, hand-crafted map

 Aesthetic Tweaks

In the top-down version I did a second pass over the generated level and changed the tiles to look more "3D". For the side-on version I took exactly the same approach, but looked for any tiles that had a non-walkable tile *above* them. These were then changed to the grass-topped tile to give it some visual interest.

ASCII maps are quick and effective for testing (and learning), but they don't "scale up" well. They're limited in functionality and are hard to edit. Once you're sick of hand-rolling maps, spend some time looking at **Tile map editors**. These are GUI applications where you can select your tiles from a palette and paint your world. You can have multiple layers, as well as attach data to layers or individual tiles. Tile data can be integrated into your game code—so things like "player start positions", or "enemy types" can be defined in the editor, rather than hardcoded in your game. We'll integrate the popular Tiled Editor in Chapter 8.

In the initial "jumping" test, the sprite falls until it touches the ground plane arbitrarily defined as "halfway down the game screen". In a tile-based level, how can we know when the player is on the ground? Conceptually, it's when the player's "feet" have collided with the top of the ground beneath them. It turns out we already check this *exact scenario* in the bowels of our `wallslide` collision detection function: `if (y > 0 && !(bl && br))` .

If the player is falling (`y > 0`) and their feet (bottom-left or bottom-right corners) are not free to move, they must have hit the ground. We'll augment `wallslide` to note *which edge* of the entity has collided with a tile in the direction it wants to move:

```
const hits = { up: false, down: false, left: false, right: false };
```

We'll then pass this information *back* from a collision check for use in our game logic:

```
return { x: xo, y: yo, hits };
```

The hit directions all default to `false` and will only be `true` if a collision occurs in the given direction. In the movement collision tests, when we test if the entity hits its "head", we now also record this in the `hits` map:

```
// Hit your head
if (y < 0 && !(tl && tr)) {
  hits.up = true;
  ...
}
```

The same goes for the feet (down), and left and right. We now understand the nature of the collision. We know when the player touches the ground, hits their head, or bumps into edges. This will be useful for other game mechanics too, such as wall jumping.

 Wall Jumping

> **Wall jumping** is a standard platform-game mechanic where the players jump, hit a wall, and jump again from midair—allowing them to go higher, rather than just sliding down to the ground. To implement it in your game, you could check if the player is pressing jump in the same frame that `hits.left` or `hits.right` is true and re-trigger a jump. We'll explore this more in <u>Chapter 8</u>.

Back in the main game code, we reset the `jumping` flag (and velocity) whenever `hits` tells us there's a solid tile beneath us:

```
const r = wallslide(this, map, xo, yo);
if (r.hits.down) {
```

```
    this.jumping = false;
    this.vel = 0;
  }
```

So far, so good. But now we have a levitational issue: gravity is *only* applied when the player is jumping—and jumping is *only* enabled when the player presses the jump button. If the player wanders off the edge of a ledge, there will be no gravity and they can walk on air. You probably don't want this. Check if the ground isn't actually there (`r.hits.down` is not `true`) any time the player is *not* jumping.

To make it feel a bit more natural, we also give a little push downwards (three units) so they don't "float" off the edge too much. This was just a trial-and-error figure that felt pretty good:

```
// Check if falling
if (!this.jumping && !r.hits.down) {
  this.jumping = true;
  this.vel = 3;
}
```

 Not Quite Natural

Why not just apply gravity all the time, like in the real world? You can! Though one tiny issue is that for each frame, gravity will push down, while collision detection will push back—giving it a small vertical jiggle. This is a bug, because we flip between `hits.down` true/false every frame. We'll fix this soon, by checking *underneath* the player. More importantly, though, not applying unnecessary forces makes it easier for us to *precisely control* what is going on—rather than leaving it up to the laws of "nature".

There's one final subtle issue with our jumping code. If the player tries to jump in a confined area, they smash their head on the roof above them. You'd expect them to rebound and fall directly back to the ground, but because the regular jumping trajectory is still being calculated, the player sticks to the roof until velocity gets high enough to push them down. To avoid this, velocity must be neutralized as soon as the player hits their head:

```
if (r.hits.up) {
  this.vel = 0;
}
```

Notice how easy it is to mess with physical laws in our game world! Once you understand how to implement things realistically, you can start thinking about how to bend the rules. Perhaps velocity *doesn't* get neutralized when you hit your head, and "roof sliding" across gaps is a core mechanic of your game? Always be experimenting and prototyping with the rules and values!

Fixing Our Time Step

We're back on track for the game jam, but our platform game has just exposed a major issue with our game loop. If you play the game on a slow computer (or your computer suddenly undertakes a CPU-intensive task) the player's jump height changes! They might not even be able to jump high enough to get up on a platform! That's not good. We glossed over this in <u>Chapter 2</u> (for simplicity's sake) but we can't ignore it when implementing forces that depend on a consistent delta time.

 Simulating High CPU Load

To mimic a high load, you can write a loop that outputs a lot of `console.log` messages in the game's main update. For example, `for (let i = 0; i < 1000; i++)` `console.log(i);` . Now play the game and hold down the space bar: notice the jump height can dip below the platform!

The reason for the inconsistency is this: the force we apply for a jump is *constant* and instantaneous, but the amount of gravity we apply is *dependent on the time that has passed* between each frame. On a slow computer more time passes, so `dt` is higher and gravity is heavier. We could compensate by considering `dt` when applying a launch force. But `dt` varies; if jumping happens on a fast frame, there wouldn't be much power. If it's during a lag, the player would get a mega jump—possibly getting stuck in a tile above them!

One solution is to use a *fixed time step* for our physics system where each update is given a constant `dt` . When there's a lag, a lot of time has passed between frames, so we call `update` *multiple times* with the constant `dt` to make up for it. We only render once after the updates are complete. Rendering is generally the most expensive part of a game loop, so splitting apart updating and rendering gives us a way to keep the game physics correct without overtaxing slow computers.

The core game loop logic in `Game.js` is the same as before: determine the time between the previous and current frames (capped at some maximum length based on `STEP` : the frame rate we desire). However, now the `dt` is *accumulated* rather than just assigned. (That is, where previously we had `dt = Math.min(...)` , we now have `dt += Math.min(...)` .)

```
// Updates and render
const t = ms / 1000; // Let's work in seconds
dt += Math.min(t - last, MAX_FRAME);
last = t;
```

The accumulation is used to store the amount of time that gets "carried over" from the last loop. Then comes the crux of a fixed time step loop: the amount of time carried over, plus the length of time between the frame, is divided into *STEP* -sized chunks. This is the *number of updates* that need to be done. For each chunk, our *scene* is updated and the *gameUpdate* function is called:

```
while (dt >= STEP) {
  this.scene.update(STEP, t);
  gameUpdate(STEP, t);
  dt -= STEP;
}
this.renderer.render(this.scene);
```

After the *STEP* -sized updates are done, the scene is rendered *once*. In a perfect world, there would only ever be one update per frame. But if there's lag in the browser, it may be two or even three (up to our maximum). But each update is a *fixed size*, so our physics calculations will behave more predictably. The elapsed time won't be exactly the size of a step, but whatever is left over gets saved for the next frame.

In addition to having a stable game loop, we also have more control over when our update and render functions are called. It can be enhanced with additional features such as "slow motion". The game will *think* it's running at 60 frames per second, but we can speed it up or slow it down so that time is mystically dilated. Add another couple of global variables at the to of *Game.js* :

```
const MULTIPLIER = 1;
const SPEED = STEP * MULTIPLIER;
```

The *MULTIPLIER* will be the ratio to dilate time by. Greater than 1 and time will slow, less than 1 and time will speed up. *SPEED* uses the multiplier to determine the rate that the game should be updated. For now, the *MULTIPLIER* is a constant, but later we'll expose it so we can modify it in real time:

```
while (dt >= SPEED) {
  this.scene.update(STEP, t / MULTIPLIER);
  gameUpdate(STEP, t / MULTIPLIER);
  dt -= SPEED;
}
```

The number of updates we do depends now on *SPEED* (which is a function of the step size and the multiplier). Each *update* still receives the normal *STEP* size, so despite the modified frames per second, internally the game will be consistent as when running at normal speed. Even if you don't want time manipulation as part of your game, setting *MULTIPLIER* to a large number can be invaluable for debugging game logic. We'll cover this in Chapter 9.

The final change to our game loop is not related to fixed time steps (or physics) at all. There's an issue with how our loop values are initialized. When we *first* call the *Loopy* function via *requestAnimationFrame*, the timestamp (*ms*) is not zero. Depending on what your scripts are doing it can sometimes be 100 milliseconds or more. This means our delta value for the first frame is *way* too high.

To prevent *update* being called multiple times unnecessarily, we'll have a separate function that properly initializes the variable.

```
const loopy = ms => {
  // ... main loop logic
};
// Initialize the timer
const init = ms => {
  last = ms / 1000;
  requestAnimationFrame(loopy);
};
requestAnimationFrame(init); // Call "init" instead of "loopy"
```

Game will schedule a call to the *init* function. This sets the real *Last* value and *then* schedules a call to *Loopy*. Problem fixed!

While we're here I also converted *Loopy* to be an arrow function: because I know we'll need to be in the correct *Game* scope later, when we implement screen transitions. Our core loop is now rock-solid, and ready to be the backbone of our physics-enabled games.

Triangles and Vectors

Trigonometry is all about the relationships of lengths and angles in triangles. When you start squinting, triangles are *everywhere*—and recognizing characteristics and behaviors of triangles is extremely important in game development. They turn up in AI for path finding and human-like behavioral responses, in simple physical properties like bouncing and reflecting, and in visual effects like lighting and particles. It's all triangles!

Thankfully, we don't have to dive too deep into math to reap some compelling rewards. Even the shallow end of the math pool gets us a long way when making games.

Building a Vector Library

Vector spaces (for the purposes of gamedev, at least) represent the game universe where things exist. Vectors are objects that model certain aspects of our game world. Pragmatically, we often use them to represent *points in space* and *physical forces*. There are some wonderful mathematical properties of (and operations we can perform on) vectors that benefit us while making games.

For example, combining vectors is an elegant way to implement physical forces (jumping force + gravity force = player trajectory). Or another example, if you apply the algebraic operation known as the *dot product* on vectors that represent the positions of, say, a *bad guy* and *the player*, the result will tell you if the bad guy is *facing* the player. Which has some obvious use cases for enemy AI. Vectors are a way of neatly modeling the world around us in code.

Vectors are often visualized by an arrow that has a length (called its **magnitude**) and a direction. Throughout this book, we've been representing points in screen space using the 2D *vector* `pos`. This has an `x` and `y` component that together show where an entity should be drawn. If we wanted to, we could also consider `pos` a vector that starts at the origin (often written `(0, 0)`, where `x = 0` and `y = 0`) and points to `x` and `y`:

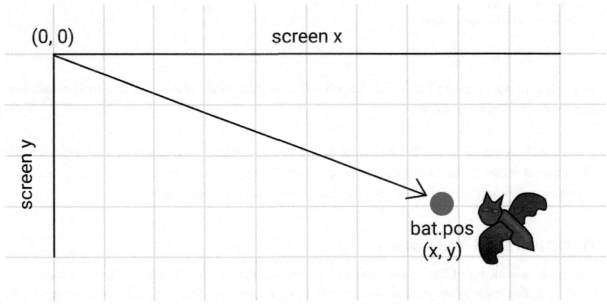

6-5. Position as a vector

The line from the origin (0, 0) to (x, y) is the *magnitude* (length) of the vector. An advantage of treating `pos` as a vector is that we can abstract common vector operations into a reusable library. We no longer need to apply every operation separately to the `x` and `y` components. We write less code, and our intentions are clearer.

So let's make a vector library that will encapsulate the concept of vectors. In this section, we'll create the library (a library inside our library!) and add some helpful methods. Then, in the rest of the chapter, we'll use the vector library to simplify and extend our physics code. The library will live in `Pop` in the `utils` folder, and will henceforth be known as `Vec.js`. At its core, it's a container that (optionally) sets `x` and `y` values:

```
class Vec {
  constructor(x = 0, y = 0) {
    this.x = x;
    this.y = y;
  }
}
```

Throughout the book, we've created many objects that would be better modeled as a `Vec`. The most obvious is the `pos` of our base library elements. We can store `pos` as a `Vec`, rather than maintain the individual `x` and `y` properties ourselves. For example, let's convert a `Sprite`'s `pos` into a vector:

```
import Vec from "./utils/Vec.js";

class Sprite {
  constructor(texture) {
    this.pos = new Vec();
    ...
  }
}
```

For the moment, nothing has changed: a sprite's position can still be altered by modifying `pos.x` or `pos.y`. Any time we need a point-like object such as `pos`, we can create a `new Vec()`. If we want to default it to a value, we can pass that in at creation time: `new Vec(10, 10)`.

Vectors can be used for more than just modeling points. A vector often represents an entity with a *direction* and a *magnitude*. In the previous image, you can see that the vector's origin point is `(0, 0)`. The direction is the *angle* of the hypotenuse of the right triangle formed from the origin and the *point*. The magnitude is the *length of the hypotenuse*. Sound familiar? It's Pythagoras again—just like our `math.distance` function. Determining the magnitude of a vector comes in handy, so it becomes the first helper method on `Vec`:

```
mag() {
  const { x, y } = this;
  return Math.sqrt(x * x + y * y);
}
```

The `Vec` class can also be extended with methods that *manipulate vectors*. A simple but useful one for us is `set` , which updates both components at the same time:

```
set(x, y) {
  this.x = x;
  this.y = y;
  return this;
}
```

Any `Sprite` 's position can be updated with a single call— `pos.set(10, 10)` . Not a huge difference, but conceptually we're now thinking about position in terms of a single tangible concept (and we can set `pos` with a one-liner, instead of two!).

 Enabling Method Chaining

Many of the methods in the `Vec` library will return `this` . `this` represents the current instance of the `Vec` . By returning itself, we end up back where we started after the function is complete. From here we can call another function, and another. For example, `pos.set(x, y).add(velocity)` would first set the position and then add a velocity vector to the original position. This *method chaining* can result in a very readable API when we need to perform multiple operations in a sequence.

Many times we want to set an entity's location to some *existing value* (for example, its spawn location). A bullet should originate at the player's current location when they press fire, or a bad guy should spawn at a location defined in our level map editor. Rather than setting positions by hand, we could *copy* an existing vector:

```
copy({x, y}) {
  this.x = x;
  this.y = y;
  return this;
}
```

The `copy` method works with *any* object that has an `x` and `y` property (it doesn't have to be an instance of `Vec`). Just like `set` , we can now use a single call rather than setting properties manually:

```
map.spawns.bats.forEach(spawn => {
  const bat = bats.add(new Bat());
  bat.pos.copy(spawn);
});
```

I think that looks a lot nicer. Let's take it even further. Once our `Vec` library becomes more powerful, we'll want to be able to use *any* object (that has an `x` and `y` property) as a vector source. We *could* create a new `Vec` and use `copy` to set the values with `new Vec().copy(objWithXY)`, but it's a bit ugly: it doesn't clearly show our intent to create a new `Vec` from a source. A nicer solution is to provide a shortcut (via a static method) at the top of the `Vec.js` class:

```
static from (v) {
  return new Vec().copy(v);
}
```

Then we can create a vector via `Vec.from(objWithXY)` without requiring the `new` operator. Handy!

Static Methods and Properties

Static methods and properties are shared between all instances of the class. As a property, this makes sense when all instances need to globally share some information (perhaps a count of all created instances). For methods, it's nice in cases where you don't need access to the instance properties, such as our `from` helper.

Having a raft of ways of initialized vector values, it's finally time to do some vector manipulation. The most common vector operation is to add two vectors together. What doing **vector addition** *means* depends on the use of the vector itself. If we're using it to denote a position in space, then addition is a *translation* from a current position to a new position. However, if the vector is a force, then it's the *combination* of forces.

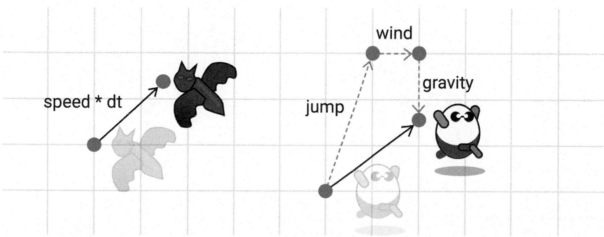

6-6. Vector addition

To add two vectors together, we sum the corresponding `x` and `y` components. Our API accepts a vector as an argument (actually, anything with `x` and `y` properties) and adds this to the current vector. This *modifies* the current vector:

```
add({ x, y }) {
  this.x += x;
  this.y += y;
  return this;
}
```

We can make a complimentary `subtract` method too. If we want to translate a sprite, we can add or subtract a translation vector to it. For example, we currently do this every time after we check for tile-map collisions. The result from `wallslide` is the *amount to translate* the sprite by—in the form of an object with `x` and `y` components that we can now treat as a vector:

```
const response = wallslide(this, map, xo, yo);
pos.add(response);
```

Another common operation is *vector scaling*. **Scaling** a vector means to make its magnitude larger or smaller by some factor. For example, if we had a vector `Vec(5, 0)` and wanted to scale it by a factor of two, we'd expect to end up with the result `Vec(10, 0)`. The magnitude of the vector has doubled.

To calculate the new vector, we multiply it by a scaling ratio. Because we want it to scale proportionately on both axes, the multiplication factor is a *scalar value* (single number) rather than a vector:

```
multiply(s) {
  this.x *= s;
  this.y *= s;
  return this;
}
```

To test that our vector has been correctly scaled, we can measure its magnitude before and after scaling:

```
const vec = new Vec(5, 0);
console.log(vec.mag()); // 5
vec.multiply(2);
console.log(vec.mag()); // 10
```

But what does it *mean* to scale a vector? Again, it depends on the context. If the vector is a force, scaling it will either strengthen or weaken the force. If the vector is a position, scaling will *project* the position along the path from the origin to the current location. For example, we could find the midpoint between two entities by adding their positions and then scaling by half:

```
player.pos
  .add(badguy.pos)
  .multiply(0.5);
```

The midpoint between two entities might be of practical use in your game. Perhaps you want to show a warning indicator half-way between you and some approaching aliens, or deploy a fancy shield that blocks incoming missiles. However, there's an issue with our operation. The `add` function *modifies* the original vector. Calculating the midpoint would result in the player's sprite being teleported to the midpoint! This is because our vector library is *mutable*: all changes are done in place on existing vectors. If we want to use the result somewhere else, we first need to *clone* the original vector:

```
clone() {
  return Vec.from(this);
}
```

Cloning will create a new `Vec` object and initialize it with the current `x` and `y` values:

```
const midpoint = player.pos
  .clone()
  .add(badguy.pos)
  .multiply(0.5);
```

Normalizing, and the Dot Product

There are several additional operations that are frequently required when making games. One is the concept of *normalizing* a vector. **Normalizing** scales a vector so that its magnitude is exactly 1. To do this, take the current magnitude and divide each axis by that amount:

```
normalize() {
  const mag = this.mag();
  if (mag > 0) {
    this.x /= mag;
    this.y /= mag;
  }
  return this;
}
```

The result of normalizing is a **unit vector** (because it would touch the perimeter of a **unit circle**—a circle with radius 1). Normalizing gives us the *essence* of the direction of a vector. Once you have the essence, you can manipulate this in consistent ways. For example, a normalized vector can be rescaled to get a specific magnitude in the given direction. Here's how to find the point exactly 50 pixels away from the player, in the *direction* the bad guy:

```
player.pos.clone()
  .add(badguys.pos)
  .normalize()
  .multiply(50)
```

The last operation we'll look at is a weird one, but one that often appears in AI behaviors—the *dot product*. The **dot product** is the *sums of the products* of corresponding components. It's calculated like this:

```
dot({x, y}) {
  return this.x * x + this.y * y;
}
```

The result of the dot product is the x components multiplied together, plus the y components multiplied together—a scalar value. Intuitively, this might seem like a strange idea, but it has some interesting properties with regards to the angle between the two vectors.

When two vectors are pointing in the same direction, their dot product is *positive*. This seems reasonable enough: if you took the dot product of a vector with *itself*, it would be the squared length of the vector. The opposite case also seems reasonable: when the vectors point away from each other, the result will be negative. And the point where they're exactly perpendicular to each other? There's nothing in common between the vectors, so the dot product returns 0!

The dot product is proportionate to how closely the vectors are pointing in the same direction. This sounds valuable when we think about applying it in our games. "If the bad guy's facing away from the player, wander around. If they're facing the player, ATTACK!"

The Need for Speed (and Direction)

Having implemented some vector manipulation, it's time to see what we can do with our new skills. Many of the properties and forces we'll use to simulate the world around us can be nicely modeled with vectors. "Roughly" simulating the world is our goal here. Mario doesn't fall back to the ground at a rate of 9.80665 meters per second for a reason: it's not as fun!

Unless you're trying to create a realistic simulation, you should consider tweaking and exaggerating your physics to make things exciting and compelling. If you're playing a futuristic racing game and the cars move as they do on Earth, it feels good ... but if the cars slide around and accelerate like a *rocket*, it feels awesome. If the cars handle like souped-up old jalopies, you'd better have some other interesting mechanic (get it?) to make it enjoyable!

6-7. The preposterously detailed engine physics of My Summer Car

 Pausing Bravedigger

For the next few sections, we'll put *Bravedigger* on the back burner and start fresh with a minimal test project. The goal of this project is to implement and validate a physics system with velocity, acceleration, gravity, and friction. Once we've confirmed our system is solid, we'll integrate it back into our physics-based platform game.

Velocity

It all starts with *velocity*. **Velocity** is a vector quantity that describes an object's speed and direction. We've been setting the player's velocity all along—based on a combination of the user's keyboard controls and a constant "speed" amount. Because we independently update an entity's `x` and `y` coordinates, we've been able to move in any direction. As we switch to a physics-based approach, we'll stop *directly* modifying `pos` and instead apply a "force" that will *indirectly* affect it.

Our project will feature a brave test pilot—an intrepid `Sprite` called `CrashTestDummy.js`. `CrashTestDummy` is our guinea pig while we work out kinks in the physics system. The main `GameScreen` consists of a `CrashTestDummy`, along with some debugging `Text` for displaying timing information to validate our physics values.

3.000 (266.67)

6-8. Crash test dummy, rolling

```
class CrashTestDummy extends TileSprite {
  constructor(vel) {
    super(texture, 48, 48);
    this.vel = new Vec(vel, 0);
  }
}
```

The key here is the creation of the *velocity vector*, `vel`. It's a `Vec` initialized with a `y` value of 0 (so it won't move up or down) and an `x` value assigned from the outside world. This will be the speed of our `CrashTestDummy` test subject.

The velocity of an object is the *rate of change of its position with respect to time*. To calculate the new position of an entity (to apply the vector force and displace our sprite) we add the individual components of the vectors, multiplied by time, to the original position.

```
update(dt) {
  const { pos, vel } = this;

  // Move in the direction of the path
  pos.x += vel.x * dt;
  pos.y += vel.y * dt;
}
```

 Using an Old Approach

We're back to individually updating properties again (rather than using `.add()` and `.multiply()`). Why? Multiplying the velocity vector by `dt` would mutate `vel`, but we need it to remain unchanged. We could clone it with `pos.add(vel.clone().multiply(dt))`, but then we have to create a new `Vec` object every frame, and the result is harder to read. I just decided to do it the old way.

To test velocity within our new project, in `GameScreen` create a new `CrashTestDummy` and assign it a velocity based on the width of the screen. By doing this, we know how long the `Sprite` should take to get from one side of the screen to the other, and we can set a timer to confirm that our velocity calculations are correct:

```
const velocity = this.w / 3; // Should be three seconds to cross the screen
this.ctd = this.add(new CrashTestDummy(velocity));
```

Every frame, we check if the `CrashTestDummy` has made it to the finish line. If so, we stop the timer running. (I also added in a reset switch so you can hit the space bar to re-start the test.)

```
if (ctd.pos.x >= w) {
  this.running = false;
}
if (running) {
  this.time += dt;
  timer.text = `${this.time.toFixed(3)}`;
}
```

This looks correct. Good enough at least! Our `CrashTestDummy` takes exactly three seconds to get from the left to the right side of the 800-pixel-wide screen, at a velocity of 266.67 pixels per second. Try modifying the frames per second (`STEP` size) in our main game loop to ensure we're running correctly at all frame rates. (Spoiler: this also seems fine.)

Velocity Bounce

The sprite's position is now the result of *applying velocity*. If we don't modify velocity after we initially set it, `CrashTestDummy` will fly off the screen, never to return. It would be nice if it bounced back when it hit an edge. Reflecting an arbitrary angle (bouncing off a surface) can sometimes be tricky—but not so much in our simple world. Because the screen edges are *perpendicular*, we only need to invert the entity's velocity on the axis that it collides with. Velocity can be inverted by multiplying it by -1:

```
// Bounce off the walls
if (pos.x < 0 || pos.x > bounds.w - w) {
  vel.x *= -1;
}
if (pos.y < 0 || pos.y > bounds.h - h) {
  vel.y *= -1;
}
```

The `bounds` is the bounding area of the entire game screen. We'll make the main game area quite large, and pass the bounds to the `CrashTestDummy` when it's instantiated. Our `CrashTestDummy` can now bounce. To test this, have the `CrashTestDummy` choose its own position (within the bounds) and velocity (between -300 and 300 pixels per second on both axes).

Because the velocities are random for both x and y, it will also move in a random direction:

```
this.pos.set(bounds.w / 2, bounds.h / 2);
this.vel = new Vec(
  math.rand(-300, 300),
  math.rand(-300, 300));
```

Now we can apply the sacred rule for showing off gamedev features: "Why have one, when you can have 30?" More is more! Add a pod of crash test dummies to a `Container` in `GameScreen` and set them free:

```
const bounds = { x: 0, y: 0, w: this.w, h: this.h };
for (let i = 0; i < 30; i++) {
  this.add(new CrashTestDummy(bounds));
}
```

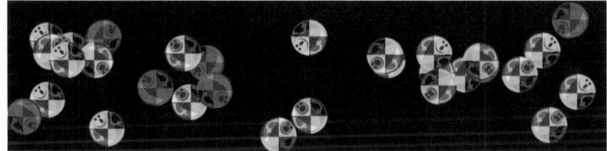

6-9. Bouncing crash test dummies

Having *direction* controlled via *velocity* starts to yield some fruit.

Acceleration

Moving things with velocity alone is fine, but *acceleration* is how we make things supercool. Where velocity represented the rate of change of position, acceleration represents the *rate of change of velocity*. Rather than just adding a constant to an entity's position, we add the amount of acceleration to velocity and accumulate it every frame. This accumulation is what gives the feeling of naturally "speeding up":

```
this.vel = new Vec();
this.acc = new Vec();
```

Acceleration is a vector just like velocity. It can be applied independently in the x and y directions. For our initial tests, we'll only apply it in the horizontal direction inside `CrashTestDummy`'s `update` (at a rate of 200 pixels per second):

```
const ACCELERATION = 200;
acc.x += ACCELERATION;

// Update velocity and position
...

acc.set(0, 0);
```

At the end of the update loop, `acc` is reset back to 0. Otherwise, we'd be accelerating acceleration! Now we can do our physics integration:

```
vel.x += acc.x * dt;
vel.y += acc.y * dt;

pos.x += vel.x * dt;
pos.y += vel.y * dt;
```

Acceleration is the rate of change of velocity with delta time, and velocity is the rate of change of position with delta time. First we add acceleration to velocity, then update position from velocity as usual. Now on each frame the value of velocity becomes larger, rather than remaining a constant. The `CrashTestDummy` starts very slowly, getting faster and faster until it hits the other side of the screen, then rebounds back elastically.

It looks pretty groovy—and that's often good enough. But to ensure we're accumulating velocity correctly, we could test it against the physics formula for displacement from acceleration— $s = ut + \frac{1}{2}at^2$ —where s is where our sprite should end up on the screen, u is the initial velocity, a is acceleration and t is time. Because we start from a dead stop, ut can be ignored, and we end up with this:

```
const expectedPos = 0.5 * ACCELERATION * this.time * this.time;
```

In the game screen, we'll add a timer and some text and freeze it after two seconds to see if we're correct. In our tests (running at 60 frames per second) we saw that, after 2.017 seconds, the sprite had moved 410 pixels. Plugging that into the equation gives `0.5 * 200 * 2.017 * 2.017 = 406`. That seems pretty close—only a few pixels off. But still, not perfect. And if we try dropping the frame rate in `Game.js`, the margin of error gets larger.

Integration

The reason for the discrepancy is due to our method of *integration*. Adding acceleration with time to velocity, then velocity with time to position, is called the "Semi-implicit Euler method[1]". It's simple, efficient, and matches our verbal definitions of acceleration nicely, but it's only as accurate as the delta step time, and is subject to rounding errors.

 More Advanced Physics

> If you want to build a serious physics engine, you should study integration algorithms like Vertlet integration and the 4th-order Runge-Kutta method (RK4). These are stable and will work well even when it comes time to implement advanced physics topics.

We don't need our engine to be too advanced, but we'd like it to work even consistently at very low frame rates. We'll tweak our integration to use an approach called *Velocity Vertlet* integration. Because this is something we'll want to do on many of our entities, it's time to drop some physics into *Pop* in a new file called *utils/physics.js* :

```
function integrate(e, dt) {
  const { pos, vel, acc } = e;
  // integrate!
  ...
  acc.set(0, 0);
}
export default {
  integrate
};
```

This method is doing exactly what we did earlier. It's a function that accepts an *entity* and the *delta time* that has elapsed and then applies acceleration and velocity to position (and finally resets acceleration to 0). Before this, we perform the Velocity Vertlet integration:

```
const vx = vel.x + acc.x * dt;
const vy = vel.y + acc.y * dt;
const x = (vel.x + vx) / 2 * dt;
const y = (vel.y + vy) / 2 * dt;
pos.add({ x, y });
vel.set(vx, vy);
```

This integration method looks a bit hairier than Euler's method, but it's not too different. It's still adding acceleration by time to velocity, then velocity by time to position. But now it's *averaging* the acceleration over frames—applying half now, and the other half next frame. The position update is calculated in the middle of an integration step, rather than on the edge, resulting in more stable updates even at very low frame rates.

Now that we can easily integrate, we should also make it easy to add forces to an entity. The

---

[1.] https://en.wikipedia.org/wiki/Euler_method

`CrashTestDummy` is currently powered by a mysterious force pushing on it to the right, and that's it. The beauty of controlling entities via forces is that they can easily be *combined* to make more interesting results. For example, the mysterious force on `CrashTestDummy` is probably a jetpack, but crash test dummies could also be subject to gravitational forces—or perhaps intermittent wind forces. Each can be added independently without knowing about the others.

For us, applying a force simply means adding it to the amount of acceleration to calculate. If you think back to physics classes, you may recall Newton's Second Law of Motion: $F = ma$. Force equals mass times acceleration. If we want to figure out acceleration, we have to solve for it. Acceleration equals force divided by mass. Most of the time, we'll omit mass from the entity and just assume everything has mass `1`, but feel free to play around and changing it!

```
function applyForce (e, force) {
  const { acc, mass = 1 } = e;
  acc.x += force.x / mass;
  acc.y += force.y / mass;
};
```

Notice that we *add* the result to `acc`. Acceleration is accumulated with each force we apply. That's why we needed to reset `acc` to 0 at the end of the integration, rather than just assign it fresh at the start of each loop. Each force is applied, then finally we integrate:

```
// Jetpack!
physics.applyForce(this, { x: 200, y: 0 });

// Gravity!
physics.applyForce(this, { x: 0, y: 100 });

physics.integrate(this, dt);
```

Impulse Forces

Accelerate is slowly build up velocity over time. Not all forces work this way: if you get shot out of a cannon, you don't take much time to get to your maximum speed! In our games, we'll frequently want to give an entity an instant boost to have them moving at the correct rate. We do this with an **impulse force**. Rather than something that accumulates over frames, it's a one-off injection:

```
const applyImpulse = (e, force, dt) => {
  applyForce(e, { x: force.x / dt, y: force.y / dt });
};
```

Applying an impulse is similar to a regular force, except you must also pass in the delta time for the current frame. The `applyImpulse` method removes the time that would normally get multiplied inside the `integrate` method; the force gets directly transformed into velocity. You use an impulse wherever you want a one-off kick, rather than a constant buildup:

```
if (mouse.released) {
  physics.applyImpulse(this, {
    x: 400,
    y: 0
  }, dt);
}
```

For example, a bullet will instantly be moving at its maximum speed as soon as the player clicks the fire button. Applying an impulse uses the regular `applyForce` under the hood. Therefore, other forces that affect the bullet (impulses or regular) still work as expected.

Friction

Without an opposing force, our sprites would keep accelerating and drifting though the void of space forever. Even with small amounts of acceleration, that will quickly become uncontrollably fast! Something needs to slow us down, and that something will be *friction*. For games that aren't set in space, we need to calculate the friction generated when an entity is in contact with a surface.

The formula for friction is $F = -1\mu Nv$, where F is friction, μ is a coefficient for resistance of the surface, N is the *normal vector* (perpendicular force) of the surface, and v is the velocity vector. That's a lot of things to do just to slow us down a bit. Time to "fake it until we make it" again (we'll figure it out correctly in the next section).

How about, instead of real friction, we temporarily violate our rule of messing with `vel` directly and apply a **dampening force**. It's not really a force as we know it; it's just a trick to scale down the final velocity vector by a value from 0 to 1. The closer the value is to 1, the lower the friction. (We'll put physics constants at the top of the file so you can quickly tweak them.)

```
const FRICTION = 0.95;
...
vel.multiply(FRICTION)
```

The value you choose *radically* changes how the sprites move. Very close to 1 feels like you're skating on ice. Lower, and you're suddenly stuck in mud. You also may have to increase the acceleration power to fight the opposing friction. Striking a perfect balance between power and friction is the key to making something that handles nicely. Optimum values vary dramatically depending on the requirements of your game.

Figuring Out the Best Values

Figuring out the best values for our faux-physics system is great fun and can result in some happy, unexpected accidents. Don't forget the tip "double or halve it!" when hunting for interesting settings.

More Accurate Friction

The dampening method for applying friction is simple and easy, but really it's a cheat. Gamedev is all about cheating *when you can get away with it*, but there are some serious problems with our fake friction. A big one is that it doesn't consider the timestep at all. If you're running at a low frame rate, friction will be calculated less often, and the sprites will slide around more.

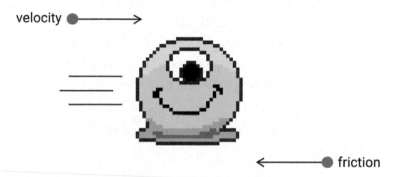

6-10. Friction as a force

Let's move closer to the original equation for calculating kinetic friction force, `F = -1μNv` . `-1` is the inverse. `μ` is fine too: it's the coefficient constant we want to resist by. Higher equals more resistance. `v` is the *direction* of velocity. The only thing left is `N` , the surface normal. In the image above, the surface normal is a vector pointing perpendicular to the ground. Our ground is flat, so the surface normal points straight up and doesn't affect the horizontal force. We'll ignore it.

The idea is to get the vector that's pointing in the opposite direction to the sprite (that's why it's -1), and apply a set resistance force in that direction. We can find the "opposite direction" by scaling the velocity vector by -1: `vel.clone().multiply(-1)` . If we used that, the equal-and-opposite force would stop the sprite dead. To apply a specific `μ` value, we first need to `normalize` to get the unit vector and *then* multiply by our friction coefficient:

```
const friction = vel.clone()
  .multiply(-1)
  .normalize()
  .multiply(200);

physics.applyForce(this, friction);
```

Velocity isn't being modified directly, but through a force. Our entities will slide the same regardless of frame rates. Other real-world forces can be emulated in the same manner. The beauty of a physics-based system is this ability to combine simple rules to define the overall complex behavior of your game world. In many games, you'll just want to keep things simple: friction, gravity, maybe some air resistance. But you get to be God here, and you write the rules. Don't forget to go crazy from time to time.

Gravity-based Platformer

We have all the tools to integrate physics into our games. As we saw earlier, gravity is a downward force (a force with no `x` component). Of course, it doesn't *have* to be downwards, or constant; you can make gravity work however you want! But now, thanks to friction, when the `CrashTestDummy` reflects off the bottom of the screen it will struggle to return to its original position. Force is being dissipated and our crash test dummies "bounce".

```
const friction = vel.clone().multiply(-1).normalize().multiply(200);
const gravity = { x: 0, y: 500 };

physics.applyForce(this, friction);
physics.applyForce(this, gravity);
physics.integrate(this, dt);
```

Having covered velocity, acceleration, and friction, we can reintroduce these concepts into *Bravedigger*. Our game's forces of nature will affect how the player moves. However, forces are not the *only* things that affect the player in the games we've been making.

Our level's tile map is made of solid bricks; gravity shouldn't be strong enough to push us right through the ground. We need our physics integration to *work together* with our `wallslide` (and related collision detection functions) to put entities in their correct spots.

Skipping the Physics

You can think of the `wallslide` collision detection method as being the opposing *ground reaction force* to our character's *contact force*. But it's not implemented as a force at all: it's just cheating and using our old system of modifying the `pos` variable manually. You *could* model it with a real force—but honestly, because of the simple nature of a platformer world, it's *much* easier to get the precise feel you're after by taking manual control.

Remember that our collision detection algorithms work by us providing a displacement amount we *want* to move. In return, it tells us how much we *can* move. Rather than updating `pos` directly in `integrate`, we need to get the amount we *want* to move back from it so we can pass it to `wallslide`:

```
const vx = vel.x + acc.x * dt;
const vy = vel.y + acc.y * dt;
const x = (vel.x + vx) / 2 * dt;
const y = (vel.y + vy) / 2 * dt;
vel.set(vx, vy);
acc.set(0, 0);
return { x, y };
```

The result from the integration is where physics thinks we *should* go. `Wallslide` considers this and returns its own opinion. *That* is the displacement amount we add to `pos`:

```
let r = physics.integrate(this, dt);
r = wallslide(this, map, r.x, r.y);
pos.add(r);
```

With physics and tile-map collision working together, the only remaining challenge is choosing the physics constants that feel good in the game. It can be "fun" getting values that work exactly how you'd like. It's the double-edged sword of using a physics system: having the world dictate how everything moves is magical and powerful, but comes with the cost of surrendering precise and exact control.

It's best not to be too dogmatic. Where possible, you shouldn't modify velocities and positions directly … but gamedev rules were meant to be broken! If you *need* to stop velocity dead in its tracks to get a sensation or effect you desire, then break the rules. If it feels good, do it.

Billiard Ball Physics

Adding basic physical properties to your games gives fluidity to platformers and shoot-'em-ups. But it can be taken further! If you take the simulation further—and your game's core mechanics rely on it—then you have a **physics game**. In physics games, generally *all* forces and responses are determined by the physics engine. (For example, we don't delegate responsibility out to a `wallslide`, like a collision handler.)

Implementing a system to handle arbitrary shapes in our library (like polygon sprites and convex terrain) is beyond the scope of this book. (In the next section, we'll cheat and use a third-party library to do it for us.) But if we impose some restrictions, we can implement some nice physics-based mechanics without getting into "hard math" territory.

Our primary restriction is that we have to treat all entities as *circles*, rather than rectangles. Circles are just easier to deal with: we don't have to worry about detecting collisions with rotated rectangles. With that in mind, we'll implement a simulation of balls moving on a billiard table, pinging and reflecting off each other as they collide.

The setup will be a handful of crash test dummies placed randomly around the screen:

```
this.bounds = { x: 0, y: 0, w: this.w, h: this.h };
this.balls = this.add(new Container());
for (let i = 0; i < 30; i++) {
  const b = this.balls.add(new CrashTestDummy(this.bounds));
  b.pos.set(
    math.rand(48, this.w - 96),
    math.rand(48, this.h - 96)
  );
}
```

The bulk of the collision detection and resolution is done in the `GameScreen`'s update. Here we loop over all of the balls and check them for collisions against *all other balls*. We do with this in a nested *for* loop:

```
const balls = this.balls.children;
for (let i = 0; i < balls.length; i++) {
  const a = balls[i];
  for (let j = i + 1; j < balls.length; j++) {
    const b = balls[j];
    // Check for collisions
    ...
  }
}
```

This nested loop is an efficient way to check each child against all others. The inner loop starts from `i + 1` so that we only check each pair of balls against each other once. Now we can do collision detection and resolution. The first step is detection:

```
// Check for collisions
const diff = b.pos.clone().subtract(a.pos);
if (diff.mag() > a.radius + b.radius) {
  continue;
}
```

This is our standard circle-based collision test. We say there's a "collision" if the magnitude of the position offsets (*a.pos* and *b.pos*) are less than the *sum of the circle's radii*—just like our shoot-'em-up in Chapter 3. If there's no collision, we'll move on to the next pair of balls.

Collision Resolution

Now comes the tricky part. The two entities are colliding. Up till now, when things have collided we've made them explode and die—problem solved. But now we need them to react less violently. We need to adjust their positions so they're not colliding, and adjust their velocities so they're moving away from each other—in the correct direction, with the correct speed.

The first step is to separate the two entities so they no longer overlap. To do this, take the vector between them, find the point exactly in the middle of that vector, then adjust each position relative to the midpoint such that they're no longer overlapping.

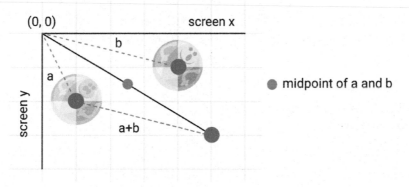

6-11. Finding the midpoint

To acquire the midpoint between the two balls, add the positions together and divide by two:

```
const mid = a.pos.clone().add(b.pos).divide(2);
const normal = diff.normalize();
```

To move the balls apart, first normalize the *diff* vector between the balls and displace them *away* from the midpoint. Remember that normalizing gives us only the *direction* between the two points, with its magnitude scaled to 1. We can use this to move an exact number of pixels in that direction. Multiplying by *radius* gives us the correct amount to move. For the first ball, we *add* this to the midpoint; for the second ball, we *subtract* it. In pseudo-code it would look like this:

```
a.pos = mid - (a.radius * normal)
b.pos = mid + (b.radius * normal)
```

If we did these calculations with our vector library, there would be lot of cloning for the midpoint and normal vectors. This would be costly in terms of unnecessary objects, and wouldn't read very nicely either. It's another case where it's probably better to do it ourselves:

```
a.pos.set(mid.x - normal.x * a.radius, mid.y - normal.y * a.radius);
b.pos.set(mid.x + normal.x * b.radius, mid.y + normal.y * a.radius);
```

The *a* entity has been moved a bit in one direction, the *b* in the other. Because they both moved apart *radius* pixels, they no longer overlap and sit just next to each other. Now the balls are in the right spot, but their velocities still have them moving on their original courses. To rectify this, we take the *difference* between their current velocities, *projected along the normal vector* between them:

```
let power = (a.vel.x - b.vel.x) * normal.x;
power += (a.vel.y - b.vel.y) * normal.y;
```

Taking the sum of the axes' power, we alternatively add and subtract it to the entities' velocities—just as we did for adjusting the positions. They now reflect off each other and ricochet away.

```
const displacement = normal.multiply(power);
a.vel.subtract(displacement);
b.vel.add(displacement);
```

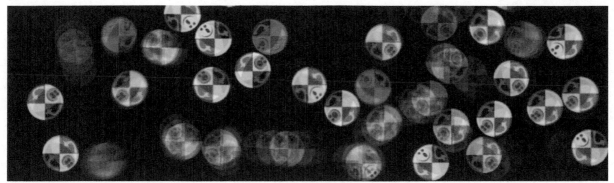

6-12. Bouncy balls

Using principles of vector manipulation, we can create some satisfying real-world effects. At the very least we could make a good game of snooker.

Polar Coordinates

We've seen how using vector properties can help us model real-world moving objects ... but what do the components of our velocity vectors actually represent? At what speed is something moving if its velocity vector is `{x: 150, y: 85}` ? At what angle is it traveling if its velocity is `{x: 0.7, y: 0.7}` ?

In our bouncing billiard balls example, some sprites were moving at, say, a 30 degree angle. So there must be *some* value of `x` and `y` we can use to move in *any* desired direction. Yes! It turns out it's about `{x: 0.866, y: -0.5}` to move at 30 degrees at a speed of 1. This `x/y` representation is referred to as the **Cartesian coordinate system** (specifically as the **rectangular coordinate system** because we're in two dimensions).

In the real world, we don't talk in terms of `x` s and `y` s. We like to think about things in terms of more familiar angles and speeds. We need a different representation—namely, the **polar coordinate system**.

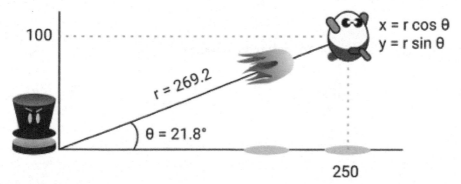

6-13. Polar and Cartesian coordinates

Thankfully, converting between the two systems is straightforward. When we have a scalar that is the radius (the magnitude, or speed to move by) and an angle (in radians), we retrieve Cartesian components like so:

```
x = r cos θ
y = r sin θ
```

And when we want to convert *back* from Cartesian to polar coordinates, there are two distinct operations—both of which we've used before in the "Moving, and Shooting, Towards a Target" section from <ins>Chapter 5</ins>:

```
r = √ x² + y²
θ = atan2(y, x)
```

Using Pythagoras' theorem, we can calculate the hypotenuse of the triangle formed (which represents the radius, or speed, or distance) by our coordinates. This just happens to be our `math.distance` function. Similarly, the *angle* is calculated by taking the arc tangent of the coordinates, and is our `math.angle` function. We can use whichever representation is more natural for the task at hand:

```
this.dir = math.randf(Math.PI * 2);
this.speed = math.rand(50, 150);
```

In this example, our `CrashTestDummy` sprites are assigned a random direction between 0 and 2π (0 to 360 degrees), and a random speed. They aren't moved by a velocity vector, but via their *angles and speed*. We use the formula above to convert them into `x` and `y` values to add to position:

```
pos.add({
  x: Math.cos(dir) * speed * dt,
  y: Math.sin(dir) * speed * dt
});
```

And we'll sync the sprite's rotation to match the direction:

```
this.rotation = this.dir + Math.PI / 4;
```

Offsetting Rotation

The `rotation` property is offset by the amount $\pi\,/\,4$. This is because the graphics file was drawn with "up" facing 45 degrees away from 0 radians. The offset syncs the sprites so they're facing forwards as they move.

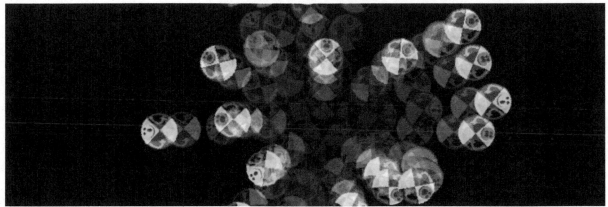

6-14. Polar crash test dummies

`x` and `y` versus speed and angle are two ways of representing the same thing. Which you choose to work with depends on the situation. For example, polar coordinates are more natural when we want our entities to be controlled by steering, like a car: turning the steering wheel doesn't move the vehicle, it only changes its direction.

```
this.dir += controls.x * 0.8 * dt;
```

Increasing or decreasing the `dir` property is all we have to do to steer! If you combine this with the acceleration we implemented earlier, you can create some extremely satisfying car sliding mechanics.

Physics All the Things

"Hey, hey, MomPop Games!" It's Guy. Again. "Did you recover from your false start? Got a game to show me?" he enquires as he takes over your laptop and starts playing. "Hmm, what's with all this platform-game nonsense? What kind of sport is that?"

He looks at your blank stare.

"I told you the theme was 'Let's get PHYSICAL', right? It's supposed to be about *sports*. That's the pun—physics, physical ... Sports. You get it? Oh man, that's a shame. You should really read the website instead of listening to me, you know."

He has a point.

You consider your situation—having to start all over *again* at this late stage in the competition. It'd be hard to transform *Bravedigger* into some kind of sport. You reply, "Oh, this—no, this is just the base for an idea I'm fleshing out. It's, um, golf, but with … penguins. Penguin Golf. It's called *Pengolfin'*, and it's fully physics-based."

He looks at you suspiciously, with a raised eyebrow, as he rises and silently moonwalks out the door. Forget about him, we still have time to get an entry done for this game jam! We just need a little bit of third-party help.

Physics Libraries

Recreating accurate, real-world physics is not an easy task. So far, our efforts have been fairly simple approximations of how things "kind of" move. If we were to continue to build on our custom system, we'd quickly hit some really difficult (albeit, quite interesting) problems around collision resolution, and how to accurately detect collisions between rotated entities.

If we had more time, we might start delving into these meaty topics (look up the *Separating Axis Theorem* if you're keen)—but we're in the middle of a game jam, so we we'll repeat a well-worn gamedev adage: "Make games, not engines!"

There are some excellent JavaScript options for us when it comes to simulating a *rigid-body system*. **Rigid-body** means the points that make up the object don't get deformed by external forces—but we'll think of it as "our player object is solid, has mass, and will react appropriately when hit by another object". Many game frameworks have real physics options baked in, so we'll need a stand-alone library that we can integrate with Pop.

 Do You Need a Real Physics Engine?

You should consider carefully if your game really needs a full-blown physics engine. They simulate chaos; they're unpredictable. If you've ever played *Angry Birds*, you'll likely have encountered a time where the game declares "LEVEL FAILED" even though you *know* the teetering pillars will topple given a couple more seconds. With a physics system, it's hard to know when things are stable, and it's hard to control *exactly* how everything will interact together.

One of the most common physics libraries known in 2D game development is a C++ project called *Box2D*[2]. This has been ported to many languages, including several efforts in JavaScript. Of these, *Planck.js*[3] is a well maintained effort.

However, I feel that *Box2D* tends to feel very "C++"-ish and verbose in JavaScript. There are a few more modern and idiomatic options available to us. *P2.js*[4] and *Matter.js*http://brm.io/matter-js/ are two great projects that have been under active development for a long time. We're going to run with Matter.js. It's well maintained, fun to use, and easy to integrate. It's important to note that the basic concepts and features apply to nearly all physics engines. Once you master one, it doesn't require a lot of effort to get up to speed with any other.

Penguin Golf

We don't have a lot of time left in the game jam, so we need to think fast. Something simple, but fun and addictive. *Pengolfin'* will involve a side-view, mountainous golf course. The player will angle and fire their penguin and try to get it in the hole in as few "strokes" as possible. To make it more interesting, we'll also make randomly generated terrain. To maintain the penguin theme, the terrain will actually be icebergs—so badly aimed strokes will land the penguin ball in the ocean, after which it's returned to the tee.

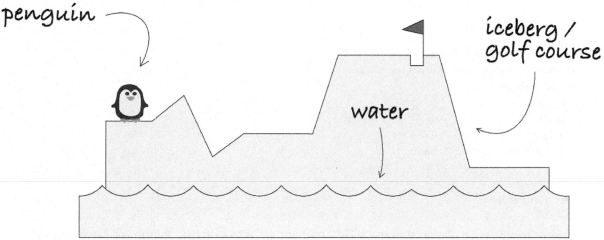

6-15. Pengolfin' sketch

Matter.js

To get a feel for what a physics engine can do, we're going to start with a minimal version without even using our Pop library at all. Matter.js includes its own renderer that's perfect for debugging. Once we're satisfied it can produce the results we want, we'll figure out how to sync up the Matter.js models with our sprites to be rendered with *our* renderer. That's essentially our goal: syncing the bodies from a physics library to Pop entities. The physics library does the heavy lifting, and we draw sprites on top of it.

---

2. http://box2d.org/
3. http://piqnt.com/planck.js/
4. https://github.com/schteppe/p2.js

Starting from scratch, we'll pull in the components we need from Matter, and spin up a new *engine*:

```
import { Engine, Bodies, World, Render } from "matter-js";
const w = 800;
const h = 400;

// Set up the physics engine
const engine = Engine.create();

Engine.run(engine);
```

Engine is the main workhorse of Matter.js. It performs all the calculations for physical interactions and responses between *Bodies* (objects like circles, rectangles, and other polygons) in the *World*. Matter is designed both to be used standalone, or in other game libraries such as Pop. In standalone mode (or when debugging) we can use its *Render* object to render wireframes of the physics bodies:

```
// Debug render it
const render = Render.create({
  element: document.querySelector("#board"),
  engine: engine,
  options: {
    width: w,
    height: h,
    showAngleIndicator: true
  }
});
Render.run(render);
```

A renderer requires an element in the HTML page as a container, the engine we created, and accepts a bunch of options that affect how the world works. We'll specify the width and height of the world as well as showing some extra debugging indicators. If you run the code, you'll have a full-fledged physics engine—but there's nothing in the world yet.

```
// Create some bodies
const course = Bodies.rectangle(400, 30, 300, 50, { isStatic: true });
```

The *Matter.Bodies* object contains a collection of factory methods for creating physics bodies. You can create circles, rectangles, trapezoids, polygons, and complex shapes from vertices. The factory methods all also accept an *options* object for specifying a body's physical properties, like mass, density, friction levels—all sorts of goodies that simulate objects in the real world.

Our rectangular body we have created (with *Bodies.rectangle*) is located at coordinates (400,

300). It's 300 pixels wide and 50 pixels tall. The only extra option we've specified is `isStatic`. A static body is not affected by physical collisions, and it doesn't fall to the ground under the pressure of gravity. It's as solid as a rock.

Now that we have the earth beneath our feet, we'll drop a whole boatload of bouncy balls on it, just to see what happens:

```javascript
const balls = [...Array(50)].map(() => {
  const radius = Math.random() * 25 + 5;
  const x = Math.random() * w;
  const y = Math.random() * -1000;
  const options = {
    restitution: 0.7
  };
  return Bodies.circle(x, y, radius, options);
});
```

A circle body requires an x/y location, as well as a radius. As far as options go, we set the ball to have a *restitution* of 0.7. **Restitution** means how elastic and bouncy a body is. 0 means the body is perfectly inelastic—it doesn't bounce at all. 1 means the object will bounce back with 100% of its kinetic energy … and is *ludicrously* bouncy.

 Other Stuff to Play With

"Restitution" is just one of the fun properties we can play with. Check out the properties on `Matter.Body` in the documentation and see how messed up you can make things!

Bodies need to be added to the world before they're processed in the engine. To set our balls in motion, add everything to `engine.world`, passing an array to `Matter.World.add`:

```javascript
// Add them to the world
World.add(engine.world, [course, ...balls]);
```

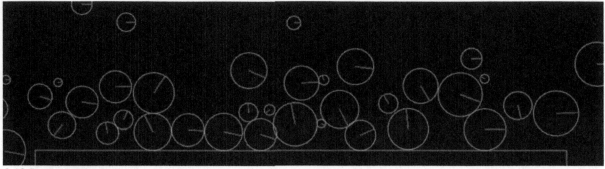

6-16. Bouncing wireframes

I'd say that was a successful test. Now let's see how this might integrate with a Pop game. To establish a base for *Pengolfin'*, start a new project using the familiar `GameScreen` approach. Create some mouse controls too—because our game will be controlled largely by mouse. Also give `GameScreen` a way to restart a level:

```
// Main.js
...
const game = new Game(800, 400);
const controls = {
  keys: new KeyControls(),
  mouse: new MouseControls(game.renderer.view)
};
function playHole() {
  game.scene = new GameScreen(game, controls, playHole);
}
playHole();
game.run();
```

`Main.js` is, as always, the entry point for the game. We'll keep track of the score here too, but now the Matter.js engine creation code we played around with will become part of the responsibility of `GameScreen`.

Syncing with Our Library

The physics engine is doing all the hard work of figuring out where things go and how they move. All we have to do is *draw it all*. To marry Pop and Matter.js we'll create entities as usual with Pop, but also give each entity a corresponding Matter body.

The Matter body will be created and attached to the Pop entity as a property called `body`. In an entity's `update` method (that runs every frame) we'll set the `rotation` and `pos` properties to match the values of the Matter body. The physics system calculates where things should be, and we copy the results back to our Pop entity. To get things started, we'll make the boring-est golf course ever—a flat rectangle:

```
import { Bodies, Body } from "matter-js";

class Course extends Rect {
  constructor(pos) {
    super(1000, 20, { fill: "#eee" });
    // Step 1: Create the body
    ...
    // Step 2: Sync the body and the Rect
    ...
    this.body = body; // store the Matter body reference
  }
}
```

One major difference between Matter's coordinate system and our coordinate system is where the pivot and anchor points are set. In Pop, an entity's position is where the *top-left* pixel should be located. In Matter, it's where the *center* of the body should be located. Likewise, the default pivot point is top left in Pop, but center in Matter. We need to account for this and offset the entity's *pivot* and *anchor* points accordingly:

```
this.pivot = {
  x: this.w / 2,
  y: this.h / 2
};
this.anchor = Vec.from(this.pivot).multiply(-1);

const body = Bodies.rectangle(0, 0, this.w, this.h, { isStatic: true });
Body.setPosition(body, pos);
```

First, we adjust the pivot point to the center, and then *copy* that point and invert it—thus giving the correct drawing offset. This now matches Matter's system. The Matter `Body` is a rectangle and the Pop entity is a `Rect` . To make the two match up, we copy the *position* and *rotation* from the `Body` to the `Rect` :

```
// Sync the Rect
this.rotation = body.angle;
pos.copy(body.position);
```

For non-static bodies, we have to copy the `body.position` and the `body.rotation` every frame in the entity's `update` function. That's all it takes to get Pop and Matter in sync! Now we can do the same for the golf-ball penguin. It's a `TileSprite` that lives in `entities/Penguin.js` :

```
class Penguin extends TileSprite {
  constructor(pos) {
    super(texture, 32, 32);
    this.pivot.x = this.w / 2;
    this.pivot.y = this.h / 2;
    this.anchor = Vec.from(this.pivot).multiply(-1);

    this.body = Bodies.circle(pos.x, pos.y, 10, {
      restitution: 0.7
    });
    this.body.torque = 0.002;
  }
}
```

Just as with the ground, to make a physics-enabled `Penguin` we offset the pivot and anchor points of the penguin and then create a `Body` —this time a circle. We've adjusted the default *torque* of the Matter.js body. **Torque** is a measure of how much *rotational force* is acting on a body. By applying a bit of torque as the penguin is created, it rolls slightly to the right. It just looks cool—that's all. `Penguin.js` has the same *update* function as the ground plane, which syncs the `TileSprite`'s *pos* to `body.position` and rotation to `body.angle`.

```
import { Engine, Events, World } from "matter-js";

class GameScreen extends Container {
  constructor(game, controls, onHole) {
    // ...
    this.ready = false; // Can the player shoot yet?

    const course = new Course({ x: 450, y: 300 });
    const penguin = new Penguin({ x: this.w / 2, y: -32 });

    // Add everyone to the game
    this.penguin = this.add(penguin);
    this.course = this.add(course);
  }
}
```

At the end of the `GameScreen` constructor, we put the engine creation code (which I cut and pasted from our initial Matter.js tests from earlier). All that remains is to add the penguin and the golf course bodies to the new `World`:

```
World.add(this.engine.world, [penguin.body, course.body]);
```

Everything is in sync! Whenever the physics bodies move, the corresponding Pop entity follows. This is just one way of many to proxy the properties of a physics body to our entities. If you have a preferred way to accomplish this task, don't be afraid to roll your own.

Event Systems

One of the big challenges when making physics games is deciding when a given "turn" or "play" has completed. In a complex system of interacting bodies, 99% of entities could all be at a standstill and at rest. Then one kinetic-energy-filled smart alec makes a final move that triggers a whole new chain reaction. Waiting for everything to be 100% stable can take a very long time—often far longer than your impatient player is willing to wait to keep playing.

Generally, there's no easy solution to this. You'll just have to "call it" at some point. In our golf game, life's a little easier: there's only one body we have to worry about (the penguin) and it's essential that it comes to a complete stop before we let the player shoot again.

How do we determine if the penguin is at rest? Perhaps we could just check its speed every frame and see if it's close to zero? You could do that by polling `body.motion`, which is a number representing the amount of movement a body currently has. If it's very close to zero, the penguin isn't moving. Unfortunately, that's not enough. If the penguin is shot straight upwards, at the peak of its trajectory its `body.motion` will *also* be close to 0. Luckily, Matter supplies us with a module to help out— `Matter.Sleeping`.

 Not Every Game Needs Sleeping

> Not every game will care when bodies are sleeping, so to avoid unnecessary computations, it's not enabled by default. This is why we had to add `enableSleeping: true` as an option when creating the main engine.

A body is **sleeping** when it has no motion and there are no pending forces acting on it. We can check our penguin and see if it's awake or asleep with the property `isSleeping`:

```
if (penguin.body.isSleeping) {
  // Player can shoot again!
  this.ready = true;
}
```

Alternatively, we could use the Matter *event system*. An **event system** is a way to manage communication between different parts of your game without each part needing explicit knowledge of the other. In this case, our `Penguin` can be informed about something that happens in the `Matter.Sleeping` system without knowing anything specific about the system itself. The `Penguin` doesn't care who decides it's sleeping; it just wants to know when it happens.

This is achieved through an event listener, specifically via the `sleepStart` and `sleepEnd` events:

```
Matter.Events.on(penguin.body, "sleepStart", () => {
  this.ready = true;
});
```

The event is registered once in `GameScreen` initialization. It's the same as how we register event listeners for mouse or keyboard events from the DOM. When the `Sleeping` module determines the penguin is sleeping, it will fire the event and call our callback function, enabling the player to shoot again.

 Available Events

There are many events available for us to listen to; have a look at the Matter *event* examples on the Matter.js website for more. If you want to listen to multiple events for the same body, you can separate them via spaces: `Events.on(body, "sleepStart collisionStart", (e) => {})`. Generally, you'll only listen to similar events in each `Events.on` statement, because the event information passed to the callback will be specific to that event. For example, collision events will have a member `e.pairs` —with `bodyA` and `bodyB` properties for the bodies involved in the collision.

Now that the sleeping logic has been delegated to the event listener, the only actual game logic we need to handle in the `GameScreen` is to check if the penguin has fallen off the edge of the screen, and if the player fired the penguin:

```
const { penguin, h, mouse } = this;
// Gone off the edge?
if (penguin.pos.y > h) {
  this.onHole();
}
// Player taken a shot?
if (mouse.released) {
  // Fire!
}
mouse.update();
```

If the penguin's `y` position is greater than the height of the game screen, we assume it fell off the edge and call the `onHole` method. This in turn calls the `playHole` function from `main.js` —which restarts the game.

Another way we could implement "falling off the edge of the world" would be to create additional

Matter bodies and position them around the edges of the screen. If we got a `collisionStart` message from any of them, we'd know the `Penguin` went out of bounds. It's not really necessary here, as our entity check is much simpler, but it highlights the benefit of mixing and matching the power of Matter.js and Pop.

Applying Forces

Just like our home-brew physics solution, Matter.js supplies a method for applying a force to a body. It's slightly more complicated than our version, because in addition to specifying the force, you must also specify the position in the world you're applying the force *from*.

```
Matter.Body.applyForce(body, position, force)
```

In our simple Pop physics, *position* isn't relevant. In a real physics system, it changes how the amount of power and torque gets applied to the body. For our golf game, it means we can hit the ball (penguin) slightly above center, so torque is applied in a clockwise direction and it gets a nice forward roll to keep it coasting after it lands:

```
fire(angle, power) {
  const { body } = this;
  Body.applyForce(
    body,
    { x: body.position.x, y: body.position.y - 10 },
    { x: Math.cos(angle) * power, y: Math.sin(angle) * power }
  );
}
```

We put the call to `applyForce` in a helper function that accepts an angle to fire at, along with the power of the shot. We convert the angle and power to Cartesian coordinates (see the earlier "Polar Coordinates" section). These inputs will eventually be supplied by dragging and releasing the mouse, but to test it out we'll just hardcode it in the main game after a mouse click:

```
if (mouse.released) {
  // Fire!
  const angle = -Math.PI / math.randf(1.75, 2.25);
  const power = 0.01;
  penguin.fire(angle, power);
}
```

The angle is a random upwards value (`-Math.PI / 2` is straight up). As it stands, you can spam the mouse button to apply the force repeatedly to make a flying penguin. It might be unrealistic (penguins can't fly: their wings are tiny!), but it's pretty funny.

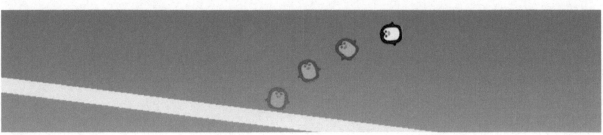

6-17. Flying penguins

Dragging Indicator

In our golf game, the player fires the penguin into the air by clicking somewhere on the screen, then dragging in the *opposite* direction they want to fire—as if pulling back a slingshot. We have to implement a slingshot.

The amount of power is determined by the *distance* the mouse is dragged. To model this (as well as visually show the player what they're doing), we create a new entity `Arrow`. It will hold the positions and states of the mouse clicks as well as draw a couple of thin rectangles for a power-and-direction bar:

```
class Arrow extends Container {
  constructor(max = 100) {
    super();
    this.background = this.add(
      new Rect(max, 4, { fill: "rgba(0, 0, 0, 0.1)" })
    );
    this.arrow = this.add(new Rect(0, 4, { fill: "#FDA740" }));
    ...
  }
}
```

The rectangles will rotate to show the direction of the shot. The `background` rectangle shows the full power range available, and the `arrow` rectangle will change width depending on the current stroke power. For the drag state, we have to track the start position where the mouse was clicked, the maximum width the display can be (this is also the constant width of the `background` rectangle), and the maximum drag distance—the amount of pixels to drag to have 100%-power shot:

```
this.pos = new Vec();
this.max = max;
this.maxDragDistance = 80;
```

A golf shot in our game is made up of two parts: clicking, and dragging. When the player clicks, we provide a *start* method to register the position and move the arrow:

```
start(pos) {
  this.pos.copy(pos);
}
```

Any dragging that's done now is in relation to this start position. This relationship is used to calculate the angle and power:

```
drag(drag) {
  const { arrow, pos, max, maxDragDistance } = this;

  // Calculate angle and power
  ...

  // Set the display
  this.rotation = angle;
  arrow.w = power * max;

  return { angle, power };
}
```

Every frame the player drags, the visualization will be updated and the angle/power data returned. The power is a number from 0 to 1, where 0 is "no power" and 1 is "full power". To calculate these we use some hopefully now-familiar math friends *math.angle* and *math.distance* to convert to polar coordinates:

```
// Calculate angle and power
const angle = math.angle(pos, drag);
const dist = math.distance(pos, drag);
const power = Math.min(1, dist / maxDragDistance);
```

The distance between the drag position and the start position is used to calculate the amount of power. If we drag further than *maxDragDistance*, the power is capped to *1* (by taking the minimum). Because we have a normalized value, we can use that to set the display width of the power bar.

The arrow is now ready to be used in *GameScreen*. When the player first presses their mouse button, we call *start* to register the position:

```
// Start your stroke
if (mouse.pressed) {
  arrow.start(mouse.pos);
```

```
    }
```

Then we have some logic to do. We can only drag and shoot when the penguin body is *sleeping* and we're ready to go. If it's all good, we check that the mouse is either being held down (*mouse.isDown*) or just released (*mouse.released*). In either case, we update the arrow with *arrow.drag* , passing the current mouse position:

```
if (this.ready) {
  if (mouse.isDown || mouse.released) {
    const { angle, power } = arrow.drag(mouse.pos);
    if (mouse.released) {
      this.fireAway(angle, power * 0.021);
    }
  }
}
```

When the player has finalized their shot, they release the mouse button and we can call *this.fireAway* with the returned angle and a scaled power. (It's scaled down because power is a ratio from 0 to 1, and a Matter.js force of 1 will send our penguin flying miles off the golf course!)

The *fireAway* method calls *fire* on the penguin, and also sets *this.ready = false* so the player can't apply more force to the penguin until it comes to rest. To give this golf game a point, we'll also create an entity that's the *hole* to try and get the penguin in. This can live in *GameScreen* : it's just a regular Pop entity on which we'll do a regular bounding-box collision test, to see if the penguin is touching it as it goes to sleep:

```
const hole = this.add(new Rect(20, 10, { fill: "#FDA740" }));
hold.pos.set(this.w - 100, 300);
```

When the penguin *stops*, we check if it's touching the hole (it doesn't count if the penguin bounces in the hole and then bounces out again). If it's touching, the hole is completed successfully. Again, we're mixing and matching our Pop and Matter.js logic: we could have also made the hole a Matter body and checked for collisions with Matter. Whatever works, works!

If there's a collision, we'll pass a flag (*true*) to indicate the hole was completed successfully, as opposed to the penguin falling off the edge of the world:

```
Events.on(penguin.body, "sleepStart", () => {
  if (entity.hit(penguin, hole)) {
    this.onHole(true);
  }
```

```
    this.ready = true;
});
```

That's the core of our game working. You can aim and fire a penguin; when it hits the hole, we're done! It's not very fun though. The problem is that the course is *very flat* and *very repetitive*. Physics games are only fun when things bounce around and interact with the environment. Let's build some more challenging courses.

Procedurally Generated Terrain

The exciting part about minigolf-style games is the wacky courses. Our game will be side-on, so the challenge needs to be in getting the penguin in the hole despite some mountainous icebergs standing in the way. There are several ways we could accomplish this.

To be honest, for the first pass when making this prototype, I took a different approach. I created a course out of several rotated rectangles that fit together snuggly. This worked fine (better than I expected, actually) but it had a couple of issues. Making levels by hand was pretty easy, but when trying to procedurally generate new levels, the math got pretty gnarly. Secondly, it was very hard to render these nicely on the screen. There's no way to "fill in" the space *between* the rectangles, so there were big holes in the middle of the iceberg courses.

I decided to bite the bullet and introduce a *new* renderable entity into Pop: a **path**. A path is series (an array) of point coordinates that join together like connect-the-dot puzzles, with the last point connecting back to the first to form an arbitrary polygon.

6-18. Canvas path

HTML5 Canvas has the concept of a path as part of its API, so it's easy to integrate into our Canvas renderer. But it's not something native to Matter.js: there'll be a couple of hoops to jump through to make that work. Additionally, when it comes time to make our WebGL Renderer, it will complicate things there too! Ah well, that's the beauty of rolling your own library: you can add things as you need them, and adapt to the situation at hand.

To display the path on screen, we need to add support to Pop's `CanvasRender.js`. The renderer will expect a "path" element to have a `path` property that's an array containing two or more points defining the path. It also expects it to have a `style` property that optionally defines a `fill` color (defaulting to `#fff`) to paint the polygon:

```
else if (child.path) {
  const [head, ...tail] = child.path;
  if (tail.length > 0) {
    // Draw the path
  }
}
```

The path is split into two parts: the "head" (first element) and the "tail" (the rest). To draw a path in Canvas, you start with a call to *beginPath*, then *moveTo* the position defined by head. From here, you *lineTo* each proceeding point, and finally call *closePath* to join up the path:

```
ctx.fillStyle = child.style.fill || "#fff";
ctx.beginPath();
ctx.moveTo(head.x, head.y);
tail.forEach(({x, y}) => ctx.lineTo(x, y));
ctx.closePath();
ctx.fill();
```

Now that we can render a path, we have to figure out how to procedurally generate our golf course, and cut that up for Matter.js. The way we'll approach it is to *slice the course up* into vertical segments. Each segment will either be flat, slope up, or slope down a random amount. The first segment will be the *tee*, and we'll choose a random segment to be the *hole*. Both of these will have to be flat.

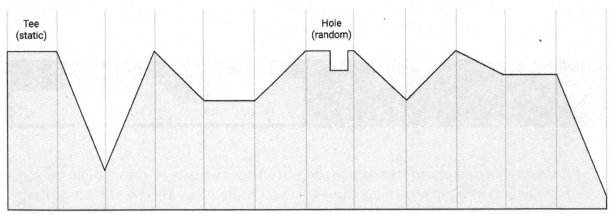

6-19. Course segments

```
class Course extends Container {
  constructor(gameW, gameH) {
    ...
    const segments = 13;
    const segmentWidth = 64;
    const xo = 15;
    let yo = math.randOneFrom([32, 128, 300]);
```

```
    let minY = yo;
    let maxY = yo;
    let holeSegment = math.rand(segments - 7, segments);
  }
}
```

The number of segments, and the segment width, have been chosen to fit nicely in the screen space. The `xo` and `yo` properties are the initial offsets for the first segment. We keep track of the height of each segment and make sure the course doesn't get too high or too low:

```
const terrainData = [...Array(segments)].map((_, i) => {
  const mustBeFlat = i <= 1 || i === holeSegment;
  if (!mustBeFlat) {
    // Randomly move up or down
    ...
  }
  return { x: i * segmentWidth, y: yo };
});

const tee = terrainData[0];
const hole = terrainData[holeSegment];
```

 Some JS Trickery

The code `[...Array(segments)].map()` is a handy JavaScript trick for creating an array of a given size that can be mapped over. If you create an array "normally" with *new Array(segments)*, the entries will be empty and are not passed to `.map()`. By destructuring the empty array we get a list of *undefined* elements that *do* get passed to `.map()`.

We create a new object for each segment to store the `x` and `y` positions of the segment point. The `x` (horizontal position) is calculated by taking the current array index (`i`) and multiplying it by the `segmentWidth`. The `y` (vertical position) depends on whether or not the segment is flat. If it's flat, the `yo` offset remains the same and adjoining points will be on the same vertical plane.

```
// Randomly move up or down
const drop = math.randOneFrom([32, 64, 152]);
const dir = math.randOneFrom([-1, 0, 1]);
// Random go down
if (dir === 1 && yo - drop > 0) {
  yo -= drop;
}
```

```
//Random go up
if (dir === -1 && yo + drop < 320) {
  yo += drop;
}
if (yo > maxY) maxY = yo;
if (yo < minY) minY = yo;
```

If the segment is *not* flat, we choose a random elevation and direction for the slope—ensuring we never get too high (`yo` must be less than 320), and never dive right through the bottom of the iceberg (`yo` must be greater or equal to 0). The maximum and minimum levels are recorded so we can calculate the total course height later.

This gives us the top surface of the golf course. To finish it off, we have to "carve" a small rectangular area as the hole. It needs to be big enough for the penguin to fall into, but not too big as to make the game too easy! We'll splice in four additional points on the flat surface of the hole segment. The four points are the corners of the hole:

```
// Add the hole
terrainData.splice(
  holeSegment,
  0,
  { x: hole.x - 30, y: hole.y },
  { x: hole.x - 30, y: hole.y + 25 },
  { x: hole.x - 10, y: hole.y + 25 },
  { x: hole.x - 10, y: hole.y }
);
```

With the top surface of the course complete, we now add two more points (the bottom-right point of the iceberg and the bottom-left point of the iceberg) to create a "base" for the course. This is calculated by going straight down from the top surface to the `maxY` value we calculated earlier. We also add an extra 52 pixels so the bottom of the course can never be too close to the water. The final point aligns horizontally with the first point (`x = 0`) so when the path is closed we get nice rectangular edges:

```
// Add the base, close the path
const { x } = terrainData[terrainData.length - 1];
maxY += 52; // "base" height
terrainData.push({ x, y: maxY });
terrainData.push({ x: 0, y: maxY });
```

The last step is to figure out the total final height of the iceberg so it can be positioned on screen correctly:

```
const h = gameH - (maxY - minY);

this.path = terrainData;
this.pos = new Vec(xo, h - minY);
```

The final terrain data points are stored on the entity as `this.path`. The `CanvasRenderer` will see the path and fill it in for us.

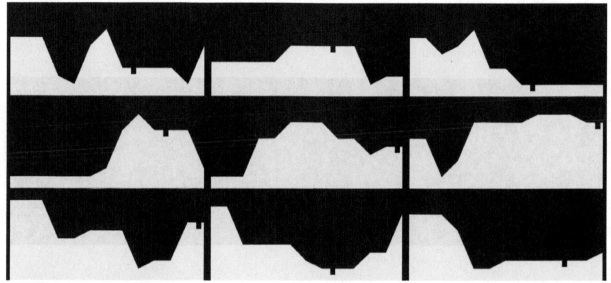

6-20. Randomly generated levels

We have an infinite golf course! Refreshing the screen gives us a new challenge each time. While we're here, we can also add in the spawn locations for the tee and the hole. We'll use these in the main `GameScreen` to position the `Penguin` and the target hole graphics:

```
this.hole = Vec.from(hole).add({ x: -15, y: h - minY });
this.tee = Vec.from(tee)
  .add({ x: xo + segmentWidth / 2, y: h - minY - 5 });
```

Having all of this information is no good if the penguin has no *physics bodies* to interact with. The iceberg level is just an image; the penguin will fall straight through it and the game will reset. We need to be able to convert our *path* into Matter.js *bodies*. To achieve this, we use the `Bodies` factory method called `fromVertices`:

```
const terrain = Bodies.fromVertices(0, 0, terrainData, { isStatic: true });
```

`Bodies.fromVertices` takes the path and chops it into a body. Sounds exactly like what we need. Only, by default, it works with *convex polygons*. A **convex polygon** is one where, if you drew any straight line through the shape, it would hit exactly two borders. If our golf course was a triangle or a simple rectangle, this would be true. But we have all sorts of dips and peaks. Our course is concave.

If Matter encounters a concave path, it will try to *decompose* the path into multiple convex polygons. But to do this it needs an additional library, poly-decomp.js[5], which we need to make available as a global function. The easiest way to do this is to put it in our `/vendor` folder and link to it from the main HTML:

```
<script src="vendor/decomp.min.js"></script>
```

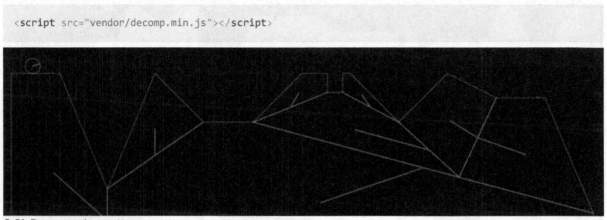

6-21. Decomposing matter

The golf course will be chopped up into multiple convex polygons that work perfectly with Matter.js. If you want to see the triangles that poly-decomp creates, re-add the debug Matter renderer. It's pretty impressive. With a course full of convex polygons, `Penguin` will bounce around just like a real penguin golf ball. Like all of our Matter bodies, we need to adjust it so it aligns with the Pop image, and now our penguin is once again forced to obey our laws of nature!

```
// Create the geometry
Body.setPosition(terrain, {
  x: -terrain.bounds.min.x + xo,
  y: h - terrain.bounds.min.y
});
this.body = terrain;
```

We're rapidly running out of time, but we have everything we need to turn this into a game now. Using the hole and tee positions, we can set the start and end points of each hole.

Then the game could use a few finishing touches. First, a score system. How about this: each shot the player takes will add one stroke to their score? Makes sense. Annnd, if they fall off the edge of the world, they get, say, a five-stroke penalty.

5. https://github.com/schteppe/poly-decomp.js

To make our game more aesthetically pleasing, we'll add a couple of arctic-themed touches. A solid blue rectangle at the bottom of the screen represents water. Each frame, this can bob up and down via a sine wave to look like a rising and falling arctic ocean:

```
waves.pos.y = Math.sin(t / 800) * 7 + this.h - 20;
```

In the dying seconds of the game jam, we'll add a CSS gradient background in *main.css* to represent the skyline … aaaand time is well and truly up!

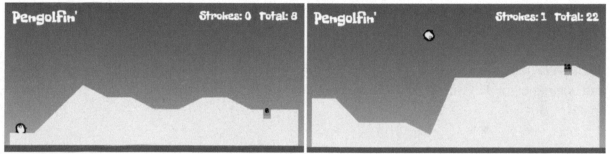

6-22. Pengolfin'

When you model aspects of your game using physical forces—whether through rolling your own, or via a full-featured physics engine—they become part of a *system*. System-based games can be extremely interesting from both a player's and a developer's perspective, as they allow for emergent behavior—interactions between simple rules that combine into complex, fascinating, and unexpected results. That means deeper gameplay for the player, and more hours lost tinkering with things for the developer. How about extending *Pengolfin'* with some more obstacles … such as moving targets to bounce things off … mountain-side trampolines … penguin multi-ball?

We Got Physical

As you consider the possibilities, there's a kerfuffle at your door, as Guy Shifty and a dozen of his minions push into your office at the same time. Guy stands before them, looking immaculate as ever. It was only one grueling weekend, but *you* look like you've been lost in the woods for a month. How does he do it?

"I just brought my people down here to show them an example of poor planning. I assume you got nothing done for the Lucky Dare Game Jam Competition in the end?"

You let the minions play some *Pengolfin'*. They try not to smile as they play.

Shifty looks moody. "Hmm, better than nothing, I suppose. But no music or sounds, no polish. And like I told you all", he barks, as he snatches the mouse from the current player and starts ushering the crew back out the door, "it's got no chance at this year's IGC."

You roll your eyes, but decide to indulge him. "What's IGC?"

"You don't *know* about the Independent Game Competition?" he replies, feigning surprise. "It's only the *biggest* indie game competition of the year. I'm entering my 'indie division' (the people I don't pay). First prize is $10,000." He looks at you coldly as he exits. "You could use that money to help you find a new place to work."

I don't know what he means by that, but it can't be good. He's right about one thing, though: having games systems and good core mechanics is not enough. We need start *polishing* our games. We need music, special effects, explosions, and sounds. It's time to roll up our sleeves and begin the grind of transforming our prototypes into games. It's time to take it to the next level!

Audio | Level 7

The human brain is so easily manipulated and enchanted by sound. Great audio has played a starring role in every influential game ever. We all have fond memories of our favorite game's theme tunes and sound effects. Audio can make or break a game. I'll say it 100 times in this chapter, until you believe me: *audio IS NOT optional*. It can't be left until the end, and it can't be an afterthought. It must be planned and developed along with the rest of your assets, in order to achieve your artistic vision.

The good news is that, because messing around with music and sound effects has *such* a dramatic impact, it's extremely rewarding to experiment with. Even some quick-and-dirty sound effects can add real "pop" to your games and prototypes—and at this stage, we need all the help we can get if we want to craft a winning IGC entry.

In this chapter, we'll cover more about sound production than we may ever need to know—from the fundamentals of adding (and producing) music and sound effects to polishing and mastering sound for inclusion in games. Along the way, we'll also make a generic asset loader so we can display a loading screen while we preload our large audio and image files.

7-1. Gaëtan Renaudeau's psychedelic rhythm game, Timelapse

Old-school Techniques

Before we explore the current state of audio in HTML5, a little history. Historically, audio has been a second-class citizen on the Web. During the period of mainstream adoption of the internet, the most frequent way you'd encounter any noise at all was via horrific-sounding MIDI tunes embedded in web pages.

MIDI is a simple format (still often used in music production) for storing song information—note pitches, note lengths, vibrato settings and so forth. A song can be encoded in MIDI format and then replayed. MIDI describes only the notes; it doesn't include any actual audio. Musicians can feed the MIDI data to their high-end synthesizers and drum machines, which will faithfully play back what was recorded.

But internet users in the '90s didn't have high-end synthesizers and drum machines. They had cheap sound cards with painful, built-in MIDI sounds. The Web during this era was a cacophony of bad MIDI jingles and pop songs played by children's toys. It was a dark, dark time.

It *was* possible to include and control audio files by dynamically including links in the head of a web page, but support across browsers was patchy. The only respite came from third-party Flash plugins. Flash included decent sound-effect and audio playback capabilities for use with animations and games that could be harnessed as a standalone audio player.

This gave rise to libraries that are still sometimes used as fallbacks when support for modern methods fails. The "playback via Flash" technique remained the de facto way to make sound and music on the Web until the uptake of HTML5 and the Web Audio API.

Audio on the Web

The Web Audio API[1] had its first public draft in 2011. It was several years before it became widely available, though it's now the standard way to play sounds on the Web. But it's also oh-so-much more than a simple sound player.

While older libraries could only play back pre-recorded files (perhaps with some minor processing ability, such as affecting stereo panning or modifying the volume), the Web Audio API can also manipulate and affect existing audio files, as well as generate sounds from scratch.

The API is *modular*. It accepts a variety of input sources and can route them through different audio processing units before outputting them to a particular destination (usually your computer speakers). This provides a lot of power and flexibility. That power comes at the cost of complexity. The Web Audio API is unwieldy, and has a steep learning curve.

To simplify things, there's a more "web-like" companion, the *HTML5 Audio element*, which is used in the same manner as other HTML entities—via an HTML tag within a web page:

```
<audio src="/lib/amenBeat.mp3" loop />
```

And just like other HTML entities, we can create and control them completely via JavaScript. This is one way of getting synchronized sound in our games.

Playing Sounds

Audio in games is *not optional*. I'm serious! Audio is such a very powerful mechanism for conveying action and meaning that even simple sound effects will *dramatically* improve the feel of your game.

To illustrate this, consider an example. (Of course, the example works much better aurally than in

---

1. https://webaudio.github.io/web-audio-api/

a print, so make sure to try the "plop" demo in the examples.) It goes like this. Imagine two identical circles—one on the left side of the screen, one on the right, and both at the same height. The two circles move horizontally, crossing at the center of the screen. When they reach the other side, they move back again until they reach their start positions.

Something interesting happens when we introduce a simple sound. If, at the very moment the two circles intersect, we make a "plop" sound (like a tennis racket hitting a ball), suddenly there's a strong illusion that the two circles actually *collide and rebound*! Nothing changes with the drawing code: our ears hear the sound, and our brains are tricked into thinking a collision has happened. This is exactly the kind of illusion we need to harness for developing immersive experiences.

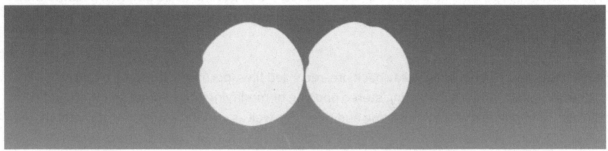

7-2. Tennis ball bounce

The plop example also demonstrates the simplest way to get some sound to play via JavaScript. Create a new `Audio` element and assign the source, in exactly the same way we'd create an `Image` element:

```
const plop = new Audio();
plop.src = "./res/sounds/plop.mp3";
```

This is equivalent to embedding an `<audio />` tag in the main web page … but created on demand when required throughout our game. The audio is loaded once and can be played back whenever we want. When the "tennis balls" collide (well, when their `x` position offsets are `< 5` pixels apart) we call `play` on the `Audio` element:

```
if (Math.abs(x1 - x2) < 5) {
  plop.play();
}
```

Besides `play`, there's a whole host of properties and operations that can be performed on the sound file. (See MDN[2] for examples.) Because we'll be using sound in *every project* (no

---

[2.] https://developer.mozilla.org/en-US/docs/Web/HTML/Element/audio

exceptions!) we'll integrate this into our core library, wrapping some of the most useful audio functions.

Create a new folder, *sound* , in the root library folder. Inside that, create a file called *Sound.js* (and expose it in Pop's *index.js*). *Sound* will be a class that accepts several parameters and exposes an API for controlling audio:

```
class Sound {
  constructor(src, options = {}) {
    this.src = src;
    this.options = Object.assign({ volume: 1 }, options);

    // Configure Audio element
    ...
  }

  play(options) {}
  stop() {}
}
```

The parameters are *src* —the URL to the audio file resource, and an optional *options* object that will specify the behavior of the sound element. This includes a default parameter *volume* —the volume level to play back the sound, from 0 (silence) to 1 (maximum loudness).

 Object.assign

Object.assign specifies a "target" object, followed by one or more "source" objects. (You can specify multiple arguments after the source target.) The properties from the source objects are all copied to the target. If there are matching keys, the target will be overwritten. We specify *volume: 1* as a default. If the *options* object also has a key *volume* , this will take precedence.

For the time being, our *Sound* class is simply a wrapper over *Audio* that exposes *play* and *stop* methods. We'll enhance it with more features soon. Each of our custom *Sound* instances will be backed by an HTML5 *Audio* element:

```
// Configure Audio element
const audio = new Audio();
audio.src = src;

audio.addEventListener("error", () =>
  throw new Error("Error loading audio resource: " + audio.src)
```

```
    false);
```

As in the tennis-ball example, we create an `Audio` element with `new Audio()` and set the location of the audio file to the `src` attribute. We also attach an event listener that will fire if any errors occur while loading (especially useful for finding bad file paths!).

Now it's time to fill out our `play` and `stop` API methods. `play` also accepts an object with options, so we can temporarily override the default settings each time the sound plays, if needed:

```
play(overrides) {
  const { audio, options } = this;
  const opts = Object.assign({ time: 0 }, options, overrides);
  audio.volume = opts.volume;
  audio.currentTime = opts.time;
  audio.play();
}
```

After merging any options in the function parameter with the `Sound`'s default options, pull out the final `volume` value and set it on the audio object. By default, the `time` option is set to 0 (the very beginning of the audio file) and the `Audio` element's `currentTime` is set to `time`

In our tennis-ball example, we can switch in our new `Sound` class rather than hand-roll a new `Audio` object. Because both our API *and* the `Audio` element have a `play` method (and we're happy with the default options), the only change we have to make is to change our creation code:

```
const plop = new Sound("res/sounds/plop.mp3");
```

Let's make our game a whole lot noisier. *Pengolfin'* is just crying out for some audio attention—starting with a catchy theme tune! Have a listen to it. I hope you find it suitable for our game, because it's the one we'll make ourselves a little later in this chapter. Load the `Sound` assets the same way we load `Texture` assets. In the constructor function of `TitleScreen`, create an object to group the sounds and load our title song, which is located at `res/sounds/theme.mp3`:

```
const sounds = {
  plop: new Sound("res/sounds/plops.mp3"),
  theme: new Sound("res/sounds/theme.mp3", { volume: 0.6 })
};
```

Keeping Things Tidy

As with texture assets, we define it at the top of the file. It isn't necessary to store all our references together in a *sounds* object. We could assign it directly to a variable (*const theme = new Sound("...");*), but it helps to keep things organized.

By default, our sounds are played at the maximum volume. If everything plays at maximum, there's nowhere for us to go if we end up with some sounds that have been recorded quieter than others. (For more on this, see the "Mixing" section later in this chapter. Also see the "These go to eleven[3]" scene from the mockumentary *This is Spinal Tap*.)

To give us some breathing room, we play the theme song with a volume of 0.6 (60% of the maximum). Eventually, we'll also want to give ultimate control of the volume to the player via a settings menu. After you've defined the sound, it can be played as soon as the game loads, in the *TitleScreen* constructor:

```
sounds.theme.play();
```

A title screen, complete with a snazzy audio accompaniment. However, if you press the space bar to start the game, you'll notice that the title song continues playing in the main *GameScreen*. Stop it with the Audio API method *pause*. We'll wrap this in a helper method that we'll call *stop* :

```
stop() {
  this.audio.pause();
}
```

I'm calling it *stop* rather than *pause* because the *play* method restarts the audio from the beginning every time, and the net effect is the same as stopping the audio. I'm not sure this was the *cleanest* implementation, but it's the most common use case in games, so I'm sticking with it. The most logical time to stop the theme song is after the player presses the space bar (before we leave the screen):

```
if (controls.action) {
  sounds.theme.stop();
  this.onStart({..});
}
```

---

3. https://www.youtube.com/watch?v=4xgx4k83zzc

Playing SFX

Our system isn't just for playing songs. It works equally as well for playing sound effects—when a player shoots, walks, or collects a power-up. Add the `Sound` in the entity's class file, and call `play` as required.

While we're here, we may as well start building on the basics of our sound library. The first addition is a property to indicate if a given sound is *currently playing* or not. We might not want to call `play` again (for example) if the sound is already playing. To implement it, we need to keep track of a few related actions and events.

The `playing` property is a boolean flag on the `Sound` object. It's initialized to `false`, just after the other sound options have been defined. At the end of the `play` method, set the flag to `true`:

```
this.playing = true;
```

And at the end of the `stop` method, set it to `false`:

```
this.playing = false;
```

This takes care of user actions that start and stop a sound. But we also have to know *when* the sound has reached the end (when it stops playing on its own). Thankfully, the `Audio` element fires an `ended` event especially for this case. Track this in the same way we did for the `error` event:

```
audio.addEventListener("ended", () => this.playing = false, false);
```

Each `Sound` object now has an accurate `playing` flag that we can use in our games. For example, to only play the theme song if it's not already playing, just ask:

```
if (!sounds.theme.playing) {
  sounds.theme.play();
}
```

The last bit of core functionality we'll add is the ability to modify the *volume* of the sound, even if it's currently playing. To do this, add `volume` getter and setter methods to the `Sound` prototype to report and set the `Audio` element's volume:

```
get volume () {
  return this.audio.volume;
},
set volume (volume) {
  this.options.volume = this.audio.volume = volume;
}
```

Notice we also store *volume* in the *set* method as the new *default volume* of the sound. This is so that if we set the volume with *theme.volume = 0.5*, any future *play* calls will also be at volume *0.5*.

Repeating Sounds

By default, all of our sounds are **one-shot**. They play through from start to end, then stop. That's perfect for most effects (like power-up twinkles and collision explosions). Other times, we'll want sounds to loop over and over.

The obvious case is for music loops. You can have a short snippet of a song—say, 16 or 32 beats long—that repeats many times. Looping can also be employed for game sound effects that have to play for an indeterminate length of time. For example, a jetpack should be noisy whenever it's activated. A bass-heavy *woooosh* should be blasting for as long as the player is holding down the jetpack button.

To facilitate this, add the *loop* property as one of our possible options when creating a *Sound* instance. If looping is set to *true*, we'll apply it to the *Audio* element (via its corresponding *Loop* property):

```
if (options.loop) {
  audio.loop = true;
}
```

Then we'll define it in the options object when making our game's loopable sound element:

```
const sounds = {
  swoosh: new Sound("./res/sounds/swoosh.m4a", {volume: 0.2, loop: true})
};
```

For our test, if the player is holding down the up button (*controls.y()* is less than 0), the jetpack is applying its upward force and the relevant *woosh* sounds should play:

```
// Player pressed up (jet pack)
```

```
if (controls.y < 0) {
  sounds.swoosh.play();
  ...
}
```

Argh, what is this?! If you test out this version, you'll notice our jetpack has become a lot noisier—but not in a good way. What's happening is that for *every frame* the user accelerates, the `play` command is issued and the sound restarts from the beginning, creating a horrible stuttering mess. The solution is to guard against this by using the `playing` property:

```
if(!sounds.swoosh.playing) {
  sounds.swoosh.play();
}
```

Because the "loop" option is set to true, the sound will play continuously. Even after the user has let go of the up key. Oh dear. To fix this, you need to `stop` the sound if it's *playing* and the user *isn't* trying to use their jetpack:

```
// controls.y is not less than 0
else {
  sounds.swoosh.stop();
}
```

Polyphonic Sounds

In the last section, we witnessed the situation where accidentally hitting `play` on a sound every frame resulted in unpleasant, stuttered playback. One question you might ask is why it was stuttering and not creating a discordant, clamorous cacophony—a thousand jetpacks sounded at once?

The answer is that the `Audio` element is **monophonic**. It can only generate one sound at a time. Which sucks for us: we'd prefer a **polyphonic** system that can play several instances of the sound simultaneously. Imagine your game has shooting. If the firing rate is faster than the length of the sound file, each time the player fires, the previous sound will be cut off by the next.

Luckily, the Audio API is capable of playing multiple monophonic `Audio` elements at the same time. We can fake a polyphonic `Sound` by creating *several* `Audio` elements with same audio source. We then play them one after the other! This is known as a **sound pool**, and is something we'll want to be able to reuse easily. Let's add it to the library as `sound/SoundPool.js`. The pool will be an array of identical `Sound` instances:

```
class SoundPool {
  constructor(src, options = {}, poolSize = 3) {
    this.count = 0;
    this.sounds = [...Array(poolSize)]
      .map(() => new Sound(src, options));
  }
}
```

The structure of the *SoundPool* is very similar to the API provided by *Sound* . The only difference is it requires a parameter that is *poolSize* : the number of copies of the sound to add to the pool. The *SoundPool* constructor holds an array (of length *poolSize*) where each element is mapped to a new *Sound* object. The result is a series of sounds with exactly the same source and options:

```
play(options) {
  const { sounds } = this;
  const index = this.count++ % sounds.length;
  sounds[index].play(options);
}
```

Each time *play()* is called, we get the index of the current sound in the sound pool. This is done by incrementing the *count* , then taking the remainder of the number of sounds in the pool, looping over and over the array in order. We then play it with any options provided, exactly the same as if we called *play* on a *Sound* element directly.

If we want to call *stop* on the sound pool, we need to iterate over each sound and stop them all:

```
// stop ALL audio instances of the pool
stop() {
  this.sounds.forEach(sound => sound.stop());
}
```

And that's our polyphonic sound pool. It's used the same way as the regular *Sound* —except with extra "phonic"! To really hear the effect, we'll play our plop sound repeatedly every 200ms:

```
const plops = new SoundPool("res/sounds/plop.mp3", {}, 3);

const rate = 0.2;
let next = rate;
game.run(t => {
  if (t > next) {
    next = t + rate;
    plops.play();
  }
```

```
});
```

It sounds fine with a `poolSize` of 3—but set it lower and you'll hear the stuttering from earlier. The `poolSize` should be set on a case-by-case basis in a way that's optimal for your game. If you set it too small, you'll hear the sounds being cut off. If you set it too large, you'll be wasting system resources. It's best to go for the smallest value possible that still sounds good.

Randomly Ordered Sounds

Like game design, **sound design** is about intentionally sculpting an experience to meet an artistic vision. When sound design is done well, the players often won't even notice; it's just natural and engaging. If it's done badly, however, it will drive them crazy! The most sure-fire way to make your players go loopy is to repeat an audio phrase over and over and over. The human brain is excellent at recognizing patterns, and also quick to tire of them.

This is usually a problem in games when a *single sound* is used for a core mechanic that might happen hundreds (or thousands) of times during play—such as shooting a weapon, or the sound of footsteps. In the real world, each footstep will sound ever so slightly different. Different surfaces, different room acoustics, different angles of impact ... they all combine to subtly alter the pitch and tone that hits our ears.

Luckily for us, the human brain is also easy to trick. We don't need *too* much variation to break the monotony. If we create a few different samples with slightly different sonic characteristics, and play them in a random order, the result will be enough to fool the player.

We'll call this approach a "sound group". A **sound group** is a manager for randomly selecting and playing one from a bunch of `Sounds`. It can go in the `sound` folder as `SoundGroup.js`:

```
class SoundGroup {
  constructor(sounds) {
    this.sounds = sounds;
  }
}
```

The `SoundGroup` expects an *array* of objects that have `play` and `stop` methods (so, either `Sound` or `SoundPool` objects from our library). To add one to a game, define the `SoundGroup` by supplying the list of `Sounds` to choose from:

```
const squawk = new SoundGroup([
  new Sound("res/sounds/squawk1.mp3"),
```

```
    new Sound("res/sounds/squawk2.mp3"),
    new Sound("res/sounds/squawk3.mp3")
])
```

If you preview each of the audio files individually, you hear that they're various takes on a "penguin" squawking. (Honestly, I have no idea what sound a penguin actually makes; it's just me and a microphone. Jump ahead to the "Sound Production" section if you want to see how it's done!) It's the small variations that we're looking for to create a more natural effect. The number of unique sounds you'll need will depend on the situation. A few is enough for *Pengolfin'*, as the sounds don't happen too often. But more is always better.

Next we need to add the *play* and *stop* methods. *stop* is easy: it's the same as *SoundPool*, where we loop over the sounds and stop each of them. And *play* is only slightly more complicated:

```
play(opts) {
  const { sounds } = this;
  math.randOneFrom(sounds).play(opts);
}
```

It chooses a random element from the *sound* list and plays it. Now, whenever the penguin hits a surface with force, it squawks out one of the random variations by calling *squawk.play()*.

This approach is simple, but you can build on it to suit your games. For example, you could implement a round-robin approach for selecting the next sound (rather than just randomly), or even create a strategy that combines the two: it chooses randomly, but never plays the same sound twice. Whatever you can do to break up a monotonous repeating sound will be greatly appreciated by your players!

An Asset Manager

Assets are resource files that must be loaded to be used in a game. Because we've been running the games locally (serving them from our own computer to our browser) everything loads up pretty much instantly. But when we release our games to the wide world, they'll live on a server in the sky where others can play them.

Downloading large files over the internet can take a considerable amount of time. What happens if we try to play a sound or render a sprite that hasn't loaded yet? At the very least, we'll have invisible sprites or silent audio! Not a good first impression. To remedy this, we should display a **loading screen**—a progress bar, or animation—so the player knows *something* is happening, and we can build up some excitement for the game to come.

An **asset manager** is used to facilitate this and handle the loading of assets. We no longer need to create raw `HTMLImageElements` (via `new Image()`) or `HTMLAudioElements` (via `new Audio()`) directly, but can instead let the asset manager do it for us. When we want an image, we'll ask the asset manager for it: `Asset.image("res/images/tiles.png")`.

Dependencies

ll of the required files can be known before the game starts, thanks to the JavaScript module system. When a module is required, any dependencies of that module are also required. This generates a *tree* of all the required source code files. If we define our assets at the top level of our source file, we can keep track of necessary files as the tree is being traversed.

Our asset manager will be called `Assets.js`, and becomes another part of the Pop library. It will manage the loading, progress reporting, and caching of all our game assets. Here's the skeleton for our first pass at an API for loading game assets:

```js
const cache = {};
let remaining = 0;
let total = 0;

const Assets = {
  image(url) {
    // Load image
  },
  sound(url) {
    // Load sound
  }
};
```

We define some local variables to keep track of the state of the loading files: a key/value `cache`, and a couple of counters to keep track of progress. The exported API contains methods to load an image (`Assets.image(url)`) and a method to load a sound file (`Assets.sound(url)`). Shortly, we'll also add some event listeners to inform external users of the loading progress.

The asset manager does some housekeeping operations that are homogeneous regardless of the type of asset to load: checking the `cache`, updating counters, and so on. We'll extract this into a function called `load`:

```js
// Helper function for queuing assets
function load(url, maker) {
```

```
  if (cache[url]) {
    return cache[url];
  }
  const asset = maker(url, onAssetLoad);
  remaining++;
  total++;

  cache[url] = asset;
  return asset;
}
```

There's quite a lot going on in this little function. It revolves around the `cache` object that's defined at the start of the file. `cache` acts as a hash map that links URL strings to DOM asset objects. For example, after we've loaded a couple of files, the cache may look like this:

```
{
  "res/images/bunny.png": HTMLImageElement,
  "res/sounds/coins.mp3": HTMLAudioElement,

  ...
}
```

If we ask for the same URL twice, we get the object from the `cache` and don't bother loading it again. This is the `if` check at the start of the `Load` function: if the cache key already exists, return the asset straight away, and we're done.

 Browser Caching

> It would obviously be really bad to load an image ten times if it's used in ten different entities, but in reality the browser itself has been acting as a cache for us already. It remembers if we recently loaded a file and retrieves it from its own cache.

If the key isn't found, the asset needs to be loaded. The `remaining` and `total` counts are incremented. `total` is just for our records (so we can calculate a percentage for showing a progress bar on the loading screen) and `remaining` will decrement every time an asset loading completes. When it gets back to 0, everything is loaded.

The `Load` function requires a second parameter called `maker`. `maker` is a *function* that will do the actual asset creation. We'll have one for images and one for sounds (and more later, if required—for example, to load JSON as an asset). The output of `Load` will be the *reference to the asset*—so we can return this directly from our `Assets.image` API:

```
// Load an image
image(url) {
  return load(url, (url, onAssetLoad) => {
    const img = new Image();
    img.src = url;
    img.addEventListener("load", onAssetLoad, false);
    return img;
  });
}
```

The image loader returns the result of calling `Load` . The parameters we feed it will be the user-supplied URL, and the function that creates an `HTMLImageElement` and sets the source. It then attaches an event listener that will fire as soon as the image is done loading. When the `Load` function calls our image loader function, it supplies us this function to call when loading is done. This is what enables our asset manager to keep track of what remains to be loaded.

 Higher Order Functions

A function that accepts a function as a parameter, or returns a function as a result, is called a **higher-order function**. A normal function abstracts over values, acting as a black box operating on numbers and strings. A higher-order function abstracts over *actions*. They let you reuse and combine behavior which can then become the input for even more complex combinations. For our purpose, higher-order functions let us abstract the concept of monitoring the state of a loading asset.

The key step for our asset manager is that a `maker` function *must* call the `onAssetLoad` function (which we'll define shortly) as soon as loading is done. For an image, we attach the function to an event listener that's called when the image's built-in `Load` event fires.

Now that we can preload, how do we work this into our library? Ideally, we'd prefer not to change how the end user makes games with Pop, so we'll take care of this under the hood, in `Texture.js` :

```
import Assets from "./Assets.js";

class Texture {
  constructor(url) {
    this.img = Assets.image(url);
  }
}
```

If you compare before and after, not much has changed: the work of creating the DOM element and setting the source attribute has been moved to the asset loader, rather than directly in the library. Existing games that use *Texture* will still continue to work as they did before.

Now we need to do it all over again for sound files. Again, we use the *Load* helper method, but we create a new *Audio* element. An audio file is loaded (enough to play some audio, at least) when the *canPlay* event fires. Because this event can potentially fire multiple times, the event handler should be removed after the first time it's called:

```
// Load an audio file
return load(url, (url, onAssetLoad) => {
  const audio = new Audio();
  audio.src = url;
  const onLoad = e => {
    audio.removeEventListener("canplay", onLoad);
    onAssetLoad(e);
  };
  audio.addEventListener("canplay", onLoad, false);
  return audio;
}).cloneNode();
```

This is the same idea with our *Image* loader, but with one slight difference: at the end, we call *cloneNode()* to create a clone of the *Audio* node. If we didn't do this, the same reference would be returned each time. If we used the reference as part of a *SoundGroup* , every time we restarted *one* sound, *all* sounds would reset.

As with *Texture* , we can update *Sound.js* to use the manager to load the asset:

```
class Sound {
  constructor(src, options) {
    ...
    // Configure the Audio element
    const audio = Assets.sound(src);
    ...
  }
}
```

Asset Manager Events

So far, we've gained nothing from moving asset loading to an asset manager. To make it useful, we need a way to expose some events for us to listen to while the assets are loading. We won't run our game until the asset manager gives us the go-ahead:

```
Assets.onProgress((done, total) => {
  console.log(`${done / total * 100}% complete`);
});

Assets.onReady(() => {
  // Remove loading screen & start the game
  titleScreen();
  Game.run();
});
```

The function in *onProgress* will get called after each individual resource loads, and the function in *onReady* will get called once (and only once) when *all* resources are loaded. The event management coordination is done inside the *onAssetLoad* function that gets called by the "maker" functions we created above.

```
const readyListeners = [];
const progressListeners = [];

let completed = false;

function onAssetLoad(e) {
  if (completed) {
    console.warn("Warning: asset defined after preload.", e.target);
    return;
  }

  // Update listeners with the new state
  ...
}
```

The asset manager gets a flag, *completed* (which notes if everything loaded) as well as two new arrays for storing any callback functions that get registered from our game. As each asset completes, it calls *onAssetLoad* . We start with a sanity check: if we've already decided everything is loaded, it warns us if we have a new file outside our system. (This could happen if we declared a new *Texture* object dynamically inside an entity.) The warning will let the library user know they should move the declaration up and out of the entity class so it can be properly preloaded.

```
// Update listeners with the new state
remaining--;
progressListeners.forEach(cb => cb(total - remaining, total));
if (remaining === 0) {
  // We're done loading
  done();
}
```

Otherwise, we decrement the count of remaining files to load. First, we call all functions in *progressListeners* and keep them posted with how things are progressing. If there are 0 remaining files, we set *completed* to true and call any callback functions in *readyListeners*, via a *done* function:

```
function done() {
  completed = true;
  readyListeners.forEach(cb => cb());
}
```

The last step is to expose a way to add callbacks via the Assets API. All we have to do is add the callback function to either the *readyListeners* or *progressListeners* array. For *onReady*, we also check if *remaining* is 0. If this is the case, the game doesn't have any assets to load at all, so it calls *done* itself:

```
onReady(cb) {
  readyListeners.push(cb);
  // No assets to load in this game!
  if (remaining === 0) {
    done();
  }
},

onProgress(cb) {
  progressListeners.push(cb);
},
```

onProgress and *onReady* will now notify us on the state of the world. We'll use *onReady* to prevent a game from running before all its assets are loaded by integrating it with our *Game.js* helper. Only after the "ready" event fires can we start the main loop:

```
import Assets from "./Assets.js";

class Game {
  run(gameUpdate = () => {}) {
    Assets.onReady(() => {
      // Normal game loop
    });
  }
}
```

This is a simple asset loader that could be improved in several ways. We could introduce more error handling capabilities, as well as take on more responsibility for any cross-browser differences with various file formats. It could even be extended to let us load assets in batches rather than needing to load everything up front. However, it will serve us well enough for most projects, and we can be confident that everything will be loaded when serving our games to our players.

Sound Production

That's enough messing around with housekeeping details. We came here to make some noise. But wait a minute: how do you actually *make* noise? I mean, where does the sound come from? How can we capture or generate it? How can we modify it? How can we make it sound *good*? The answer is **sound production**! It's an expansive and supercool field all of its own. We'll borrow some of the techniques and essentials for making our games sound as good as they look.

Tools and Software

There's a long history of using computers to generate sound. Much of today's modern music production is now done in software, but early software synthesizers (such as Csound[4] from 1985) could only work offline—with long programs fed in as input and (some time later) raw audio files generated as output. Since then, computers have become vastly more powerful, and your laptop can now run a recording studio's worth of real-time software synthesizers simultaneously without breaking a sweat. This has opened up a huge market for off-the-shelf software synths that run the gamut from faithful recreations of classic audio hardware to wacky and original inventions.

 Deep Note

The famous THX "Deep Note" that played at the start of movies was generated offline via a script and then recorded onto high-quality tape to be played in cinemas. However, the composer (programmer Dr James "Andy" Moorer) used random numbers as part of the score. He was never again able to reproduce the exact, well-known original.

---

4. "http://csound.github.io/

7-3. Hybrid software/hardware studio

These days, it's most common that audio software is one of two kinds—a host or a plugin. A **host** is the workhorse of your music creation environment. It lets you record, sequence, and cut/copy/paste *the model* of sound. You can record notes and play them back with any audio plugin. **Plugins** are individual synthesizers (or effects) that will work across hosts. These define what sounds you can make, and how you can process them.

Of the hosts, there are two main types (though the distinction is often murky): **digital audio workstations** (DAWs) and **sound editors**. DAWs are to music creation what IDEs are to coding. They let you compose, edit, assemble, arrange, and effect your audio creations in a single application. Sound editors generally focus on tweaking, editing, and mastering your final sound rather than generating new sounds.

The original DAWs attempted to copy the analog tools that had been used in music studios for decades. They can record and play back multiple audio tracks at the same time, which can be mixed and modified individually. Back when disk space and processing power were limited, a modest home computer would struggle to play back more than a couple of high-quality audio files, so early DAWs like Pro Tools[5] were a combination of expensive audio hardware and software. As computers got faster and cheaper, more raw audio processing could be done purely in software.

[5.] https://en.wikipedia.org/wiki/Pro_Tools

Because early 8-bit home computers were so limited in power, they relied on dedicated sound chips to produce music and effects. To score and compose songs, the computer musician would use a **music tracker**. Trackers worked very differently from analog, multi-track recorders. They did have multiple "tracks" of sounds that played back simultaneously to make a song, but rather than long, continuous audio recordings, they were made of instructions for the built-in sound chips. The 16-bit era extended this to also allow sound **samples** (short sound files) to be sequenced.

For example, there might be a *sample* for a kick drum. Using an instruction like `C-5 01 15` would play a C note in the 5th octave, using the `01` instrument sample, at volume `15`. Because the samples were so small, long compositions took up much less space. Additionally, player software could be embedded in games, allowing songs to change dynamically in response to the state of the game. A huge music scene (the **tracker scene**) grew from the early trackers that continues to this day.

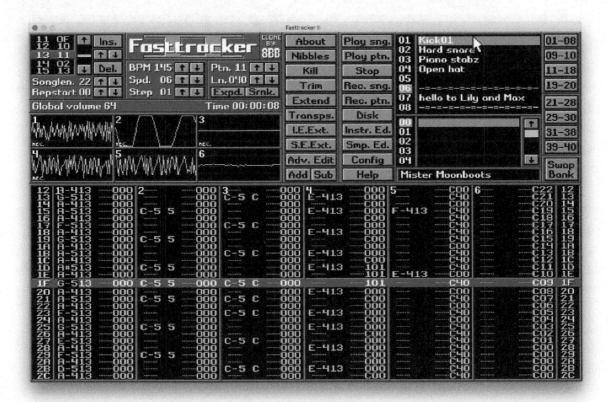

7-4. FastTracker II

Today, most DAWs are a hybrid of traditional, multi-track recorder, MIDI editor and music tracker. Cubase, Logic Pro, and Ardour (open source) follow the traditional multi-track recording approach. Max MSP (or the open-source equivalent Pure Data) follows in the footsteps of

CSound—but in real time, and with GUI. Re-noise, Sun Vox (open source), and FL Studio are more closely related with music trackers than multi-track recorders. Ableton Live and BitWig Studio are good examples of DAWs that broke away from early software music packages and focused on music performance and experimentation. They're extremely popular with DJs and electronic music producers.

7-5. So many DAWs

Sound-effect Generators

Actually, let's not get ahead of ourselves. DAWs are heavy, serious packages—especially if you just want a few quick sounds for your game. One far less intimidating piece of software that should be a part of every game developer's audio toolkit is a **sound-effect generator**. Sound-effect generators are great fun to play with. They're standalone synthesizers (that is, not a plugin for a DAW) designed to make it *absurdly easy* to create random, 8-bit sound effects such as explosions, pickup noises, power-up effects and more—no experience necessary!

7-6. Bfxr making some effects

There are many sound-effect generators, but the most well-known one is called Sfxr[6] by Tomas Pettersson (aka DrPetter), released in 2007. Since then, there have been various clones for different platforms, such as Bfxrhttp://www.bfxr.net/, a Flash port you can try on the Web. Load up the sound generator and hit "randomize" until it makes a sound you want: it can't get any easier than that! If you find a sound you kind of like, but it's not perfect, hit the "mutation" button to get other similar sounds. And if that's not quite right either, get tweaking the hundreds of parameters!

[6.] http://www.drpetter.se/project_sfxr.html

That Sounds Familiar

Sound-effect generators are extremely fun and practical, but you're *not* going to win any awards for originality using these sounds. The ease and popularity of effects generators means the results are very recognizable. If you just don't have time to improve them, then go for it! Otherwise, consider adding extra effects (or layering them with other sounds) in your DAW or sound editor to make them original again!

Samples and DIY Recording

The job of *game creator* requires you to wear many hats. One of them is a "Foley artist" hat. A **Foley artist** creates sound effects and incidental sounds. If an actor puts keys in their pocket, the Foley artist makes the jangly sound. Often the *method* of producing the sound doesn't relate *at all* to what's seen on screen. Flapping a pair of leather gloves for flying bat wings, or punching some Corn Flakes for walking on gravel: a Foley artist does whatever it takes to create the *illusion* of natural sounds.

Getting the perfect sound to match an action in your game will require a lot of searching and testing. But often you won't have that kind of time: you just need to get some sounds in the game *right now*. The tried-and-true method for making sounds fast is … **mouth sounds**! Humans are pretty good at making noise, and what easier way to get *kind of the sound you're after* than gurgling directly into your computer microphone?

You don't need to be a beat-box expert to get usable effects. With even the smallest amount of tweaking, you can get some very effective results. They also act as excellent placeholders and references while you develop your game. Some sounds (such as those of the undead groaning zombies in *Minecraft*) stay there forever.

The first thing you'll need is a *microphone*. Your computer likely has a built-in microphone, or you can use the mic in your cellphone earbuds. Anything that lets audio in. Next, we need some software for recording. You probably also have something already on your computer to take audio notes, but we'll need to level up and use a **sound editor**.

A sound editor is the Photoshop of audio—the Swiss army knife of sound. It lets you record, cut, paste, tweak, and polish your audio files. The best free, cross-platform sound editor is Audacity[7]. It's been around for a long time, and although it feels a bit clunky in comparison to some of its expensive rivals, it's very capable, and more than adequate for our needs.

---

[7] http://www.audacityteam.org/

To prepare for recording, create a new sound file (*FILE -> NEW*) and select your audio input device. (It should be correct by default, but there's a small icon of a microphone, with a dropdown box listing all the possible input methods.) You can also choose to record either stereo or mono audio, but stereo is the default. The human voice is a monophonic sound source (and many microphones are mono), but it's best to work in stereo for when we do post-processing effects that apply individually on each channel.

Then hit the red circular record button. Audio data should be filling the screen—and if you make some noise, it should be clearly reflected in the waveform. We're in business. Start making some noises: bloops, beeps, swooshes, squelches. Whatever you need!

If we're going to start polishing up *Pengolfin'* for the IGC, we should start with some general penguin sounds. I'm not 100% sure what "general penguin sounds" are, but we at least need some penguin grunts and squawks as it flies around, colliding with mountains and such. We'll also want a solid *thwack* when propelling the projectile. We'll record a ruler swatting a phone book to get that.

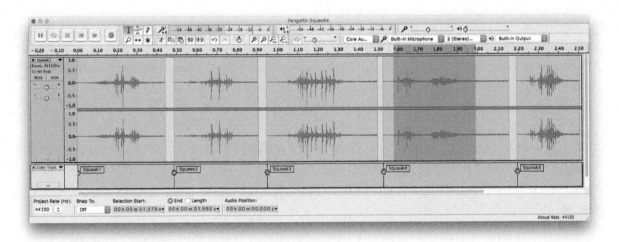

7-7. If a penguin falls in a forest

After you've done a bunch of squawking, grunting, and thwacking, hit the stop button and you'll have something to work with. Play the audio back and listen for promising candidates. Also keep your ear out for possible issues with the audio—crackling or popping or background noises. These can be easy to miss if you're not paying close attention.

Don't Go to Eleven

For the best quality, you want to be as loud as possible without causing "clipping". **Clipping** occurs when the sound level goes above the maximum capacity of the recording system. Any data outside of this range will be chopped off. If you zoom in close and notice flat areas in your audio, it has clipped and will sound distorted. If you record too quietly, you'll have more noise (background hiss) in the final result. Record raw sounds as cleanly and loudly as possible while avoiding any clipping.

Cropping and Editing

With source material in hand, we can start chopping it up and "effecting" it. Start by selecting the area that contains a sound you like, with a generous amount of space before and after. Copy it, then create a new window and paste it in. We need to find good *start and end points* for the sample. This can be important, because if you're not careful you can end up with very audible "click" sounds.

There are two ways to avoid this. One is to zoom in extremely close—as far as your audio editor will allow—and cut the waveform at a **zero crossing**. This is the point where the waveform crosses over from positive to negative, or negative to positive. The volume level here is 0, so we don't get a click. Removing everything before the zero crossing will give us a nice clean start to our sample.

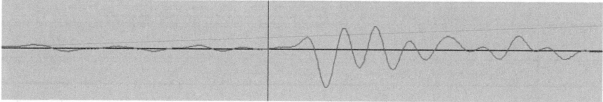
7-8. Finding the zero crossing

The other way we can achieve this is by adding a tiny fade at the beginning and end of the sample. To do this, zoom in quite close and select a very short section at the start of the sound. Then click on *Effect* in the main menu and select *Fade In*. The start of the selection is attenuated to zero (silent), and it linearly rises to the original volume. You can do the same at the end of the sample, but with *Fade Out*. The fade length should be short enough not to be audible, but avoid any clicks or pops.

Often your sound will naturally have a long tail, where the sound has finished and is fading out to silence. Because of noise introduced along the recording signal path, it's a good idea to have a fade-out that's quite long too. Select the area where the sound has become *almost* silent and drag until the end. Fade out this entire section to create a noise-free transition.

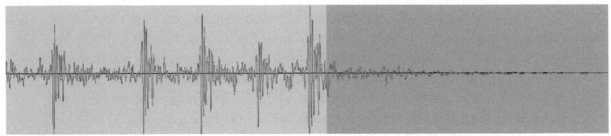

7-9. Fading out a sample

Layering Sounds

An excellent tip for making impressive audio effects is to **layer** multiple sounds that make up a single effect. The swoosh-thwack for launching our penguin can be beefed up with additional sounds. To make a swoosh-ier swoosh, I recorded swinging a broken car radio aerial. To make a thwack-ier thwack, I mixed in a bass drum sound for some low-end punch. I snapped a DVD-R in half to get a nice *crack* sound. Then I layered in a very faint sound of rolling thunder that I found copyright free on FreeSound.com. Finally, I added a wobbly sound from Sfxr. The result is the swooshiest, thwackiest sound you've ever heard.

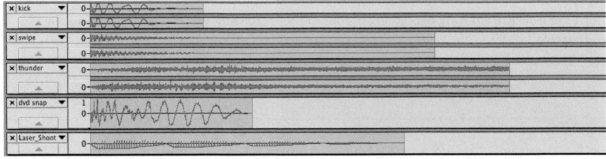

7-10. Audio layers

Layering (combined with mixing and effecting) can turn pedestrian sounds into beasts. Experiment relentlessly, and remember to always listen to your effect in context with your graphics. Sometimes sounds that seem like they should be perfect just don't work in a game, while other things you never dreamed would work end up bringing your game to life!

Zany Effects

Getting good source material is the best way to ensure a great end result ("garbage in, garbage out", as they say). If you're stuck with something less than stellar, or you just want to see how far you can push your recordings, then sometimes you can strike gold by getting wacky with audio effects.

Most audio editors will have a selection of built-in effects (usually with the option to install third-party plugins for more variety). The best thing you can do when starting out is go nuts with the built-in effects and learn what they all do! You'll probably go massively overboard with them. Back up often, and every once in a while go back and make sure you didn't lose anything that made the original special.

When making effects for games, some commonly useful effects are pitch-shifting and delays. **Pitch-shifting** means making a sound play at a different pitch than it was recorded at. It can produce great results when shifting in either direction: shift *down*, and our penguin-squawks sound like dinosaur growls; shift *up*, and our penguin becomes a lot more comical. Pitch-shifting also makes things you record not sound like you—which can help if you're embarrassed when listening to your own voice!

Delays are when a sound is fed back to itself to produce echoes, chorus, and phaser effects. A nice chorus or phaser effect will fatten up a dull sound or make it more futuristic. Echoes will change the feeling of the "space" in a game. Be consistent with sounds that are supposed to be playing in the same space as each other.

Don't be afraid to chain effects either. Reverse your sound, pitch-shift it up a couple of semitones, overlay a fat swirling chorus … BOOM! As with any software, it'll take a while to learn what all the tools do and when's the best time to use them. Sometimes you'll conjure up an effect that sounds absolutely fantastic in your editor, but doesn't work aesthetically with your game. Toss it out and save it for another project! Sounds must contribute to the aesthetic of your game.

Mastering Effects

Before you go too crazy with effects, you should ensure your raw recordings are as usable as possible. There's a handful of core effects and techniques that are used to make more professional-sounding effects and recordings. These subtle (less zany) post-processing effects are often used as part of a track's *mastering* phase (that we'll look at more later), but can also help to clean up and improve the raw input.

Firstly, if you recorded the sound too quietly, you can use a volume amplifier (*Effect -> Amplify* in Audacity) to bring the overall level up. Amplifying raises the level of all sounds equally. If you do too much, the loudest part of the sound will clip and create distortion. To avoid this, you can use the *normalize* effect that will amplify the sound as much as possible without clipping.

Often, this still isn't good enough. A lot of times you won't be able to make the quiet parts of your sound loud enough without clipping the loud parts. The solution is to apply an **audio compressor**. A compressor magically reduces only loud parts of your sound file (you can define what "loud" means on a sound-by-sound basis). It then applies an overall *makeup gain* so the entire sound becomes louder without introducing clipping.

This Is Not the Same as File Size Compression!

Don't confuse audio compression with file compression. This has nothing to do with file size, and everything to do with audio volume!

Audio compression is a black art, but is really important for making your music work in a variety of playback environments. Done well, compression can make your overall mix louder, more impressive, and more "professional". But if you overdo it, the sound can lose clarity and *punch*, or introduce too much background hiss.

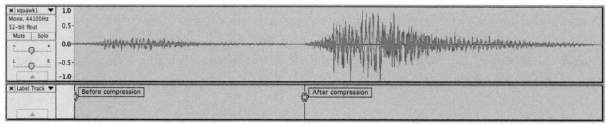

7-11. Audio compression

Another essential effect—probably *the* essential effect—is *reverb*. **Reverb** adds a slight echo to a recording, giving it a feeling of space. As humans, we rely on natural reverb for locating sound sources in our environment. If you clap your hands in a large concrete hall, it sounds very different from clapping your hands in your carpeted bedroom. Your brain uses reverb to understand direction and distances. Using this in your games can be very powerful. Using it in your music can make things sound more natural and real and (like singing in the shower) can make things sound better.

The final core effects you should be familiar with are **equalizers** (EQs) and **filters**. These might not always be necessary (and filters can also be abused as a creative effect). They're familiar fixtures of most home stereos, and involve selectively boosting or cutting certain frequency ranges in the sound.

Filters come in a variety of types. The most common filters are the **high-pass** (reduces low frequencies), **low-pass** (reduces high frequencies), and **band-pass** (reduces high and low frequencies, leaving the middle area untouched). There are thousands of filter plugins available, and they're an excellent tool for radically shaping a sound. Even our humble mouth sounds can sound like massive explosions with a chunky, low-pass filter, some heavy compression, and a wash of echoey reverb.

These are the main DSP effects for improving and sculpting good raw sounds. During this phase, you must carefully and constantly A/B test any changes you make to ensure you're actually improving things. However, when it comes to effects for creative purposes, there are no rules and no limits—so feel free to apply as many effects as extremely as you can!

Recording Tips

For the purposes of game development, we can happily adopt the "whatever works" approach to sound design: whatever gets good noises in our game is good enough. But sound design is also a field with a long history, and there are lots of rules of thumb and general guidelines to help us achieve better results …

Use the Best Gear You Can Get Your Hands On

There's a world of difference between the microphone in your laptop and a Neumann U87 (which will set you back several thousand dollars). You can pick up a decent microphone pretty cheaply these days. Just remember that a microphone captures *analog sounds*, which need to be converted to *digital* for use in our games. Just like the mic, the *analog-to-digital converters* in your laptop are generally pretty average. Some microphones include their own converters (if they plug directly in via USB, for example). Otherwise, you'll need to get an *audio interface*.

Also be aware that there are different *types* of microphones—primarily *dynamic* and *condenser* microphones. Condensers are great for recording vocals, because they're *extremely* sensitive and can pick up a wide frequency range. But they're generally more expensive and may require *phantom power*—a 48-volt power source often supplied by mixing desks and preamps. If it plugs in via USB, it'll be ready to go out of the box.

Find a Quiet Recording Environment

It's easy to ignore a lot of the day-to-day noises that surround us. Sometimes you won't even notice they exist—until a passing car or a sneezing roommate ruins an otherwise fantastic recording. Be mindful of the sounds around you, and try to record in the quietest part of your house—during the dead of night!

Watch Your Signal Level

When recording, keep a close eye on the input level of your sound source. If it's too low, you'll be capturing too much background and signal-chain noise. If it's too loud, you'll get clipping that, in most cases, will render the recording unusable. Most recording software has level indicators that include a red light that remains lit if any clipping occurs so you know you've gone too far.

Reduce the Echo

Even in the dead of night, there's a hidden source of noise that will mess up your sounds: **room reverb**. Any time you record, you pick up the natural reverb of the room you're in. A good way to test this is to stand in the center of the room and clap (once) sharply and loudly. Reverb is the sound bouncing around the room, reflecting off the walls, slowly decaying. In a room with poor sound absorption you'll hear a *flanging* robotic effect. That's bad for sound recording. (Even a room with beautiful natural reverb might not be what you need for your effects; and you can't remove the reverb after it's recorded.)

To fix the echo, get creative! You need to dampen the sound reflecting off of hard, parallel surfaces. Pull up your bed mattress and lean it against the wall. Hang blankets around the room. Litter the ground with sweaters. Pull books half out of the bookshelf to create uneven surfaces. Try the clap-test again after each change. The "deader" the sound, the better.

Music for Games

We've already put on the Foley artist hat—and we're making this whole game from scratch by ourselves—so why not take it all the way and be the musician too? Music is a very important (and often neglected) aspect of game creation. It's sometimes added as an afterthought, or omitted entirely—which is a grave mistake! Music is a powerful and efficient tool for establishing mood and feeling, for building tension and excitement, and for controlling the pacing of a piece. The movie industry knows it, the big game studios know it—and you should know it, too!

There are various options when you want to get sound in your games. The easiest is to grab some pre-made tracks with a suitable copyright license and plonk it in. The problem with this approach is that anyone else can use that track for their game too, and there's no chance of getting any variations or changes made to the track. It's often obvious and distracting when a game mixes song sources, so choose this path at your peril.

The next option is to find a game music composer and work with them. This might not be as difficult as you imagine: there are lots of aspiring game musicians out there looking for a chance to feature their work in finished games! If you look on popular game developer forums—such as TIGSource[8] or Reddit Gamedev[9]—you'll find many musicians looking for projects. Collaborating with others can be very rewarding and fun. Be sure to lay out expectations clearly at the beginning (and establish milestones to track progress) to avoid wasting each other's time.

If you want original music but don't want to start collaborating with others, the only choice left is

[8] https://forums.tigsource.com
[9] https://www.reddit.com/r/gamedev

to do it yourself! Yes! Your first efforts might not go platinum, but the reward will be a game that's *completely* your own creation! There are *many* music-making packages available and (like choosing a text editor or an IDE) the one for you will be a personal choice. If you don't have a lot of experience, you can start with GarageBand or Mixcraft—which offer drag-and-drop music creation from a stack of pre-packaged loops. After that, you'll have to try them all and see what you like. My personal favorites are Ableton Live and SunVox.

Creating a Track from Scratch

Pengolfin' needs a theme song that's fitting for a fun-filled carnival on the South Pole. Most likely it should be in a major key (as otherwise it would be a *sorrow-filled* carnival in the South Pole), with a simple melody played in some kind of quirky, squishy bell or plucky sounds. Something bright and happy. I've chosen to make our theme song in SunVox. SunVox is an audio tracker that's free and open source, available on many platforms (including mobile devices), and has some built-in synthesizers—enabling us to make a whole song with no extra requirements.

Trackers let you sequence sounds in a spreadsheet-like matrix. Each row plays one at a time, and any sounds on the same row will play simultaneously. Each cell determines which sound triggers, at what note. The main advantage of trackers—back when computer memory was measured in kilobytes—was that a small number of sound samples could be reused and arranged into a full song. It's less important these days, but trackers are still fun to use and easy to program.

To kick things off (drum-based pun there), we'll make a simple beat. Honestly, you can play *any* percussive sounds at regular intervals and they'll sound good. But starting with a stock-standard beat will be more familiar to your listeners, and you can tweak it from there. We'll go with the ol' *boom-ka-boom-ka* beat. Play a bass drum (also called a "kick drum", because real-life drummers use their feet for it) on every beat, a snare drum in between beats, and a closed hi-hat (*chht*) over the top of both of them:

```
        1   2   3   4   1   2   3   4
Kick:   X - - X - - - X - - - X - - -
Snare:  - - X - - - X - - - X - - - X -
Hi hat: - X - X - X - X - X - X - X - X
```

When you play this back, it sounds like this (if *you* sing the *boom-kas* and a *friend* does the *chts*):

```
        1   &   2   &   3   &   4   &
you:    boom    ka      boom    ka
friend:     cht     cht     cht     cht
```

Rock and roll! Let's transpose this into SunVox. Because we're never playing the bass and snare at the same time, we could put them in the same *channel* (a column in the matrix)—but for clarity we'll separate them. Each row represents one beat, every four rows is a bar (the first beat of a bar is colored slightly differently). In each cell you can place one note by pressing a keyboard key. This will determine the pitch. For drum sounds, it's best to use their original pitch (which is generally the C note).

To make a sequence, first put SunVox in "edit" mode (to toggle), then place a kick drum sound in the first cell of the first channel. Then move down to the 5th row (the second bar) and place another, then the 9th row (the third bar) ... and so on. Play it back: you've just made *the classic* four-on-the-floor drum loop! In the next channel, add a snare sound and put it between the kick drums (on beats 3, 7, 11 ...). Finally, add a hi-hat on every second row. You've got yourself a beat.

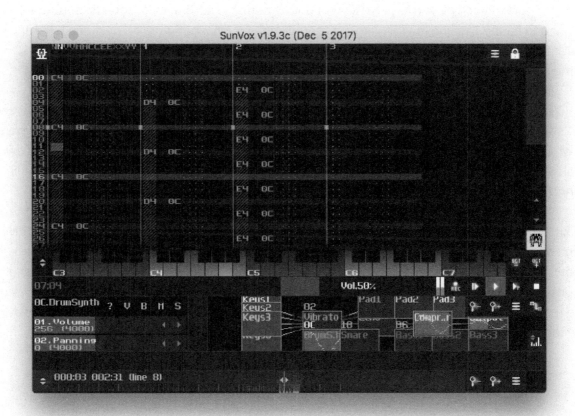

7-12. Rocking out with SunVox

It's time for the most important ingredient in our theme song—the melody. This is what we want to get stuck in people's heads and have them associate with our game. This is the time for magic. Select a synthesizer sound you like and start pressing keys on your keyboard until you make something catchy. Alternatively, just sequence some random things until you get something useful. (The safest approach is to space these evenly apart, on the drum beat.) Easy!

Making Music

This sounds like a pretty hand-wavy description of writing music. But seriously, plopping any old thing down will often sound better than you expect. It will take years of musical training to understand *why* it sounds good (or how to make it sound like you want) but you've been listening to music your whole life and have picked up the basics by osmosis. I promise.

Once you have a melody, it's time for a bass line. The bass line tends to follow the rhythm of the drum beat: it's the glue between the beat and the melody. It needs to sit well with both. It's easiest to start with the same note as the melody, and play one note per bar. We'll add a tuba-like *oomph-ah* on each bar to make a bass line that feels fun.

That's all we really need! Each page of notes in a tracker is called a **pattern**. The patterns can be arranged into a complete song. Our song arrangement will start with only the melody pattern, followed by the full song repeated four times. Humans like their music in multiples of four: four beats to a bar, played a multiple of four times. When you're a pro, you can make some 5/4-time polyrhythmic jazz … but to begin with, keep it simple.

What Else?

This is a very simple song, and maybe you're wondering what else you could add? After a melody and bass line, the next most common addition to a song is a "pad". A **pad** is a rich sound like orchestra strings. It sits in the background and fills up the sonic space without making things sound cluttered.

The theme song is done; it's ready to be exported for final *mastering* in our audio editor. As it stands, the song ends very abruptly (there's no nice fade out, or ending). That's what we want, because the final song will be imported in our game as `new Sound("res/sound/theme.mp3", { Loop: true })` and will loop around nicely when it gets to the end.

Music is about sequencing and layering sounds. The ideas behind making a song in *any* music package (or even in real life, with real instruments) will be similar to what we've done with SunVox, even if the user interface is completely different!

The Web Audio API

After using synthesizers in music packages like SunVox, you might start wondering, "But *where* does the sound come from?"

It's kind of wizardry—summoning a sonic soundscape out of thin air. The original hardware analog synthesizers worked by combining electronic *oscillator* circuits that produced periodic recurring signals: if you cycle the circuit twenty thousand times a second, you're producing an *audible* sine wave! These raw waveforms can then be mixed, re-routed, and filtered (removing certain frequencies, boosting others) to shape individual notes and create interesting timbres and effects.

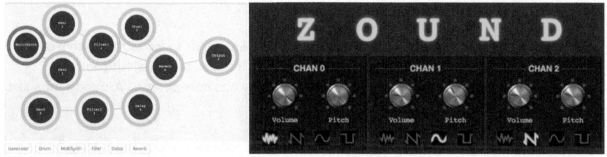

7-13. Web Audio API synthesizers

Software synthesizers emulate this process in code. Modular synthesizers have basic components (oscillators and filters) that can be networked in a myriad of ways to create complex musical systems. The system consists of a series of black-box modules that perform different audio tasks. Each module has one or more inputs and one or more outputs. They can be connected together to make more complex effects (which also can be packaged to form *new* black-box modules).

The Web Audio API provides a collection of these **digital signal processing** (DSP) components for generating and manipulating audio. The components (called **audio nodes**) are networked to form an *audio routing graph* capable of all manner of sound processing magic. The primary audio *sources* for the graph are either `Audio` elements (sound files), or *oscillators* that generate pure tones. The primary output will usually be the *master destination*—the user's speakers.

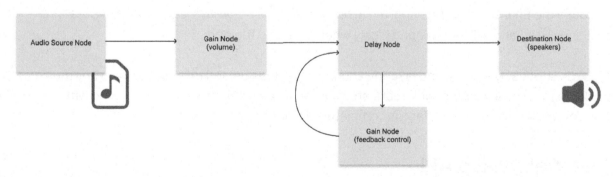

7-14. Web Audio API graph

Web Audio API

I won't sugar-coat it: the Web Audio API is daunting and complex and a bit weird. As a result, there are many hoops to jump through to get things working the way you might expect. It *is* powerful, though, and it has some really nifty features. If you like the idea of wrangling audio in weird and wonderful ways, then it's worth reading the spec and diving in further.

To work with the Web Audio API, we require an audio *context*, which is similar to the `Canvas` graphics context. This is available in the browser as `window.AudioContext`:

```
const ctx = new AudioContext();
```

Once you have an instance of the `AudioContext`, you can start to make the graph connections, which is the only way to get work done. The Web Audio API is all about `connect`-ing modular boxes together:

```
const master = ctx.createGain();
master.gain.value = 0.5;
master.connect(ctx.destination);
```

Our first audio node is a `GainNode`. A `GainNode` is created with the helper method `ctx.createGain()`. Gain is a module that attenuates *or* boosts its input source. It's a volume knob. All audio nodes have a `connect` method for joining the audio routing graph (as well as a `disconnect` for leaving it). The parameter for `connect` should be another node. In our example, the `GainNode` is connected to a special node `ctx.destination` —which is the main audio output (your speakers!).

Audio Nodes

There are many basic audio nodes, and they're all instantiated via helper methods off the audio context (such as `ctx.createGain()`) rather than directly with `new GainNode()` —as they can only exist with a reference to the current audio context.

Audio nodes are controlled by tweaking their `AudioParam` parameters. Each node will have zero or more parameters that are relevant to its functionality. A `GainNode` has only one `AudioParam` — `gain`. By setting the node's `gain` value (`gain.value`) to 0.5, any input will come out half as loud as it went in. `AudioParam`s can be set directly, or can be scheduled and automated over time (see the "Timing and Scheduling" section).

Oscillators

To generate sound magically out of nothing, the `ctx.createOscillator()` function creates an `OscillatorNode` audio node. The oscillator works like its hardware equivalent—repeating over and over fast enough to generate a cyclical waveform that we can hear (well, assuming we set the `frequency` audio parameter in the human hearing range, or that you're a bat).

 Look After Your Ears

> Protect your ears: you can't buy a new pair! While working with the Web Audio API, you'll inevitably connect a node to the wrong place and end up with a feedback loop that will be *very, very loud*. If you're wearing headphones, this can damage your hearing. Always work at a reasonable level, and add gain nodes with initial low volumes while you test new things.

```
const osc = ctx.createOscillator();
osc.type = "sine";
osc.frequency.value = 440;
osc.connect(master);
osc.start();
```

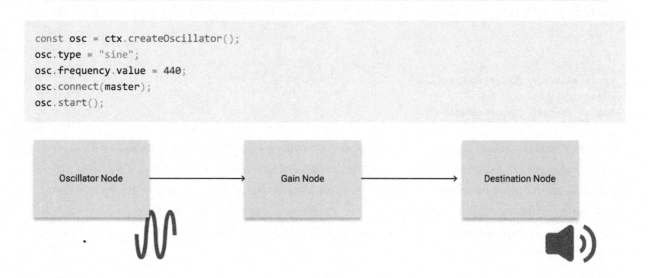

7-15. Oscillator audio graph

This creates a pure *sine wave* at a frequency of 440 Hz (the musical note A, called the "pitch standard"). The oscillator is connected to our volume node, which is connected to your speakers. The `type` property defines the shape of the repeating wave. The default is `sine`, and others include `square`, `sawtooth`, and `triangle`. Try them out. (I think you'll find `square` is the best.)

The audio parameter `frequency` determines the pitch and is measured in hertz (Hz). Humans generally can hear between 20 Hz and 20,000 Hz. Try them out. (Just watch your volume: don't damage your ears!) Listening to pure tones can quickly become unpleasant, so we'll stop the sound as soon as you hit the space bar:

```
game.run(() => {
  if (keys.action) {
    osc.stop();
  }
});
```

 You Can't Restart a Stopped Oscillator

Once you stop an oscillator (or other sound buffer, as we'll see shortly) you can't start it again. This is the weird nature of the Web Audio API. The idea is to remain as stateless as possible by simply creating things as you need them. Under the hood, things are optimized for instantiating large quantities of new audio objects. We'll see how to handle multiple notes shortly.

A single oscillator is very annoying, but it's a start. The beauty of modular audio systems is the ability to compose simple nodes into a complex timbre or effect.

Combining Oscillators

A far more interesting sound can be made from two oscillators. (In fact, many famous, old-school analog synthesizers contained only two oscillators, usually along with a white noise generator.) To combine the oscillators, just create a new one and also connect it to `master`. The settings need to be different, as otherwise it'll just be the same sound but louder!

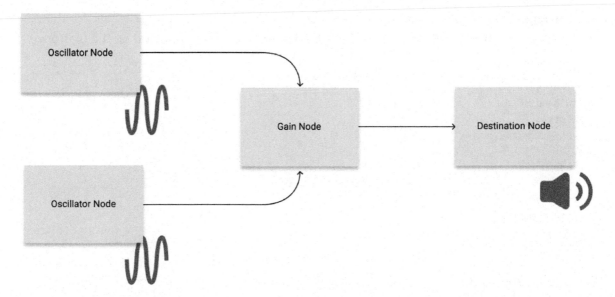

7-16. Combining oscillators

```
const osc2 = ctx.createOscillator();
osc2.type = "square";
osc2.frequency.value = 440 * 1.25;
osc2.connect(master);
osc2.start();
```

Here we have a square wave playing at a frequency 1.25 times higher than the sine wave. This ratio sounds nice. (Actually, it's a ratio of 5/4, which happens to be a "major third" above the original A note.) It's connected to our master gain. If we were going to extend this mini-synth, we would want to create its own "output gain" node, so the volume of both oscillators could be controlled with one audio parameter, without affecting anything else in the audio graph.

Moving into Our Library

As mentioned, the Web Audio API is reasonably complicated and powerful—so it's actually quite difficult to make a lovely API without sacrificing that power. In our library, we'll just expose a couple of helpful things—the audio context, and a master gain node. For the rest, you'll have to roll up your sleeves and do it yourself.

Create a new file at `sound/webAudio.js`. It will export an object with a `hasWebAudio` flag (so we can test before we use it), along with `ctx` audio context and `master` gain node:

```
const hasWebAudio = !!window.AudioContext;
let ctx;
let master;
```

`ctx` and `master` are initially undefined. They'll be "lazy loaded" the first time we ask for them. This is so we don't create an audio context if it's not needed, or not supported on the platform:

```
export default {
  hasWebAudio,
  get ctx() {
    // Set up the context
    ...
    return ctx;
  },
  get master() {
    return master;
  }
};
```

The first time you ask for `ctx`, it will run the getter function and create the context and gain nodes, and connect to the user's speakers:

```
// Set up the context
if (!ctx && hasWebAudio) {
  ctx = new AudioContext();
  master = ctx.createGain();
  master.gain.value = 1;
  master.connect(ctx.destination);
}
```

Everything should connect to the `master` gain node, rather than directly to the speakers. This way, it's possible to implement overall volume control, or mute/unmute sound. Anywhere we want to do Web Audio work, we can grab a reference to the global context or connect nodes to the `master` gain node:

```
const { ctx, master } = webAudio;
```

An extension of this approach would be to make two additional gain nodes—say, *sfx* and *music*—both connecting to `master`. Any sounds would connect to the relevant channel and could be controlled independently in your game.

Audio Element as a Source

Oscillators can be useful for making quick sound effects, but your game probably won't be generating sound from scratch in real time; it'll be playing kick-ass sound samples and rockin' some tunes you made earlier. Although this is already possible via the `Audio` element, we can't do real-time effects on them until they're part of the audio graph.

For this purpose, there's `ctx.createMediaElementSource()`. It accepts an `Audio` (or `Video`) element as input and converts it to a `MediaElementAudioSourceNode`, which is an `AudioNode` that can be `connect`-ed to other nodes!

```
const plopNode = ctx.createMediaElementSource(plops.audio);
plopNode.connect(master);
```

This is the simplest way to get a sound into the Web Audio API world if it's already loaded as an `Audio` element. In this state, it's easy to apply some cool sound effects to it and do other audio post-processing (which we'll do shortly).

Source as an Audio Buffer

The `MediaElementAudioSourceNode` is easy, but a bit limited in its abilities: it can only do what a regular `Audio` element can do (play, stop … that's about it). A more powerful, programmatic element is an `AudioBufferSourceNode` . An `AudioBufferSourceNode` can play back and manipulate in-memory data (stored in an `AudioBuffer`). It offers the ability to modify the detuning, playback rate, loop start and end points, and can be used for dynamically processing a buffer of audio.

The downside is it's harder to set up and use. You need to load the sound from a file in a special format, then decode it as a buffer, and finally assign the buffer to the `AudioBufferSourceNode` . *Then* it can be used in our audio graph. We'll treat the sound buffer as a new asset type; it's a good test of our asset loading system. `Asset.soundBuffer` will do the heavy lifting of loading the file and decoding it:

```
soundBuffer(url, ctx) {
  return load(url, (url, onAssetLoad) => {
    ...
  });
},
```

What should we return for a "buffer", though? An image returns a new `Image` , and audio returns a new `Audio` element. A buffer is weirder: it doesn't have a handy placeholder we can easily return before loading. This is the perfect use case for a JavaScript *promise*. A **promise** is a promise. "I promise I'll give you a buffer … eventually."

```
fetch(url)
  .then(r => r.arrayBuffer())
  .then(ab => new Promise((success, failure) => {
    ctx.decodeAudioData(ab, buffer => {
      onAssetLoad(url);
      success(buffer);
    });
  }));
```

We're using `fetch` to grab a sound file from a URL. The `fetch` function happens to return a promise too—so we can use `.then()` to wait for the result of fetching. This is the beauty of promises: you can combine them and handle all asynchronous tasks in a consistent manner.

When `fetch` returns, we extract the result as an `arrayBuffer` . (Other possible functions include `text()` and `json()` , depending on the type of file you're fetching.) The result of this is an `arrayBuffer` that we can decode as audio using `ctx.decodeAudioData` . This is an asynchronous operation, so we create a new `Promise` to wrap the callback function (so everything stays in promise-land).

A promise takes a function as a parameter, and this function is called with two of its own functions— `success` and `failure` . When the functionality you want to accomplish is complete, you call one of these functions to *resolve* the promise and get on with things.

That's part one done—making an *AudioBuffer* . Part two is to make an *AudioBufferSourceNode* to play it. These are lightweight nodes like oscillators: you create them each time you want to play a buffer. In *sound/SoundBuffer.js* , we'll make something that acts a lot like a regular *Sound* , but has a default *output* node to connect to:

```
class SoundBuffer {
  constructor(src, options = {}) {
    this.options = Object.assign(
      { volume: 1, output: master },
      options
    );

    // Configure Audio element
    const audio = Assets.soundBuffer(src, ctx);
    ...
  }
}
```

By default, it'll connect to our *webAudio.master* gain node—but you can override this in options any time you call *.play()* :

```
play(overrides) {
  const { audio, options } = this;
  const opts = Object.assign({ time: 0 }, options, overrides);

  audio.then(buffer => {
    // ...
  });
}
```

In *play* , we collate our options and get a reference to the promise from our asset loader. Because it's a promise, we can call *.then* to retrieve the audio buffer. (Once a promise is resolved, calling *then* will give us the same result each time. It doesn't load anything again.) To play the buffer, we create an *AudioBufferSourceNode* with *ctx.createBufferSource* :

```
const source = ctx.createBufferSource();
source.buffer = buffer;
source.volume = opts.volume;
if (opts.speed) {
  source.playbackRate.value = opts.speed;
}
source.connect(opts.output);
```

```
source.start(0, opts.time);
```

This again mimics `Sound`, but there are some new abilities. One is to set the `playbackRate` so we can alter the pitch on each play. This is great for varying sound effects like bullets and walking as we did earlier, without requiring any additional sound files.

Effecting a Sound Source

Once we have a source audio node ready and loaded (be it in the form of an `Oscillator`, `MediaElementAudioSourceNode`, or `AudioBufferSourceNode`) we can start making some effects to spice up our sounds. Audio effects are made by routing audio sources through one or more modules. We've already seen one "effect"—a simple gain node volume control. Cooler effects just require more modules linked together! There are several Web Audio API nodes that are helpful for making a variety of DSP effects:

- `GainNode` (`createGain`): volume control
- `DelayNode` (`createDelay`): pause before outputting the input source
- `BiquadFilterNode` (`createBiquadFilter`): alter the volume of certain frequencies of the input source
- `DynamicsCompressorNode` (`createDynamicsCompressor`): apply audio compression to the input
- `ConvolverNode` (`createConvolver`): use convolution to apply a reverb effect to an input source.

We're going to create an "underwater in a cavern" effect for *Pengolfin'*. When our penguin ball falls into the water off the edge of the screen, the theme tune switches from a bright crisp sound to a gurgling underwater effect. The effect will consist of a filter, a delay, and a gain node connected together. The filter dampens the high-frequency sounds, and the delay and gain work together to make a feedback loop to make an underwater-y echo.

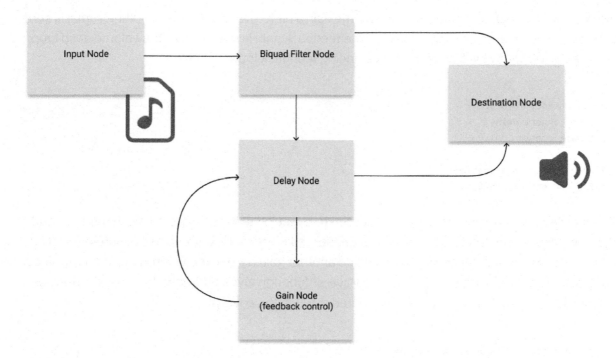

7-17. Audio graph for our effect

```
function inACavern(ctx, destination) {
  const filter = ctx.createBiquadFilter();
  const delay = ctx.createDelay();
  const feedback = ctx.createGain();
  ...
  return filter;
}
```

Our effect generator will be a function that returns the filter node. This is the audio node to connect source sounds that we'd like to have effected. The filter will be connected to a node specified in the destination parameter. Now our effect can have an input and output to the audio graph.

```
delay.delayTime.value = 0.2;
feedback.gain.value = 0.5;
filter.type = "hipass";
filter.frequency.value = 650;
filter.Q.value = 5;
```

Next is the fun part: figuring out some nice parameters for the components. Don't overthink it to begin with; just try any old values and see what sounds cool. These values can also vary over time (see the next section on scheduling). Once you have something that works, it's time to connect everything up. The delay and feedback gain connect to each other so that any input is delayed for

200 milliseconds (0.2), then dampened by the gain a bit (0.5) and then the resulting signal is *sent back* to the delay, and the cycle repeats. The feedback gain is set to halve the volume each loop; setting this closer to 1 will create a never-ending feedback loop.

```
delay.connect(feedback);
filter.connect(delay);
feedback.connect(delay);

filter.connect(destination); // "Dry"
delay.connect(destination); // "Wet"
```

The filter (which is our input) is also connected to the delay to kick things off. Both the filter and the delay are connected to the output destination, so there's a mix between the pure filtered sound and the feedback echo. (You could add another gain here if you wanted more fine-grained control.) The effect is ready to go. Our `inACavern` function gives us a new "black box" effect we can use elsewhere. Sounds can now be routed through the cavern!

```
const effect = inACavern(ctx, master);
theme.audio.disconnect(master);
theme.audio.connect(effect);
```

By connecting and disconnecting sounds to effects, you can create unique-feeling spaces in your game. Our effect is pretty over the top. Sometimes you want this, but most of the time you should apply the "less is more" rule: you don't want an effect to jump out and break the player's immersion.

Timing and Scheduling

Timing is everything with audio. A sound that's out of time (even by a few milliseconds) will sound very wrong to our brains. (That's why it's easy to tell when someone is bad at playing the drums.) The Web Audio API has a sophisticated timing system for scheduling sounds to play in the future. It's a pretty tight drummer.

The key for scheduling sounds revolves around the `ctx.currentTime` property. This is a high-precision timer that's used to offset *future* events. Everything we've done so far has been spur of the moment. Our `SoundBuffer`s start playing as soon as we call `play`, because under the hood they call `source.start(0)` —which means "play right now!" Using `currentTime`, we can schedule it for later:

```
source.start(ctx.currentTime + 1)
```

The timer is measured in seconds, so the above code will request that the audio starts playing *exactly* one second in the future. The precision of the audio system means that, if you schedule a bunch of notes to play an equal distance apart (say, 60 seconds / 250 BPM = 0.24 seconds apart), you'd be playing at a steady 250 beats per minute!

```
const bpm = 60 / 250;
const note = bpm / 2; // 1/2 beat notes
```

We want to play a bunch of notes, all "on the beat". We'll make a function that takes the note to play, the time to start, and the note length. If you want, you can double the oscillator for a nicer synth sound as we did above:

```
const playNote = (note, time, length) => {
  const osc1 = ctx.createOscillator();
  osc1.type = "square";
  osc1.frequency.value = note;
  osc1.connect(master);
  osc1.start(time);
  osc1.stop(time + length);
};
```

The key parts to playing a note are the `start` and `stop` times. A note will turn on when we tell it to, and turn off half a beat later. To make something musical, we have to schedule a note exactly `bpm` seconds apart. We'll make a loop that's eight bars long, with each bar playing four beats:

```
const time = ctx.currentTime;
for (let i = 0; i < 8; i++) { // 8 bars
  const offset = time + (i * (bpm * 4)); // bar offset

  playNote(A, offset + bpm * 0, note); // beat 1
  playNote(C, offset + bpm * 1, note); // beat 2
  playNote(G, offset + bpm * 2, note); // beat 3
  playNote(D, offset + bpm * 3, note); // beat 4
}
```

It's not likely that you'll want to make a whole song this way (though it's certainly possible, and might make for an interesting game mechanic if the song is tied to actions in your game!). But it can be useful for making sound effects. Try changing the beats per minute from 250 to 1250: suddenly our arpeggio is a cosmic ray-gun effect.

Ramps and Modulators

Scheduling is not just for generating and triggering sounds. A more common use case is for applying smooth *ramps* to audio parameters. When modifying an audio parameter (such as a gain value) we can modify it directly (with `master.gain.value = 1`), which shifts the volume level instantly. Often this is undesirable, and we need parameters to move smoothly over time. This is a **ramp**. There are two types of ramps in the Web Audio API: linear and exponential.

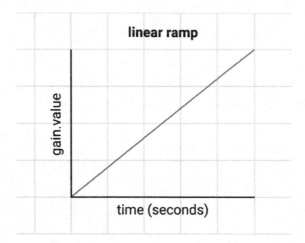
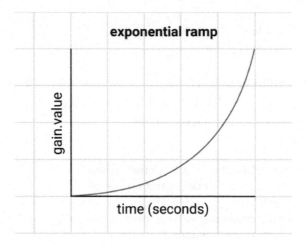

7-18. Linear vs exponential ramps

 Liner vs Exponential

> Generally, exponential ramps sound smoother and more natural to the ear when applied to frequency changes. For other parameters (such as volume), it depends on your needs. I usually use exponential ramps for fades, but you need to try it out for yourself.

Ramps can be tied to *any audio parameter*. If it's attached to a gain node, it can act as an automated fade-out effect, which is much nicer than simply cutting out when our game changes screen. The *fade* function will take a value to fade *to* and a length of time to fade over:

```
function fade (to, length) {
  const { master, ctx } = webAudio;
  const now = ctx.currentTime;
  master.gain.setValueAtTime(master.gain.value, now);
  master.gain.linearRampToValueAtTime(to, now + length);
}
```

Before a ramp will work, you must call `ctx.setValueAtTime` first (that is, you can't just directly set the value). `setValueAtTime` accepts two parameters: the value you wish to assign, and the scheduled time to set it. We want it *right now*, so use the `ctx.currentTime`.

To create a ramp, we use the `AudioParam` method `linearRampToValueAtTime` —which ramps, linearly, to a value, at a time. It accepts the destination value to slide to, and how long it should take. We make this relative to when we started (`ctx.currentTime + length`). The Web Audio API takes care of smoothly automating the volume change over the time period we specified.

```
master.gain.value = 0;
fade(1, 2.5);
```

Ramps ramp, oscillators oscillate. When oscillators oscillate fast enough, we can hear them. However, a smoothly undulating waveform has other purposes too. The output of an oscillator can *control other audio parameters* in the same way a ramp does—allowing for some really radical effects. A very slow oscillator (from around 0 Hz to 20 Hz) is called a **low frequency oscillator** (LFO), and can be used to modulate parameters like frequency (for a vibrato effect) and volume (tremolo), or affect parameters like delay time and filter amounts:

```
const lfo = ctx.createOscillator();
lfo.frequency.value = 2;
lfo.connect(osc.frequency);
```

This is really just scratching the surface of what musical madness you can sculpt by combining nodes and scheduled parameters. The more you play with arranging nodes, the more you get a feel for how the various modules will interact—and you'll have greater control. Until then, you can make some really cool sounds even by accident.

Post Production: Mixing and Mastering

The technical side of adding sound effects and music to our game is done. But before we push our audible creations out to our eager fans, we should consider one last piece of the audio puzzle: the mystical arts of mixing and mastering.

As we mentioned earlier, **mixing** refers to setting the volume levels and spatial positioning of all the `Audio` elements that play at the same time. This can be harder than it seems: your game is dynamic, and you don't have total control over which sounds will play at any given time. The important thing is to make sure your sounds all work well together and none stand out too much.

 Checking Volume Levels

It's a good idea to script a bunch of sounds in your game to play in loops at varying times to ensure they're all *about* the correct volume. Anything that sticks out too much will probably end up as a source of annoyance to your players.

When using the Web Audio API, the easiest way to handle mixing settings is to attach a `GainNode` wherever you want some volume control. If you were doing this in the analog world, it would be the equivalent to patching your source into a giant *mixing desk* full of sliders—the kind of thing you see in the movies whenever someone is "in the studio".

The gain node becomes the master volume of the sound, and can be dampened, boosted, muted or faded over time. But volume changes alone may not save the day. If you have a sound effect that's in the same frequency range as a prominent part of your music track (or other sound effects), it can become "lost in the mix". A common way to fix this is to give your sounds their own area in the frequency spectrum. Using a filter or EQ effect, you can boost and cut frequencies so that a given sound is the most prominent in that frequency range.

```
const backgroundNoiseFilter = context.createBiquadFilter();
backgroundNoiseFilter.Q.value = 0.2;
```

Vary the `frequency` and `Q` values (**Q factor** describes the width of the frequencies affected) and listen to the results. Depending on your values, the effect can be extreme. If you were in the studio, these parameters would likely be available via a series of knobs right above the volume sliders: that's how important they are! If you connect these parameters to an LFO to vary them over time, you'll hear some classic music filter sweeps.

The default filter type is "low-pass". It leaves low frequencies alone and cuts the high frequencies, and is good for pushing high-frequency sounds into the background. Alternatively, boosting with a "notch" or "high-pass" filter around 2000 Hz tends to push sounds more forward in the mix so they stand out.

At this stage, it's good to have someone play through your game while you listen on a variety of sound systems: your kick-ass stereo, cheap computer speakers, ear-bud headphones … anything with speakers. It's easy to become immune to audio issues over time, so you need to come in with some fresh ears. In particular, you should listen out for sounds that jump out too much (especially high-frequency sounds), as they'll quickly annoy the heck out of your players. Filter them in your audio editor or with a `BiquadFilterNode`!

Once you're happy with the overall mix, it's time for a spot of Web Audio API-powered mastering. **Mastering** is applying the final touches and polish to the entire output—adding subtle effects that make the audio feel more cohesive and complete, making things pop. Mastering is usually part of music production, but the same principles apply for sound effects too. For example, adding a subtle overall reverb effect can make everything jell—as if everything was recorded in the same physical space.

Despite being a ubiquitous effect, the Web Audio API doesn't come with a simple built-in reverb. This isn't an oversight. Reverb units are snowflakes, each with their own distinct nuances, and sound designers and audio engineers will have their individual favorites. To be flexible, the Web Audio API includes a *convolver unit* that models physical spaces (real or virtual) by using short sound impulses. The shape of the impulse "decaying" over time is fed into the convolver. A pure impulse that is played and re-recorded in a huge cathedral will have a long resonant decay shape. An impulse in an anechoic chamber (a special room that's designed to completely absorb reflections of sound) will have practically no decay at all.

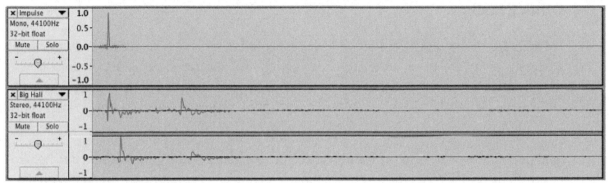

7-19. Impulse response of a large hall

This decay shape determines how the pure frequencies of the input impulse (the first track in the above figure) map to the output frequencies (the second track). This mapping can then be "applied" over your game audio sources. The result is a reverb that sounds as if your game is being played *inside* that huge cathedral space (or that anechoic chamber). The impulse responses can be recorded in real-world spaces, or can be generated in code.

 Used in Film

> This technique is a favorite of filmmakers. They'll often record impulses on their movie sets so that actors can overdub dialog after shooting. A convolution effect will then be added to make the overdubbed vocals sound as if they were recorded on location.

Thanks to the modular nature of the Web Audio API, standalone effects can be created and reused as if they were a standard module (as we did with our `inACavern` effect). An example of a third-party offering is the `simple-reverb` package[10] which programmatically creates impulses to make its reverb. You can import this and connect it to other modules just like a `Gain` node:

```
import SimpleReverb from "simple-reverb";
```

---

10. https://github.com/web-audio-components/simple-reverb/

```
...

const reverb = new SimpleReverb(context, {
  seconds: 2,
  decay: 1
});
out.connect(reverb.input);
reverb.connect(reverbGain);
```

 Other Effects

You can also create some nice effects by feeding multiple copies of a module's output back into its input after small random delays (with `ctx.createDelay()`). Depending on the amount of delay (and the amount of feedback) you can create some interesting chorus, flange, and delay effects.

Finally, and depending on the range of sounds used in your game, some compression can help to tighten everything up. It boosts the low-end sounds and reduces the high-end sounds. With the Web Audio API, this is done with the `DynamicsCompressorNode` created by `ctx.createDynamicsCompressor`:

```
const comp = ctx.createDynamicsCompressor();
comp.threshold.value = -20;
comp.knee.value = 30;
comp.ratio.value = 15;
comp.attack.value = 0.1;
comp.release.value = 0.25;
```

Listen with headphones (or good speakers) and set the compressor to some extreme values to hear the effect on the original audio source. The idea of a compressor is to squish the audio together so the overall level can be boosted without clipping and becoming distorted. This "boost" isn't part of the compressor node by default—so generally, a compressor will be attached to another `GainNode` before being output.

Mastering is like visual post-processing effects in your game: it won't change the core mechanics, but it can change and improve the feel. Mixing and mastering work together to get the most out of your raw materials and allow the sound to sit in your game in a way that's natural, and that's impressive for your players.

Fade to Silence

It's hard to stress just how important sound is. Put sound in your games. Even some simple effects generated from a sound-effect generator, or mouth sounds squelched into a microphone, will dramatically improve things. There are no excuses. Once you've seen how transformative sound can be, start thinking about it as an important aesthetic choice. Audio is an incredibly expressive medium, and your choices will alter the emotions your players experience.

You're blasting out your latest Web Audio API-powered track that will feature in your entry for this year's IGC, when Old Lady Wassername (the co-working space owner) enters, looking sad. She calls everyone over to the center of the room. You turn off the music.

"Listen, kids. I've got some bad news. I'm behind on the building rent. Apparently *Exploitative Games, Inc.* has put in an offer to take over the space, so if I can't get $10,000 by the end of the month, I'm afraid we'll have to close down."

This is not good. Some of your fellow co-workers practically grew up here; it's their home. Where will they go? After considering the news for a few moments, you slowly rise to your feet. "I will get you the money," you boldly declare. "I will win the IGC game-of-the-year prize and use it to save our co-working clubhouse!"

"Ha!" snaps Guy Shifty, who—ninja-like as always—materializes in the doorway. "I've seen your work. You don't have a *chance*! But I'll tell you what: let's make it interesting. If your game ranks *above* our game, we'll withdraw our tender for this office space. If not, then I'm turning this clubhouse into my 'clone factory'—where I steal indie game ideas and add free-to-play elements and loot boxes to them. And I'll start with *SquizzBall*, *Bravedigger* and *Pengolfin'*. Ha ha!"

He's morphed from a regular corporate evil guy into an '80s movie supervillain. Well, it's time for us to rise to the challenge. We've still got a lot of work to do if we want to save the day—but thanks to our new-found audio skills, we can at least do it to a rockin' sound track.

Bringing a Game to Life with "Juice"

Level

8

> *In game development, the first 90% of a project is a lot easier than the second 90%. — Tim Sweeney, Founder of Epic Games*

Everything we've been learning has been building up to this chapter. If we have any chance of winning the IGC, saving the clubhouse, and taking down Guy Shifty, *this* is where we have to do it. This is where we transform *Bravedigger* from a scrappy proof-of-concept prototype into a full-blown game. Although we now have the ability to make games, they don't yet feel like the ones we know and love. That's because they're missing something important. They're missing "juice".

Juice is the *magic dust* that we sprinkle liberally on our projects to bring them to life. It's an umbrella term that houses a plethora of tricks, tips, and techniques for improving the feel of games: smooth tweens and jarring screen shakes, sparkly particles, over-the-top explosions, and all manner of visual effects. We're also talking about sneaky game design tweaks, physics hacks, and camera techniques for making our game mechanics *pop*, and for making our players feel powerful and awesome.

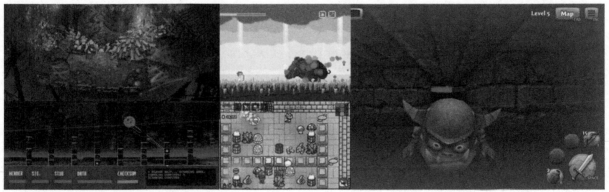

8-1. Some juicy game effects

The beautiful part of this chapter is that there's very little completely *new* knowledge required to elevate our "prototype" to a "game". We've put in the hard work, and we understand intimately our core components and know they fit together. The grueling foundation-building phase is complete; the rest is just thinking up crazy ideas!

 Juice?

The term "juice" gained popularity after a gamedev talk titled *Juice It or Lose It*[1], by Martin Jonasson and Petri Purho. This talk, and the video The Art of Screenshake[2] by Vlambeer's Jan Willem Nijman, are mandatory viewing for any aspiring game developer looking to turn their boring prototypes into delightful experiences.

From here onwards, we won't be making many big changes to our game library. Our codebase facilitates the implementation of almost anything you can imagine. Sure, there are still plenty of creative tweaks to add—but the further we journey, the more you'll be on your own. Your ideas are unique and interesting and will make your games stand out from the crowd. For each "standard" effect we discuss, it's up to you to start thinking about *how else* they could be implemented, and how they might be abused and mutated to make them your own.

Screen Effects

There's some "low-hanging fruit" when it comes to adding juice. We're talking about effects that are pervasive, impressive, easy to implement, or just plain mandatory! We'll start with some screen effects that apply to the entire game (rather than a single area or entity). These tend to come from the real world—or at least, the *televised* real world. Many of gaming's juicy tropes—screen shakes, lighting effects, camera techniques—all rely on things we recognize instinctively from film and television.

Screen Shake

A screen shake event occurs when an *immensely powerful* natural force rocks our entire world—when an explosion or impact is potent enough that our game's camera operator *can no longer control the stability of the shot.* The entire view wobbles and shimmies for a short time until order is restored and the shake subsides.

Okay, from a practical point of view, screen shake is just moving the viewport randomly by a few pixels every frame. But it's a nice effect. The amplitude and duration of the shake influences the feeling of immenseness. Naturally it's an effect that's ripe for overuse, and recently there's been a bit of "screen shake backlash". Some people will now caution you against overdoing it. But they're wrong. More is more!

Screen shake needs to affect every game entity and background element (though usually the HUD elements and foreground elements stay fixed). The easiest place for us to implement screen shake is on the camera object itself. Each frame, we'll move the camera randomly, decreasing the amplitude of the movement until the effect is over. "Random" movement isn't strictly the way a real camera would move if it were filming in an earthquake. (It wouldn't instantly switch positions, but would have smooth—though extremely rapid—movement.) But it's chaotic enough for us.

The guts of the effect will be called from the `Camera.js` update. The camera position is offset

---

1. *https://www.youtube.com/watch?v=Fy0aCDmgnxg*
2. https://www.youtube.com/watch?v=AJdEqssNZ-U

every frame, decreasing in power as it settles down:

```
// Do shake!
pos.add({
  x: math.randf(-shakePower, shakePower),
  y: math.randf(-shakePower, shakePower)
});
this.shakePower -= this.shakeDecay * dt;
```

 Without a Camera

> If you aren't using a *Camera* object in your game, the same logic will still apply: just
> randomly offset the root parent container that holds everything you need to shake.

There are two variables that control the epicness of the shake: *shakePower* and *shakeDecay*.
They are defaulted to 0 as properties on the *Camera*:

```
this.shakePower = 0;
this.shakeDecay = 0;
```

When we need the game to explode, we call the *shake* function to set the events in motion. The
two parameters available will be power (amplitude) and duration (in seconds). From these we
determine the decay rate of the shake to ensure it runs for correct length:

```
shake(power = 8, length = 0.5) {
  this.shakePower = power;
  this.shakeDecay = power / length;
}
```

From anywhere in the game you can call *camera.shake()* to get a "default" shake, or you can
specify your custom power and/or duration—for example, *camera.shake(20, 3.5)* for a massive,
long shake! With the properties set, we apply the above shaking logic every frame until
shakePower is no longer above 0:

```
_shake(dt) {
  const { pos, shakePower } = this;
  if (shakePower <= 0) {
    return;
  }
  // Do shake!
  ...
```

```
  }
```

Of course, this `_shake` helper also must be called from somewhere. We do it in the `update` method, after focusing on the camera subject:

```
update(dt, t) {
  super.update(dt, t);
  if (this.subject) {
    this.focus();
  }
  this._shake(dt);
  ...
}
```

Screen shake makes getting hit feel so much more powerful. Each striking blow rocks us to our very core—and suddenly we understand the severity of the situation and will be more careful in the future not to get hit again.

That was easy … screen shakes are done, right? Nope. As always, there's an edge case. (To be honest, I didn't even find this case until halfway through a game jam!) Because the screen shake effect is tied to the camera position, any *other* camera tricks will also be displaced permanently each frame. This becomes an issue when we implement smooth camera panning later on, because the shaking motion *also* gets smoothed out. Instead of a violent explosion, we get a gentle sliding.

Thinking about it, it's probably not wise for us to steal control of the camera position as we did. So plan B is to *undo* the previous frame's shake amount at the start the next frame. Any movement we apply will be erased, and there'll be no unexpected offsets for the user of the library.

```
this.shakeLast = new Vec();
```

We'll start with a vector that will hold the *previous frame's* shake amount. Rather than just adding the shake directly to `pos`, it's first stored in the `shakeLast` variable (and then added):

```
_shake(dt) {
  ...
  shakeLast.set(
    math.randf(-shakePower, shakePower),
    math.randf(-shakePower, shakePower)
  );
```

```
    pos.add(shakeLast);
    ...
}
```

The shaking logic hasn't changed, but now we have a reference to the amount of shake we applied. If we want to "erase" the shake, we can then subtract it from the current camera position:

```
_unShake() {
  const { pos, shakeLast } = this;
  pos.subtract(shakeLast);
}
```

Finally, every frame the camera can be "unshook" *before* doing any focusing or moving:

```
this._unShake();
if (this.subject) {
  this.focus();
}
this._shake(dt);
```

Randomly moving the camera provides us with a cool screen shake, but if you wanted to, there are ways we to improve it further. A more natural shake movement can be achieved if we replace `Math.random` with a smooth noise function like Perlin or Simplex noise. (There are JavaScript libraries around for this. I often use simplex-noise.js[3]). You can also get a nice effect by messing with the camera *rotation* as well as the translation.

Alpha support

Changing gears a little, the next bit of juice isn't really juice at all. **Alpha compositing** is partially "blending" an image with its background in order to make the image look transparent. It's an infinitely useful effect that we really need to add to our library. Luckily it's well supported by the Canvas API. In Chapter 2, we covered the Canvas operation `ctx.globalAlpha` . In this section, we'll integrate that into our main `CanvasRenderer` .

We need to support transparency on both our `Container` items, as well as individually on any children of the container. The first case we'll handle is for the `Container` in situations when its `alpha` is set to 0. This is the same as when `visible === false` . Here we can save some CPU time by just ignoring any children and exiting the render function:

---

3. https://github.com/jwagner/simplex-noise.js

```
if (container.visible === false || container.alpha === 0) {
  return;
}
```

If `alpha` is defined, wrap the `children` rendering in another `save … restore` block and set the `globalAlpha` for these rendering operations. After all of the container's children are drawn with the correct alpha level, we pop the context stack so the original alpha level is restored.

```
// Set the alpha level for the children
if (container.alpha) {
  ctx.save();
  ctx.globalAlpha = container.alpha;
}
// Render the container children
...
// Pop the context stack
if (container.alpha) {
  ctx.restore();
}
```

That's fine for the container's alpha level, but we also want the ability to specify a *per-child* alpha setting too. For example, if we want our player `Sprite` to be translucent, we can assign `player.alpha = 0.5;`. All we have to do to implement this is set the `globalAlpha` before we render the child. It's not necessary to wrap this in another `save … restore` because each child node is *already* rendered in its own block.

```
if (child.alpha) {
  ctx.globalAlpha = child.alpha;
}
```

Having the ability to set the alpha is the key to a lot of juicy effects. In this chapter, we'll use it for fading particle effects, smooth screen transitions, and (in the very next section), screen flash!

Screen Flash

Screen shake perfectly represents an explosive event: but not everything needs to be an explosion. I guess.

Imagine that, in the deep recesses of a darkened, arcane tomb, you discover a time-worn wooden chest. Carefully you prize open the lid to reveal the munificent treasures inside. It momentarily floods your field of view with a wondrous, blinding, treasure-filled light. It's a *screen flash*!

A **screen flash** emulates a flash of lightning that briefly saturates the world (and hopefully fills the player with awe). The screen flash is a great tool for indicating that something important has happened—something the player should be aware of. It tends to be useful for highlighting events that aren't directly related to the action. For example, collecting the final piece of a puzzle that unlocks the level. The player may already have collected a haul of keys—but only the last is special. The screen flash shows that something bigger than just finding yet another key just happened.

To get flashy, we'll create a big opaque rectangle that covers the entire camera viewport—the sudden appearance of which represents the blinding flash. Quickly it fades away until it's gone. This sounds quite similar to a screen shake, but it's slightly more complex, as there needs to be a new entity (the rectangle object) that's added to and removed from the scene.

```
this.flashTime = 0;
this.flashDuration = 0;
this.flashRect = null;
```

We have two variables to track the flash: a countdown timer (how much time remains), and a duration (so we can calculate the correct alpha value). Throughout gameplay, we can flash the player with `camera.flash()`, just as we called `camera.shake()` for screen shake:

```
flash(duration = 0.3, color = "#fff") {
  if (!this.flashRect) {
    const { w, h } = this;
    this.flashRect = this.add(new Rect(w, h, { fill: color }));
  }
  // Set flash properties ...
}
```

The first step is to create the `Rect` rectangle if it doesn't exist and add it to the scene. Its width and height should match the viewport width and height of the camera itself. Next, we set the properties for timers and the rectangle. (I've set the fill color to pure white— `#fff` —but your game may call for a specific hue.)

```
this.flashRect.style.fill = color;
this.flashDuration = duration;
this.flashTime = duration;
```

Just as we did for screen shake, we'll add a helper method that's called from `Camera` 's update method. If there's no flash rectangle, there's no flash happening, so we leave ...

```
_flash(dt) {
```

```
const { flashRect, flashDuration, pos } = this;
if (!flashRect) {
  return;
}


...
}
```

Otherwise, we decrease the timer and handle the flash logic:

```
const time = (this.flashTime -= dt);
if (time <= 0) {
  this.remove(flashRect);
  this.flashRect = null;
} else {
  flashRect.alpha = time / flashDuration;
  flashRect.pos = Vec.from(pos).multiply(-1);
}
```

If the timer is done (`time <= 0`), we remove the rectangle and set the `flashRect` reference to null. (I've made the decision to add and remove a new rectangle for each flash. Alternatively, you could *always* have a rectangle there and just make it not visible so the renderer ignores it.) If the timer is still running, we set the `alpha` value. Because `time` is decreasing, the ratio with `flashDuration` approaches zero and the rectangle fades out.

The last line is very important. It updates the rectangle's position to be the inverse of the camera's position. If we didn't update it every frame, the edges of it would appear as the player moved around and the camera panned. We need the *inverse* of the camera's position because it's a child of camera. Remember that if the camera moves left, all of the child elements will seem like they're moving right. By multiplying by -1, we get the position we'd need to set something for it to appear in the top-left corner.

That's it for flashing. Our screen flash is perfect for when *Bravedigger* has cleared a room. At the end of this chapter, we'll expand our world into many rooms—and the flash will indicate that we've unlocked the door to exit the level.

```
// Got all pickups.
if (this.pickups.children.length === 1) {
  camera.flash();
  this.score += 5;
}
```

Screen flash is a handy effect. Despite briefly taking over the entire screen, it actually feels quite subtle. It's a great indication that something big has happened—without shifting the focus of the player.

Hit Stop, Hit Lag (Time Dilation)

In Chapter 6, we fixed our timestep. Now we can *abuse* our timestep. As part of improving our main loop to work correctly with our physics system, we introduced a constant called `MULTIPLIER` that scaled the game loop time to be faster or slower than "real time". What if `MULTIPLIER` wasn't a constant, but a variable we could modify as part of a game mechanic? That would be pretty cool *and* easy to implement. Just convert it from `const` to `let`, then expose it (via a getter/setter) from our main `Game.js` class:

```
get speed() {
  return MULTIPLIER;
}
set speed(speed) {
  MULTIPLIER = speed;
  SPEED = STEP * MULTIPLIER;
}
```

And what purposes could it serve? Controlling time is not a power to be sneezed at! First, we could just use it to improve debugging. Running speed is now a variable that can be controlled via the keyboard. You could assign some shortcuts to double or halve the speed while you work on other mechanics. (Having a shortcut to dramatically slow the game is *unbelievably* handy. We'll implement this in Chapter 9!)

Time dilation could also be a feature of your game. Certain pickups or events (say, taking damage) could slow down time temporarily—giving you super-human, Matrix-like powers to avoid obstacles and enemies. For something more ... um, over the top ... let's *constantly* modify the speed with a sine wave:

```
this.time += dt;
game.speed = Math.max(0.8, game.speed + Math.sin(this.time / 0.3) * 0.05);
```

This might make your brain melt, but it's probably not going to be relevant to too many of your projects.

A more practical use is for imparting a feeling of the "weight" of an action, by very briefly—*almost* unnoticeably—slowing down time. The moment the player, say, fires a rocket, we pause the game for just a few frames. The entire world buckles under the physical force of the player's action. It's a very subtle enhancement that you only really notice when you take it away.

```
this.add(new Timer(0.1, p => game.speed = p * normalSpeed))
```

This modifies the game speed over 0.1 seconds using a timer system that we'll create shortly. Combining hit lag with the particle effects (which we'll also create shortly), you can concoct a huge, physical reaction that imparts a real sense of tangible weight to your game's action.

Animations, Tweens, and Easing

Our eyes and brains are specialized machines for spotting discrepancies. We become alarmed and suspicious when something moves abnormally—which is great for survival, but makes life tough for gamedevs. We have to be careful *how* we move things in our games. Thankfully, human brains also really enjoy smooth, fluid, natural motion, so the solution is simple: animate everything smoothly, with *tweening*.

The term **tweening** originally comes from cartoon cell animation, where skillful animators would draw the important poses (or **key frames**) of an animation. Then less experienced (or at least, less well-paid) illustrators would be employed to fill in all of the "in between" frames (or "tweens") to get the correct number of drawings for the desired frame rate, and to morph smoothly between each key frame.

In the context of 2D game engines, tweening means something slightly different: it generally refers to moving smoothly between *two values* over time. The value could be a property in our system, like `pos`. A tween might move an entity from the bottom left to the top right of the screen over a duration of, say, ten seconds. But tweens aren't just for positions. They're used whenever you need some value to change smoothly over time—such as alpha (fading out a title graphic to invisible), or color hue.

If we make it easy to tween properties, we'll be more inclined to animate more of our game, making everything juicier!

Normalization and Lerping

Before we can run, we have to learn how to lerp. **Linear interpolation** (often called **lerp**) is a classical math function that converts a value from a bounded domain (some minimum and maximum values) to the domain `[0,1]`. The idea is to *project* any range as a ratio from 0 to 1. When we convert everything into the 0 to 1 range, we say our values are **normalized**. From here, we can apply all manner of funky math formulas over it to make interesting function curves.

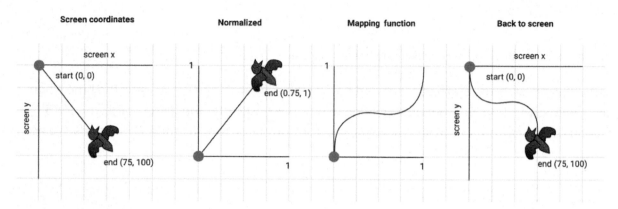

8-2. Normalizing values

Normalized values can be manipulated and transformed using common functions that modify the linear output in interesting ways. If we have a function that takes a linear input and produces a "bouncing" curve, for example, we could apply it to a y coordinate of an entity to bounce a basketball. Or we could apply the same function to *scale* for a weird stretchy-sprite effect. When everything is in the same domain, the functions can be composed and combined and reused from effect to effect and game to game.

 Not Just for Animation

Once you have such library functions at your disposal, you'll find them applicable to almost every aspect of game development—from making smooth animations with "easing" (covered shortly), to implementing AI rules, procedural map and level generation … and lots more!

To get a normalized value, we apply the linear interpolation formula. This effectively determines where the current value lies in relation to the minimum and maximum values. (*lerp* is another *math* function, so add it to *utils/math.js* and export it so that it's available on the *math* object.)

```
function lerp(x, min = 0, max = 1) {
  return (x - min) / (max - min);
}
```

Imagine we have a range from 1 to 3. Our *min* value is 1 and our *max* value is 3. Let's say that our current value (x) is 2: *lerp* will give us *(2 - 1) / (3 - 1) = 1 / 2 = 0.5* . We get the value 0.5 (or 50%) because 2 is exactly halfway between 1 and 3. Value normalized! The idea of a "range" is applicable to many scenarios. For example, we can compute the current progress percentage of any animation over time:

```
const perc = math.lerp(currentTime, startTime, endTime);
```

Here, *startTime* is the starting scheduled time of the animation and *endTime* is the time when the animation ends. If we want an animation to start 1 second after the game starts, run for 5 seconds (a range from 1 to 6) *and* the game has currently been running for 4.75 seconds, we get a value of *0.75* (or 75%):

```
var perc = math.lerp(4.75, 1, 6); // 0.75
```

The animation should be 75% of the way through. This value can then be used to calculate the position/color/whatever of the element we're animating. What about if the current time is greater than the maximum? The returned value will be greater than 1. Often this is undesirable, so we clamp it:

```
const perc = math.clamp(math.lerp(x, min, max), 0, 1) // never overflows 0 - 1.
```

Lerping gives a linear range between 0 and 1. We can use that value directly on properties that operate in this domain (for example, in our library *alpha* ranges from 0 to 1), but in most cases we want to *project* the value into a different game dimension. For example, to project from 0.75 to "three-quarters of the screen height, in pixels". To transform from the lerped value to the world domain, use the slope-intercept formula: $y = ax + b$.

Here, x is the value we received from lerping, while a is the value we want to *scale to* (that is, the range of the domain, *max - min*) and b is the amount we want to *translate by* (the offset of the range, or *min*). As a real example, I've created a title screen for the game. The title text animates from outside the top of the screen into its rightful place.

8-3. Lerping the title text

```
title.pos.y = 150 * math.clamp(math.lerp(t, 1, 6)) + 10;
```

Our time domain is from 1 to 6 seconds. Our screen space domain is from 10 to 160 pixels. Once the game has been running for `1` second, the title's `y` position will lerp smoothly from pixel 10 down to pixel 160 (150 + 10) over 5 seconds (when `t` will be `6`). The ability to convert between domains like this is the basis for many gamedev tricks—the most ubiquitous of them being "easing", which we'll cover shortly.

A Generic Timer

A quick aside. Coding up our smooth animation with lerp is not overly complex, but if we have to hand roll our animations, we'll get sick of the extra state variables and timers that are required just to move something. If it's not easy to add new tweens, we'll avoid doing it at all and our games will lose precious juice. We should simplify the process and stick it in the library.

 How Would You Do This?

Before we add it, take a couple of minutes to think how *you* would abstract the idea of a tween? What would the API look like? How would you create a new one and control what properties are tweened? As usual, there isn't one "correct" answer.

Our idea will be to abstract things at a slightly higher level, and implement a **generic timer** that will be controlled via the regular update system. The timer's job is to holler at us once per frame, announcing how much of the timer has elapsed (from 0 to 1, just like our hand-rolled lerp—and just like our onProgress system for asset loading). When it does this, we can project the tween properties using our transformation formula y = ax + b .

Timer.js is a root element in the library that doesn't extend any other Pop class. It's like an *entity* that doesn't have a renderable aspect. It accepts a duration property for the length of the timer, and an onTick function that will be called every frame with the current progress ratio from 0 to 1.

```
class Timer {
  constructor(duration = 1.0, onTick) {
    this.duration = duration;
    this.onTick = onTick;
    this.elapsed = 0;
    this.dead = false;
    this.visible = false;
  }
}
```

The Timer has an update function that our system will call for us when we add the Timer as a child to the scene. If the progress ratio gets above 1 (finished), we set the dead property to true . Just like a regular entity, the timer will be removed from the scene hierarchy and will no longer be called:

```
update(dt) {
  const { duration, onTick } = this;
  this.elapsed += dt;
  const ratio = this.elapsed / duration;
  if (ratio >= 1) {
    onTick(1.0);
    this.dead = true;
  } else {
    onTick(ratio);
  }
}
```

To use the timer, create a new instance with a duration and a callback function. To have the timer's update method be called from the main game loop, it needs to be added to the scene. It doesn't matter *where* in the scene hierarchy; any old container is fine. (You could even augment the Game class to accept a helper method especially for timers if you like.)

```
this.add(new Timer(2, p => console.log(p)));
```

Are Timers Really Entities?

Honestly, I think this timer-as-an-entity is a bit of a hack: it should probably exist outside the scene graph. But it's simple, and there's something nice about treating all elements of game engine as equal. Also, it would be easy to break this out as a separate subsystem in the future if we found it problematic. But at this stage, juice is our primary goal—and this is an easy way to get it.

Our callback function (a `console.log` with the current progress) is called every frame. After two seconds the timer is "dead" and no longer active. A timer can be used wherever we need some delayed action in our game. Because the progress ratio is passed to us every tick, it's also useful for tasks that are normally linearly interpolated—such as tweening.

```
this.add(new Timer(3, p => icon.alpha = p));
this.add(new Timer(3.5, p => icon.pos.x = p * 300 + 100));
```

Here we add two animations that run at the same time. The first fades the icon entity's alpha property from 0 (invisible) to 1 (fully opaque) over three seconds. The other animates the `x` position from offset 100 to offset 400 (300 pixels distance) over 3.5 seconds.

Sometimes we'd also like to be notified when the timer has expired. This is useful for triggering another tween after the initial one has completed (for example, for constructing larger sequential animations) and in non-tweening cases (such as "spawn a new enemy after three seconds").

Like `onTick`, an `onDone` callback is a new parameter given to the `Timer` constructor and stored as a property on the class. A timer is done when the ratio we calculated gets to 1. We've kept the original call to `onTick` with 1.0, in case your animation code needs to know about that too:

```
if (ratio >= 1) {
  onTick(1.0);
  onDone && onDone();
  this.dead = true;
}
```

The final feature we'll add is an optional delay *before* the animation begins. The `onTick` won't be called until the delay has elapsed. Then the timer works the same as before. This is helpful, for example, in orchestrating concurrent animations.

```
if (delay > 0) {
  this.delay -= dt;
```

```
    return;
  }
```

The parameter `delay` is also passed to a new `Timer`. In the `update` function, we don't do anything until the delay timer has reached 0. Then we proceed as usual. Our timer system is handy for tweening properties, but also invaluable for sequencing general events in your game.

Easing

Okay, back to animating. The timer's progress is *linear*, so when we apply it to a property like an entity's position we get a constant-speed animation. Boring. In the real world, things don't move linearly. They start slowly, accelerating to a maximum speed, before decelerating gently towards a resting position. And even *that's* a bit boring. More exciting is if it *springs*. Then it doesn't even stop at the correct target spot: it *overshoots* the target, rocketing back and forward constantly until all its momentum is lost. That's juicy.

In the animation world, this is known as **easing**. It looks way more juicy than linear animation. There are many common functions for easing behaviors of various levels of coolness. Some situations call for subtlety, but of course most should be over the top!

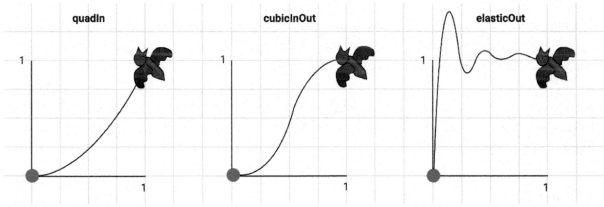

8-4. Various easing curves

With linear easing, each step on the `x` axis results in an equal step on the `y` axis. If we apply a mathematical function to `x`, we can affect the change in `y`. A nice "curvy" function produces a smoothly accelerated animation. Depending on where the slope change is greatest (at the beginning or the end) we say an animation *eases in* (accelerates at the beginning), *eases out* (decelerates at the end), or both—*easing in and out*.

Easing Functions Without the Timer

Our timer gives us a normalized linear range to supply to our easing function. If you want to use the easing functions in other situations (not using our timer) you'll need to do the normalizing yourself with `clamp` and `lerp` : `const x = clamp(lerp(value, min, max), 0, 1)` .

This is where the beauty of our normalized values starts to shine: we can create reusable and widely applicable behaviors. It's good to build up an anthology of easing functions, ready to be summoned as the animation requirement arises. They can live as part of our `utils/math.js` file, in an object called `ease` :

```
const ease = {
  // easing functions here!
};
```

Our first easing function will be called `quadIn` . It will be accessible as `math.ease.quadIn` . Rather than the linear `y = x` , it will be a quadratic curve on the input value:

```
quadIn (x) {
  return x * x;
}
```

If the input value lies on the extreme left, the output is the `min` value—0. On the extreme right is the `max` output 1 (same as with linear interpolation). But in between we get some interesting results that are *not* linear. Instead, they follow the formula `x * x` . Applying this to an entity—such as our title text—causes a slow acceleration at the beginning of the tween:

```
x => title.pos.y = math.ease.quadIn(x) * 330 - 30;
```

The `quadIn` effect begins with smooth acceleration and ends with an abrupt halt. But we want the opposite for our title text: it starts off screen (so we don't care if it accelerates) and should *decelerate* gently into place. For this, we need to invert the function, like this: `y = 1 - ((1 - x) * (1 - x))` . Progress runs from 1 to 0, so we subtract one from it to get it back to the correct range. This gets uglier as the formula get more complex. A cleaner way is to make use of the existing "ease in" version:

```
quadOut(x) {
    return 1 - this.quadIn(1 - x);
```

```
}
```

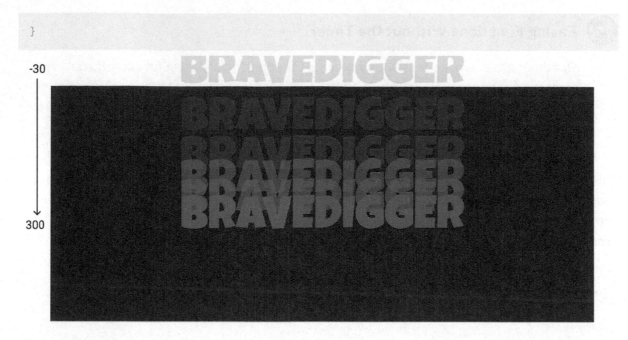

-30

300

8-5. Easing the title

Visualizing Curves

It can be hard to picture the curves in your head if you're experimenting. You can test out your formula on Wolfram Alpha[4]. In the main text box, enter the query `x * x from 0 to 1`. Most JavaScript math functions also work; just omit the `math.` prefix!

The quadratic curves are nicer than straight linear animations, but they're quite subtle—and this chapter is *not* about subtlety. Time to take things to higher power—the third power:

```
cubicIn(x) {
    return x * x * x;
}
```

Better! The cubic curve is steeper and it takes longer for the animation to accelerate, which exaggerates the effect. You can take it further by raising to any power. (Using `Math.pow` will make the code cleaner: `return Math.pow(4, x);`.) And just as with `quadOut`, we can make `cubicOut`—a function that calls `cubicIn` with an inverted input.

Now that we have acceleration (ease in) and deceleration (ease out)—how about both? Often we'd like our entities to both accelerate when they start *and* decelerate as they end. The solution

---

4. https://www.wolframalpha.com

is not fancy: just combine them by calling *ease in* for the first half of the tween (when the progress is less than 50%), and *ease out* for the second half. The only adjustment we have to make is to scale the range so the effect is squished into half the space. We do this by doubling the progress, doing our effect calculation, and halving the result:

```
cubicInOut(p) {
    if (p < 0.5) return this.cubicIn(p * 2) / 2;
    return 1 - this.cubicIn((1 - p) * 2) / 2;
}
```

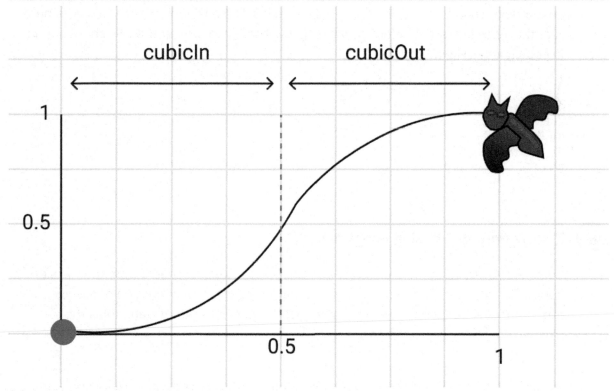

8-6. Combining in and out easing functions

Grafting two functions together like this might feel a bit inelegant. It's effective, but not very "mathematics-y". Surely there's a single function that does both? Yep, there is! An example of an all-in-one function that eases in and out is *smoothstep*. Smoothstep[5] is an intriguing function that follows a nice "S" curve between 0 and 1. Outside this range it's *not* so helpful, so we `clamp` it to keep it in check:

```
function smoothstep(x) {
    return math.clamp(x * x * (3 - 2 * x));
}
```

[5.] https://en.wikipedia.org/wiki/Smoothstep

```
  }
```

Smoothstep (like its more aggressive partner in crime, *smootherstep*) is widely used in the gamedev world, and is a great addition to your bag of tricks. But it's *still* not as zany as we need for our title page. We need something preposterous and wild!

```
pow(2, -10 * x) * sin((x - 0.4 / 4) * (PI * 2) / 0.4) + 1 from 0 to 1
```

Is that crazy enough for you?! Put this in Wolfram Alpha and you'll notice the graph's y value actually extends beyond 1—a couple of times! If we tie this to a position property in our game, it will *go past* the intended target before bouncing back. That's why we get the overshoot bouncy effect. In code it looks like this:

```
elasticOut(x) {
  const p = 0.4;
  return Math.pow(2, -10 * x) *
    Math.sin((x - p / 4) *
    (Math.PI * 2) / p) + 1;
}
```

 Robert Penner's Easing Functions

"Wait, did you make up that formula?" you ask. Nope, it's a copy-paste from the classic Robert Penner's Easing Functions[6]. Almost anywhere you hear a mention of easing, you'll find these functions. There are more cool functions to explore (and tools for creating your own) on his website.

That's more like it: that's juicy! Time to tween up a storm in our title screen. We'll slide in some of our screen elements with our gently easing animations. The crowning point will be our title logo text. Rather than a single `Text` element, we'll break it into *individual letters*. Each letter will be sprung into place with a bounce and a random delay. Adding small amounts of randomness (combined with smooth animation) is a very effective technique for wowing your players. Just what we need in a splash screen:

```
"BRAVEDIGGER".split("").map((c, i) => {
  const ch = this.add(new Text(c, ui.title));
  ch.pos.set(i * 40 + 150, -i * 20);
  // Bounce it!
```

[6.] http://robertpenner.com/easing/

```
   ...
});
```

The title is broken into individual characters with the `split` function and then mapped as `Text` entities in the scene. They don't have to be `Text` entities: if you wanted something fancier, you could even make them `TileSprite` elements with a fancy, unique bitmap font.

```
// Bounce it!
this.add(
  new Timer(
    1,
    p => ch.pos.y = elasticOut(p) * 320 - 150,
    null,
    math.rand(10) * 0.1;
  ));
```

Each character gets a timer that runs for one second. The timers start after a random delay (of `math.rand(10) * 0.1` seconds) and then the text elements elastically spring into place with `elasticOut`.

Animating HUD elements is a fantastic way to add juice: bouncing and popping elements make everything seem more alive and exciting. Look over someone's shoulder when they're playing *Candy Crush*: *every* HUD element is wobbly and bouncy. Combined with the simplicity of our timers, there's no excuse not to animate anything and everything you possibly can.

8-7. A bouncy title screen

Particle Effects

A dust cloud, a swarm of floating lights, massive explosions, speed lines, smoke, 1-UP and floating coins, shock waves, mysterious gaseous auras, magic fairy dust ... we're talking about **particle effects**!

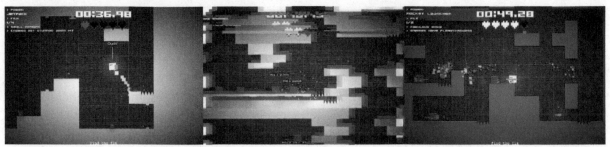

8-8. The juicy particle effects of Rémi Vansteelandt's Glitchbuster

Like screen flash and screen shake, particle effects have roots in entertainment media rather than real life. Early cartoonists invented some great tricks to convey the feeling of exaggerated movement and momentum that are still used in cartoons and games today: agitrons, briffits, swalloops, doozex, grawlixes, indotherms, and squeans. (Okay, these might be not-so-serious names from the cartooning guide *The Lexicon of Comicana*, but they're very appropriate.) Particle effects often require long descriptions, such as "lines drawn around a head to show shock and surprise", and "clouds of dust that hang in the wake of swiftly departing character".

In real life, there aren't a lot of (visible) particles. Smoke and fire, yes ... but flying comical sweat droplets when nervous, or horizontal straight lines when moving with speed, not really. Generally, particle effects are used to exaggerate and enhance a feeling or mood that's intangible or invisible. They're extremely important for setting our game's ambiance and helping us tell our story.

 Performance Using Canvas

As we look at more intensive particle effects, our primary choice of technology—namely, our Canvas renderer—starts to show its weakness. Very impressive particle effects are often comprised of *a lot* of individual particles. In AAA games, we can be talking about *millions* of particles, using sophisticated blending techniques. Technologies like OpenGL and WebGL are designed for this sort of processing; Canvas 2D, less so. It's still very capable for modest amounts of particles, but if you need the big guns, consult the next chapter, where we discuss rendering in WebGL.

1-UPs

1-UPs are, you know, when you collect a pickup awarding you an extra life! A happy sound effect goes "bling", and above your head—where the pickup used to be—is some text that says "+1". The text floats upwards and fades out. You now have one more ... you're one up.

There's a million variations on the 1-UP, and mostly they signify that you just earned something. Perhaps instead of text it's a spinning coin or star graphic. Sometimes it might not rise upwards, and sometimes it doesn't fade out. But at its core it's a single particle. We're going to create our 1-UP particle effect in a *Container* . As part of the class constructor we accept a renderable node. It can be anything—a *Text* element, a *Sprite* , a *TileSprite* … it's flexible. But just so there's always *something*, we'll add our own yellow square if no renderable item is specified (which is useful if you're just prototyping something):

```
class OneUp extends Container {
  constructor(display, speed = 2, duration = 1) {
    super();
    this.add(display || new Rect(30, 30, { fill: "#ff0" }));

    ...

  }
}
```

Whatever we pass in as a display node will be added as a child to the *Container* . If *display* is null, we create a small *Rect* and use that. There are also two additional parameters, *speed* and *duration* , for the speed of the rising element and how long the entire effect should last. Because it rises straight upwards, we model its velocity as a vector with 0 horizontal offset and *-speed* vertical offset. The *duration* is stored twice, as we did with screen flash: one is a timer, the other the maximum length for calculating the opacity of the display node.

```
this.vel = new Vec(0, -speed);
this.duration = duration;
this.life = duration;
```

The *update* function is pretty dull—nothing we haven't done before. Add the velocity to the position, set the alpha, and if the timer is done, the 1-UP is dead!

```
update(dt) {
  super.update(dt);
  const { life, duration, pos, vel } = this;

  pos.add(vel);
  this.alpha = life / duration;
  if ((this.life -= dt) <= 0) {
    this.dead = true;
  }
}
```

We'll add a *OneUp* instance any time the *getPickup* function is called from *GameScreen* . To make it fancy, we'll create a coin animation as a *TileSprite* so a spinning coin rises up from our open treasure chests:

```
const coin = new TileSprite(texture, 32, 32);
coin.anims.add("spin", [6, 7, 8, 7].map(x => ({ x, y: 3 })), 0.05);
coin.anims.play("spin");
```

To use the coin as a `OneUP`, we pass it in and set its position to where the player is currently positioned. The coin appears, rises up, fades away, and is gone.

```
const one = this.add(new OneUp(coin));
one.pos.copy(player.pos);
```

Firework Particles

If one particle looks cool, 50 particles look ... 50 times cooler—and with no additional effort. When each element is given slightly different parameters for direction, life, speed, and color, magic happens! Our plan is to have two classes. One is `Particle`, which is a single particle element. The other is `ParticleEmitter`, which will be responsible for managing all of the little particles. For our generic `Particle`, we'll copy-paste our `OneUp.js` code. It will be almost identical, though slightly more customizable.

Like `OneUp`, we'll default it to a `Rect` if not told otherwise. The big differences between our `OneUp` and our general `Particle` is that its options need to operate in a *random range* (so each is slightly different).

```
class Particle extends Container {
  constructor(display, options) {
    ...
    this.vel = new Vec();
    this.life = 0;
    this.alpha = 0;
    ...
  }
}
```

A `Particle` is the individual element that makes up the effect. It's our `OneUp` but with a random velocity (direction) and life span. The particle's properties will be reset each time the particle is used by the particle emitter:

```
reset () {
  this.vel.set(math.randf(-5, 5), math.randf(-5, -10));
```

```
    this.life = math.randf(0.8, 1.5);
    this.pos.set(0, 0);
  }
```

The particle's velocity is set to a random x and y direction: between plus/minus 5 in the x direction, to give a nice horizontal spray, and between -5 and -10 in the y direction, so the particles will always start traveling upwards. This is because we're going to apply *gravity* to them to make them fall downwards and shower like fireworks. Likewise, `life` is set to a random time between 0.8 seconds and 1.5 seconds so each particle lives for different amounts of time.

Improving the Fireworks

These numbers are hardcoded. Your homework is to make them parameters. There are dozens of possible tweaks and features you can add to each particle. If you have a flexible way to describe one (and not hardcode the values), you end up with a system that will be reusable across many games in many different situations.

```
if (life <= 0) {
  return;
}
this.life -= dt;

if (gravity) {
  vel.add({x: 0, y: gravity * dt});
}
pos.add(vel);
```

In `update`, we move the particle in a similar manner to `OneUp`, except with a simple gravity system like the one from Chapter 6. Each frame, we add a gravity force to `vel` that in turn is added to `pos`. Note that when `life` is 0, we *don't* set `dead` to true as we'd normally do. This is because we'll reuse "dead" particles in our emitter.

The beauty of a particle effect is that, once you've defined the rules for a single particle, you just make a whole bunch of them—and suddenly, everything looks great! To transform the individual particles into some real fireworks, we'll make a `ParticleEmitter.js` class whose job it is to instantiate and hold the elements, as well as to start the effect (at the correct screen position) whenever we need a shower of particles:

```
class ParticleEmitter extends Container {
  constructor(numParticles = 20, display) {
    super();
```

```
    this.particles = [...Array(numParticles)]
      .map(() => this.add(new Particle(display)));
  }
}
```

The `ParticleEmitter` holds on to a bunch of particles (20 by default). They lie dormant until we need the effect to start, which happens when we call `play`. This repositions the effect and calls `reset` on each of the particles. Resetting a particle brings it to life (with random parameters)—resulting in a nice, explosive firework.

```
play(pos) {
  this.pos.copy(pos);
  this.particles.forEach(p => p.reset());
}
```

8-9. Heart-shaped particles after taking spike damage

Even simple rectangles can be effective for blood, fire, and explosions. With a `Sprite` (or animated `TileSprite`!) you can have convincing smoke, fire, snow, or dust clouds. And they don't have to be huge, eye-catching effects. Some of the best uses of particle effects in games are very subtle—a puff of dust when the player starts running, or when hitting a wall hard. Leaves and grass rustle and fly as the character runs by. These kinds of details the player often won't consciously pay attention too, but they add to the overall aesthetic of the game.

Camera Tricks

The camera object in our game was created so we could conveniently control what we see on screen—just like a real-world film camera. If our level is larger than the viewport, the "camera" will follow the player, keeping them *exactly* in the center of the screen. Ex-act-ly.

But human camera operators don't do that—especially when filming live action events, like news or sports. They can estimate and predict where the subject will move, but they don't know precisely what will happen. They have to react to sudden changes, making smooth adjustments to their position. And even if they *could* acquire superhuman, pixel-perfect reflexes, that's not how they'd follow the action. Even for scripted television shows (where each movement is dictated in advance) the camera operator will smoothly pan, minimizing any unnecessary movements and leading the viewer's eye to important details, hinting at action off screen, building suspense ...

Smooth Camera Motion

Before we start thinking of artistic uses for our game cameras, we need to fix up the basics. Our robot-powered camera is not "realistic". It needs some of our lerping and easing knowledge to be juicier. In our current implementation we already call `camera.focus()` to determine where the camera should be pointed. To create the illusion of a more human-ish camera operator, we instead take a *mix* between where the camera is currently pointing and where it *should* be pointing:

```
function mix (a, b, p) {
  return a * (1 - p) + b * p;
}
```

The core of our camera motion will be the `utils/math.js` function `mix`. Mix is like an inverse `lerp`: it takes a bound, `[a, b]`, and computes a value inside this bound with a mix percentage (unlike `lerp`, which *gives* us the percentage). If we supply a percentage of 0, the output is 100% of `a`. If the input is 1, the output is 100% of `b`. And if `p` is 0.5, you get the average of `a` and `b`. It gives us the *mix* between the two.

In our old system we determined where the camera needed to be and set its `pos` so that it centered on the subject:

```
focus() {
  ...
  pos.x = x;
  pos.y = y;
}
```

With `mix`, we can simulate the camera operator lag by mixing between where we currently are and where we should be. We add an easing factor variable and then use this to mix:

```
focus(ease = 1) {
  ...
  pos.x = math.mix(pos.x, x, ease);
```

```
    pos.y = math.mix(pos.y, y, ease);
}
```

By mixing between the two values, the result is somewhere in the middle. Modifying the `ease` factor will change how quickly the camera converges on its target. 1 means "full destination" (the camera has the same behavior as before, and instantly snaps to the subject) and 0 means it would never move.

 Let it Scroll

Our test level is not bigger than the screen, so there's no scrolling. Either make the game size smaller in `main.js`, or make a bigger map! While you're at it, you might want to temporarily remove or disarm the bad guys in the game. They can get really annoying when you're trying to test things!

The easing factor is set to a low value so the `mix` favors the current position of the camera over its destination—and there's a nice, natural drift as the player moves. The `easing` setting (which we default as `this.easing = 0.03` when the camera is created) gets passed to `focus()` every frame in the camera's `update` function:

```
update(dt, t) {
  ...
  if (this.subject) {
    this.focus(this.easing);
  }
}
```

If you make the `easing` too small, the player can get away from the camera (and therefore not be able to see what's ahead), so it needs to be reasonable. But a slight delay greatly enhances the feeling that your player is moving so fast that the camera operator can't quite keep up. You can even modify the easing value depending on factors like the velocity of the player.

Camera Tracking Box

The easing feels a lot more smooth and natural than our previous robo-auto-zoom, but it's still not how a *real* camera operator would frame a shot. For example, if the player stands on a platform and starts jumping up and down, the camera probably *wouldn't* bob up and down to follow their motion. As long as the camera could see the entire jump, it would just stay still to avoid making the viewers feel sick. Only when the player makes a dash too far from the center of the view would the camera operator begin following them again.

How exactly this works in a 2D game depends largely on personal preference and artistic vision, and (again) varies on a game-by-game basis. Once you start examining classic games, you'll find scores of variations on camera tracking techniques. Some games will do everything they can to minimize camera movement. Some will keep the vertical movement stable until it "snaps" up when you jump up to higher platform. Some will push ahead so you can see more of what's coming at you. And some will dynamically zoom and pan to keep the most action visible without directly centering on the player.

 More on Tracking

Essential viewing/reading on the topic is a fantastic talk/article by Itay Keren titled *Scroll Back: The Theory and Practice of Cameras in Side-Scrollers*[7]. You can find it in both video and blog-post formats; both are brilliant, and visually illustrate how the player character has to move to start pushing the camera in many classic games.

The tracking camera we'll implement will be designed to take a bit of movement out, but keeping the player largely in the center of the screen. We'll have a tracking box—an invisible rectangle—in the center of the screen. While the player stays within the confines of the box, the camera will be stationary. If it pushes past the edges of the box, the camera will start following again.

The dimensions of the tracking box are set via a helper called `setTracking` inside `Camera.js`. It's primarily a setter for our `tracking` vector, but if you check the sample code, we also enhance this to add a visible bounding box for debugging purposes.

```
setTracking(w, h) {
  this.tracking = new Vec(w, h);
}
```

In the `Camera` constructor, we'll set the tracking box: `this.setTracking(96, 72)`. By default, it's quite small: just 96x72 pixels from the center (on either side of the center point—so effectively doubled, but still small). The reason is that our test game viewport is fairly small too, and the size of the tracking box determines how far ahead we can see when moving. If it's too large, the player won't get enough warning about enemies and traps.

```
focus(ease = 1, track = true) {
  ...
}
```

We add a `track` property to our `focus` call. Sometimes we might need to ignore the tracking

---

7. https://www.gdcvault.com/play/1022243/Scroll-Back-The-Theory-and

box, but we'll want it to be true by default. Inside the *focus* function we decide if we should move the camera or not. If we determine the player is *inside the tracking box*, we ignore the calculated centering values and set them back to the original position:

```
if (track) {
  if (Math.abs(centeredX + pos.x) < tracking.x) {
    x = pos.x;
  }
  if (Math.abs(centeredY + pos.y) < tracking.y) {
    y = pos.y;
  }
}
```

The calculation for determining if the player is inside the tracking box is fairly easy, as we already calculate the center of the screen when we do a regular *focus*. If the center of the screen is less than the size of the tracking box, we revert our movement amounts and the camera stays stationary.

Testing this in-game reveals we've achieved the effect we're after. Take your player to a platform and jump up and down: the camera does not bob up and down. If you move horizontally, you can find the point where the camera starts to push along with you. If you turn and walk in the other direction, the camera waits until you hit the opposite edge.

In the example code, there's also a commented out `Rect` entity in `Camera.js`, and some additional code to position it. This is a debugging rectangle to visually show the tracking box area. It's good for getting things set up, but in general it's better to turn it off to make sure it actually feels good in the real game. This is how the players will experience it.

Platformer Tricks

Every genre of game has its staple effects. In this section, we're going to look at some tried-and-true tricks for juicing platform games. Even if you're not making a platform game, it's worth checking out, as you'll find much of the content is applicable to aspects of almost any 2D game. The core of what follows is about making the player feel *powerful*.

In the game *Half Life*, if you're confronted by more than two enemies at the same time, all but the closest two will just run around randomly, never attacking you. In the Vlambeer game *Luftrausers*, the first few enemies when you start will *deliberately* miss you when they fire. In *many* games, your last bullet will do double damage, and your last health point counts as two points (providing opportunities for some exhilarating survived-by-the-skin-of-your-teeth moments).

Games aren't reality! Juicing your game is often about making the player *feel* more skillful. It's not exactly *cheating*. We have to remember that we aren't simulating reality. We're crafting an experience. Anything that we can do to make that experience feel better needs to go in the game.

Invincibility Blinking

Fun action games maintain a balance between calmness and chaos, between safety and terror. A frightened player is a captivated player! But too much intensity, for too long, becomes exhausting. A way to provide some relief is via temporary player *invincibility*—a period of time where the player can't be attacked or hurt. It's usually triggered after taking damage (so you don't get double-damaged) or via bonus pickups. Invincibility is a chance to catch your breath, settle down, take stock and prepare for the next surge in action.

There are two parts to invincibility. One is to be invincible; the other is to be *visibly* invincible.

The first part will be highly game-specific. A timer (either one of our generic timers, or a dedicated variable) tracks the player's invincibility. Any hit detection (or enemy attack decisions) needs to first check this value. As an example, we'll add some new properties to `Player.js` : `invincible` (a timer), and `hp` for the player's hit points. When hit points are 0, the player is dead and when `invincible` is above 0 they can't be hurt.

```
hitBy() {
  if (this.invincible > 0) {
    return false;
  }
  this.hp -= 1;
  if (this.hp <= 0) {
    this.gameOver = true;
  } else {
    this.invincible = 1.1;
  }
  return true;
}
```

The function `hitBy` will be called from our `GameScreen` collision detection code when the player is hit by something dangerous. First it checks the `invincible` timer before doing anything else. If the player is invincible, the hit is discounted (and the function returns `false`). Otherwise, the player loses a hit point and (if they aren't dead) gets the power of invincibility for 1.1 seconds. In our main game code we call the function whenever a player is hit by something:

```
// Called any time a player is hit
playerWasHit(baddie) {
  // But can the player BE hit at the moment?
  if (player.hitBy(baddie)) {
    this.setHearts(); // Yes! Update the player lives display
    camera.shake();
    // But are they dead?
    if (player.gameOver) {
      this.state.set("GAMEOVER"); "GAMEOVER"// Yup :(
    }
  }
}
```

If the player is invincible (which we determine by calling *hitBy*), nothing should happen and the game continues as normal. If they *aren't* invincible, they lose a hit point—and are potentially game-over'd. In our game, the only way to become invincible is to get hit by a bad guy, but you could also grant invincibility by setting the timer variable after the player, say, finds a special pickup.

The second part to invincibility (the part you can juice) is the *visual representation* of being invincible. Historically, there are two ways to show that a player is immune to attack: blinking between the normal player graphic and either a blank frame or a "white mask" silhouette frame.

Blinking on or off is the simplest: it doesn't require any additional assets, and we've done it before. Based on the *invincible* timer value, toggle the entity's alpha between 0 and 1 (or its *visible* property on or off) using the "remainder toggle" technique from Chapter 4. The best place to do this is at the bottom of the player's *update* method:

```
// Animations
if ((this.invincible -= dt) >= 0) {
  // (Or DON'T floor it for a fade!)
  this.alpha = Math.floor(t / 0.1) % 2;
} else {
  this.alpha = 1;
}
```

The other common approach is to flash between the normal sprite and a solid silhouette of the character. This is done similarly to blinking on and off, but instead of changing the *alpha* value you update the *frame* reference to point to the modified player sprite.

8-10. Silhouetted Bravedigger

When using our `anim` system, you can create copies of the existing animations but point to the modified sprites. If you're tweaking sprite frames by hand, you can relatively offset all of the silhouetted frames from the originals. For example, if the original graphic is at frame *{x: 1, y: 0}* and the masked frames are on the row below it, you can do this to toggle between the two:

```
this.frame.y = Math.floor(t / 0.1) % 2;
```

 Why Not Just Adjust the Tint at Runtime?

Some game engines allow you to modify your sprite's tint and brightness settings at runtime. In such a system, you could programmatically alter the sprite graphic to be a "flash" without needing extra assets. Our renderer uses HTML5 Canvas, which has poor performance for pixel-by-pixel access. It's far more efficient (though less flexible) to bake your effects in and load separate assets.

Jump Forgiveness

In olden-day cartoons, the evil-but-ineffectual antagonist chases our hero towards a precipice of a giant chasm. A sneaky side-step at the final moment deceives the bad guy, sending him over the edge. Not yet understanding the grievous error he's committed, he continues to sprint magically in mid air. Several seconds later, the truth dawns on him. His jog slows to a halt, and he plummets hilariously to his demise.

Reality is less funny. Gravity doesn't kid around—and we've programmed our characters to obey the laws of gravity. The very first frame the player steps over the edge of a tile, they begin falling and can no longer jump. It turns out that—just like real-life gravity—this sucks. The player's brain expects their avatar to spring to victory, only to find they're 1/60th of a second too slow and are now dead. Obviously they *wanted* to jump, so why didn't the stupid character jump?!

Perhaps it's not reality, but giving the player the benefit of the doubt in these situations will result in happier players. Once you test it out for yourself, you'll also rue games that don't do the same. It just doesn't *feel* fair. And we're all about "feels". Of course, it makes our code a bit scrappier having to cheat like this. We need (as always) a timer that starts ticking whenever the player has gone off the edge. If they jump quickly enough, we allow the jump:

```
this.falling = true;
this.fallingTimer = 0;
```

On the player there's an extra timer variable (`fallingTimer`) that starts counting down the moment the player *should* be falling. If they haven't jumped by the time this timer expires, they're the proverbial cartoon antagonist—and they fall. The length of timer significantly alters the feel of the game. We'll make it a global constant at the top of the file while we play with it:

```
const JUMP_FORGIVENESS = 0.04;
```

If you make it too long, it's too forgiving. It becomes obvious to the player that you're cheating. And it looks weird because you can walk on air. (Try setting it to a very large value and see.) The timer logic happens after we determine the player should be falling (when both their left and right feet are on "walkable" tiles):

```
if (left && right) {
  this.falling = true;
}
```

Rather than simply set `falling` to `true` , we replace it with our forgiving timer. If `fallingTimer` has previously expired (`<= 0`) we initialize it to our `JUMP_FORGIVENESS` value. Then the `falling` variable will only become true if the player keeps passing our "should be falling" test after the timer has drained:

```
if (this.fallingTimer <= 0) {
  this.fallingTimer = JUMP_FORGIVENESS;
} else {
  if ((this.fallingTimer -= dt) <= 0) {
    this.falling = true;
  }
}
```

Because the `falling` and `fallingTimer` variables are now linked, you also have to be sure to reset the `fallingTimer` to 0 whenever you set `falling` to `false` (which we do when `r.hits.down` is `true` on our player). Otherwise, the next time the player starts to fall, the timer will already be halfway through draining and the forgiveness time will be inconsistent.

Be sure to play test this in action *a lot*. Because it happens quickly, it can be hard to see the effect. But if you slow down the game (by modifying `MULTIPLIER` in `Game.js`), it's clear that the character *should* be falling but isn't. Don't worry too much about reality; only worry about how it feels. If you find you fall too much when you expect to jump, up the forgiveness. If it starts to feel like cheating, lower it.

 Bounce Forgiveness

In *Bravedigger* we can continue to jump by holding down the fire button. In many games, you have to release the button before you can jump again. In this case you have the *reverse* of our not-falling problem. Often the player will re-hit the fire button a few frames *before the player touches the ground*, so they won't be able to jump yet. Some "landing forgiveness" could be applied here too: the jump action gets triggered once they land, and the character jumps as the player intends.

Knockback

We saw earlier that screen-shake is an effective and over-the-top way to convey a physical impact. Often we want something a bit more subtle, localized to the actual site of the strike. "Knockback" is the answer. **Knockback** is when a character gets, um, knocked back. For example, if a bullet strikes a player from the left, the force flings them violently in the direction of the impact. (They might also get lifted off the ground. That's just how immense the pressure was!)

8-11. Knockback path

It's a suitably unrealistic trope of 2D games, but it serves a couple of important purposes. It underpins the magnitude of the event (adding a sense of weight to enemy attacks), and it gives the player a bit of breathing space so they can fight back. This helps *us* (as devs) as much as the player, because it also handles collision resolution for us. Imagine that a zombie manages to munch on the head of the player. The player is stunned. Before they have a chance to fight back, the still-colliding zombie follows its AI rules and attacks them *again*. The player is trapped forever.

Knockback helps us out by breaking apart the collision. We don't have to do careful edge logic (like we do to support wall sliding in tile-map collision) to push a player away to exactly the right pixel. We just propel them away with force! Like all effects, you should only include a mechanic if it supports the narrative, aesthetic, and feel of the game. But it also looks pretty cool, so why *not* add it in! As our platformer player is controlled via our physics functions, implementing knockback is just a matter of applying the correct impulse when the player is hit. But in which direction?

One idea is to take into consideration the direction of the entity that caused the knockback. In the `GameScreen` , when there's a collision with the player, we also pass along the *entity* to the `hitBy` method on `Player.js` . This can then be used in a `knockback` function to calculate an angle to be knock-backed in:

```
knockback(e) {
  const { vel, acc } = this;
  const angle = entity.angle(this, e);
  const power = 400;

  ...
}
```

Now we have the angle between us and them. Still, which way should we knock? Well, after testing a bunch of things, the one that felt coolest to me was to take the horizontal direction from where we were struck, but push straight up on the y axis. To give the most impact, we first zero out our `vel` and `acc` amounts to make sure this hit is the most important thing that happens to us and we aren't just slowed down a little (or rocket-jumped if we were hit from behind):

```
vel.set(0, 0);
acc.set(0, 0);
const dir = new Vec(Math.cos(angle), -1).multiply(power);
physics.applyImpulse(this, dir);
```

Wall Jumping

Oh boy, another mechanic that *sounds* easy, but is booby-trapped with a nest of edge cases. Even without the edges, it's quite a challenge making a wall jump that feels natural and fun with your control system. But in-game, it's really enjoyable, so we'd better give it a shot.

A **wall jump** is when the player leaps into the air and hits a vertical wall. Rather than slide face-first into the earth, they push off parkour-ninja style—propelling themselves upwards and effectively *doubling* the height of their regular jump. Many wall jumps can be done in succession to scale the sides of walls. It defies the laws of the conservation of momentum, but obeys the laws of juicy platforming fun.

 Quirks

Wall jumping can be hard to perfect inside a physics-based system. Often players will discover bugs in such systems and use them to their advantage. That's not always a bad thing though. The ability to "rocket jump" in the original *Quake* series supposedly arose from exploiting the way the physics engine worked. You either have to thoroughly test this mechanic in *every* possible obscure location, or just label any discovered bugs as "features"!

Here's the plan for implementing wall jumping. If you're falling and hit a wall:

1. Record which side (left or right) you hit a wall

2. Start a short "forgiveness timer" that says you're on the wall.

If the forgiveness timer is ticking:

1. Stick to the wall (no steering)

2. On jump, bounce off in the *opposite* direction of the wall.

That's it for the first pass. The forgiveness timer is necessary, as the player will rarely be able to press jump at the *exact* frame they hit a wall. In the same way that our jump forgiveness worked earlier, it feels much nicer if we predict what the player might be intending to do, rather than punishing them for not having robot-like reactions.

```
this.wallDir = 0;
```

```
this.wallTimer = 0;
```

Our two variables work together for tracking wall jumping, and are initialized to 0. The logic for manipulating them goes in the player's update code. We'll take over the part where we're already checking for wall hits:

```
if (r.hits.left || r.hits.right) {
  vel.x = 0;
}
```

And now we can wire in some wall jump code. Every frame we will reduce the `wallTimer`. When it's above 0, it's active. Otherwise, it's inactive:

```
// Wall jump detection
this.wallTimer -= dt;
if (r.hits.left || r.hits.right) {
  this.wallDir = r.hits.left ? -1 : 1;
  if (this.falling && this.wallTimer <= 0) {
    // Can wall jump...
    this.wallTimer = JUMP_WALL_FORGIVENESS;
  }
  vel.x = 0;
}
```

We know the player is hitting a wall (because of `r.hits`). If they're *also* falling, they're eligible for wall jumping. If it isn't already, we set the `wallTimer` to our `JUMP_WALL_FORGIVENESS` constant (which we'll default to 0.4 seconds). During this time, we should also stop the player's normal horizontal movement so they stick to the wall. (We forbid movement if `wallTimer > 0 && x !== wallDir` —that is, if they're trying to move away from the wall.)

This is optional, and you should test it in your game. But if the `wallTimer` is long and you continue to allow horizontal steering, the player can steer away from the wall and it looks like you're doing a weird, midair jump. At any rate, if the player presses the jump button, there are now some additional things to consider.

```
const canWallJump = falling && this.wallTimer > 0;
const canJump = !falling || canWallJump;
if (action && canJump) {
  if (canWallJump) {
    // Do wall jump
    ...
  } else {
    // Do normal jump
  }
```

```
   ...
 }
 this.falling = true;
 this.wallTimer = 0;
}
```

There's a difference between regular jumps and wall jumps, so we figure out which we need to perform. Normally, the player can jump only when they aren't falling. For a wall jump, they *must* be falling. The difference between the two jumps is how we push the player upwards. The impulse you use will depend on your game. We'll create a constant for it (`JUMP_WALL_IMPULSE = 500`) and apply it both upwards *and* away from the wall:

```
...
physics.applyImpulse(
  this,
  { x: JUMP_WALL_IMPULSE * wallDir * -1, y: -JUMP_IMPULSE },
  dt
);
```

At this stage, you might feel like you're done. But testing it out in the dreaded "real world" reveals an infestation of bugs. Wall jumping is rampant, and the game character is leaping upwards too much (even when you don't want it to). Perhaps you were just dodging a flying projectile and happened to touch the wall. If an accidental wall jump sends you flying directly into *another* projectile, you're going to be unimpressed.

It was our design choice to trigger successive jumps by holding down the fire button. This feels great on the ground, but it's not right for wall jumping. The desire to wall jump should be *explicit*. We'll mandate that the player has to release the button before they can do a wall jump. We'll check it with a flag on the player called `releasedJump` (defaulted to false). Any time the player *isn't* holding down jump, the variable gets flipped to true:

```
if (!action) {
  this.releasedJump = true;
}
```

This becomes an additional requirement for our `canWallJump` test:

```
const canWallJump = falling && this.wallTimer > 0 && this.releasedJump;
```

Finally, after executing a jump, we reset the flag:

```
...
this.falling = true;
this.releasedJump = false;
```

That eliminates a lot of the random bouncing, but there's still another pesky situation that's harder to remedy. The essence of the problem is that, *every time* you're in the air and touch the vertical edge of a tile, you can wall jump. If you try to run and jump up to a platform and you happen to scrape your foot on side of the tile on the way up—the algorithm counts that as a wall jump, projecting you backwards *away* from the direction you want to jump.

Perhaps we could check the tile map and not allow wall jumping off the *top tile* on a wall. Hmm, but then you couldn't wall jump off the edge of a floating platform (which is fun), so we'd need to check that too. It's getting complicated. Time to roll out the hacks! The problem case only appears when the *time* between jumping and hitting the wall is very small—so we'll just mandate a minimum time from jump to wall jump. After jumping, record the current time, `t` :

```
...
this.releasedJump = false;
this.jumpedAt = t;
```

And before setting the `wallTimer` , check that enough time has passed since jumping. After playing extensively with the current physics setup, I've decided that 105 milliseconds feels pretty good—as it eliminates most of the false wall jumps but doesn't prevent any intended wall jumps:

```
if (this.falling && this.wallTimer <= 0 && t - this.jumpedAt > 105) {
  this.wallTimer = JUMP_WALL_FORGIVENESS;
}
```

There are many other jump mechanics you can implement (and thankfully most are simpler than wall jumping). Many platform games allow *double jumps*, where you can perform a second magical midair jump. Some games have varying-height jumps: tapping the button briefly doesn't jump as high as holding down the button for a long time (or holding run and jump at the same time). Like wall jumping, these can be constructed out of a couple of timer variables and a bunch of testing and tweaking.

More Tiles

Having juiced our game entities, it's time to turn back to the game level itself. Adding features to the level is not the same as adding juice. It's modifying the core mechanics of your game—which has knock-on effects for how you'll design levels and how you want your players to enjoy the game.

Coming up with a unique and distinct set of level mechanics can set your game apart, but there's also a wealth of existing platforming-game staples for you to draw on. We'll implement two: *cloud tiles* and *disappearing tiles*. I've chosen these two because they demonstrate very different ways to implement tile mechanics. Clouds can be done by updating only our collision detection code, whereas disappearing tiles require us to modify the tile map itself.

 Using a Common Vocabulary

Another advantage of using tried-and-tested tiles is they make handy game design tools. Most players will already be familiar with them and don't need to *learn* how they work. Striking a balance between zany new mechanics and the common vocabulary of gaming history is all part of the game design challenge.

Cloud Platforms

No, not *that* kind of cloud platform—you know, like fluffy clouds in the sky! **Clouds** are one-way tiles where the player can jump up from underneath and pass through them without hitting their head. As they fall back down, however, their feet will land *on top* of the platform which now appears to be solid. That may sound nonsensical—I think the idea is that you're jumping up *in front* of the cloud, as if it has some three-dimensionality. But anyway, it's a nice mechanic for encouraging the player to move vertically upwards using minimal horizontal screen space.

8-12. Cloud platforms

Because clouds alter how the player collides with tiles, there will be updates to the `wallslide.js`
movement code. Clouds are a completely new type of interaction, so they require their own flag
in the tile `frame` metadata definitions too. In most cases, they act like normal `walkable` tiles and
the `cloud` flag will then be used for cloud-specific situations.

```
{ id: "cloud", x: 5, y: 3, walkable: true, cloud: true }
```

A cloud tile is also walkable. The player will pass freely through it *unless* they're currently falling
and their feet hit the top of the cloud. And our collision code already handles a case for when the
entity's feet hit the top of a tile. This check can be augmented for when one of the tiles has the
`cloud` flag:

```
// Hit your feet
if (y > 0) {
  const isCloud = tiles[BL].frame.cloud || tiles[BR].frame.cloud;
  if (!(bl && br) || isCloud) {
    ...
  }
}
```

Shorthand

TL , *TR* , *BL* , and *BR* represent the top-left, top-right, bottom-left, and bottom-right points of the entity.

When the player is falling and their feet hit a cloud, they'll snap to the top of the tile as if it's solid. Perfect, right? Nope, edge-case time! What if the player *starts* falling while their feet are in the middle of a cloud?

8-13. Stuck in the cloud

A cloud tile becomes a solid as soon as an entity starts falling. The collision-checking code is stateless, so there's no way to know if the player was touching the cloud *but not falling* in the previous frame. For frame-perfect collisions, this *could* be managed on the entity itself (storing and clearing a flag when touching a cloud). But we'll be a bit slack and approximate. We'll say that a cloud is only solid if the player is "close" to the top of tile:

```
tileEdge = tiles[BL].pos.y - 1;
const dist = tileEdge - (bounds.y + bounds.h);
if (!isCloud || dist > -10) {
  hits.down = true;
  yo = dist;
}
```

We were already checking how many pixels the entity needs to be displaced upwards when it hits a solid tile. Now we add an extra stipulation that a cloud is only solid if that distance is less than 10 pixels from the top. 10 pixels is pretty arbitrary, but feels good when playing. Make it much more and the player "snaps" upwards awkwardly; but make it much less and they can miss the top of cloud and fall right through.

Disappearing Tiles

Many cool platformer tile mechanics require modifying the tile map itself. The **disappearing tile** is such an effect. It's a normal (solid) tile until the moment a player steps on it. Like a jungle trap from an Amazonian adventure film, stepping on the tile triggers it—and it begins to disintegrate. Shortly afterwards, it crumbles into thin air. Any adventurer slow-witted enough to be dilly-dallying around will plunge into the dangers below.

Disappearing tiles can force a player to keep moving, or to carefully consider their path through a map (with the tiles acting as a single-use bridge). It's another great tool in our game-design toolbox.

To make a bridge tile "disappear", we need to modify it in our `TileMap`. Remember that a `TileMap` keeps all of the tiles as an array of `TileSprite`. To change an element in the array, we have two options. The first is to create a new `TileSprite` and splice it into the `children` array (removing the old one and inserting the new one). The second is to update the properties of the existing `TileSprite`.

The latter sounds easier: we can just make one tile act like another by modifying its `frame` properties! But there's a hitch. When we create a new `TileMap`, the `frame` data is assigned directly from the data we pass in. Until now, we've been passing a *reference* to the tile data. The same object is used for every tile of the same type. If you update the properties for one tile, it will change for *every* tile of that type!

This can be used for some neat effects—such as making a sea of animated tiles just by changing the frame index in the metadata. (Try it. It's cool!) The downside to using a reference is that we can't have the *per-tile* frame state that's needed for disappearing tiles. We don't want to change one tile only to have *all* tiles disappear. To fix it, we'll *clone* the tile `frame` before we pass it the `TileMap` constructor:

```
// before: level.map(i => tileIndexes[i])
level.map(i => Object.assign({}, tileIndexes[i]))
```

For every cell in our level, we clone the tile data with `Object.assign`. Each tile gets its own, freshly minted tile data copied from the `tileIndexes` metadata templates. These can be updated and manipulated individually without affecting other tiles of the same type. We create a new tile with the bridge graphic, as well as a new flag, `bridge` :

```
{ id: "bridge", x: 0, y: 5, bridge: true }
```

 Memory Usage

There's a trade-off for maintaining state per-tile: memory. Rather than a single frame object for each tile type, there's as many objects as tiles. We'll discuss implications of this in the next chapter, when we talk about performance.

The next step is to figure out when the player is stepping on a bridge tile. We're already getting the tiles under the player's feet when we determine if we should be falling or not. We can expand this to also check bridges:

```
const left = map.tileAtMapPos(leftFoot);
const right = map.tileAtMapPos(rightFoot);
...

// Check for bridges
[left, right].forEach(t => {
  if (t.frame.bridge) {
    map.makeDisappearingTile(t);
  }
});
```

If one of the tiles underfoot is a bridge, we send it off to the level map (`Level.js`) for processing. All of a tile's important properties are contained in its *frame* reference: the tile type ID, the graphic cell offset, and any properties. To make a tile disappear, we only need to switch its graphic frame reference to point to a blank cell and change its `walkable` property to true. However, the idea isn't that the tile disappears *instantly*, but that it crumbles over time—so that the player has a chance to escape:

```
makeDisappearingTile(t, duration = 1) {
  if (!t.frame.bridge || t.frame.counter > 0) {
    // not a bridge, or already disappearing
    return;
  }
  t.frame.counter = duration;
  ...
```

```
    }
```

The `makeDisappearingTile` function will be responsible for converting the given tile *temporarily* into a functioning bridge. After some duration (one second by default) the bridge tile transforms into an *empty* tile.

 A Little More Help

> We're playing with the level's tile metadata templates a lot here, so to help out we make another small function like `getIdx` from Chapter 5. This one, that returns the `tileIndexes` template for a given tile id: `const getTile = id =>`
> `this.tileIndexes.find(t => t.id === id);` .

To control the bridge tile timing, we introduce some shenanigans. Our `TileSprite` needs to update itself every frame by counting down its `counter` timer until it gets to 0. This behavior is not part of a normal `TileSprite`, so it has to be added. *But* ... there's *already* an `update` method on `TileSprite` for handling animation.

We could create a new subclass of `TilesSprite` (something like `BridgeTileSprite`) and then switch out the tile instances in the parent `TileMap`. But we're feeling plucky. We're going to do a little JavaScript tomfoolery and temporarily proxy the existing `update` method through our new one, just until the bridge tile disappears:

```
const update = t.update;
t.update = function(dt, t) {
  const { frame } = this;
  update.call(this, dt, t);
  ...
};
```

The plan is to hold a reference to the existing `update` functions, create a new one to do the bridge handling, then revert it once the bridge has disappeared. Inside our new `update` function, we can take care of the important work of acting like a bridge tile:

```
frame.counter -= dt;
if (frame.counter < duration * 0.33) {
  frame.x = getTile("bridge").x + 1;
}
if (frame.counter <= 0) {
  // Switch to empty tile!
```

```
    ...
  }
```

When the timer is two-thirds complete (`duration * 0.33`), we switch out the graphic for the next `x` frame. This will be a "crumbling" version of the initial bridge. (If we wanted, we could have more frames of animation in here too. One is enough to signal to the player that they have only a short time to move.) When the timer gets to zero, the bridge tile becomes an empty tile that the player can walk (and fall) through:

```
// Switch to empty tile!
this.frame = Object.assign({}, getTile("empty"));
this.update = update;
```

Finally, we can't forget to remove our proxy function by restoring the original `update` method. The bridge tile has now become a normal empty tile, and the transformation is complete.

Trigger Areas and Doors

With a bunch new tile mechanics at our disposal, we need to expand the world beyond a single dungeon room. We need some *doors*. Just like in the real world, **doors** are magical portals to places that we can't be sure exist when we aren't in them. To use a door in the real world, we have to manually turn a door handle and pull a heavy plank of wood. In the game world it's easier: we touch a *trigger*.

A **trigger** isn't something fancy: it's just *a container for a function*. We model it as an entity that has no renderable aspect, so it can still be "collided with" using our standard collision detection code. When an entity collides with a trigger, it *triggers* the custom function to perform an action. That action may be to spawn new enemies when the player enters an area, or to start a particle emitter, or to signal the end of a level is reached, or to change screens when the player passes through a door … and so on. Triggers have a million and one uses!

A Trigger (defined in `Trigger.js`) is an object with a position and bounding box, plus a reference to the custom function:

```
class Trigger {
  constructor(hitBox, onCollide) {
    const { w, h, x = 0, y = 0 } = hitBox;
    this.pos = new Vec();
    this.w = w;
    this.h = h;
    if (x || y) {
```

```
    this.hitBox = { w, h, x, y };
  }
  this.onCollide = onCollide;
 }
}
```

It kind of looks like a `Sprite` but it doesn't extend anything in our system, and it won't be rendered by `CanvasRenderer`. By giving it either a width and height, or a full `hitBox` property (`w` , `h` , `x` and `y`), it acts exactly like a `Sprite` , in that it works with our collision detection functions. There's no magic in `Trigger` . To use it in a game, we have to *manually* check for collisions using the `entity` helper methods `hit` or `hits` . If there's an overlap, we *manually* call the trigger's `trigger` function. That's it.

```
// Touched a door
entity.hits(player, triggers, trigger => trigger.trigger());
```

The `trigger` function makes sure there's an `onCollide` function to execute, then executes it:

```
trigger() {
  if (this.onCollide) {
    this.onCollide();
  }
}
```

What the `onCollide` function does is up to you. One use is to call the `GameScreen` 's "level change" function to move to a different level—effectively creating a portal to another part of the game map:

```
const door = new Trigger({ x:12, y: 11, w: 22, h: 30 }, () => {
  // onChangeLevel is in scope from `GameScreen`
  onChangeLevel(this.level, this.spawnPos);
});
door.pos.copy(doorLocation);

door.level = 2;
door.spawnPos = { x: 5, y: 4 };
triggers.add(door); // `triggers` is a Container
```

The door has a hit box that's just a bit smaller than a tile. We assign some metadata to it: the level number to move to, and the player's spawn position when the new level loads. But we can store *any* information on a trigger and use it after it fires. You could also make a special `Door` class that extends `Trigger` and accepts the appropriate metadata.

For debugging purposes, we'll add a flag that (when true) will display the hit box as a rectangle—so we can check that they're spawning in the correct place and trigger correctly on contact. Give the trigger a `children` array and add a child `Rect` that's the same size as the `hitBox`. The `children` array will be detected by `CanvasRenderer` and the child `Rect` object is displayed:

```
constructor(hitBox, onCollide, debug = false) {
  ...
  if (debug) {
    const box = new Rect(w, h, { fill: "rgba(255, 255, 0, 0.5)"});
    box.pos.set(x, y);
    this.children = [box];
  }
}
```

 Triggers

Triggers can be more advanced than simple collidable entities. With a little more state management, they could be made to only trigger "onEnter": that is, the function would only be called when an entity *first* touches the trigger (and not on subsequent frames if the collision continues). Similarly, "onExit" only when the player *leaves* a trigger area. This gives more depth to a trigger element and opens it up for more game design purposes.

With triggers, disappearing tiles and cloud tiles added to the game, hopefully you can see what's required to extend our core system into something bigger. The main advantage of rolling your own game library is the ability to dive into the internals and add new things you need. You can start with any cool idea you want to implement, and not be dependent on a list of features supplied by a third party.

Dialogs and Screen Transitions

Now that the game's getting bigger, the players need a way to pause and restart—and a way to modify any other custom settings we think they might need. While we're at it, we might also like to display some *non-player character* (NPC) dialog boxes—say if our game has a shop where we can buy upgrades.

8-14. The trading system in Maschinen-Mensch's 'Curious Expedition'

These types of tasks are achieved with *modal dialogs*. **Modal dialogs** are pop-up boxes filled with text, which cover part (or all) of the game screen and prevent the background action from continuing until the player is ready to get back to playing.

There are two approaches we could take. One is to use HTML and CSS to create menus that are *external* to the canvas world. The other is to recreate UI widgets and behaviors using the game library. There are pros and cons for both approaches, and neither is a clear winner.

Native CSS/HTML	Our game library
Large collection of existing widgets	Must create *every* widget from scratch
Accessible, consistent	As accessible and consistent as we make it
Styled via CSS	Styled like other game screens
Must pass information and events between the game and the dialog	Is part of the game
Input method is browser-ish (no gamepads by default)	Input method matches game
Requires reloading any necessary game assets	Uses the same assets from our game
Requires a full browser environment	Can be used in any deployment target our renderer supports

In either approach, dialogs are interruptions to the usual game loop. The player will go bananas if they pause the game and then we shoot them in the background. But sometimes we want certain elements (such as pacing enemies) to continue even when dialogs appear. For maximum flexibility, we'll handle the dialog life cycle ourselves within our *State* management.

Pause Dialog

As much as it pains us, sometimes you just have to put a game down. Otherwise we'd miss our train stop again and get fired for being late. If your game can't be left unattended, it needs a pause dialog. In our system, a dialog is like a scene within a scene. It's self-contained, and appears as a smaller window over the existing (paused) scene.

Our approach will be to handle the rendering of the dialog ourselves (rather than using HTML and CSS). The pause dialog is a simple *Container*. We can add whatever child entities we want to display (*Rect* s, *Sprite* s, *Text* , *Image* s ...) and handle input the same as any old scene. The tricky part is how we create, update, and display the container in our *main game flow*.

```
class PauseDialog extends Container {
  constructor(controls, onClose) {
    super();
    this.onClose = onClose;
    this.controls = controls;
    // Draw your dialog!
    const bg = this.add(new Rect(400, 400, { fill: "#000" }));
    bg.pos.set(20, 20);
    ...
  }
}
```

I'm leaving it up to you to design a beautiful *PauseDialog* . It probably at least has a background rectangle to draw on top of—but it's your call. The *PauseDialog* is instantiated with the input controls, along with any events it needs to react to (exactly like a regular *scene*). All dialogs should have an *onClose* event, as this will be called to resume the normal game flow.

The dialog class will also have an *update* function. It's here where we check to see if the player has hit the escape key (key code 27). If so, we call another method (*close*) to get out. The reason we do this in a separate place (rather than simply calling *this.onClose* inline) is that later, when we add more settings to our game, we can delegate the actions as needed, and the *update* function doesn't get too messy.

```
update() {
  const { controls } = this;
```

```
    const exit = controls.key(27);
    if (exit) {
      this.close();
    }
  }
```

The dialog box is a container and an entity in our system. To get it out of the scene hierarchy, we set the *dead* to *true* and call the *onClose* callback provided from the user:

```
close() {
  this.dead = true;
  this.onClose();
}
```

That's the dialog box itself. Now we have to wrangle it inside our game flow. For this, we'll have a new state called "PAUSED". In the first frame of the state, we instantiate a new *PauseDialog* (via a factory method called *makeMenuDialog* that we'll discuss below). The trick for pausing our game is to call *update* on the *dialog entity* each frame, but we don't call *super.update* on the *container itself*. We're selectively deciding what is updated (the dialog box) rather than updating all the children (the rest of the game). By not calling *super.update*, none of the other children of *GameScreen* will get updated—so the game is paused.

```
case "PAUSED":
  if (state.first) {
    this.dialog = this.hud.add(this.makeMenuDialog(dt));
  }
  this.dialog.update(dt, t);
  break;
```

To get into the *PAUSED* state, we wait until the user presses the escape key. This needs to be done anywhere where pausing is possible. If we put it after the main state-handling switch statement, we'll be able to pause any time in the game.

```
if (!state.is("PAUSED") && controls.key(27)) {
  controls.reset();
  state.set("PAUSED");
}
```

All that's left is to actually create a *PauseDialog*. A dialog requires we pass a callback function that runs when the dialog is closed. After the user exits the dialog, we call *state.back()* —which restores the previous state and previous state *time* so the player resumes where they left off.

```
makeMenuDialog() {
  const { controls, state, player, screens } = this;
  return new PauseDialog(controls, () => {
    state.back();
  });
}
```

The implementation of our pause screen and settings menu is also the basis for *any* game dialog: speech bubbles, upgrade shops, level selectors, post-level summaries, or crafting screens.

Fading Screens

The game is starting to feel like a *game*. One last piece of juice we'll add is to improve our screen transitions. We'll replace our "smash cut" (instantly switching to a new view) with a nice fade between scenes, just like on TV.

A screen transitions requires a *source* scene and *destination* scene that we fade between. If you've used video editing software, you're probably aware that there are many types of transition effects. Most of them are really annoying and cheesy (I'm looking at you, "star wipe"). The most subtle and suitable are "fade-to-black", and "the dissolve". We're going concentrate on the dissolve: smoothly cross-fading between source and destination scenes.

Conceptually, it's pretty easy: one scene is fully opaque (the source), one scene is fully transparent (the destination). We inverse their `alpha` over time until the destination is fully opaque. The destination has become the source. Practically, there are a few things we need to modify in our `Game.js` to cater for our "dual scenes" approach. Rather than setting the `game.scene` property directly (as we've been doing to switch scenes), we add a `setScene` function to set up our transition:

```
setScene(scene, duration = 0.5) {
  if (!duration) {
    this.scene = scene;
    return;
  }
  this.destination = scene;
  this.fadeTime = duration;
  this.fadeDuration = duration;
}
```

This function takes our new destination scene and a `duration` of time to fade. If the duration is 0 (or a falsy value) we keep the existing behavior of not fading between scenes and just switch `this.scene`. Otherwise, we keep a reference to the `destination` scene and establish our (hopefully now familiar-looking) ratio-timer system for cross-fading.

After the source `scene` is rendered in the main game loop, we check for a `fadeTime`. If it's greater than 0, it means we're doing our cross-fade logic.

```
renderer.render(scene);

// Screen transition
if (fadeTime > 0) {
  const { fadeDuration, destination } = this;
  const ratio = fadeTime / fadeDuration;
  scene.alpha = ratio;
  destination.alpha = 1 - ratio;
  renderer.render(destination, false);
  ...
}
```

The source scene ratio goes from 1 to 0, and the destination scene is inverted, 0 to 1. The destination scene is rendered over the top of our source scene. Be sure to set the `clear` flag to `false` so that it *doesn't clear the background* (the source scene) before rendering.

```
if ((this.fadeTime -= STEP) <= 0) {
  this.scene = destination;
  this.destination = null;
}
```

The `fadeTime` timer is reduced each frame. When we're at (or below) zero, fade is complete. The destination scene becomes the source scene and we free up the `destination` variable and the next scene plays on. Test out the effect between our title screen and the game: it ties the two scenes together, and adds that extra bit of polish.

Designing Levels with a Level Editor

Hand rolling our *Bravedigger* level maps as we've been doing is great fun. Seeing grids of 0s and 1s rendered on screen as colorful tiles and characters is strangely rewarding. But if you have more than a few simple levels, it's time to start thinking about a *level editor*. A **level editor** is a specialized graphical tool that speeds up designing levels for your game. A good editor will let you freely and quickly experiment with design ideas, providing tools to sketch out, iterate, and improve levels via an intuitive interface. We're going to need this if we want to get a large amount of quality content into *Bravedigger*.

There are two main approaches to level editors: either create a bespoke editor for your specific game, or use an off-the-shelf level-editing package. As always, there are pros and cons to both. Creating your own custom editor *can* be a great choice (especially if you're making an unusual game that doesn't fit well into a generic editor). A custom editor can reuse the game's rendering and logic code, so it's not like starting from scratch. As a bonus, if it works well enough, you can even release it to your community of players who can make and share their own new levels!

However, it's going to take time. Any time you spend creating a level editor is time you *aren't* spending on the game itself. It's important to understand the limits of available generic tools before you go down the (very enjoyable) rabbit hole of rolling your own.

Tiled: a Level Editor

For 2D games (especially grid-based games), one of the most popular level-editing tools is the free and open-source Tiled[8] map editor. Tiled lets you paint levels with brushes (rather than hand-placing them in code as ASCII!). It supports features like flood-filling, copy-pasting tile areas, bulk replacing tiles, as well as advanced features like *terrain brushes*—where specially constructed tile sets can automatically be painted with correct borders between, say, sand and water.

In addition to tile placement, Tiled also allows you to add *extra metadata* and objects into the levels that can represent game data like player spawn points, position (and abilities) of baddies, value of pickup objects, and level goal requirements. (For example, if you need to find "X" number of crates to finish a level, you can specify the "X" in a Tiled map's properties.) Fewer elements need to be hardcoded into our game code, so experimenting with *game design* is easier.

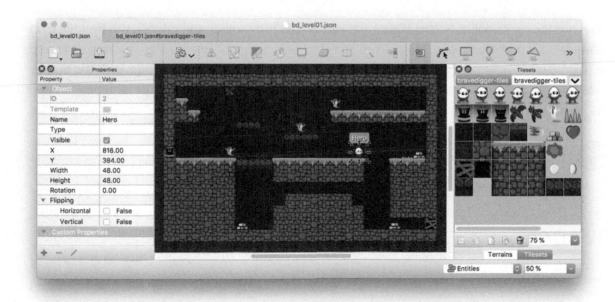

8-15. Bravedigger in the Tiled editor

8. http://www.mapeditor.org/

Where to Get the Editor

Head over to the Tiled website and follow the link to the *download* page to get the editor for your system. I was using version 1.1.1 at the time of writing, but everything that follows should be fairly similar for future versions and other editors. Tiled is a "name your own price" title—so you're free to name $0, but the author Thorbjørn Lindeijer has been working tirelessly on Tiled since 2008, and any money received is used for making it better. Win-win!

Once installed, you'll be greeted with a blank editor. The first thing to do is to create a *new map*. Upon hitting the *new map* icon (or *File -> New* from the menu bar), Tiled will ask you some questions about your world. Change the *Tile size* properties to 48x48px (or whatever your tile size is!) and set the *Map size*. This is going to vary on each level of our game. For the first level, we'll choose the amount that fits exactly into one screen (with no scrolling)—25x16—giving us a game screen size of 1200x768. Sounds good.

The next thing to do is get our tile sprite sheet image file into the editor. On the right side of the screen, there are several panels: *Layers, Tilesets, Properties*. Under the *Tilesets* panel, click the *new* icon to add a tileset to the map. Find the `res/images/bravedigger-tiles.png` file. Check the box "Embed in map". When you hit *ok*, the tileset is added and the image should be chopped up so that each tile aligns with the grid.

Now the fun part begins. Select the *stamp* tool on the top toolbar and choose the first tile icon. Now click around the screen. Magic! You can start designing out the level as you want it to appear to the player. If you make a mistake with a tile placement, you can erase things with the erase tool. You can also select ranges to cut and paste, do a "magic wand" select of matching tiles, and flood-fill tiles.

 Custom Brushes

By default, all stamping and filling operations use the tile you selected from the tileset. However, if you have the *stamp* tool selected and *right-click and drag* an area of a map, this selection becomes a custom brush. You can then re-stamp this pattern or use it to fill an area. This lets you very quickly sketch out a level with repeated elements.

Once you're happy with how your level is shaping up, use *File -> Save as* to get it to a place we can load from our game. By default, Tiled saves as XML with the custom *.tmx* file extension. But we are JavaScripters, so JSON is more natural for us. In the export screen, change the dropdown box from *Tiled map files (.tmx)* to *Json map files (.json)*. Recent versions of Tiled have started storing the level cell data in a compressed format to keep the file size low. It's possible to decompress this in JavaScript, but it's easier if we just keep our big ol' levels in plain ASCII. To do this, you need to modify the map *Properties* on the left side of the screen. Change the setting *Tiled Layer Format* from "Base64 (zlib compressed)" to "CSV". Now we're good to go.

Create a new folder— `Levels` —inside the `res` assets area of our game and save the file as `bd_Level01.json`. Once you've saved, you'll notice the file name in the editor changes, and the extension is now `.json`. This means that any changes you make will now automatically be reflected every time you hit save, which is fantastic: the fewer steps between editing and seeing results in your game, the better.

Loading a Tiled Level

The Tiled JSON file can be loaded into our game and converted into a level format that we transform into game entities. We'll create a new type of `TileMap` level class to hold our Tiled level. Our asset manager currently doesn't know about JSON files, so the first step is to add this to the library's `Assets.js` loader:

```
json(url) {
  return load(url, (url, onAssetLoad) =>
    fetch(url)
      .then(res => res.json())
      .then(json => onAssetLoad(json))
      .catch(e => console.error(e))
  );
}
```

We can asynchronously load a JSON file via the **Fetch API**. `fetch` loads a file and returns a promise for us. The loader system handles the preloading the same way as the `Image` and `Audio` assets. However, for our game we're not going to load all of the levels in one go. We'll load them as needed. If we end up with hundreds of levels, this will speed things up at the beginning. (We could also consider some kind of hybrid system, where we load levels in batches.)

```
const level = 1;
const levelUrl = `res/levels/bd_level${level}.json}`;
Assets.json(levelUrl)
  .then(json => this.setupLevel(json));
```

When `GameScreen` is created, we'll load level 1. The level number will eventually get passed in when we make some more levels. Because the JSON file is loaded asynchronously, we can't display the level until it's loaded. Instead, we start in a new state ("LOADING") and display a loading message. Once it's done, we can parse the level data and move to the "READY" state, where things can continue the same as our synchronous (in-memory) levels.

The next thing to do is to figure out what all this JSON is that we get from Tiled. Honestly, the *specifics* of this next section are not too interesting. The key is the *idea*. Regardless of whether you're using Tiled or another tool, you'll have to figure out the *data transformation*. It's all about transforming the editor's output into a format we can use in our `TileMap`.

In our project, we'll create a new class `TiledLevel.js` that will be a replacement for `Level.js`. It will still extend `TileMap` and will do all of the things our `Level` was doing. But any level information we were hardcoding (such as the layout and dimensions of the tiles, and the tile properties, like `walkable` and `clouds`) come from the Tiled editor.

`TiledLevel` is specific to our game. It will expect our Tiled levels to have certain objects with specific names and types. But parsing a Tiled JSON file is something we can make generic to every Tiled file. To do the parsing, we'll create a function `utils/tiledParser.js` and add it to our library. It will take as input a Tiled JSON file and return as output a plain object with the metadata about the map (as well as a couple of helper functions for extracting information we need for the game).

 Reverse Engineering

To figure out the Tiled level format, I just opened the JSON in a text editor and reverse engineered it! Thankfully, it's pretty straightforward and well laid out, and the documentation on their website is pretty good. So if you want to integrate more advanced Tiled features, you just need to figure out how to transform the saved file structure into a format you can use.

```
function tiledParser(json) {
  const {
    tilewidth: tileW,
    tileheight: tileH,
    width: mapW,
    height: mapH,
    layers,
    tilesets
  } = json;
}
```

The first part of the parser extracts and renames the level data. What we've been calling `tileW`, Tiled calls `tilewidth`, and what we've called `mapW`, Tiled calls `width`. We also pull out the layers we defined in the editor. For a Tiled level to work out of the box with our game library, we've decided to enforce a couple of naming conventions: the main level layer *must* be called "Level", and the main objects layer *must* be called "Entities". If they don't exist, we throw an error and give up:

```
// Layer-fetcher-helper function
const getLayer = name => {
  const layer = layers.find(l => l.name === name);
  if (!layer) {
    throw new Error(`Tiled error: Missing layer "${name}".`);
  }
  return layer;
};
// Get our main level
const levelLayer = getLayer("Level");
```

The next step is to get all of the tile properties so we can correctly create our `TileSprite` elements that make up the map. We assume that there's only one tileset and it's in the first index. (In the sample code, we wrap this in a helper like `getLayer`, so you get an error in the console if it doesn't exist.) The tileset object contains information we can use to get the number of cells in the tileset image. This way, we can map over the level data and transform the cell information to a format that mimics our existing `frame` object—with `x`, `y` and any extra metadata properties.

The next step is more transformations: converting the tile information into something we can use in `TileMap`:

```
// Map the Tiled level data to our game format
const props = tileset.tileproperties; // tile properties: walkable, clouds, etc.
const tilesPerRow = Math.floor(tileset.imagewidth / tileset.tilewidth);
const tiles = levelLayer.data.map(cell => {
  const idx = cell - tileset.firstgid; // Get correct Tiled offset
  return Object.assign({}, props && props[idx] || {}, {
    x: idx % tilesPerRow,
    y: Math.floor(idx / tilesPerRow)
  });
});

return { tileW, tileH, mapW, mapH, tiles };
```

Again, the *specifics* of this transformation are not particularly interesting. It's just the result of a rough reverse-engineering of the Tiled output file. One thing that *is* very important for us is the contents of `tileset.tileproperties`. This is where tile properties like `walkable` and `clouds` are set. Each tile that's returned in `tiles` will contain its `x` and `y` indexes *plus* any metadata supplied by `props` (which are merged into the tile object using `Object.assign`).

To create the metadata inside the Tiled editor, click in the tileset area on the tile you want to change (for example, any blank tile that the player can walk in the tile selector) and then on the left side of the screen in the properties list create a new "Custom Property" called `walkable`. Make it a boolean value and check it to `true`. No longer do we need to maintain it in code (which we used to do with `tileIndexes`). We can do everything inside the level editor!

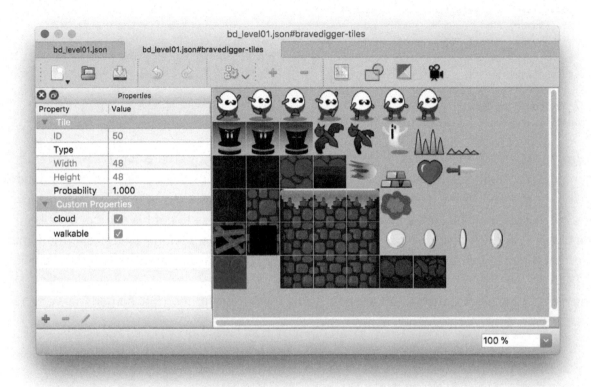

8-16. Custom properties for a cloud tile

We have all of the information we need to create a `TileMap` instance and display it on screen:

```
class TiledLevel extends TileMap {
  constructor(json) {
    const { tileW, tileH, mapW, mapH, tiles } = tiledParser(json);
    super(tiles, mapW, mapH, tileH, tileW, texture);
  }
}
```

Being able to edit a level in Tiled and see the results on screen instantly—combined with the ability to define tile types (such as `walkable`)—means you can easily try out new level design ideas. Also, it means it's easier to work with a dedicated level designer—who only needs to know how to put things together in Tiled, but doesn't need to know how your code works!

Tiled Objects and Properties

The background level is beautiful, so now it's time to fill it with some entities. Previously in `Level.js`, we set all of our spawn points in ASCII by hand. Now we can do it directly in the editor by creating a new *layer*. We can place *objects* anywhere in this layer. A Tiled "object" is just a data definition—with a width, height, position, and any additional metadata you might want for your game. Our goal is then to transform the *object* definition into a Pop *entity*.

In the *Layers* section on the right of the screen, click the *new* icon and select *Add Object Layer*. This is where we'll define the location and types of all our bad guys (and the player). Rename the layer to "Entities" (we'll use this ID later) and select the *Objects* tab so we can start adding things.

All of the icons on the top right of the top toolbar are for manipulating Tiled objects. One option is to draw entities using the *Insert Rectangle* tool. You can click anywhere on the map and draw out a rectangle to act as a spawn location. Because our tile graphics also contain our player and bad guys images, we can use the *Insert Tile* tool (the picture icon) to stamp them around the layer (rather than just using abstract rectangles).

Click the *Insert Tile* tool, select a tile that represents the entity you want to create (we'll start with the player graphic), and then click it's spawn point on the map. A new object is added to the *Objects* list. Each object can have a *name* and a *type*. Because there's only one player, we'll give them a name `Hero`. (Again, this ID will be used when we load the level.) Next, we'll do the same for some pickups. Click on the treasure icon, stamp it on the map, and this time give it a *type*, `Pickup`. Do the same again for type `Ghost`. Add a bunch of pickups and ghosts wherever you like!

8-17. Entity properties in Tiled

We can extract this data from the Tiled JSON and then get our spawn points. From the *Entities* layer we get the `objects` and pull out the information we might be interested in. We also have to subtract the object's height from it's `y` position to get its *actual* location—because (for reasons that are very confusing) Tiled positions objects from their *bottom-left corner* (instead of the top-left corner, like everything else):

```
const entitiesLayer = getLayer("Entities");
const entities = entitiesLayer.objects.map(
  ({ x, y, width, height, properties, type, name }) => ({
    x,
    y: y - height, // Fix tiled Y alignment
    width, height,
    properties, type, name
  })
);
```

We also create a couple of functions (`getObjectsByType` and `getObjectByName`) that will extract objects by name or type. These functions are returned from the parser so we can use them in `TiledLevel` when we want to get the spawn locations and other details. If you're using an editor other than Tiled, you'll need to write this transformation of "editor-object to Pop-entity" yourself.

```
getSpawnLocations(data) {
  return {
```

```
    player: data.getObjectByName("Hero"),
    baddies: [
      ...data.getObjectsByType("Ghost"),
      ...data.getObjectsByType("Bat"),
      ...data.getObjectsByType("Totem")
    ],
    pickups: data.getObjectsByType("Pickup"),
    doors: data.getObjectsByType("Door")
  };
}
```

Tiled objects not only define *positions* but also *metadata*, which is stored in the object's `properties` . Any *Custom Properties* that are set on the object (like how we added `walkable` to individual tiles) will show up here. There are *many* uses for custom properties; we're using them to define how doors work in the game. In the first level, there's one door, which has the following custom properties defined:

```
spawnX: 4
spawnY: 12
toLevel: 2
```

When we create a door trigger, we pass it these parameters. And when the player hits the trigger, we know which level to load, and where to position the player (so they're standing next to the door they entered). This is just one use for custom properties. They can also be used to set the speed and direction of bad guys, pickup health amount, damage levels—anything and everything! The more you can jam into the custom properties, the more you can play and experiment with level design from the comfort of the Tiled editor.

Game State and Serialization

Before we call it a day, we'll quickly look at how to manage moving between levels. In previous chapters, we saw how to pass data between scenes so that we could manage high scores. This is more serious though. In our game we need to move from level to level (creating a new `GameScreen` each time) and when we *return* to a previous screen, we have to restore its state. We can't have the player kill all the bad guys, run out the door and back again, and magically all of the bad guys have respawned (well, unless you *want* that to be a feature).

Just like recording high scores, our `main.js` will have to hold the *global state* for our entire game session. Here we'll store things like scores, player HP, current level bad-guy positions and other data—anything that's maintained across levels:

```
const defaults = () => ({
  level: 1,
  doors: { "1": true },
  data: {},
  hp: 5,
  score: 0
});


let state = defaults();
```

The *defaults* are returned via functions, because our state will also contain a couple of JavaScript objects. And by creating them from scratch in *main*, we avoid the problem of mutating existing ones when we start a new game. The two objects are *doors* and *data*. *doors* is a list of the levels that the player has unlocked. Because they start at level one, the door "1" is unlocked—so when they get to level 2 they can get back again!

 Cheat Codes are Handy for Testing

While testing the game, you can unlock more doors by default so you don't have to beat all the enemies a million times. Better yet, hook up a cheat code to unlock the current level so that your player community can one day find it and feel like kings!

The *data* object is the one we want to talk about in this section. This will be where we store the current level progress so that the player can move between levels and return to a room with the same configuration as when they left: same pickups, same bad guys, in the same place. To do this, we *serialize* the level data. **Serialization** is converting the state of a running system into a data format that can be stored. At any time in the future it can be *deserialized* and be as if it continued from the point it was serialized. It's a save game.

We need to convert our running state into something that *exactly* resembles the output of the *tiledParser* function. The serialized data can then be loaded as if it's just another level. There are only six fields we need to fully serialize our level. We pull them out of the current running game and return them from a new method in *TiledLevel* :

```
serialize(game) {
  const { player, pickups, baddies, triggers } = game;
  const { mapW, mapH, tileW, tileH, children } = this;
  ...
  return { mapW, mapH, tileW, tileH, tiles, spawns };
}
```

Some fields (*mapW* and *tileW*) are easy: they're the values stored on the current level. But for `tiles` , we have to be a little careful. The tile data may have changed since the level was originally created (perhaps there were bridge tiles that the player disintegrated). We have to *map* the current world back to raw data that mimics our old `tileIndexes` frame data:

```
const tiles = children.map(({ frame }) => Object.assign({}, frame));
```

It's just the inverse of how we set it up! We pull the *current* frame data out and copy it to a new object. However, `spawns` is a tiny bit more tricky. It involves looping over the relevant containers and converting the children back to the correct format. For example, `pickups` only require `x` and `y` locations to be created and would be serialized like this:

```
pickups.children.map(({ pos: { x, y } }) => ({ x, y }))
```

Once the entire level is serialized, it can be stored in our `gameState` 's data object (`gameState.data[gameState.level] = map.serialize()`). When it comes time to *load* a level, we check if there's *already* data for this level. If there isn't, we load the level from the network via our asset manager. If there *is*, we pass the `data` value directly to `setupLevel` (we've made it a JavaScript promise with `Promise.resolve` so we can treat both cases the same) without doing any JSON parsing:

```
const levelUrl = `res/levels/level${gameState.level}.json`;
const serialized = gameState.data[gameState.level];
const level = serialized
  ? Promise.resolve(serialized) // Load serialized level
  : Assets.json(levelUrl);      // Load from the network

level.then(json => this.setupLevel(json, !!serialized));
```

By mimicking the `tileParser` function, we don't care if the level comes from a URL or from memory or from disk or wherever. The data can be saved to the server or to the browser's *localStorage* cache, so progress can be tracked even when the player reloads the game.

Got Game

This chapter was about adding lots of common juicy game elements. But gaming lore is deep and wide. We haven't even scratched the surface of the surface. Study (and steal) juicy mechanics and tips from other games, movies, and cartoons—and always be thinking about how you can juice your game in its own, unique way. Do it well enough and one day might even see your *own* inventions ripped off in others' games. Then you'll know you've made it!

Putting the finishing touches on the final level of *Bravedigger*, you stand up for a little victory dance: you've taken the clunky prototype and transformed it into a magical catacomb adventure—complete with particle effects and screen shakes and oh-so-much juice.

Just then, your celebration dance gets a little out of control and you crash into the indoor plant in the corner of the office. From out of the plant tumbles a small microcontroller with what looks like ... an attached camera. Guy Shifty is spying on our progress! Outraged, you lift the camera to your face and gnash your teeth, before dropping the camera to the ground and crushing it with your foot. This means war!

Optimizing & Packaging

"Hey, MomPop Games," whispers a nervous-looking, hoodie-clad figure you recognize as one of Guy Shifty's coders. "We just wanted to give you a heads-up about IGC. Shifty saw how your *Bravedigger* game was shaping up, so he's got us working on *multiple* games that he's going to enter in *multiple* categories! I think you'll have to beat him on desktop *and* mobile. Otherwise, he says he wins the bet. I gotta go. Good luck."

Great, more work for us, and we don't even know *how* to get things out into the world yet!

A game only exists once people can *play it*. This requires two things: it must run at an acceptable frame rate, and it must be available for people to download or install. And for us, at this stage of our career, the first part is kind of optional. A finished game that runs horribly is worth *10,000 unreleased prototypes*. If this is your first (or second, or maybe third) game, then worry about game ideas, rather than game performance.

Once it's finished, you can launch it out into the world—to Steam, Itch.io, the App Store, or Google Play. It's exciting and cool to imagine tens, hundreds, even thousands (dare we say *millions*!) of people enjoying your hard work—sharing it with their friends, or streaming it on the internet! It makes you want to make *more* things. Actually *releasing* a game is the only way to start building up a community of players (and fans!) who'll then be more interested in your future games. Getting your game out the door establishes the habit of *finishing your projects*—which is the hardest gamedev skill of them all.

You can't just ignore performance forever, though. At best, a poorly performing game will elicit angry feedback from players. At worst, it can hurt your artistic vision for the project. (It sucks to have to scale back a big idea because of performance limits.) When it comes time to improve your code, measure everything before you change anything, target the big wins first, and make sure the fixes actually improve things for the environments you plan to deploy to.

Debugging

Before releasing to the world, we have to squash as many bugs as we can. You likely have your standard assortment of webdev debugging techniques. (If not, or if you want a refresher, *JavaScript: Novice to Ninja*[1] has a great chapter on debugging, covering the console logger and debuggers for web apps.) But game debugging is a slightly different beast. It's difficult to comprehend the state of a system accurately when things are moving so fast. Some old, faithful debugging tricks (like `console.log(player)`) aren't practical at 60 frames per second, as things just scroll away in a sea of messages. A few `console` statements inside a nested loop in the main game loop is a sure-fire way to make your browser unresponsive and crashy!

---

[1]. https://www.sitepoint.com/premium/books/javascript-novice-to-ninja-2nd-edition

But the trusty logger is still a very efficient go-to weapon in the early stages of a bug hunt, even in a tight loop. One trick is to *conditionally* log messages by introducing temporary global variables to reduce the sea of messages to a small pond.

```
window.tmpLogCount = 0;
```

Instead of logging every frame, create expressions that log only certain frames. This is particularly applicable when you *kind of* know when a bug happens, but can't pinpoint it precisely.

```
update () {
  ...
  baddies.forEach((b, i) => {
    if (i < 2 && t > 2 && ++tmpLogCount < 20) {
      console.log(i, b);
    }
    ...
  });
}
```

In this example, we only log the first two bad guys (`i < 2`), with a maximum of 20 messages each—but only *after* two seconds have elapsed (`t > 2`). This might look contrived, but it was actually used to hunt down a logic bug in the baddie AI state code. (It turned out to be a variable typo in the "attack" logic for `Bats` , those pesky Chiroptera.) Using global variables (even temporarily) might feel icky, but it does provide some rudimentary control via the browser console itself. At any time, you can reset the temporary counter and get another 20 messages:

```
tmpLogCount = 0;
```

It's certainly not fancy, but it's fast and easy!

Console Tools

The `console` debugging object has a few more tricks up its sleeve than simply logging messages, and some are particularly helpful in gamedev. For example, `console.clear()` can be used to clear the current console output. If you're logging your sea of messages and temporarily only care about a certain message, a `console.clear()` before logging means only what you're interested appears at the top. It can even be hooked up to a keyboard shortcut in your game if you want to clear the console while you're playtesting.

Depending on the structure of the variables you're logging, `console.table` can be very useful for outputting tabular data. This method takes a JavaScript array or object and prints it as a cool table (rather than the regular, expandable tree-view representation). This is especially useful if you need to copy-paste values out to another document:

```
console.table(entities);
```

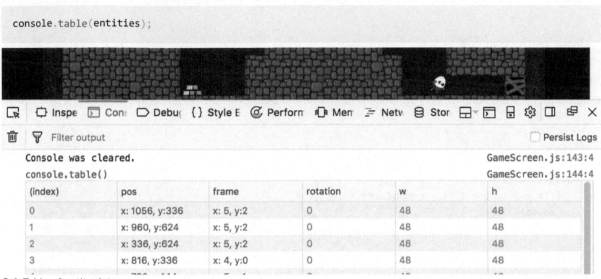

9-1. Table of entity data

Another powerful tool for finding bugs in your codebase is `console.assert`. This allows you to *assert* that something is in the state you expect. Normally this is true, so the statement does nothing. If the asserted expression is false, something's gone wrong and it prints a warning to the console. For example, our library deals a lot with *entities*. To be an "entity" you need to have a `pos` object and a width and a height (`w` and `h`). We can assert that this is true (for example, in our `utils/entity.js` functions):

```
console.assert(e.pos && e.w > 0 && e.h > 0, "Entity has wrong shape");
```

If the entity doesn't have the correct "shape", a warning is thrown and we know we've passed in something incorrect.

There are other console methods that are useful for profiling code execution times, and we'll talk about them shortly. Just remember that `console` statements may not be supported in certain environments (such as older browsers) and logging a lot of messages can slow down the browser, causing poor performance. Be sure to remove any console statements before you deploy your game!

Browser Debugger

Modern web browsers include some excellent tools beyond `console.log`. Most include JavaScript "debuggers" as part of their standard developer tools. **Debuggers** are *The Matrix* of live code manipulation. They let you pause execution of a running script, inspect and change values, and move step by step over each code instruction. You can also set **breakpoints** on individual lines of your code: before the JavaScript engine evaluates this line of code, everything will stop and the state can be examined and edited.

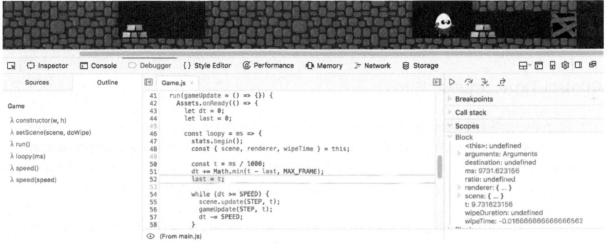

9-2. Browser debugger

We won't cover the usage of debuggers here. If you've used a debugger in low-level languages like C, they'll be very familiar. Otherwise, check out your browser's documentation for tutorials and explanations of all their features. Being able to pause the page and take a magnifying glass to every game object and variable can be a lifesaver when you can't figure out why your sprite is appearing in the top-left corner all the time. (Spoiler: it's because something had become *NaN* when I typed *bat.x* instead of *bat.pos.x* .)

Before we leave the debugger, there's one useful hint that helps when you want to examine the state of the world at some point in code: you can also *programmatically* trigger the debugger:

```
if (pos.x > 100 && isNaN(pos.y)) {
  debugger;
}
```

The keyword *debugger* will trigger the browser's debugger and pause the current game flow. In this state, you can add *watch* variables and step through the rest of the code. You can press "play" to continue the game—just like a regular breakpoint. In fact, it's the same as setting a breakpoint inside the *if* statement, but has the advantage that you can quickly add it in code without having to find it in the browser console's source-code list.

A Confession

Confession time. Debuggers *feel* like they should be the correct answer to all your debugging needs. But in practice, I don't use them as much as I probably should. Games are constantly changing, and it's often not obvious *when* you need to halt execution. And if you knew the exact conditions that triggered a bug, you probably already would've figured out what the bug is!

Control Time, Squash Bugs

A more game-specific debugging technique is to *slow down time*! It's difficult to follow values and actions when they update 60 times every second ... so why not slow down the game to two frames per second? We showed how this is possible in the last chapter. There, we used it as a game mechanic, but it's also a tool for closely examining frame-by-frame movement.

As a general-purpose debugging system, running at two frames per second is not great. It could take *hours of playing* just to get to level 2! However, if we tie frames per second to keyboard shortcuts, we run at normal (or even faster than normal) speeds until we reach the area of interest. Another keypress and we go all "Slow Mobius", and the hunt for bugs is on!

Where to Put This

I'll integrate a keyboard shortcut handler in the game's `main.js` file, but it might be something you'd like to put in the main game handler so it's available to any game you're developing. Just make sure it's only enabled for debug builds of your game (or behind a well-hidden cheat code). Otherwise, your players will exploit it!

```
game.run(() => {
  slowmo(controls.keys);
});
```

Each frame we call a function, `slowmo`, with the keyboard handler. Here we can check if our shortcut keys are pressed. If so, we can modify the game frame rate via `game.speed`:

```
function slowmo(keys) {
  if(keys.key(49)){
    game.speed += 0.25;
    keys.key(49, false);
  }
```

```
    ...
}
```

49 is the ASCII keycode for the 1 key. If it's pressed, we increment the game speed by 0.25. We also then *clear* the key press so it doesn't fire over subsequent frames: you have to re-press it to speed it up more. A game speed of 1.25 will be 25% faster than normal.

```
if(keys.key(50)){
    game.speed = Math.max(0.25, game.speed - 0.25);
    keys.keys(50, false);
}
if(keys.key(51)){
    game.speed = 1;
}
```

We can also add handlers for the 2 key (ASCII keycode 50). In this case we slow the game down by 25%, with the slowest possible speed being 0.25. You can change the amounts and minimums if you want to go even slower. Just keep it above 0! The final case is the 3 key (ASCII keycode 51). This resets the speed back to 1.

Debug Overlay

Often the most useful way to display fast-changing information is via a display on the screen itself. If you draw whatever you're interested in as *text* on screen, it will (unlike `console.log`) happily update at 60 frames per second. Many games will include a keyboard shortcut that you can press to see debugging information in real time. This is useful for game developers, but sometimes also for players—providing them with a tool for gathering information about any issues they're experiencing, thus helping with feedback.

9-3. Debug messages

As the game's developer, often you just need to check some value that you suspect is not correct. We can already draw text on screen. Add a new `Text` entity to the scene and set the text to the variable you want to investigate. Combined with "slowmo" from above, it's a very fast way to verify things are in the state you expect. If you already have a text element (say, for the player's score), you can even just hijack that!

```
scoreText.text = `${ vel.x.toFixed(2) }:${ vel.y.toFixed(2) }`;
```

 toFixed

The JavaScript number method *toFixed* will output a fixed number of decimal places (truncating or adding as needed). This is often desirable so that numbers don't flicker as the number of digits changes. You can also make some utility methods to pretty-print values for you!

Taking over a text field is adequate for some emergency bug surgery, but it's not a permanent or extensible solution. Ultimately, you want the screen to be toggle-able and display a lot more information. And we have a way to do that—via a modal dialog box we made last chapter. Depending on your environment, it can either be done completely using *pop.Text* entities or as plain HTML.

Profiling

We're happy we've removed the critical bugs from *Bravedigger*, but the game still isn't running smoothly, and we're quickly running out of time to get our IGC entry in. What's next?

Even though computers are ludicrously fast, they still only have 16 milliseconds to do *all* game processing and rendering. Any longer and things stop animating at our silky-smooth 60 frames per second. At this stage, it's tempting to dive into our codebase and refactor any aspect we *think* might be causing slowdown or unnecessary load. But wait! Before you change *anything*, take some time to **profile** your game—that is, take measurements—to ensure you're fixing something that is actually broken. Likewise, take some time to measure how your changes really affect performance.

 Beware Generic Programming Wisdom About Performance

Be wary of generic programming wisdom—often just superstition—that worked on a particular system, a long time ago. The Web changes incredibly fast, and tricks that are silver bullets one day can be performance destroyers the next.

Adding an FPS Counter

There are two measurements that are necessary to keep an eye on during development: memory, and frames per second. Actually, when we say "frames per second", a more important measure is usually the *number of milliseconds* it takes to render each frame (often abbreviated as "ms"). If you have a beefy machine that can easily render more than 60 frames per second, you won't realize when this number falls, as long as it remains above 60. However, you *will* see the millisecond count going up.

These measures should always be displayed on screen—or at least be easily accessible. They're your canary in the coal mine—your early-warning system for spotting performance bottlenecks. Say you add a new AI sub-system and suddenly your frame rate takes a hefty dive. With easy access to that data, you're more likely to spot the culprit early on. Most modern browsers have built-in tools available for displaying these frame-per-second and millisecond values as overlays over the entire browser. In Firefox, this is a debug option you can enable from `about:config` (set the `layers.acceleration.draw-fps` option to `true`). In Chrome, it's available from the developer tools in the "rendering" settings, as "Show FPS meter".

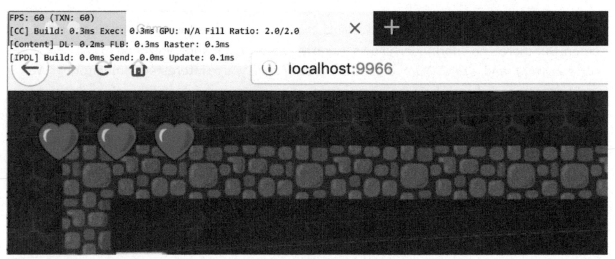

9-4. Native browser FPS stats

The browser tools are good for measuring the *overall browser performance*—including all the garbage collection and other housekeeping it has to do itself. To get more specific information about our game (rather than the whole browser) we can inject our own performance counters and display them on our game screen. We'll integrate the excellent and well-known FPS counter Stats.js[2]. Stats.js, made by JavaScript graphics wizard Mr Doob, displays a cool little widget that lives on the web page our game runs in. It includes measurements for FPS, milliseconds, and (in Chrome) memory usage. As a bonus, the measurements are also displayed as a bar graph over

---

[2] https://github.com/mrdoob/stats.js/

time so you can see when dips and peaks occur.

60 FPS (55-60)   2 MS (1-9)   7 MB (5-8)

9-5. Stats.js

To use Stats.js in your project, either download the JavaScript file from the Mr Doob's repository (and link it in your HTML file), or install it via npm with `npm install stats.js` . The crucial code areas we'd like to track are around the main game loop, so we'll include Stats.js in the `Game.js` helper:

```
import Stats from "stats";

const stats = new Stats();
stats.showPanel(1);
```

By creating a new `Stats` instance and calling `showPanel` , we have the neat little UI box on screen. But there's no information shown inside it. To report statistics, you need to call `stats.begin()` and `stats.end()` *around the area of code* you're interested in monitoring. We want to put it around our whole main game loop—but you can move that if there's something particular you were concentrating on (say, just the `scene.update` method):

```
const loopy = t => {
  stats.begin();
  ...
  stats.end();
  requestAnimationFrame(loopy);
};
```

Stats.js is a cute and useful widget that's always good to have running once your game moves beyond its *initial prototype* phase. There's nothing worse than losing half a day hunting for a performance issue that you didn't notice you introduced while coding half asleep at 3 a.m.!

Measuring

Most of the time, the "don't worry about it" approach to performance is the best choice (*especially* for your first few games). Time spent tweaking performance is time lost crafting an experience for your players. However, sometimes the two are entwined—and poor performance hurts your artistic aspirations. In these cases, it's time to get to the root cause of the problem. It's time to *measure*.

Finding out *exactly* where your code is spending most of its time is the first step to making things faster. It's easy to waste an absurd amount of time rewriting a system to be more efficient, only to discover that the improvements have minimal impact on the overall performance. Measure twice, cut once!

There are tools in the browser to help us out. A very fine-grained approach is to add **performance timers** around parts of your code you suspect might be more expensive than they could be. The idea is to record the time *before* and then the time *after* you run the suspect code. The *difference* is how long it took to execute.

There are two options for doing this: `Date.now()` and `performance.now()`. `Date.now()` returns the number of milliseconds since the UNIX epoch in the '70s. That's pretty old-school—which isn't an issue in itself. It's just that we recently got a better tool in the form of `performance.now()`. This is a high-resolution timer that returns the number of *microseconds* (as the fractional part) since the page loaded. The increased precision makes it much better for accurate benchmarking. However, if for some reason you *only* have `Date.now`, it'll do!

```
const start = performance.now();
map.path.findPath(s.x, s.y, d.x, d.y, path => {
  this.path = path || [];
  const end = performance.now();
  console.log(`Pathfinding took ${end - start} ms`);
});
```

Above is an example of a performance timer for our ghost pathfinding code from Chapter 5. Whenever the ghost searches for a new path, it also logs the amount of time it took to find it. Running this code returns various values (dependent on the complexity of the maze), but even our quite simple levels return results like `Pathfinding took 13.8799992 ms`. 13.8799992 milliseconds is not *huge*, but it may be a little surprising—as we only have 16-ish milliseconds per frame. If you tried to update your path every frame (especially on large levels) you'd certainly have a performance problem.

Performance timers are good at the micro level, but when you just want a general idea of how your code is performing (and where bottlenecks might be happening) at the *macro* level, the go-to tool is your browser's *profiler*.

A **profiler** runs performance timers over *all* of your code as it runs. In your browser (usually under the *Performance* tab in your developer tools) you start a profiling session and then just play your game for a while. When you stop the profiler, it displays a torrent of information about where CPU time was spent, how much memory was consumed, when the browser paused for garbage collection, and a lot more.

The profiler can be quite intimidating, because there's just *so* much information returned. It's hard to figure out exactly what it all means. Some information is quite useful even from the overview: the min and max FPS and the "shape" of memory usage can quickly help you find problem areas. If you see an area in the charts where FPS drops, you can select that area to see all of the JavaScript calls (in the **call tree**) and memory allocations that happened during that time. Zooming in on the **flame chart** (a special type of chart that clearly identifies frequent code paths) for expensive-looking areas will give you an indication of what is taking so long.

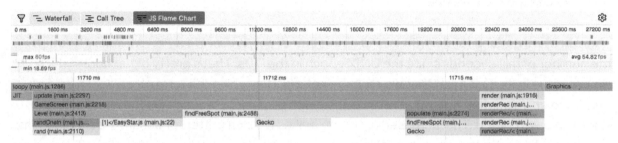

9-6. Performance flame chart

In the chart above, I've zoomed in on a frame that seemed to take a long time. You can see that half of it is *render* (as you'd expect), but the other half is the pathfinding `findFreeSpot` function we tested earlier!

The profiler also measures memory usage over time. If the chart continually rises as you play the game, it means you have a memory leak. If the chart rises and falls in a zigzag pattern, you don't have a leak, but you may be encountering excessive garbage collection lag. **Garbage collection** (GC) is when the browser cleans up all of the memory references that are no longer needed so it can be allocated somewhere else. Depending on how much memory is collected, this can take a considerable number of milliseconds and can surface in your game as a noticeable lag.

This is where we can see some of the consequences of our `TileMap` allocation strategies. Originally, we only assigned a tile metadata *reference* to each tile in our maps. When we needed per-tile data, we changed it to *clone* the metadata information for each tile. If you try each strategy on a large map you can clearly see the difference in memory usage in the profiler. However, in general this isn't a big problem. Memory is relatively plentiful, and we aren't constantly creating and destroying tiles, so we won't be suffering excessive garbage collection penalties.

If you're seeing a lot of time given to "GC" in the flame tree (or if you're noticing lags in the browser), it probably means there are too many objects being created and destroyed. There are ways to reduce this—such as implementing an object pool (which we'll cover shortly).

If you're just trying to examine a particular aspect of your code, there's another helper for identifying code calls amongst the endlessly long *call tree* and the overwhelming flame chart. The `console` logger also contains a method `timeStamp`. It accepts a label as a parameter: `console.timeStamp("findFreeSpot called.");`. The label will appear highlighted in the call tree, allowing you to quickly target specific code.

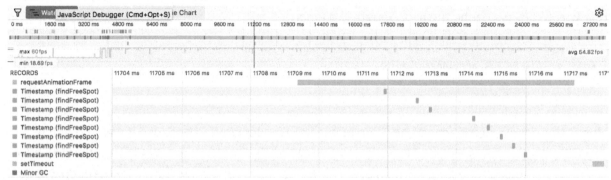

9-7. Profiler timestamp

The browser vendors are constantly improving tools for measuring performance bottlenecks, and they have a lot more functionality than we've covered. If you want to explore further, *Front End Performance*[3] and *Performance Tools*[4] are two good books for general webdev performance—most of which is applicable to our projects too.

Speeding Up Your Code

In the olden days, video games were written in assembly language (or if the devs were lazy, C). Every instruction to be executed was scrutinized for possible cycle reduction. There were esoteric tricks and mystical hacks for squeezing out every last drop of performance. Then computers got more powerful, and we got to spend more time on our *ideas* than on our *performance wizardry*. But there are still limits. When your frame rate starts falling, you have two choices: either cut features, or put on your robe and wizard hat and make things faster.

Looping Over Arrays

"Looping over arrays? What the heck are you talking about?!" you may be muttering. But wait—there's a point! This is a small warning about accepting the wisdom of the crowd without question. There are many tips and tricks that people dogmatically expound that are no longer beneficial—and sometimes *even detrimental*. This is at least partly because, historically, browser

---

[3.] https://www.sitepoint.com/premium/books/front-end-performance
[4.] https://www.sitepoint.com/premium/books/performance-tools

performance has a poor reputation. But JavaScript engines have improved hugely in recent years. A classic example of advice that's no longer useful involves *caching array length* in a `for` loop.

There are many, many ways to loop over the elements in an array. They all have slightly different performance characteristics. Looping over entities in your game is something that happens a lot—often inside the core game loop. As people became interested in JavaScript performance, they benchmarked the various methods and came up with some *best practices*. A fundamental rule was to *always* cache the array length in a loop:

```
for (var i = 0; i < arr.length; i++) {
  arr[i] *= 2;
}
```

Here's the simple, non-cached `for` loop (it uses a `var` declaration because it was the olden days). Each element is accessed and its value doubled. The performance issue was that the array length was recalculated *for each element*. This made `for` loops slow. A better approach was to *cache* the length in a variable inside the loop:

```
for (var i = 0, len = arr.length; i < len; i++) {
  arr[i] *= 2;
}
```

In this version, the array length is stored in `Len`. The loop was found to be much faster. Although the code is a little more complex, it was worth it for the performance gains. And then times changed. Running these loops in a test on JSPerf[5] today (on my machine, at least) netted these results:

```
non-cached 169,106 Ops/sec
cached 168,919 Ops/sec
```

It's so close as to be negligible. It's even veeeery slightly faster (on my machine, at least) *not* to cache it! The browser does it for us via an "internal cache lookup". The point is, test things for yourself. Don't rely on your hunches or things you heard or what someone on Stack Overflow told you. Test it! Always measure on your *target* deployments, and if the performance difference is negligible, use the clearest code.

[5.] https://jsperf.com/

JSPerf

JSPerf is a site for building benchmarking tests for related pieces of code to see which is faster. Many people can run the same test. The results are combined, allowing you to see if a clever trick will work *everywhere* or only on some specific platforms or browsers.

Unfortunately, clever (or less clear) coding tricks may still be necessary. In our library (and throughout the book) we've been playing fast and loose with a few constructions that we *know* have performance considerations. The first is our liberal use of *array comprehension methods* inside our core loops:

```
update(dt, t) {
  this.children = this.children.filter(child => {
    if (child.update) {
      child.update(dt, t, this);
    }
    return child.dead ? false : true;
  });
}
```

I happen to be fond of the functional programming style of array comprehension methods like `map`, `filter`, `forEach`, `some`, and `every`. I also run JSPerf tests on them every once in a while to see if the browsers have made them fast yet. They haven't. Perhaps one day in the future they'll be the fastest. (They're already an order of magnitude faster than when they were first introduced—and they're still a reasonably young addition to JavaScript.) As it stands today, they're *considerably* slower in all modern browsers.

Sacrificing Style

With the `update` function, we've *already* sacrificed some functional programming style in favor of performance. If performance hadn't been a factor, I would have broken it into two parts: a `map` to do the update, and a `filter` to remove `dead` entities. But old habits die hard, and the scary thought of looping over the array *twice* lead to this mashed together version.

Not only is this much slower (even on modern browsers), but we're also reassigning `children` to a freshly created array *every frame* for *every container*—and to top it off, it introduces a gotcha into our library. If an entity in a container tries to add another entity to the *same* container, the new entity is *not* included as part of the currently running `filter` execution. Because the result of filtering overwrites `children` , the new entity is lost.

We can transform this into an old-fashioned `for` loop that and slices out any dead entities (and keeps any new ones) by mutating the existing `children` array:

```
for (let i = 0; i < this.children.length; i++) {
  const child = this.children[i];
  if (child.update) {
    child.update(dt, t, this);
  }
  if (child.dead) {
    this.children.splice(i, 1);
    i--;
  }
}
```

Sometimes the old ways are the best ways! The reason I didn't suggest this from the start was that I felt the functional-style approach was clearer in our code's *intent*. It's a balancing act: we'd most likely opt for the best performance of the clearest code in a general game library that was used by other people. If it was just for our own game, then … we'd profile it.

Object Pools

JavaScript manages the computer's memory for us through a garbage collection system. We don't *ask* for memory, we just create strings and arrays and objects whenever we want. The garbage collector notices this, and when something goes out of scope (and isn't needed anymore) it periodically frees up the memory for us.

We don't have any choice about *when* the collection happens, or how long it takes. Depending on how much work it has to do, the garbage collector can be busy for a long time—enough to cause a visible lag in our game. One way we can fight this lag is with an **object pool**. Rather than mindlessly creating new entities whenever we need one, we create *a whole stack of entities* up front. These are held as a *pool*.

If we need a new entity to display on screen, rather than saying `baddie = new Baddie()` we say `baddie = pool.getBaddie()` . The pool manager will look around, find a bad guy who isn't busy and give him to us to use. Because the entity is still in scope (it's being held in the pool), the garbage collector never tries to free that memory. There's less work for the garbage collector, and less lag for us.

More Memory Hungry

This approach has the side effect of requiring more memory at any given time. In general, though, it's worth the sacrifice!

We've already written an object pool, and it's already being used in our library. In Chapter 8, we created a *particle* that was controlled by a *particle emitter*. Particles have a very short shelf life. In a game with a lot of particle effects, you'll be spawning millions of instances, who survive for a few seconds and then are gone. Instinctively, we created a cache of `Particles` at the start of `ParticleEmitter.js` :

```
this.particles = [...Array(20)]
   .map(() => new Particle());
```

For the small explosion effect, we created 20 particle objects and stored them in an array. Each time the effect played, they would do their dance and then fade away. To make them dance again, the `ParticleEmitter` `reset` each particle:

```
this.particles.forEach(p => p.reset());
```

That's the idea of an object pool at its core. I like to take this simple, manual `ParticleEmitter` approach when there's a lot of creation churn—that is, lots of created and destroyed entities. But it's also possible to abstract the idea of an object pool so it can be used more generally. The pool will be initialized with a *function* to create new objects and a maximum number of items to be held. Then it can be used like this:

```
// Create a pool of gunshots
const shots = new Pool(() => new GunShot(), 10);
```

The `shots` variable will be a pool of ten `GunShot` objects (which happens to be a plain old `TileSprite` that's drawn on screen for `life` number of seconds). In the game, the pool can be used by calling the factory method `create` :

```
const shot = shots.create(life, x, y);
camera.add(shot);
```

The primary difference between creating objects *in place* and getting them out of a pool lies in where you pass the parameters for creation. Because an object in a pool is reused over and over, there needs to be a `reset` function to get it back in pristine condition. This is exactly what we did with `Particle` . When you ask for an object form the pool, the pool manager will find a "dead" entity, call `reset` (with any parameters you pass) to put it in place and then set it as not dead:

```
class Pool {
  constructor(creator, num = 10) {
    ...
  }
  create(...args) {
    ...
  }
}
```

In the constructor is where we create our first batch of objects. We use the `creator` function (that the user passes in) to make an entity, set it to `dead`, and store it as a child:

```
this.creator = creator;
this.children = [...Array(num)]
  .map(() => creator())
  .map(e => {
    e.dead = true;
    return e;
  });
```

When the user wants a new entity, they call `create`. This finds the first "dead" entity in the pool, and calls `reset` on it before giving it back. Hey presto, a new object:

```
let next = this.children.find(c => c.dead);
if (!next) {
  next = this.creator();
  this.children.push(next);
}
if (next.reset) {
  next.reset(...args);
}
next.dead = false;
return next;
```

However, if there *are no dead entities*, the pool manager creates a new one and adds it to the pool. The pool grows. Many object pool implementations will resize (usually by doubling) when the pool is full, and create the new entities at once. If you find your pools are filling up too often, you can implement this (or just start with a larger pool)—but be sure you *profile* your changes to ensure you have the best solution for your game!

This is a very simple object pool, but it accomplishes the goals of avoiding garbage collection costs when creating and destroying large sums of entities.

Faster Collisions with Spatial Partitioning

One of our core tenets for creating a game is to "respond to collisions". We started doing this in Chapter 4 with AABB testing. Checking if two bounding boxes overlap is a fairly inexpensive operation on its own. But applying it to test if *any* entity hits *any other* entity works in $O(N^2)$ time. Its performance is proportional to the square of the size of the number of inputs, so each additional entity becomes quadratically more taxing. You may have even skipped straight to this section because you've already discovered that you don't need *huge* numbers of sprites before your FPS starts to nosedive.

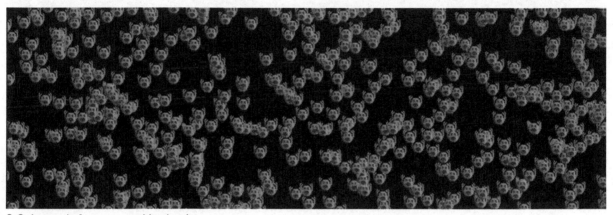

9-8. A crowd of scary pumpkin ghouls

For the handful of entities in *Bravedigger*, nobody's is going to crack a sweat. But if we have a huge crowd of entities—like a hoard of pumpkin ghouls—then checking to see which pumpkins overlap will be CPU intensive. To get our $O(N^2)$ operation down to something more manageable, we can employ **spatial partitioning**, which requires storing objects in a *spatial data structure*—one where the elements are organized by their *position* in the game world.

Added Complexity

We're introducing considerable complexity and overhead to solve our performance problem. These algorithms are effective in certain situations that will be game-specific. Often the overhead of creating and updating the data structure every frame can take *more* time than our brute-force approach. Always *measure* to ensure changes are for the better.

There are many data structures we could use, but the easiest to understand and implement is a *grid-based spatial index*. It's a way to model our 2D world as a 1D hash table. It works like this:

Create a *coarse grid* (for example, 80x80 pixels) that overlays our game world.

2   Every time an entity moves, add it to the correct grid cell.

3   Only check collisions between entities *in the same cell*.

9-9. The world as a coarse grid

Intuitively, it makes sense: don't even bother checking for collisions for things that are far away. We maintain a map of cells that have at least one entity in them. Each cell stores the entities as a JavaScript `Set` . To check for collisions, we can loop over each map cell and look at the set. If there are two or more entities, we loop over them and do our regular collision testing:

```
Object.values(hash.entities).forEach(set => {
  if (set.length < 2) {
    return;
  }
  // Do regular collision test against these entities.
  ...
});
```

This seems pretty incredible. Depending on the size of the cells, the number of entities, and how spread out they are, there are *vastly* fewer entities to check for collisions. The flip side is that we now have a lot of overhead to maintain about the grid hash table. Also we need to write it. Add `utils/GridHash.js` and start a new class, `GridHash` :

```
class GridHash {
  constructor(cellSize) {
    this.entities = {};
    this.cellSize = cellSize;
  }
}
```

This contains the map that will be the hash table for holding entities, along with a reference to the cell's size (in pixels). Before we can put an entity into the map, we need to figure out how to compute a *hash key*. This will be the key to the `entities` map:

```
hash(pos) {
  const { cellSize } = this;
  return [Math.floor(pos.x / cellSize), Math.floor(pos.y / cellSize)];
}
```

The `hash` function transforms a `pos` position into a `cell` reference as a key. The key will be a bit sneaky: it's an *array* (not a string) that points to the cell that the entity should be sitting in. Because it's an array, we can also use the key later for doing logic. Once we have a hash key, we can look up the `entities` map and add new entities. If it's the first entity in that hash location, we create a new JavaScript `Set` . (Sets are lists that can't have duplicate entries. If you add the same entity twice, it will only have one occurrence of it.)

```
_add(hash, ent) {
  let cell = this.entities[hash];
  if (!cell) {
    cell = new Set();
    this.entities[hash] = cell;
  }
  cell.add(ent);
}
```

`_add` is a helper method that we'll use internally to add entities into the grid. The next step is to figure out the hash key for a given entity. We could just pass a `pos` and use the `x` and `y` location to get a cell reference, but the image below highlights an issue with this.

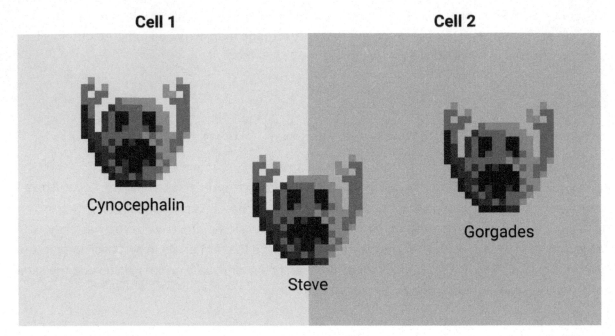

9-10. Steve, at an intersection

Our entities are free-range: they're not constrained by our artificial grid boundary walls! They can straddle multiple cells. Steve might be colliding with Cynocephalin *and* Gorgades. The trick is that, when we insert an entity into the grid, we add it to *every cell* it's touching. Steve goes in "Cell 1" *and* "Cell 2". This requires figuring out the minimum and maximum points of the `Sprite`'s hit box (using `entity.bounds`) and adding the entity to the `Set` of each cell:

```
insert(ent) {
  const b = entity.bounds(ent);
  const min = this.hash(b);
  const max = this.hash({ x: b.x + b.w, y: b.y + b.h });

  // Figure out where to add/remove the entity
  ...

  ent.hashMin = min;
  ent.hashMax = max;
}
```

We have the bounds of the entity and store the hash keys on the entity itself as `hashMin` and `hashMax`. We keep these on the entity so we're easily able to look up an entity and *remove* it from the grid (without having to search through *every* entity in the entire `entities` map). It also means we can check to see if we've changed cells since the last update:

```
// Figure out where to add/remove the entity
if (ent.hashMin) {
  // Entity hasn't changed cell
  if (min.toString() === ent.hashMin.toString()) {
    return;
  }
  this.remove(ent);
}
```

If the entity is in the *same* cell as before, we're done and can leave. (The hash key hasn't changed. We're using `.toString` which is a bit dodgy, but it works. You could implement an `equals` function to make it nicer.) Otherwise, it means the entity has *changed* cells—so we should remove it from cells it was previously touching (which we'll do shortly).

Now we can get down to inserting ourselves into the correct cells. Because it's possible that an entity spans over several cells in either direction, we cover the *range* of cells and use our `_.add` helper to add ourselves to each corresponding hash key location:

```
// Add entity to each cell it touches
for (let j = min[1]; j < max[1] + 1; j++) {
  for (let i = min[0]; i < max[0] + 1; i++) {
    this._add([i, j], ent);
  }
}
```

That's the hard work over. *Every time an entity moves*, you need to re-call `hash.insert(entity)`. This figures out the cells that the entity will be touching, and adds a reference to each of the `Set`s. The `remove` function works almost identically to `insert`, but in reverse. It uses the entity's own hash references to loop over the range of cells and remove them from each:

```
const min = ent.hashMin;
const max = ent.hashMax;
for (let j = min[1]; j < max[1] + 1; j++) {
  for (let i = min[0]; i < max[0] + 1; i++) {
    const hash = [i, j];
    // delete entity from this cell
    ...
  }
}
```

For each cell the entity was in, remove the entity from the `Set` (with `cell.delete`). If it was the *last* entity to be in that cell location, we delete the whole map entry (with JavaScript's `delete` operator). Now the cell will not appear when we try to loop over all entities:

```
const cell = this.entities[hash];
cell.delete(ent);
if (cell.size == 0) {
  delete this.entities[hash];
}
```

At the very end of the *remove* function, we also clean up our entity by removing the *ent.hashMin* and *ent.hashMax* references. That's the entire grid functionality done. It can be hard to hold this model in your head, so play with the example code and examine the contents of the map (with a handful of static entities).

In the code included, there are thousands of small *Sprites*. They jiggle around randomly. Whenever they move, their *alpha* is set to a low value (they're un-lit). Then we use hash map *forEach* loop from the start of this section to iterate over each *Set*. To check for collisions, we do a nested *for* loop, ensuring we only check each entity against each entity once (that is, we don't check A vs B *and* B vs A). When there's a hit, the *Sprite* is illuminated:

```
const ents = [...set]; // Convert to regular array
for (var i = 0; i < ents.length; i++) {
  const a = ents[i];
  for (var j = i + 1; j < ents.length; j++) {
    const b = ents[j];
    if (entity.hit(a, b)) {
      a.alpha = 1;
      b.alpha = 1;
    }
  }
}
```

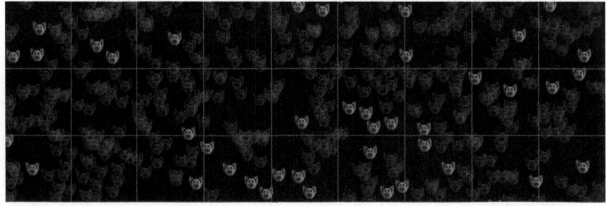

9-11. Pumpkins who have some space

In the example code, try changing the settings at the top of the file. They'll have an enormous effect on the performance of our algorithm.

```
const useHash = true;
const cellSize = 80;
const numSprites = 1000;
const hash = new GridHash(cellSize);
```

If you set *useHash* to false, it does our regular *brute force* O(N^2) collision calculations. Setting this to true, you'll see how much more efficient the grid approach is (for *this* case where there are a lot of evenly spaced entities).

There are many other similar algorithms that are good if your game has different characteristics. For example, a **quad tree** works with buckets like our grid approach, but instead of equal-sized cells, they can be independently sized (in a tree): when there are few entities in an area, that area grows. When there are *too many*, the area is split in two halves. This works well when your entities are not evenly spaced apart. It's fun to implement, but in practice, the grid approach will usually get you far enough.

Speeding Up Rendering

Honestly, the performance fixes thus far have been small fry. In the *overwhelming* majority of cases, your bottleneck will be in rendering. Even with a small viewport like 1024x768px, you need to push over *three quarters of a million* pixels—every frame, sixty times a second. That's a lot of pixels. Anything that can be done to speed things here will have a tangible impact on the game's performance.

Don't Render Off-screen Entities

CanvasRenderer doesn't discriminate: anything you ask it to draw, it will draw—even if that thing isn't inside the player's viewport! Is that a problem? Let's test it. *CanvasRenderer* uses the browser's *Canvas* implementation for drawing *Sprites* via the *drawImage* API call. If we set up a simple loop to draw a ton of images, we can do some performance testing and figure out what *Canvas* is doing for us, and how we can speed things up.

```
const rects = [...Array(numDraws)].map(() => {
  // Disk point picking - pick a random point in a circle
  const angle = Math.random() * Math.PI * 2;
  const radius =  Math.sqrt(Math.random()) * (canvas.width - w) * scale;
  return {
    x: (canvas.width / 2) + radius * Math.cos(angle) - (w / 2),
    y: (canvas.height /2) + radius * Math.sin(angle) - (h / 2),
    w,
    h
  }
}
```

```
});
```

Our test will be done using plain `Canvas` (not inside our renderer) to see if there's a performance cost for asking it to render things off screen. Perhaps `Canvas` magically takes care of this issue for us? (Spoiler: it doesn't). To test, we'll draw a whole lot of simple images inside a circular area (using a technique called *disk point picking*). We'll test first with a small area that fits on a single screen, and then with a large area (where many of the rectangles will be off screen).

```
const start = performance.now();
rects.forEach(({x, y}) => {
  if (x < -w || y < -h || x > canvas.width || y > canvas.height) {
    return;
  } else {
    ctx.drawImage(img, x, y);
  }
});
const end = performance.now();

console.log("Time taken for %i images is %f", numDraws, end - start);
```

If the bounds of the image are outside the canvas area, we `return` and do nothing with the image. Otherwise, it goes to `drawImage`. As hinted, this has a *huge* impact on the time taken for rendering. It's not one to one (that is, `Canvas` is doing *some* magic to keep the drawing time down for non-visible images). But the more off-screen entities there are, the faster it is to render when we check the viewport boundaries.

Any time we have large levels, most of the world enemies and tiles will be outside the camera viewport. Adding a check for out-of-bounds entities will speed things up significantly. Our approach will be this: in `CanvasRenderer` we'll look for our `camera` (this will be a child node that has the `worldSize` property). Anything that's *inside* this we'll do a bounds check on, and only draw things that appear inside the camera view:

```
export default function isInCameraView(e, camera) {
  return e.pos.x + e.w >= -camera.pos.x &&
    e.pos.x <= -camera.pos.x + camera.w &&
    e.pos.y + e.h >= -camera.pos.y &&
    e.pos.y <= -camera.pos.y + camera.h;
}
```

`CanvasRenderer` will import this helper function `isInCameraView`. It performs exactly the same test as earlier, returning `true` if it's visible and `false` if not. The only issue with using this code is that our renderer *doesn't know which element is the camera*. To fix that, we look for it when we render a `Container`'s children. If it's a camera, it gets passed along to `renderRec`:

```
if (child.worldSize) {
  // "child" is a Camera
  renderRec(child, child);
} else {
  renderRec(child, camera);
}
```

Then, at the top of the *renderRec* main drawing function, we can bail out early if the entity isn't in the camera's viewport:

```
if (camera && !isInCameraView(child, camera)) {
  return;
}
```

If you create a large level with a lot of tiles (and add *Stats.js* from earlier in this chapter) you can clearly see the huge difference this makes to performance. Our game worlds can suddenly become a lot more massive! We'll improve this even further shortly when we get to *TileMap enhancements*.

Canvas Tricks

The Canvas API was initially designed by Apple for generating images from code. Circles, rectangles, and arcs could be mixed together to make graphical components for UI elements. Rendering didn't have to be *ludicrously* fast, as images would be cached upon creation. But naturally, *any* technology that allows a bitmap image to be manipulated will be abused by game developers for the purposes of rendering games!

Canvas is intuitive, simple, and fun, but it's not the fastest way to get pixels on screen. (See the WebGL section that follows.) There are some tricks we can use for speed improvements. However, as with the general JavaScript code tricks, results can vary *wildly* by environment—and environments are themselves in constant flux. Today's "best practices" are tomorrow's performance pitfalls. Always test, and if in doubt, favor readable code over small or inconsistent speed-ups.

An example of such a trick is "don't render half-pixels".

```
ctx.drawImage(image, 100, 50);
vs
ctx.drawImage(image, 100.333, 49.9995);
```

I'll admit, this is a performance improvement that I *assumed* (there's that dangerous word again) would have been magically fixed by brave and relentless browser developers many moons ago. In some browsers, on some operating systems, there's little difference between the two. On other systems—such as my test Linux laptop running Firefox—the non-rounded version is 30% slower than the rounded version. Thirty percent! This is because the browser employs *sub-pixel* rendering—and calculating the correct antialiasing for each pixel is an expensive operation.

 Fun Fact

> To ensure we don't have a sub-pixel rendering cost in our renderer, we round the position: `ctx.translate(Math.round(child.pos.x), Math.round(child.pos.y)`. Our initial version of the `CanvasRenderer` code did *not* round the positions but was later updated. The change was not actually for performance reasons, but because of graphical glitches introduced when rendering `TileMap`s where 1-pixel gaps would sometimes be visible between tiles. Rounding turned out to be a double win!

Canvas (like most technologies on the Web) is in a state of constant change. The API is slowly enhanced with exciting new features as time goes on. The new `addHitRegion` functionality allows you to turn elements of your scene into DOM-like elements that receive events, such as `mouseover` and `click`. The `filter` allows post-processing style effects to be applied to the entire view: `blur`, `contrast`, `hue-rotate`, and loads more. The `OffscreenCanvas` interface provides a canvas that can be rendered off screen for use with web workers (to speed up rendering and perform effects).

Support for these features, however, is extremely patchy. That's one of the reasons we've tended to stick to simple, `drawImage`-type operations: they're universal (which also means it's easier for us to create alternate renderers). If you're experimenting or deploying to specific, well-known environments, it's worth examining and keeping track of their status as support grows.

A useful technique we can apply even before `OffscreenCanvas` is widely available is to *layer* multiple `Canvas` elements. Rather than have a single `Canvas` element, we have *several stacked on top of each other*. This might sound like several times the CPU cost, but it depends on your game. If the bottom element contains a static background, for example, it only needs to be drawn once. The mid-ground game elements could be drawn on another element and moved around to produce a parallax effect. Then only the foreground elements need to be cleared and drawn every frame.

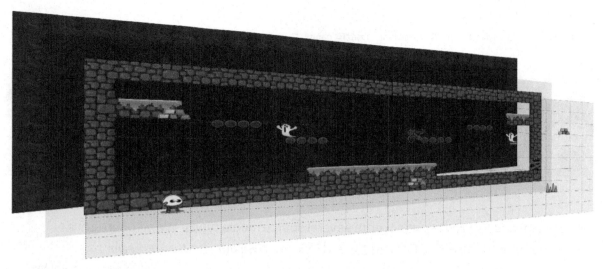

9-12. Back, mid, and foreground layers

Additionally, a technique called **dirty rectangles** can be employed, where only *parts* of a scene are cleared and updated each render. For an aging but still relevant guide to layering and dirty rectangles, check out Adam Ranfelt's "Optimize HTML5 canvas rendering with layering[6]".

Layering can also be done on a single target canvas. If you have elements in your game that are composed of several drawing operations, it's possible to render them down to a single element that can be reused. A common use case for this is an entity made up of several *combined images*, or an asset or effect generated using `Canvas`'s primitives. Rather than a sequence of `fillRect`s, `drawImage`s and `arc`s, they're done once, to a new rendering context:

```
const spiral = document.createElement("canvas");
spiral.width = 128;
spiral.height = 128;
const c = spiral.getContext("2d");
for (let i = 0; i < 8; i++) {
  c.fillStyle = `hsl(${i * 40}, 50%, 50%)`;
  c.beginPath();
  c.arc(64, 64, (8-i)*8, 0, Math.PI * 2);
  c.fill();
}
```

The new element, `spiral`, is not part of the DOM. It's a reference to a new canvas element that we've drawn a bunch of colorful circles on. With this reference in hand, we can re-draw it as often as we like without having to re-render each circle:

---

6. https://www.ibm.com/developerworks/library/wa-canvashtml5layering/

```
for (let i = 0; i < 200; i++) {
  ctx.drawImage(spiral, math.randf(w), math.randf(h));
}
```

9-13. Canvas as a media type for drawing

This works because `drawImage` accepts several source media types. We've been using `ImageBitmap` throughout this book (regular HTML images), but `SVGImageElement`, `HTMLVideoElement`, `HTMLCanvasElement` (and soon, `OffscreenCanvas`) are also acceptable! We can treat the `Canvas` elements just as we've been treating our image assets. They can be created and modified at any time, then used in place of a regular image. Additionally, we could even sneak this into our `CanvasRenderer` system by setting the `spiral` canvas element as the `Texture`'s image!

TileMap Enhancements

`TileMap`s are containers filled with potentially *vast* amounts of `TileSprite`s to render—probably more than any other container in your game. Certainly more than anything else in *Bravedigger*. So far, we've taken the cavalier approach of *drawing all the things!*—so now might be a good time to reflect on some possible improvements. We've already made our library not render off-screen elements, so we should be fine to render massive worlds, right? Let's say we had a gigantic map that was 1000 tiles wide and 1000 tiles deep. 1000x1000 is one million. *One million tiles*, for which we perform an AABB overlap test, every frame, to see if we should draw it or not.

We happen to know more about the internal structure of a `TileMap`. It's not just a collection of random sprites: it's a carefully organized *grid* with known tile and map dimensions. Rather than check each tile to see what *doesn't* need to be displayed, we figure out the subset of tiles that *do* need to be rendered!

```
let children = container.children;
if (container.mapW) {
  const { tileW, tileH, mapW } = container;
  children = [];
  ...
}
```

The plan is to just keep a subset of a `TileMap` container's `children` that are in the screen view. To do this, we figure out the tile offsets that match the top left of the screen, and only include "one screen's worth" of tiles as children:

```
let idx = 0;
const xo = (offset.x / tileW) | 0;
const yo = (offset.y / tileH) | 0;
const xt = Math.floor(w / tileW) + xo;
const yt = Math.floor(h / tileH) + yo;
for (let j = yo; j < yt; j++) {
  for (let i = xo; i < xt; i++) {
    children[idx++] = container.children[j * mapW + i];
  }
}
```

Our rendering time for a large map is now enormously reduced. However, you'd expect to see the frame rate for a `TileMap` now be constant, regardless of map size. But it's not. If you measure it, you'll find that massive maps take more CPU time than small maps. What's going on? Remember that our `TileSprite` has an `update` function. It gets called for every tile—and a million tiles equals a million function calls! There are two possible fixes. One is to create a new type of minimal tile (say, `SimpleTileSprite`) that has *no update function* and just includes the minimum amount of support necessary for your game. Another, quicker fix is to just *not update* `TileMap` children by default (unless a special flag is set):

```
update(dt, t) {
  if (this.updateTiles) {
    super.update(dt, t);
  }
}
```

Now a small map and a *gigantic* map have the same CPU requirements. If you're making extensive use of huge maps for your game, there are even more things you could do to speed things up. Our default implementation is a generic solution for rendering our sprites as `TileSprites`. A `TileSprite` is a `Sprite`, but with added support for animations. If your game doesn't need animated tiles, there's a ton of memory and update cycles that get lost to this extra support.

Another simple enhancement we could make is to not render any *blank* tiles. If we have a tile that's completely transparent graphically, we shouldn't bother calling `ctx.drawImage` at all. If a map is composed largely of blank tiles (which is likely if you're rendering multiple `TileMap` layers—one as a background, and one or more as a foreground) this can can be a considerable CPU-saver:

```
{ frame: { x: 0, y: 0, walkable: true, blank: true }}
```

Having added the tile metadata, it can now be checked inside the renderer. If it's `blank`, don't bother calling `drawImage`:

```
if (!frame.blank) {
  ctx.drawImage(..);
}
```

At this point, it's worth re-measuring your game's performance. Is it acceptable? Do you need to squeeze out some CPU cycles? Looking at our current `TileMap` render system with Firefox's *Canvas capture frame* feature, we can see that there's still some room for improvement. Capturing a random frame gives the following output for a tile:

9-14. Firefox's Canvas capture frame

The tool is showing that these five canvas instructions are being executed for *every tile* in the `TileMap` we're drawing. If we wanted to save even more cycles, we could work around the general rendering case for `TileMap` children altogether and create a new core type `TileMapSprite`. Do you need to scale the tiles in your game? If not, get rid of that! What about manually calculating the `drawImage` position parameters so you don't need the `translate` calls? Heck, you then wouldn't even need `save` and `restore`! This is the beauty of "rolling your own". We can optimize things for *our specific game*. It doesn't need to be general and work for everybody's projects. We *wrote* the `TileMap` system, and we can change anything about it we want.

A WebGL Renderer

At the start of the book I claimed that abstracting the rendering operations into a dedicated rendering system would allow us to make alternate implementations for different environments. Specifically, I said we could even make a *WebGL Renderer*, and promised that it would be superfast. I said that.

And it's true, but we won't cover it in depth here, because WebGL is a vast and dragon-infested subject. Included in the codebase is an experimental branch with a `WebGL2Renderer` for rendering `Sprite`s and `TileSprite`s. It's a simplified version of our renderer, but it provides an example of how a more complete renderer would be built out.

Canvas 2D	WebGL2
5.800000042654574	1.9999999785795808
6.600000080652535	1.2000000569969416
5.599999916739762	1.7000000225380063
6.900000036694109	2.100000041536987
6.399999954737723	1.7999999690800905
8.000000030733645	1.500000013038516
6.199999945238233	2.3999999975785613
6.900000036694109	1.500000013038516
5.600000033155084	1.7000000225380063
6.300000008195639	1.39999995008111
5.800000042654574	1.9000000320374966
6.199999945238233	1.8000000854954123

9-15. TileMap frame renderering with WebGL2

WebGL is a browser implementation of OpenGL ES (OpenGL for Embedded Systems), which is an API for rendering 2D and 3D graphics. It's fast because it's designed to run on your GPU (rather than on your CPU). The GPU is a purpose-built circuit for rendering games. For us it is, anyway! The idea of WebGL is to manipulate data and paint pixels as fast as possible.

A common misconception is that it's inherently a 3D API. It's not—but if you're clever, you can pass it data that represents a 3D object. And if you're good at math, you can calculate lighting and shading and make the object realistically look like it has depth. But you have to do all that yourself, as the API doesn't help you out at all. It can really only do two things: model a triangle, and color in each pixel inside a triangle.

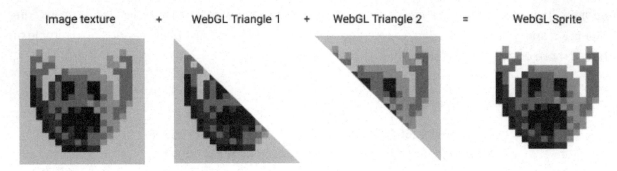

9-16. A WebGL sprite

If we put two triangles together, we have a rectangle. And if we color in each pixel with a color we sampled from a texture image, we have a 2D sprite! That's the idea. In practice, it's far more complex than the Canvas API, because it's running on completely different hardware (using a different programing language) via an API that (by necessity and history) is archaic and extremely stateful, requiring an absurd amount of boilerplate code.

But it's really fast.

Its speed comes from the fact that the processing of pixels happens on the GPU via compiled programs, called **shaders**. Shaders are written in a C-like dialect called **GLSL** (OpenGL Shading Language). The two main types of shaders are *vertex shaders* and *fragment shaders*. Vertex shaders can alter the position of vertices in the data you pass—usually for the purposes of applying perspective (for 3D), and transforms (moving sprites around) as well as for doing lighting calculations. After vertex calculations are done, data is passed to the fragment shader for rendering.

```
uniform sampler2D img;
in vec2 uv;
in vec2 pos;
out vec4 col;

void main() {
  vec4 tex = texture(img, uv);
  vec4 hueShift = vec4(sin(pos.x), sin(pos.y), 0, 0);
  col = tex + hueShift;
}
```

Above is an example of a WebGL2 *fragment shader*. It gets compiled into a program that runs *once per pixel* (well, technically, once "per fragment") every draw call. The job of the fragment shader is to say what color the pixel should be. It does this by setting an *out vec4* variable (I called it `col` above) to RGBA values. For example, `col = vec4(0, 0, 1.0, 1.0)` would set a polygon to be opaque blue (no red or green, full blue and full opaque).

Instead of a solid color, our fragment shader gets a *sampler2D* (a texture to draw) called `img`, as well as details about *which part* of the texture needs to be drawn for this pixel (named *uv* here—a standard variable name for texture coordinates). Inside the `main` function, we get the value of the texture at the `uv` coordinate. If we were to set `col` to this value, we'd have a normal rendering of the image. But fragment shaders can do so much more! In a 3D world, this is where we could apply the shadows and lighting—but it can also be used for special effects.

In our example, we *hue-shift* the colors depending on where on the screen the sprite appears. The red and green components of `hueShift` are set as the sine of the position of the sprite. And we leave the blue and alpha alone (`0`). Adding this vector to the normal texture will change the color of the sprites:

9-17. WebGL shader effect

GLSL has many built-in operators for manipulating pixels. Our example uses `sin` and `texture` (a function for extracting a pixel color from an image), but there are all sorts of mathematical and matrix operators (many that we've implemented in `Pop.math` too, like `clamp` and `smoothstep`), and vector operations (including the `dot` and `cross` functions).

Fragment shaders can create all sorts of amazing visual effects that can be applied either per-sprite or in *post-processing*. **Post-processing** is applying an effect over the *entire screen* after everything is drawn. The way it works is to apply "draw two triangles to make a rectangle" trick—but stretch it over the entire viewport. The game-screen canvas can be passed as an image to the post-processor to implement effects like motion blur, vignettes, and bloom effects.

9-18. Vignette, motion blur, and color separation effects

If you want to dive into it, check out the experimental `WebGL2Renderer` in this book's codebase (start by playing around with the fragment shader in `defaultShaders.js` !), and read through the excellent online reference >WebGL2 Fundamentals[7]. Once you numb yourself to the boilerplate and get a feel for GLSL, it's quite addictive. Knowledge of WebGL fragment shaders is also highly transferable to many game engines and libraries. Unique shader effects can really help define the aesthetic feel of your game.

Getting on Devices

It's coming down to the wire. We have to get our games packaged and shipped over to the IGC voting committee or we won't even be in the race against Shifty. Until now, we've been running our games in the web browser. This is very satisfying (normally only boring web pages go in browsers, not awesome games!) but the browser is not the traditional home of games for some of out-of-touch potential customers, who scoff that "*Real* games are supposed to be standalone apps that I install from Steam, or play on my game consoles and mobile devices!"

Naturally, the ubiquity of JavaScript (along with recent improvements to the language and ecosystem) is on our side once again. With a bit of massaging and tweaking, we can run our games in *all* the places people expect games to run—as standalone executables across platforms, on mobile phones, even on game consoles ... the places where people are more comfortable *paying* for games!

Getting on devices is rewarding, but it can be a bit frustrating. Each platform and walled garden has its own hair-pulling quirks and infuriating hurdles. Things improve at the same rate as they decay: new ways to deploy to new targets spring up, and old, faithful ways gather bit rot and stop working. It's the nature of life on the cutting edge!

 Research

One of the best places to search for up-to-date information on device deployment options is on *other game library forums*. After all, no matter which library we use, we *all* want our games on as many devices as possible! The HTML5 Game Devs forumhttp://www.html5gamedevs.com/ is a great source for such updated tips and tricks.

Besides the technical challenge of deploying to locations where JavaScript isn't a first-class citizen, there's also the design challenge of making things feel *natural* in each environment. It's obvious when someone has just ported a desktop game to mobile. The controls and style often

---

[7] https://webgl2fundamentals.org/

feel jarring—or worse, unusable.

Many early mobile phone games had extremely poor virtual joypads, making it obvious that mobile wasn't the intended target for the game. Similarly, players of desktop games expect things like gamepad support, and are fairly intolerant of obvious mobile-to-desktop ports! Even though it can be a trial just getting your games to *run* in a certain environment, if you neglect the user experience expected for that platform, all your effort will be for naught.

Gamepad Controls

Sometimes you just need to step away from your computer screen and relax on your couch. You don't want to stop playing your game, of course, so you'll need to add gamepad support. Playing on a game controller is one of those things that feels a bit magical when you implement it in your web browser. It's pretty easy to do, too, thanks to the **Gamepad API**. The Gamepad API is a little odd compared to other browser APIs, because it was made for *games*, not *web pages*. Most of the Web is event-driven, yet the Gamepad API works via *polling*. Does this remind you of anything?

```
* Loop
  - get user input <- The Gamepad API Knows it!
  - move everything a tiny bit
  - react to collisions
```

We have to manually check the *state* of the controller directly in our `update` function, rather than via mouse- or keyboard-like event handlers. There *are* some events fired by the API, but they're just for handling when controllers are plugged in and removed. We'll create a controller input for our games that works with Xbox and PlayStation USB controllers (though it'll also work for most other controllers, too), and then look at a library to do some more grunt work for handling things more generally.

Button 0
Button 1
Button 2
Button 3
Axis 0 & 1

9-19. Xbox controller buttons and axes for Bravedigger

Basic handling works for all standard controllers. But the buttons and analog sticks on one controller might not match those of another controller. To accommodate this, the Gamepad API has the notion of **mappings**. It's pretty tedious for us to collect all the mappings ourselves, so it's best to use a third-party library for more complete support. For now, though, let's add a new controls class, *controls/GamepadControls.js* :

```
class GamepadControls {
  constructor() {
    this.controller = null;
    this.controllers = {};
    ...
  }
  handler({ gamepad }, connecting) {
  }
}
```

As game controllers are connected, they'll be added to the `controllers` object. For simplicity, we'll also expose one of them as the *primary* controller, which will be accessible via `controller` . The `handler` method will process all of the "connections" and "disconnections" events triggered when we plug in, or pull out a game controller. At the bottom of the constructor we can add the event listeners:

```
window.addEventListener("gamepadconnected", e => this.handler(e, true));
window.addEventListener("gamepaddisconnected", e => this.handler(e, false));
```

The *gamepadconnected* and *gamepaddisconnected* events, which are part of the Gamepad API[8]. *gamepadconnected* , will be called when a controller is plugged in *and a button is pressed*. You need to interact with the controller before it's detected. This is to stop browser fingerprinting, for the sake of privacy.

```
handler({ gamepad }, connecting) {
  const { controllers } = this;
  if (connecting) {
    controllers[gamepad.index] = gamepad;
    this.controller = gamepad;
  } else {
    delete controllers[gamepad.index];
  }
}
```

When the handler is called, we can extract the *gamepad* item. If it's connecting, we add it to the *pads* object and set it as the primary *pad* . Otherwise, we delete it from our list. Now the controllers are available to be polled in our update loop:

```
const controls = {
  keys: new KeyControls(),
  gamepads: new GamepadControls()
};
```

In our platform game, we handle the keyboard events to set the *jump* , *fire* , and horizontal movement (*x*). We leave this code in place, but then augment it with the gamepad values:

```
const { controller } = controls.gamepads;
if (controller) {
  const { axes, buttons } = controller;
  const threshold = 0.21;
  if (axes[0] < -threshold) x = -1;
  if (axes[0] > threshold) x = 1;;
  jump |= buttons[0].pressed;
  fire |= buttons[1].pressed;
}
```

The gamepad exposes *buttons* and *axes* . To map the jump and fire actions, we do a bitwise *or* with the existing keyboard values (so you can either press the keyboard fire key *or* *buttons[1]* —the B button on my Xbox controller). The *axes* are *analog values* that map to floating-point values from -1 to 1. In our game, our game character is digital: he's either running or he's stationary. With some games, you'll *want* the floating-point values—for example, to determine how sharply to turn a corner in a racing car game. But we transform the axis value into either -1 or 1 whenever the axis value goes over a threshold (0.21). The threshold prevents very

8. https://developer.mozilla.org/en-US/docs/Web/API/Gamepad_API/Using_the_Gamepad_API

small values from the controller accidentally making the character move.

Just like in our keyboard controls, we can move some of the boilerplate into helper functions inside `GamepadControls` to keep our game code nice and clean. We'll make equivalents of `KeyControls` getter properties for checking if the `A` or `B` controller buttons are pressed. You can extend this to include more buttons as your games require.

```
get actionA() {
  return this.action(0, 11);
}

get actionB() {
  return this.action(1, 12);
}
```

Like our keyboard helpers, we'll group *multiple* buttons under the same action: button 0 *and* button 11 will both trigger our `actionA` property. The reason for this is that while most general controllers will report button 0 as the primary button, on the Xbox controller the primary button—button `A` —is ID 11. To group them together we check if *any* of the buttons are currently being pressed:

```
action(...buttons) {
  const { controller } = this;
  if (!controller) return false;
  return buttons.some(b => controller.buttons[b].pressed);
}
```

Likewise, a similar function can return the axis as either a -1, 0, or 1. This can then be used to implement `x` and `y` direction getter properties:

```
axis(id) {
  const { controller, threshold } = this;
  if (!controller) return 0;
  if (controller.axes[id] < -threshold) return -1;
  if (controller.axes[id] > threshold) return 1;
  return 0;
}

get x() {
  return this.axis(0);
}

get y() {
  return this.axis(1);
```

```
  }
```

In the final game code, handling the gamepads is done with the same API as the `KeyControls` (here we are still using the `or` operator to modify our existing keyboard values):

```
const { gamepads } = controls;
if (gamepads.controller) {
  x |= gamepads.x;
  jump |= gamepads.actionA;
  fire |= gamepads.actionB;
}
```

Controlling the character with an Xbox controller is immensely fun—and it makes showing your games to your friends way more impressive, too! If you want to explore controllers further, dive into Andrzej Mazur's Gamepad API Content Kit[9]. Additionally, the axes and buttons we chose work for most controllers, but there are many, many models of gamepads around, and we don't want to do all the mappings ourselves by hand. I'd recommend you check out Eric Lathrop's html5-gamepad[10] for a more complete, drop-in solution.

Mobile Web Tricks

An easy way to run our game on mobile devices *without* needing any crazy deployment tricks is to run them on the device's mobile web browser. This approach used to be prohibitively slow, but advancements in phone hardware and browser engines make it a tantalizing deployment target.

Our penguin-based golfing extravaganza, *Pengolfin'*, seems like our best bet for a mobile conversion that could take on Guy Shifty's team and give us a fighting chance in the IGC mobile category. It only needs some control tweaks to become a mobile game. Instead of clicking and dragging to fire the penguin, we'll implement touch controls so it works like that game about annoyed birds. People seem to *love* games that involve flinging birds around.

Because our test environment uses a web server to serve the game (thanks to the `Budo` web server), you can also browse it on your phone—as long as you're connected to the same Wi-Fi network as your computer.

```
npm start
[0000] info  Server running at http://192.168.1.161:9967/ (connect)
```

If you browse to the corresponding URI on your mobile device, it will load and display it. But you'll

---

9. http://end3r.github.io/Gamepad-API-Content-Kit/
10. https://github.com/ericlathrop/html5-gamepad

notice a few issues. It looks really small, the screen bounces around when you try to drag the penguin, and you can't drag the penguin. To fix the first point, your immediate reaction might be to turn the phone to landscape mode. This does makes it bigger, but it doesn't fill the screen. To improve the situation, we'll add some helpful HTML meta tags in the `index.html` page that instruct your device on how to display the page:

```
<meta name="viewport" content="width=device-width,
  initial-scale=1.0, maximum-scale=1.0, minimum-scale=1.0,
  user-scalable=no, minimal-ui" />
<meta name="mobile-web-app-capable" content="yes">
<meta name="apple-mobile-web-app-capable" content="yes">
```

The first, `viewport` tag has a bunch of content hints that set the scale of the game so it correctly fills the amount of space on the screen. It also prevents the user from pinch-zooming it to a different size. Different devices support different settings, and the "best practices" for these change regularly. It's a good idea to raid other libraries from time to time to see what's new and what's old. (For example, "minimal-ui" is now deprecated on the latest versions of iOS, but we leave it there for backwards compatibility until we're sure it's not necessary.)

The `mobile-web-app-capable` and `apple-mobile-web-app-capable` tags tell Android and iOS phones that the web page is an *application* and not just a boring old website. This means they can be added to your home screen (and will then launch in real, full-screen mode) and can have icons and other application data associated with them.

 PWAs and the Web App Manifest

This idea is being extended with the *Web App Manifest*[11] and *Progressive Web Apps*[12]. Hopefully, in the coming years, these will be the silver bullets that propel web apps to (and beyond!) the status of their native counterparts. We certainly should be keeping an eye on them for opportunities to integrate them with our games.

The meta tags fix the display, but we still have an issue with *Pengolfin'*. The screen loads in portrait mode, but it's really a landscape game. It's hard to enforce this rule (although this will change when Web App Manifest support rolls out). An old but trusty trick is to display an overlay over the game when the phone is in portrait mode and remove it when it's in landscape mode. We won't enforce that on our game—because it plays fine in portrait mode—but we'll put a message at the bottom of the screen recommending the player rotate their phone:

---

11. https://developer.mozilla.org/en-US/docs/Web/Manifest
12. https://developers.google.com/web/progressive-web-apps/

```
<div id="popup">
   Landscape mode is better!
</div>
```

The overlay will be a simple element that's hidden by default in CSS. While we're playing with CSS, we'll also add the `touch-action: none` directive to the main game canvas. This prevents the regular panning and dragging from occurring when the user drags their finger, and it stops the "page reload" gesture from being triggered ... at least on some devices. For others, we'll fix it in the code:

```
#board canvas {
   touch-action: none;
   width: 100%;
}

#popup {
   display: none;
   width: 100%;
   position: absolute;
   bottom: 0;
}
```

The overlay is set to `display: none` by default. We use CSS Media Queries to determine certain things about the page. If we detect that it's in `orientation: portrait` mode, we override the popup overlay's CSS to be visible:

```
@media screen and (orientation: portrait) {
   #popup {
      display: block;
   }
}
```

Touch Controls

Pengolfin' looks more like a real mobile game now, but we still can't actually play it. We need some *touch controls*! Mobile phone touch controls revolutionized how we interact with content. Just like desktop games, the best mobile games are well aware of the importance of natural, satisfying control systems.

9-20. The intuitive controls of Enclave Games' Flood Escape!

 Emulating Mobile Devices on Desktop

It's possible to get an idea of how your game will look and feel on mobile devices from inside your desktop browser. For example, Chrome has an *Emulate touch events* feature, and Firefox a *Responsive Design Mode*. Most modern browsers let you emulate phones and tablets to facilitate responsive web design, but we can piggyback on these features for testing our games before deploying to real mobile hardware.

Luckily for us the *Pengolfin'* controls don't need to be very different from our `MouseControls`. We want the same system, only with a finger instead of a mouse. To save us some work, we'll use `controls/MouseControls.js` as a base for our slightly more general version, `controls/PointerControls.js`. `PointerControls` has *exactly* the same API as the mouse. Although this works well for our game, it ignores more impressive and complex behaviors of touch controls such as multitouch. Again, luckily for us, we don't need multitouch for this game, so we can drop *PointerControls* in without changing *any* of the game code:

```
// Handlers
document.addEventListener("mousedown", e => this.down(e), false);
...
document.addEventListener("touchstart", e => this.down(e, true), false);
document.addEventListener("touchend", e => this.up(e, true), false);
document.addEventListener("touchmove", e => this.move(e, true), false);
```

To add touch controls, you have to listen for the *touchstart* , *touchend* and *touchmove* events. They're analogous to *mousedown* , *mouseup* and *mousemove* . We put the event listeners right below the existing mouse ones, then to each handler function we pass an extra parameter, *true* , to indicate it's a touch event:

```
move(e, isTouch) {
  this.pointerPosFromEvent(e, isTouch);
}
```

Inside the *move* and *down* handlers (*up* doesn't do anything with the event itself, so it's not necessary) we relay the *isTouch* flag to the *pointerPosFromEvent* helper (this was formally the *mousePosFromEvent* function). It's the same as before—still mapping an event to an *x* and *y* position on the page. The only information it really needs in order to do this is the *clientX* and *clientY* event properties. For touch events, these are located in the event's *touches* array. If it's a touch event, we also call *preventDefault* to stop the screen from being dragged on devices that don't support *touch-action: none* from earlier.

 No Multitouch

We're only handling the *first* touch action in the array: *e.touches[0]* . If you'd like to add multitouch support, you need to consider the entire list.

```
pointerPosFromEvent(e, isTouch) {
  if (isTouch) {
    if (!e.touches || !e.touches.length) {
      return;
    }
    e.preventDefault();
  }

  const { clientX, clientY } = isTouch ? e.touches[0] : e;
```

```
    // Existing calculations to set pos.x and pos.y
}
```

To extract the `clientX` and `clientY` values, we destructure it from either `e` (the event itself) for mouse events or `e.touches[0]` if it's a touch event. The rest of the function converts these values into our screen position exactly as it did before. If you run the game on your phone, you'll see you can drag and fling our penguin!

Deploying to Mobile

In order to create your mobile apps from your JavaScript code, you'll need to install (and keep updated, along with developer licenses and SDKs) Android Studio (for Android devices) and/or Xcode (for iPhones). If you don't have a Mac and you want to deploy to iPhone … well, you need to get a Mac. There are cloud services that can do it, but I can't vouch for them. (I've researched a couple, but they always seem to be very marketing-heavy and so I end up not trusting them!) If possible, it's easier to buy a secondhand Mac mini and stick it in the corner.

One of my favorite projects for getting games onto mobile devices used to be Ejecta[13] by Dominic Szablewski (creator of the Impact.js library). It's billed as a "Fast, Open Source JavaScript, Canvas & Audio Implementation for iOS". When it was released in 2012, it was by far the best way to get your Canvas game on iOS. It took the insanely clever approach of re-implementing the Canvas API in OpenGL (what?!), and executing your code in a JavaScript Virtual Machine. It skirted around the limitations of the WebView provided by Apple, and it was *fast*. Even my ancient iPhone 3G was pushing out 60 fps, no problem!

The downsides to the project are that it's iOS-only, and it only supports a subset of normal browser behavior. Notably, there's no HTML or CSS support, and only a few necessary event handlers. If you're using our Pop library and only targeting iOS, check it out. I still think it's a good, fast, reliable way to deploy games.

However, since 2012, mobile browsers have slowly been getting faster and more capable. There have long been solutions that "run a web page as a native app", providing a full browser environment. But until recently, they just weren't fast enough to run intensive games. These days, you can get impressive performance from them, and they're a viable deployment target.

The most well known of these solutions is Apache Cordova[14]. It lets you create mobile apps with HTML, CSS, and JavaScript and install them cross-platform—on iOS, Android, Windows Phone and more. Setting it up and actually deploying to these targets can take a bit of work, but once

---

13. https://github.com/phoboslab/Ejecta
14. https://cordova.apache.org/

you have each platform figured out, it's easy to create a workflow for building releases of your game for each. There are lots of steps and details involved in the initial project setup, and it's best you follow along with the documentation. But the short version goes like this:

Firstly, install the global Cordova command line tools:

```
npm install -g cordova
```

Next, create a new Cordova project with `cordova create`:

```
$ cordova create bravedigger net.mrspeaker.bravedigger Bravedigger
$ cd bravedigger
```

The `create` command takes the path of the project (`bravedigger`), a reverse domain-style identifier (I've used `net.mrspeaker.bravedigger`) and a name (`Bravedigger`). This will generate a web-based app skeleton with the project home page at `www/index.html`.

Finally, add the platform or platforms you'd like to target:

```
$ cordova platform add ios
$ cordova platform add android
```

These steps take a while, as there are lots of things to download! I'd recommend only installing one at a time. And the first time you do this, make sure you can successfully compile and deploy to each platform. If you're targeting iOS, you should also install the Ionic WKWebview plugin, which uses (and fixes a bunch of issues with) iOS's WKWebView—and is much faster than the default UIWebView:

```
$ cordova plugin add cordova-plugin-ionic-webview
```

Finally, you can build and run the project on your selected platform:

```
$ cordova build android
```

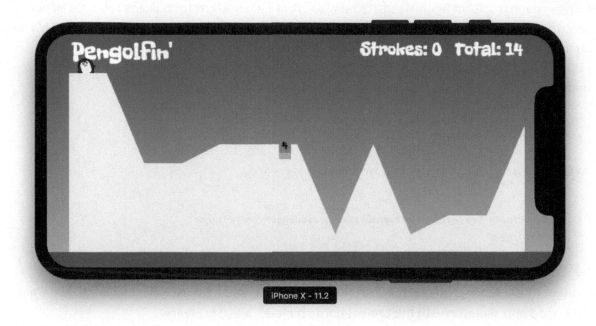

9-21. Running on the iOS simulator

This will run the emulator and start the application. You can edit the HTML file and refresh to see the changes. From there, you can deploy to physical devices, as well as create release packages to upload to the app stores for distribution.

Desktop Executables

That takes care of our mobile game entry for IGC. Now we have to package up our desktop entry, *Bravedigger*. Take a game that runs in a browser, wrap it up as a native application, and voilà—it suddenly feels more professional! It feels like a "product" rather than a web page. It can be downloaded and sold like a product. It can be uploaded to Steam. It can be burned to a CD-ROM … if that's your thing!

There are several options for packaging and distributing JavaScript applications as standalone executables. Two of the biggest players in this space are NW.js[15] and Electron[16]. They both work in a similar way: you put your HTML and JavaScript somewhere, and they run your game as if it's a native app.

Of the two options, Electron is the more popular. It has a huge community and a vast number of famous applications built on it (including Twitch, Slack, and Skype). NW.js is the older of the two,

---

15. https://nwjs.io/
16. https://electronjs.org/

however, and has a simpler setup. It's always worth testing out alternatives yourself rather than relying on popular opinion. Having said that, my opinion favors Electron, so we'll go with that here!

Electron works well with the npm ecosystem we're using (as does NW.js), so it's easy to integrate it with our existing game projects. The magic of Electron is that it bundles up a *full web browser* and displays it in a native window. This means all of our web tricks—including Canvas and gamepad support—will work without modification.

To start, install Electron as a development dependency for our project:

```
npm install electron --save-dev
```

You can then start the app by running `npx electron .` (`npx` is part of `npm` and is used for executing binaries, which the Electron browser window is). To make it part of our build system, you can add a new script command that can be run with `npm run play` :

```
"scripts": {
  "play": "electron ."
},
```

The `.` is the folder in which the Electron app is located. If you try it now, it will run Electron, but it will show an error page, as we haven't defined the app's main process. This is `main.js` by default (but you can change it in `package.json`). The Electron app revolves around the `app` and `BrowserWindow` objects defined by `electron` . `app` allows you to react to events about the application itself. Generally, you'll wait for the app's `onready` event and then create a new `BrowserWindow` :

```
const { app, BrowserWindow } = require("electron");

let win;
function createWindow() {
  win = new BrowserWindow({ width: 1366, height: 768 });
}

app.on("ready", createWindow);
```

This will create a new application and display an empty screen. There's a lot of options (and some boilerplate) for properly handling the app screen. Check out the Quick Start guide[17] to get a feel for what's possible, and which events you should be handling.

[17.] https://github.com/electron/electron-quick-start

By default, Electron just displays files from your local file system, in the same way your browser—via the local file protocol—would do if you double-clicked on an index.html file on your computer (resulting in a URL such as `file:///home/mrspeaker/index.html`). For this to work with our game system, we need to give permissions to load files locally:

```
<script>
  try {
    const webFrame = require("electron").webFrame;
    webFrame.registerURLSchemeAsPrivileged("file", { bypassCSP: true });
  } catch(_) {}
</script>
```

This approach doesn't require a dedicated server, and so is a good choice when distributing your final game. Alternatively, we could continue working with the `Budo` server we've been using to serve our files, images, and levels throughout this book. To get the equivalent functionality with Electron, we can use the `Budo` API inside `main.js`:

```
const budo = require("budo");
budo("./src/main.js", {
  port: 9966,
  serve: "index.js",
  browserify: {
    transform: [[ "babelify", { presets: ["env"] }]]
  }
}).on("connect", ev => {...});
```

This starts a server using the same parameters as our `package.json` specifies when we say `npm start`. If we tell the `BrowserWindow` to load the HTML file via the server (rather than the file system) we have the same environment as our web browser via `win.loadURL("http://localhost:9966/index.html")`. The advantage of this approach is our live reloading and regular setup keeps working so it's easier to develop and make modifications.

When it comes time to distribute your application, there are some steps you have to do to bundle your files with the Electron prebuilt binaries (for the platforms you want to target). It's a slightly hairy process, so check out the Electron documentation for a step-by-step guide. There are also some excellent projects (such as Electron Builder[18]) that are quite simple to get started with. Electron Builder streamlines the packaging process so it can be integrated into your workflow.

Getting on the Stores

Our games are done and ready to be sent off for judging at IGC. But then what? We've been so

18. https://www.electron.build/

focused on beating Shifty that we forgot to make plans for our game release! Now that the hard work is over, the *real* hard work is set to begin. We have to find some customers (paying or otherwise) and get our games into the hands of potential fans! For that, we'll need *distribution*, and we'll need to do some basic marketing.

The world of video game distribution has changed radically over the last ten years, and continues to present new challenges to wannabe gamedev superstars. For the foreseeable future, the distribution juggernaut for desktop games is Steam[19]. Where once upon a time "making it" meant having your product for sale as a physical box on the shelves of Evil-Mart, today success is being featured on the Steam home page, or building a thriving community in Steam's Community Hub pages. Steam is the big league.

It's not all rosy though. Every distribution method has its costs and benefits. Steam's costs is $100 per game to launch (though you get it back after $1000 in sales). A bigger cost is that it's a saturated market. Where previously getting on Steam meant you were almost guaranteed success, today anybody with $100 can get on there, so you can't just coast. You'll have to stand out from the crowd!

To get started, you need to head to the Steam Partner page[20] to sign up for the Steamworks Distribution program. Once you've done that, the easiest way to get your game working with Steam is to integrate Greenheart Games' reenworks[21]. This add-on gives you access to a number of important SteamWorks APIs from JavaScript.

But that's Steam. What if you don't even care about Steam? Steam is so *last year*. You just finished your first game (or you're just doing this for fun) and you don't want to get bogged down in this quasi-corporate world. You didn't get into this biz to do biz! You want to do your own thing. Where else can you release your games?

If you time traveled back to 2007, you wouldn't be making your opus in HTML5. You'd be making it in Flash. And you'd be launching onto Flash portals like Kongregate[22] or NewGrounds[23], where you'd bask in the temporary glory of being featured on the home page, garnering hundreds of thousands (or millions!) of plays, and receiving acclaim from an adoring public. Alas, those days are gone, but it's not all bad news. These sites have largely made the shift from Flash to HTML5, and they can still generate a decent amount of page views.

---

[19]. http://store.steampowered.com/

[20]. https://partner.steamgames.com/steamdirect

[21]. https://github.com/greenheartgames/greenworks

[22]. https://www.kongregate.com/

[23]. https://www.newgrounds.com/

There are also some up-'n'-coming game sites that are rapidly growing in popularity. They tend to be more modern (in terms of web technology and tooling) than the old portals, but they're not yet *giant* drivers of organic traffic. Time will tell. You need to do your own research, as the goalposts shift regularly. Itch.io[24] is one such lo-fi indie game place to be. It costs nothing to use, and you can host your games there. You get to choose the percentage split of sales between you and itch.io. And the sale amount can be $0 if you're just looking for some free hosting.

Another similar indie-gamedev–friendly site is Game Jolt[25]. It's also free to use and host, and any sales are split between you and Game Jolt, based on whatever split you'd like—up to a *maximum* of 10%. Very reasonable!

A platform that leans more towards the Steam side of the distribution spectrum is GOG[26]. It used to be called *Good Old Games*, and featured good … old … games. Now it's a distribution platform for games and movies—and it features some impressive, big-name titles, all DRM-free. You can submit your game for inclusion on their site, but it needs to be accepted—and that's not easy. But if you manage to jump over their entry hurdles, you'll get some amazing coverage!

For mobile games, the two big players are Google Play and the Apple App Store. Google Play requires you to register as a *publisher* (it costs $25) and ensure your game meets their launch specifications. For the Apple App Store you need to join the *Apple Developer Program*, which costs $100 per year. Both services take a 30% split of your hard-earned money. That's life.

The world of digital distribution changes rapidly—so make sure you keep your eyes peeled for any new potential markets that might work well for your genre of game.

Releasing to the World

We game developers aren't particularly social creatures (and especially not social *media* creatures). But marketing is a necessary evil of the game-making process. In a perfect world, everyone who might like your game would magically find out about it. Unfortunately, game discovery is a giant problem: there are lots of games, and there are lots of gamers. Marketing is all about reaching an audience that might care about *your* game.

Marketing efforts should begin as soon as you have a demo-able prototype. If you've been working through this book sequentially and are just about to hit the "deploy to world" button, I'm afraid you've left it way too late! (Sorry, I should have mentioned that earlier.) You need to be pushing your game and building some "buzz" long before you release. Otherwise, you run the risk

24. https://itch.io/docs/creators/faq
25. https://gamejolt.com/marketplace
26. https://www.gog.com/

of launching to the sound of crickets.

 Buying More Lottery Tickets

There's a naive idea that often floats around the game development world—that if your game is *really good* it will sell itself. Word of mouth will spread like wildfire, and your community will come to you. Yes, it *can* happen. But you *can* win the lottery, too. Marketing is the act of buying more lottery tickets.

The good news is that it's not *hard* to do some grassroots marketing. It's just time-consuming. Choosing the best place to invest your efforts will depend on you and your game. You need to build up your own community. You have to target people who might be interested in your style of game. This means posting your game updates and progress on Twitter, Facebook, your website (or on Tumblr or WordPress if you don't have one), and Reddit (you'll need to do some research to find the most appropriate sub-reddits to post to).

9-22. Butterscotch Shenanigans: masters of community building

If you have a bit of charisma, get it out there! Try streaming or recording some of your development process. The gamedev team *Butterscotch Shenanigans* make some great games, and many people learn about them from their awesome podcast. Building a community takes love and time, and this bunch are masters of it!

You can also post to game development forums (like TigSource[27] and eddit GameDev[28]) and IRC/Slack channels. If your game is unconventional, then target the non-game communities that might enjoy it. Put analytics (such as Google Analytics) on anything you can, so you can tell which communities are the most interested.

Wherever you post, you need to *wow* people. Or at least *entice*, *surprise*, or even *confuse* them. As long as you don't *bore* them. This might be the only interaction they ever have with your

[27.] https://forums.tigsource.com/
[28.] https://www.reddit.com/r/gamedev/

game—so if you can pique their interest with a cool or unusual screenshot, animated GIF, or piece of concept art, then there may be a chance of them sticking around to find out more.

If you've got some good screenshots, be sure to hashtag them with #ScreenshotSaturday (on Saturdays, naturally)—and add #gamedev too. Sometimes your fellow gamedevs can be your biggest advocates.

As your launch day approaches, research a list of game review websites and YouTube "influencers" you can contact. (Don't take a scattergun approach: find sites that review or stream games in the style of the one you're releasing.) Set up a website for your game featuring a trailer video, or at least some very good screenshots, with prominent links to where people can buy the game.

You should also prepare a **press kit**—a package containing all the information that reviewers might need for reviewing your game. Logos, screenshots, descriptions, contact information—even a pre-written PR piece. Anything that makes a reviewer's life easier. A great template is available at presskit()[29] to get you started.

When you know your launch date, set it to release in all the stores and *spam everyone you can* (as appropriate). A week before launch, contact all the people on your list of review sites, and then contact them again on release day. You only have one shot at this, and a good review can create an avalanche of word-of-mouth coverage.

Ultimately, marketing is just about *standing out from the crowd*. Checklists and "best practices" can be helpful, but their value is limited. They may have worked for the *first* person who did it, but a million others have since copied them and the tricks have lost their impact. People love to be surprised, entertained, delighted. All of the elements that make an entertaining game also make an entertaining marketing campaign. If you can come up with a twist or a hook, you might have a chance to propel yourself out of the ocean of same-ol'-same-ol' game launches and get noticed. Good luck!

Game Over

You've make it through the hardest part of gamedev—the grind from initial prototype to finished game. The polishing and juicing, the bug fixing and performance improvements, establishing deployment workflows and dealing with the minutia of various app stores ... slogging through the mountain of details in order to call your masterpiece "complete".

And what if your game launch fizzles on takeoff? What if only ten people download it, and only

---

29. http://dopresskit.com/

your parents buy a copy? What if we don't win the IGC and save the day? It doesn't matter. Congratulations are still in order. You've done what very few people have managed to do: you've created and released a fully finished product. The hard-learned lessons from your first few games will serve you well. All that's left for us to do now is send off our game entries to the IGC. It's out of our hands. Time to sit back on the couch with some celebratory snacks and relax with a few rounds of *Bravedigger*.

Bonus Round: The Epilogue

In the beginning there was a loop.

A loop that trapped an external stimulus. A stimulus that caused the world to move a tiny bit. A tiny bit of movement that resulted in a collision. A collision that fed back to the world outside.

There was a game!

By starting from simple principles, you've built a full-featured game from the ground up. Where there was nothing, there now stands ... well, something. Something kind of fun. The gap between reality and the game ideas in your head has narrowed. What will you make next? A tower defense survival game? A sailboat exploration game? An RPG about librarians? It's up to you; you have all the tools you need to create entire worlds. You've reached an achievement that many strive for but very few attain. You're a game developer.

You reflect on this while sitting in your formal attire in the main function hall of the annual Independent Game Developer Competition awards ceremony. *Pengolfin'* did well: it picked up an honorable mention, while EGI's embarrassing Candy Crush clone—*Gummi Bash*—was nowhere to be seen. You now fidget nervously, moments away from the announcement of the winner of The Grand Prize in the Category of Excellence in Making Some Games.

The lights dim, and the crowd falls silent. The host strides over to the podium, opening an envelope with a flourish. "And the Independent Game Developer Competition Grand Prize in the Category of Excellence in Making Some Games goes to ..."—a nervous buzz fills the air—"Exploitative Games, Inc.—*and* MomPop Games! For the first time in the history of the competition, we have a tie!"

A tie? What?! Do we win the bet? You rise and look around, and slowly walk towards the stage.

Guy Shifty joins you, beaming his corporate smile and waving at people in the crowd. "Not bad, MomPop Games," he says out the corner of his mouth. "I have to say, you put up a pretty good fight, and certainly kept me entertained. You really showed some indie gamedev spirit. Pity you lost ... well, pity you didn't win."

"What?!" you exclaim, as you turn to him in desperation. "I beat you in mobile *and* tied on desktop. You have to give us a break. You can't shut down the coworking space!"

A ponderous expression falls over Shifty's face. "Tell you what—I'll withdraw my tender on the space so you can keep your little clubhouse open. On one condition." He stops walking and turns to you, and an impish look enters his eye. "You create a brand new game in a *36-hour, live-coding battle extravaganza* against my top five programmers and artists. It'll be like—like an underground 'game-dev-off'. Yeah! Fight Club for gamedevs! We'll have DJs and strobe lights, and I'll get some celebrities to judge the best game. Winner takes all! What do you say?"

He may be a weird and infuriating nemesis, but we certainly are being productive. I guess you'd better get busy if you want to win the competition!

[Roll Credits]

Appendix A: List of Games Mentioned

Some of the fantastic games mentioned throughout the book (in order of appearance):

- FEZ - Polytron Corporation Incorporated: http://fezgame.com/
- Braid - Jonathan Blow: http://braid-game.com/
- Game Dev Tycoon - Green Heart Games: http://www.greenheartgames.com/app/game-dev-tycoon/
- Elliot Quest - Ansimuz Games: http://elliotquest.com/
- Wanderers of Io - Przemyslaw 'rezoner' Sikorski: https://wanderers.io/
- Behind Asteroids, The Dark Side - Gaëtan Renaudeau: http://js13kgames.com/entries/behind-asteroids-the-dark-side
- qbqbqb - Przemyslaw 'rezoner' Sikorski: http://qbqbqb.rezoner.net/
- A Wizard's Lizard - Lost Decade Games: http://www.wizardslizard.com/
- Another World - Éric Chahi: https://en.wikipedia.org/wiki/Another_World_(video_game)
- DHTML Lemmings - crisp: https://crisp.home.xs4all.nl/
- Airscape: The Fall of Gravity - Cross-Product: http://airscapegame.com/
- Curious Expedition - Maschinen-Mensch: http://curious-expedition.com/
- Slither.io: http://slither.io/
- Wilds.io - Przemyslaw 'rezoner' Sikorski: https://wilds.io/
- Thomas Was Alone - Mike Bithell: http://www.mikebithellgames.com/thomaswasalone/
- Plonat Atek - Sol Bekic" https://s-ol.itch.io/plonat-atek
- zDoom - Alexis Guinamard, Guillaume Hoffmann, Raphaël Siryani: http://www.ticalc.org/archives/files/fileinfo/360/36062.html
- Cold Snap: Vegas Rules - Mr Speaker: http://www.mrspeaker.net/dev/ld31/
- Universal Paperclips - Frank Lantz: http://www.decisionproblem.com/paperclips/
- Zmore - Mr Speaker:
- Undertale - Toby Fox: https://undertale.com/
- Nuclear Throne - Vlambeer: http://nuclearthrone.com/
- Gunpoint - Tom Francis: http://store.steampowered.com/app/206190/Gunpoint/
- Hotline Miami - Dennaton Games: http://hotlinemiami.com/
- Spelunky - Derek Yu: http://www.spelunkyworld.com/
- Super Meat Boy - Team Meat: http://www.supermeatboy.com/
- Getting Over It with Bennett Foddy - Bennett Foddy: http://www.foddy.net/2017/09/getting-over-it/
- Tetris - Alexey Pajitnov: https://en.wikipedia.org/wiki/Tetris
- Flappy Bird - Dong Nguyen: http://dotgears.com/apps/app_flappy.html
- SquizzBall - MomPop Games
- Crashlands - Butterscotch Shenanigans: https://www.crashlands.net/
- Stardew Valley - ConcernedApe: https://stardewvalley.net/
- Bravedigger & Bravedigger II - MomPop Games
- FlyMaze - Franco Ponticelli: http://flymaze.ponticelli.me/
- BrowserQuest - Little Workshop (for Mozilla): ttp://browserquest.mozilla.org/

- Kerbal Space Program - Squad: https://kerbalspaceprogram.com/en/
- Mosh Pit Simulator - Sos Sosowski: http://moshpitsimulator.com/
- My Summer Car - AMISTECH GAMES: http://www.amistech.com/msc/
- Pengolfin' - MomPop Games
- Timelapse - Gaëtan Renaudeau: http://js13kgames.com/entries/timelapse
- Minecraft - Mojang: https://minecraft.net//li>
- Mad World - Jandisoft: https://www.madworldmmo.com/
- Oscillator - Mr Speaker: https://www.madworldmmo.com/
- Keep Out - Little Workshop: http://www.playkeepout.com
- Glitchbuster - Rémi Vansteelandt's: http://store.steampowered.com/app/661360/Glitchbuster/
- Luftrausers - Vlambeer: http://luftrausers.com/
- Digibots & Co. - Mr Speaker: http://www.mrspeaker.net/dev/game/digibots/
- Flood Escape - Enclave Games: http://flood.enclavegames.com/

CPSIA information can be obtained
at www.ICGtesting.com
Printed in the USA
BVOW07s0127160218
508302BV00003B/15/P

9 780994 182616